PRAISE FOR THE AUTHOR'S 'V2V' HISTORICAL SERIES

Mary Anne Yarde – Author of the Du Lac Series

"These are not dry dusty books whose historical characters are one dimensional. Hughes has brought these men and women back to life with her quick wit and beautiful prose. The stories she tells are fabulously descriptive, as well as at times profoundly moving. She pulled it off beautifully."

D.K. Marley – Historical Fiction author of *Blood and Ink*

"What an incredibly fascinating walk through history with such in-depth historical research. I applaud Trisha Hughes for this immense undertaking, as well as the beautiful imagery and story-telling quality of her voice. I highly recommend taking this ambling journey into the pages of this historical series"

David Baird – David's Book Blurg

"Trisha Hughes did a great job of bringing each of these Kings and Queens to life. This is the kind of book that gives you the juicy, interesting facts and ignites the flames of passion for history"

Tony Riches – Historical Author of the *Tudor Trilogy*

"I wasn't disappointed as Trisha's lively and engaging style takes us on a grand tour of those who enjoyed wearing the crown. As Trisha Hughes says 'these stories span hundreds of years of lust, betrayal, heroism, murder, cruelties and mysteries.
What more could you ask for?"

Lyn Horner – Author

"Written in a lively, never boring style, I thoroughly enjoyed this historical epic. A definite 5 stars."

Paul Bennett – Author and Book Reviewer:

"Detailed research is evident throughout the book giving the reader a full picture of the events and the larger than life people who sought for the crown of a kingdom seemingly in constant turmoil and uncertainty. A fascinating tutorial of the
period of Canute to Elizabeth,
I'm looking forward to the next book.
5 stars"

PREVIOUSLY BY THE AUTHOR

Autobiography

Daughters of Nazareth

Historical Fiction

Book 1

Vikings to Virgin – *The Story of England's Monarchs from The Vikings to The Virgin Queen*

Book 2

Virgin to Victoria – *The Story of England's Monarchs from The Virgin Queen to Queen Victoria*

The Tartan Kings - *A Powerful & Rich Story of Scotland*

Crime/Mystery

Dragonfly

Chameleon

Scorpion

VICTORIA TO VIKINGS

THE STORY OF ENGLAND'S MONARCHS FROM QUEEN VICTORIA TO THE VIKINGS

SECOND EDITION
BOOK THREE

TRISHA HUGHES

First published in Great Britain 2019 by
The Book Guild Ltd

Copyright © 2024 Trisha Hughes

The right of Trisha Hughes to be identified as the author of this work has been asserted by her in accordance with the Copyright, Design and Patents Act 1988.

All rights reserved. No part of this publication may be reproduced, transmitted, or stored in a retrieval system, in any form or by any means, without permission in writing from the publisher, nor be otherwise circulated in any form of binding or
cover other than that in which it is published and without a similar condition being imposed on the subsequent purchaser.

This work is fiction based on real events in history.

Typeset in Garamond

For my father, Ernest Joseph Gourgaud.

I miss you every day of my life.

Never forget the importance of history. To know nothing of what happened before you took your place on earth, is to remain a child forever.

Cicero

CONTENTS

Foreword   xiii

1. The Georgian and Victorian Eras   1
2. Victoria   10
3. Edward VII   119
4. George V   177
5. Edward VIII   211
6. George VI   224
7. Elizabeth II   293
8. The Circle of Blood   306

FOREWORD

In ages gone by, many kings died while they were still young men. There were battles and diseases and many were simply overthrown. But the days of regal engagement in hand-to-hand combat are over and the line of succession has a good ageing prospect these days, buttressed by sound health care and nutrition.

Interest in the British Monarchy has ebbed and flowed over the centuries depending on the reigning monarch and the controversy surrounding said monarch. Now with William and Kate's three children, as well as Harry and Meghan's marriage, interest has bloomed again showing that the monarchy has fulfilled their function over the years with great skill.

But why are we so enthralled by the British monarchy with a type of mystic reverence?

Without a doubt, there are a lot of ingredients in this spicy stew we call history and one of the questions always asked is "How accurate is it?" Are the written records and evidence that survives today regarding the billions of lives, loves and hates of people who actually existed even exact? Hillary Martel, an English writer who has twice been awarded the Booker Prize for her books, argued that 95% of the past – what ordinary people actually said to each other and felt in their hearts – has vanished. What's left is just a few stones and clods of evidence that has been caught in the sieve, and this is

FOREWORD

what historians have turned into the whole structure we call history. We simply use our imagination to capture past realities and bring them vividly to life.

For most, researching history is a mundane task. It involves cross-referencing, note taking, and more often than not remembering things that most people forget. Moments of inspiration can be few and far between and you are very fortunate if your work leads to an earth-shattering revelation.

For me, British monarchs usually fall into four categories: the Mad, the Bad, the Hopeful and the Resourceful. The Mad were self-explanatory and they have dotted history for two thousand years. The Bad were less easy to identify and are more subjective, especially when you look at King John. Not that I condone his dreadful behaviour, but perhaps there were extenuating circumstances when you look at his spendthrift elder brother, Richard 1, who used England as a cash cow to fund his crusades. And then there was Richard III who has been branded 'evil incarnate' by many. The jury is still out on Richard because his reputation may have been muddied by William Shakespeare, a loyal (and I should imagine somewhat nervous) supporter of the Tudors. Shakespeare depended on the Tudors 'benevolence' for funding and as such, he would have felt obliged to paint Richard in the worst possible light. Tudor propaganda, many historians have called it. For both John and Richard, perhaps it was frenzied ambition without the restraining hand of conscience.

The Hopeful financed the building of churches, ships, castles and custom-made masses of altarpieces and jewellery. It was a never-ending attempt to nurture their souls. Then there were the Resourceful who were opportunists who tread upon the backs of others to get what they wanted, and who perhaps walked hand in hand with the other three.

My tale is a conglomerate of accumulated facts together with my imagination, backed up by plausibility in the quicksand of history. Despite the hard work, it's been an exciting time for me, none more so than Queen Victoria's reign, rightfully called the Golden Age of the 1900s. After rambling through the centuries, we come to the final book in my trilogy – *'Victoria to Vikings – The Circle of Blood'*. You may be wondering about the *'Circle of Blood'* reference and I'm hoping it will tweak your interest enough to read my book through to the final chapter.

THE GEORGIAN AND VICTORIAN ERAS

The 1800s and 1900s were magical eras when Britain was undeniably the world's most powerful nation on the planet. It was a time of great reforms: technology, engineering, entertainment, medicine, sport and above all, sanitation. Britain was in a state of industrial euphoria and her people were absolutely besotted with mechanical gadgets.

It was also a time of a different sort of brilliance. Charles Dickens, Arthur Conan Doyle, Charlotte Bronte and her sisters virtually blossomed in this atmosphere, as did the theatre, and Britain saw a series of fourteen comic operas by Gilbert and Sullivan being performed. People were enjoying the sound of a brass band while strolling through parklands and they were being entertained by one of the many travelling circuses dominating the kingdom. Gentlemen were visiting dining clubs and the gambling establishments, called casinos, and they were becoming wildly popular.

To get a better idea of Victorian times, let's take a walk around London. Imagine an overcast day with the promise of rain to come but you've decided to brave the elements anyway. Water puddles in dark alleys and the drains have overflowed from the previous night's downpour and the filthy water is coursing down the middle of the cobbled streets. People are bundled up warmly as they hurry along in their scruffy hats and cloaks, scurrying either to work or their homes before the inclement weather arrives. Huddled under dripping eaves away from the fluttering pigeons who trickle white streaks on everything below, you would perhaps glance at the line of hideous slums stretched out ahead of you where you know thirty or more people of all ages inhabit a single room. A sedan chair rattles past, carelessly splashing water on your already threadbare clothes and the bearer curses loudly at you as he roughly pushes you aside.

There are any number of places they could be going. These days, locomotives hurtle people across the country from London to Birmingham at an astounding thirty miles per hour. By 1845, two thousand miles of railway lines had been laid and 30 million passengers are being carried around the country every year, so the wealthy could be heading for a train that will take them to the seaside. Or if business is booming, people with cash were also heading to America by steamship, only taking twenty-two days to cross the Atlantic since three major shipping lines had popped up and trade routes to India, South Africa and Australia had been established. Essentials and raw materials such as corn and cotton were arriving daily from the United States along with meat and wool from Australia.

Most days, a heavy blanket of smoke hangs over the city and the pollution gets in your eyes. The stonework of every building is blackened by it. You wrinkle your nose as a breeze brings the smell of noxious fumes from parts of the city where tanning is taking place and you know that the smell will only intensify as the day progresses unless the sky opens up and washes way the smog, the tanning stench and the smell of aromatic horse dung lying in piles in the street.

But there's a reason you're out and about today. Very soon the streets will fill, not just by permanent residents who contribute to the overcrowding feeling, but by thousands of people who are also on their way to town. You see, today is a special day. Today is one of the eight hanging days a year and you would not want to miss this social occasion. On these public holidays, the condemned are driven through the streets from Newgate prison in a wagon, taking pause for alcoholic refreshment along the way, and you would have already pushed your way to the front to get a closer view. Many arrive at Tyburn mercifully drunk, but for even the most hardened of criminals the clamour and crush would have been overwhelming.

As you watch the criminals' progress along the crowded street, you remember stories your mother told you. These stories were not Gilbert and Sullivan tales where the punishment fits the crime. Those criminals were beheaded, limbs were cut off and thieves were chained up and whipped. Others were forced to carry hot stones or wear bridles over their tongues – a favoured method for troublesome wives - and of course, witches were burnt and poisoners were boiled alive. As for murderers, they risked being hung up in a cage, usually after execution, occasionally before, so people could watch them die slowly. Like today, it was a holiday for the ordinary people who could bring their lunch and have something to tell the neighbours that night.

As usual, today's hanging will not be the final moment in the program. You would be looking forward to the scuffle afterwards between the various surgeons who vie for the smorgasbord of limbs for research after the Hangman takes the criminal's clothes as a perk. You make a silent wish that a crone or two climbs up the gibbet as well in quest of a gruesome but prized token – a hand from one of the victims. This 'Hand of Glory' gives the owner a certain amount of power and is always up for grabs (excuse the pun).

It is so crowded, smelly and noisy you will barely be able to hear yourself think.

The turn of the 18th century was a great period of urbanisation when the poor of England flocked to London in search of streets paved with gold only to find that the streets were paved with mud and there was no work to be had. London's population was around 600,000 and it was a grand, anonymous city. There were none of the social constraints of a village where everybody knew everybody's business. And there were none of the financial safeguards either with a parish that would support its native poor or family and friends who might have looked after you at home. Instead, there was gin.

Alcoholic spirits were a pretty new commodity in 1800 society, though they had actually been around for a long time. They started as a chemical curiosity in about the 10th century and by the 1500s they were being consumed by the very rich for pleasure. Then in about 1700, they hit in a major way. The reasons are complicated and involve taxation of grain and the relation with the Dutch, but the important thing is that gin suddenly became widely available to Londoners.

It's very hard to say which was bigger – the craze for drinking gin that swept the lower classes or the moral panic at the sight of so many gin drinkers wandering the city drinking away their sorrows. Often their clothes were readily exchanged for the spirit. In any case, the government decided to tax the living daylights out of it. Understandably, people simply couldn't pay the tax, so enterprising men set themselves up as unlicensed gin-sellers. When the government heard about it, they decided to pay informants to hand in these unlicensed entrepreneurs. The attempt turned ugly as a number of mobs formed to attack even suspected informants, and several people were beaten to death. Not that the informants were necessarily nice. They could, and some did, run the whole things as a protection racket. But in any case, if you were well off, you kept well clear of it all and left it to your staff to procure it for you while you went about your business or holiday pursuits.

The Victorian era was a time of unparalleled growth where the population rose from 13.9 million in 1831 to 32.5 million in 1901 despite 15 million emigrants leaving the United Kingdom to settle in United States, Canada, New Zealand and Australia, looking to start a new and better life away from the poverty and starvation of home. But while the population in England and Wales had almost doubled from 16.8 million to 30.5 million and Scotland saw a rise from 2.8 million to 4.4 million, Ireland's decreased rapidly to 4.5 million, less than half, mostly due to the Great Famine. This ticking time bomb had far-reaching consequences. The Irish blamed the British government for the famine since Britain was the only ones benefiting from any new policies while Ireland continued to suffer.

You could probably put the population increase down to the new sanitation reforms where thousands of miles of street sewers were built to try and clean up the dirty, overflowing gutters full of human faeces and waste. You didn't have to nimbly sidestep slops being thrown out the windows anymore. Soap was also fast becoming a main product in the relatively new phenomenon of advertising. With the new sewage works in full swing, the quality of drinking water improved as well and in this healthier environment, diseases were less frequent and did not spread as easily as they once had. It was the first century when a major epidemic did not occur although a cholera outbreak did take place in London in 1848, killing 10,000 people. If you were a woman, it meant you were more likely to survive your childhood as nutrition standards increased, leaving you able to produce more children. Greater prosperity allowed people to finance a marriage, which in turn meant the birth rate increased.

An increase in prosperity meant longer working hours and lighting the streets for demanding businesses became imperative if you wanted to keep the lower class from waylaying you on your way home from work. Gas lighting became widespread in industry, homes and the streets and ensured your survival for another working day.

On weekends, you could watch your favourite sport. Cricket, croquet, roller-skating and horseback riding were becoming very popular and the modern game of tennis at Wimbledon was being played for the first time in London in 1877. You could even get swept up by football mania with the beginning of FA Cup fever.

If you were well-off and needed an operation, chloroform was now available and the use of anaesthetic meant you did not have to be physically tied down to have a tooth removed anymore. More and more people were having teeth pulled and replaced with real human teeth set into hand-carved chunks of ivory from hippopotamus or walrus jaws. If you were one of the lucky ones, you could also obtain teeth from executed criminals, victims of battlefields or from grave robbers.

But with the increase of population came large numbers of skilled and unskilled people looking for work. This population increase kept wages down to a barely subsistence level. Housing was scarce and very expensive, resulting in overcrowding. Wealthy homeowners began turning their large houses into flats and tenements but landlords failed to maintain these dwellings resulting in slum housing. In this appalling environment, almost one child in five was dead by the age of five. Polluted water and damp housing were the main causes but tuberculosis remained unconquered, claiming between 60,000 and 70,000 lives. It's easy to see how diseases of all sorts popped up.

Smallpox was one of London's biggest killers and even those who were lucky enough to recover were often badly pock-marked, with patches of hair and eyelashes missing, and could also leave skin thickened as if by burns. Yet, domestic servants who had visible smallpox scars were often preferred to those with unmarked skin as this was proof that they wouldn't be bringing the disease into their new household. Early inoculation was introduced from Turkey by smallpox survivor Lady Mary Wortley Montagu in 1720 before Edward Jenner introduced mass vaccination in 1796, using a less dangerous strain of cowpox.

Britain had not always enjoyed a rabies-free status and there were several outbreaks in London during the 1750s. Dogs were commonly used to protect property and also for fighting, so snapping, snarling canines were not an unusual sight on London's streets. But between 1752 and 1759 Londoners were always on the alert for dogs (and people) with running eyes and salivating mouths. Rabies also affected London's pigs, many of which were kept in backyards. The law stated that instant destruction of a rabid pig was necessary – a huge blow for a devoted pet owner or a poor family reliant on a single pig a year.

Syphilis had become easily curable by penicillin in Victorian times and Britain had lost the fear of it that our Georgian ancestors endured. Besides abstinence, sheep-gut condoms were the only form of protection against the disease although abstinence was still more reliable. However, the confusion of syphilis with less serious infections, coupled with the fear of syphilis' deformities and madness, meant it played a more prominent role in the public imagination than the rate of other infections merited.

Throughout the 18th century it was widely believed that one woman in five was involved in London's sex trade. London was an expanding place filled with merchants, property speculators and traders of all rank and description. Many of these people made their fortunes off the back of investment in the sex trade, a sector that was growing as rapidly as the urban population was increasing. The demand for entertainment and pleasure saw the creation of numerous brothels and taverns, while many of the newly built neighbourhoods, such as Marylebone and Bloomsbury, found their spacious townhouses filling with those who made livings as prostitutes, pimps and bawds (the women in charge of brothels).

If you were a girl and you couldn't find work as a servant, prostitution was for you and many girls between the ages of 14 and 22 had no other choice. A census in 1851 showed that the population of Great Britain was roughly 18 million and roughly 750,000 women would remain unmarried simply because there were not enough men. It was a time when men like Dickens portrayed prostitutes as commodities used and then thrown away. It was a time of venereal disease and it was the time of Jack the Ripper who stalked the streets of Whitechapel searching for prostitutes he could violently murder and disembowel.

There were exceptional profits to be made on the flesh market. Highly paid courtesans such as Lavinia Fenton, Kitty Fisher and Mrs Abington abounded, as well as 'bawds' such as Charlotte Hayes who was allegedly worth £20,000 at the time of her 'retirement' and Moll King, who went on to become a property owner in Hampstead.

But if the sex trade was out of the question for you, you had to scrimp to make ends meet. With work hard to find, children were expected to help towards the family budget, often working long hours in dangerous jobs for extremely low wages. Young boys were employed as chimney sweeps and small children were used to scramble under machinery to retrieve cotton bobbins. They also had their use in coal mines, crawling through tunnels too narrow and low for adults. Children as young as four were put to work in the mines and generally died before the age of twenty-five after working sixteen-hour days for most of their lives. They could also sell flowers, matches, and work as shoe shiners and apprentices to respectable traders. Working hours were long: sixty-four hours a week in summer and fifty-two in winter while domestic servants worked eighty hours a week no matter what time of year.

Many could not afford to have children at school so most could not read or write unless the parents taught them in their spare time, if any was available. A breakfast of porridge was at five in the morning and most parents could only spare a slice of cake for the child to eat during the day, although no rest time was allotted. It was only in 1833 that a Royal Commission recommended that children aged between 11 and 18 should only work a maximum of twelve hours a day and children aged between 9 and 11, a maximum of eight hours. This act, however, only applied to the textile trade, not mining.

If you were a young male and unemployed, it was certainly not in your best interest to hang around London's docks. But if you needed work, your choices were limited so 'press-ganging' seemed your best option. Being 'pressed' into service could work out pretty well if you took to life on the waves, but it was a poor start to a naval career. However, as the poorest Londoners still sold themselves as indentured servants, the view was that press-ganging was a way of neatening up the streets and filling a gap in the labour market.

Despite all of this, Britain was feeling pretty confident compared to the state of other countries in Europe. As he'd promised, William IV had stubbornly hung on to life until his niece, Victoria, turned 18 years old on 24th May 1837 but then had promptly waved his white flag at 71 years of age and left her to it, with only one scant month up his sleeve. On that day, an emotional, obstinate, straight-talking, and rather spoilt, young woman became the Queen of United Kingdom.

Despite the shaky beginning, Victoria learned on the job and in the end, she triumphed. An entire era in human history has taken its name from her. That, among many other things, is what she accomplished.

I wonder if she had any idea of the legacy she would leave the world as she first sat on the throne beneath the soaring arches of Westminster Abbey under the gaze of thousands of people. It seemed most of London had thronged the streets well before sunrise on her coronation day hoping to catch a glimpse of their new queen, just 18 years old and less than 5 feet tall.

As the tiny teenager sat on the throne, her feet not even touching the floor, she would have looked around her and seen the immense abbey filled with aristocrats, their clothing heavy with diamonds. She would have noticed the gold drapes and the exotic carpets and her neck would have been aching under the heavy crown perched on her head.

The day of her coronation did not go off without incident. Her archbishop jumbled his lines, one of her lords tumbled down the steps when he approached to kiss her hand and she would have noticed her prime minister, half-stoned on opium and drunk on brandy, watching the ceremony in a fog. The ruby coronation ring had even been jammed on the wrong finger and her hand would have been throbbing. Later on, the ring would have to be removed with ice.

Around her she would have noticed her many advisors and none of them would have appeared confident that she could rule a nation as strong and powerful as England. But her composure was impeccable nonetheless. Her voice steady and controlled, and if the thought of becoming a queen terrified her, she gave no sign of it. She never once let on that she was aware of the enormity of the task of becoming Queen at a time when her family had been incredibly unpopular for decades and Britain was still very far from being a democracy.

VICTORIA

Born 1819
Reign 1837-1901

No one ever imagined that one day Victoria would be the queen. Her father, after all, was not the first son of a king. He was the fourth. This honour was thrust upon her by a succession of unfortunate coincidences including the deaths of family members, two obese uncles with no legitimate children and somehow her father managing to avoid being murdered by mutinous troops and lucky enough to persuade her mother to marry him, despite being a middle-aged bankrupt prince. All of these incidents ultimately left her as the only suitable legitimate candidate to assume the throne and she assumed it incompetently, and at first, reluctantly.

There was a very complicated German connection that ran through Victoria's veins. With both sets of parents and grandparents being German, it is understandable that she felt German despite being born in Britain. As such, it is easy to understand that Britain and Germany were the best of friends for a long time. In the future though, there would be a tragic failure for her grandchildren to understand one another. It destined these two nations to explode on the battlefields during the First World War as the biggest family squabble of all time. But let's not get too far ahead of ourselves.

Germany as such didn't exist when Victoria assumed her throne. The German people occupied a motley collection of princedoms, duchies and kingdoms, which were brought together during the 1860s primarily through the efforts of Otto von Bismarck. He engineered the expansion of German military might, the political triumph of Prussia, and the creation of the German Reich. He bequeathed to Europe a Germany that was thirsting for conquest.

Victoria's tangled connections with the kings, queens and lesser royals of Europe create a strong impression in our minds. It was a somewhat dysfunctional family, one held together largely by arranged marriages between close relatives, some of which turned out to be reasonably happy and many of which certainly did not. With all this interbreeding, 'difficulties' inevitably arose.

A hundred years before, Victoria's Hanoverian ancestors had been offered the throne in the last year of Queen Anne's life with high hopes of achieving a stable monarchy. What England received was the exact opposite. For all the Stuarts' misdemeanours and transgressions, they had shown enough sophistication for Britain to grant them at least *some* level of respect. More importantly, the Stuarts had shown respect for each other.

Queen Anne was the last of the Stuarts to rule England and if anyone were going to win the competition for who had the most tragic life, Anne would win hands down. In sixteen years, she had seventeen pregnancies: twelve were either miscarried or stillborn, having died weeks before in the womb and of all her children, only one survived to 11 years of age before he died as well. There was simply no one left to whom they could hand over the throne over. Well, except for the Catholic Stuarts in Italy but they were totally unacceptable. So, when Anne's last child died, Parliament began searching anxiously to find a Protestant heir to the throne rather than risk the Catholic, obstinate, pig-headed Stuarts returning from Europe. Everyone knew what the Stuarts thought of themselves. They believed they didn't have to earn a place in Heaven because they believed they were chosen by God to walk in His path on earth. They thought nothing they said could be questioned because they were 'Divine Rulers' saved through faith.

Drastic action was needed.

Frantically, Parliament went through the Stuart family tree with a fine-toothed comb, right back to James I, and they came up with his daughter Elizabeth who had married Frederick V, Elector Palantine. This finally led them to their daughter Sophia, the current Electress of Hanover. She was a part of a very German tradition of women who led the social and intellectual scene and who was rational and intelligent. As a bonus, the ready-made family in Germany looked very appealing and promising to Parliament. She seemed the perfect choice and they sat back and breathed a sigh of relief.

Sophia's untimely death came as a shock because Queen Anne was hanging on to life by a thread herself. One month after Sophia died, Anne was dead as well but thankfully, they thought, Sophia had a son to take over after her. And that's when George entered as the first Hanoverian king, George I.

George was a shy, unremarkable man who could barely speak English, and who could blame him? He'd lived in Hanover all his life. He spoke four languages, but English was his 4th. Then they heard more about George and their opinion of him took a nose-dive. He'd treated his wife cruelly, sending her into exile for adultery, rather hypocritically since he was far worse than her on that subject. He'd then refused his two children any contact her and they both resented him immensely. At the beginning of this new Hanoverian era, people experienced everything from passionate repulsion of their 'turnip king' to resignation because this was the best there was.

In a time when Britain had hoped and prayed to obtain a secure steady monarchy, the Hanovers proved to be a feisty tangle of aggressive, hot-headed family members who openly brawled with each other and bickered savagely in public.

George I and his son Prince George fought incessantly to the point that when George I died of a stroke in his beloved Hanover, his son refused to even attend his funeral. And George II's reign only started another long and turbulent era. England had already had a preview of what the Hanoverians were like but within a year, George's eldest son, Frederick, arrived from Hanover and England found that their new dynasty was actually more dysfunctional than the Tudors had ever been. If you put aside the fact that the Stuarts were Catholic, they actually began to look rather good by comparison.

As with his own father, George II and his son hated each other. George II had left Hanover with his own father, who had been ready to commence his new role as King of England, and in the process, George II left Frederick behind to show Hanover that they would not be forgotten. And Frederick never forgave him for abandoning him. He was only 7 years old as he watched his whole family disappear over the horizon and as a result, anger clouded every action in the family.

On George II's death, it would be his grandson, George III, who stepped up to the mark and from the very beginning, George was different from his Hanoverian predecessors. England welcomed him like a breath of fresh air after his feisty ancestors but George III had problems of his own. He was shy and reserved and after watching the public rantings of his father, uncle and grandfather almost on a daily basis, I'm sure he felt it was best to keep a low profile, making him a rather exemplary husband and role model for his children. But there was always something ... odd ... about George.

George reigned through the American War of Independence, The French Revolution and Napoleon's war on almost all of Europe. He suffered through the death of two of his beloved children and finally the dreadful behaviour of his eldest son and heir, Prince George. He was a widely popular king, true and loyal to his wife and family, but the disease porphyria has no favourites. Like many monarchs before him, especially in the Stuart clan, the disease took a hold of George and it left history remembering him as 'Mad King George'.

Apart for some sporadic years of his life, George III (although blind for the last ten years of his life) had been politically active. What most of the world remembers about George is the fact that he slipped in and out of lucidity and as such, fear of a royal hereditary 'madness' was always present in the minds of the British governing class. You see instability hadn't stopped with George III. His children had all shown signs of 'eccentricity' and 'self-indulgence' and with every fresh instance of peculiarity, British anxiety increased.

During George III's illnesses, the logical person to act as Regent was his eldest son Prince George, much to Britain's disgust. He was a mean, cruel man who was extremely unpopular with his people by anyone's standards.

Maturity comes slowly to some but George was slower than most. However, one thing was obvious: George liked women. His first serious affair was at the age of 17 and by the time he reached 21, he was well-known as an inveterate ladies' man who would woo his targets ardently, promise them his eternal love and then brusquely drop them like hot cakes when he tired of their charms. As far as George was concerned, variety was the spice of life.

There were very few who surpassed his reputation as a scoundrel. He was a chronic gambler and without his father's permission, wilfully married a twice-widowed Catholic actress by the name of Maria FitzHerbert (nee Smythe, nee Weld) who was, not surprisingly, six years his senior. You see, everything George did seemed out of spite towards his father and his mother.

The marriage lasted nine years until June 1794 when George sent Maria a letter abruptly telling her that her relationship with him was over. His father was demanding that he marry a rather plain German princess by the name of Duchess Caroline of Brunswick and of course he was terribly sorry. But what could he do?

No one needs to be told there were better and more sensitive ways of breaking the shocking news to Maria, but at the time George was more concerned with the massive gambling hole he found himself in. His debts had climbed back up to the extraordinary amount of £630,000 (equivalent to £58,700,000 today) and according to his father, the only way he would clear it in full, with an additional sum of £65,000 per annum (equivalent to £6,056,000 today), was if George married Princess Caroline of Brunswick. As generous as all this sounds, it was by no means to be the last time a payout of such an astonishing amount would be necessary to pay off his debts.

Although George told his younger brother Frederick that he and Maria had 'parted amicably', I'm not sure Maria would have agreed if anyone had bothered to ask her, which they didn't.

Somewhat inevitably, the subsequent marriage to Princess Caroline of Brunswick was a total disaster. Admittedly, she was not the most desirable bride for a distinguished, discerning young man like George, but sometimes women blossom with the love of a patient man. Clearly, George was not that man. He took one look at Caroline and asked for a strong brandy. It went downhill from there.

Like any girl, she would have wondered what the moment would be like when she met her future husband. My guess is George was nothing like she imagined. Caroline was heard to have said, *"he is very fat and nothing like his handsome portrait."* On the other hand, George complained that she smelt and had neglected to wash or change her dirty clothes. Not exactly the makings of a Hollywood romance.

It went from bad to worse after the wedding. In a letter to a friend, the prince claimed that the couple only had sexual intercourse three times: twice the first night of the marriage, and once the second night. That was all he could stand. As for Caroline, she claimed George was so drunk that he *"passed the greatest part of his bridal night under the grate, where he fell, and where I left him".* Nine months later however, Princess Charlotte was born and the couple officially separated with George expressing exaggerated tales of public insults perpetrated by his wife against him. Three days after Charlotte's birth, George made out a new will leaving all his property to Maria FitzHerbert and leaving Caroline one shilling.

What saved George in Britain's eyes was Charlotte. She was his only legitimate offspring and everyone was looking forward to the day when she would replace her father as the Queen of England. Her dependable husband Prince Leopold of Saxe-Coburg-Saalfeld would in effect be the king of the country, although not in name, and they would reign blissfully and solidly in the future with the laughter of many children filling the palace halls.

Charlotte had wonderful qualities that Walt Disney would have relished. She was young, intelligent, playful and beautiful, and looking at the rest of her dysfunctional relatives, she was the nation's bright and shining star, the figure on whom all British people rested their hopes. Despite a few undignified pranks in her teenage years, Britain loved her.

Her husband, Leopold of Saxe-Coburg-Saalfeld, had inherited his mother's good looks as well as her eye for a good chance. He was the correct religion and the mega-rich Russian Romanovs believed if the Coburgs married into the British royal family, they would be a useful ally to the Russians.

It took a lot of effort to convince Charlotte's father of the benefits, especially since the Coburgs were basically penniless. But eventually the wedding took place and she married her prince wearing a dress that cost over £10,000. The sleeves were trimmed with Brussels lace and her six feet long train was held in place with a diamond clasp. She wore a garland of leaves and roses dotted with diamonds on her head, a diamond necklace, diamond earrings and a diamond bracelet.

Charlotte was ecstatic and more than happy to be away from the father she hated and to have escaped marriage to some truly ugly choices, such as the short, skinny Prince William of Orange, nicknamed 'Silly Billy'.

Despite her father's trepidation, it was a very happy marriage and she was soon pregnant.

Like many of her predecessors, she suffered a miscarriage early on in the marriage but in 1817, she appeared to be carrying a baby to full term. Because of her previous miscarriage, no one wanted to take any risks with this pregnancy so it was decided she would take every precaution. After all, this was an important birth. After her father, Prince George, Charlotte was the heir presumptive to King George III's throne since no other uncle had any legitimate children.

Charlotte did everything suggested and spent her pregnancy quietly. She ate more and exercised less but when her medical team realised she was putting on quite a bit of weight, she was put on a strict diet in the hope of reducing the size of the child at birth. As you can imagine, the diet, plus the excessive 'bleeding' and 'purging', only weakened Charlotte but despite everything, the pregnancy progressed well. She was due on 19th October but when the end of October came and she had still not gone into labour, people began to worry.

Then on 3rd November, contractions started and everyone was relieved and overjoyed. But after two days of labour, no one was smiling anymore. At 6 o'clock in the evening of 5th November, meconium (a child's first faeces) oozed onto the sheets making it pretty obvious that the baby was clearly in distress. At 9 o'clock, a large stillborn son was born after a difficult and painful birth. The doctors tried to revive him but it was all to no avail. Meanwhile, Charlotte was still bleeding as her uterus had not fully contracted after the birth so her doctors removed the placenta by hand. After that, the bleeding appeared to stop.

Charlotte took the terrible news with tranquillity. After all, she was still young and she and her husband loved each other madly. They had planned on having a large family so they would just keep trying.

She took a little food before resting but as evening turned into night, at around midnight, it was obvious that something was wrong. Charlotte complained of a ringing in her ears, her heart was palpitating and she had violent stomach pains. She felt extremely cold and no matter how many blankets were provided, she continued to shiver.

Now we know that she was haemorrhaging internally and nothing would have been more disastrous than applying heat to her body. With her bed heavily covered in blankets and tucked up close to a roaring fire, Charlotte died two hours later.

That night, Leopold not only lost a much-wanted son and a beautiful wife whom he'd cherished and adored, he also lost his place on the royal snakes and ladders board. Overnight, he lost his place as the king consort and he became a royal nobody. But instead of heading for home after his wife's funeral, he decided to stay on. He continued residing at Claremont and refused to give up his benefits as a Field Marshal and Colonel along with his colossal annual income of £50,000 that he had enjoyed as Charlotte's husband and as it turned out, his decision to stay couldn't have been more fortunate for the Coburg family.

Charlotte's death caused national shock. It was as if every household throughout the kingdom was in deep mourning. A politician by the name of Lord Byron even threw open the windows of his Venice apartment and emitted a piercing scream over the Grand Canal. Charlotte was the only member of the royal family whom the people loved and with her death the credibility of the monarchy slumped dramatically. Her father, Prince George, reigning in place of his old and ill father, was lecherous, gluttonous and grossly self-indulgent and most people saw it as an unfathomable mystery how he had managed to beget such a beautiful child as Charlotte.

Thankfully her grandfather George III had no idea what was happening. By that time, he was permanently in his own mad world and no one saw the need, nor the inclination, to explain to him what had happened. But who would be the next heir to the throne after Charlotte's father Prince George was the urgent question being asked. Another child was out of the question since George had long been estranged from his wife Caroline before Charlotte was even born.

His 55-year-old brother, Frederick Duke of York was estranged from his wife as well and deeply involved with a middle-aged mistress, whom he had no intention of giving up. His German wife, Princess Frederica of Prussia, had long since been sent away to the English countryside to live permanently and that's where he intended her to stay.

The next in line was 53-year-old William Duke of Clarence who had no difficulty in producing offspring. But these ten children were by a mistress, so of course that meant none of them were legitimate or eligible.

Edward Duke of Kent, aged 51, had been living happily with his French-Canadian mistress for the past 24 years and even if she became his lawful wife, she was too old to have children.

Next was 47-year-old Ernest Duke of Cumberland, currently the King of Hanover, who had married twice-widowed Frederica of Mecklenburg-Strelitz, much to the disapproval of his mother who stubbornly refused to acknowledge her. Despite the odds, it was proving to be a happy marriage and at Charlotte's death, Ernest was the only son who was married and not estranged from his wife. But still there were no children.

Then there was 45-year-old Augustus Duke of Sussex who had twice defied the Royal Marriages Act by taking wives without his father's consent and 44-year-old Adolphus Duke of Cambridge had neither a wife, nor legitimate successors, at Charlotte's death.

Out of seven feisty young men, there was not one legitimate child who could be regarded as the heir to the throne. How could such an enormous family become extinct? It was a monumental disaster.

We've heard of panic buying but this was panic marrying at its best. The question was, which one of the overweight, almost penniless, late-middle-aged sons of George III could find a lawful wife who could then become the mother of his children and produce future monarchs.

The race was on.

Edward promptly left his mistress high and dry and set off to woo Leopold's sister Marie Luise Victoria, the widow of Prince Leiningen of Amorbach in Lower Franconia. William promptly ditched his mistress as well to search for an eligible wife elsewhere and the youngest brother Adolphus joined the sprint by marrying Princess Augusta of Hesse-Cassell, a beautiful 20-year-old who herself was a great-granddaughter of King George II of England.

For William, finding a bride wasn't as straightforward as his brothers' quests had been. At his advanced age, he knew it wasn't going to be easy especially when they found out he came with a huge gambling debt to boot.

Seeing his brothers already way in front of him in the race, he made repetitive hurried proposals of marriage to an heiress who in turn repeatedly turned him down. He then tried a rich heiress in Brighton and when she turned him down as well, he went down the traditional royal path of seeking a bride among the royal stud farms of Protestant Germany. To his surprise and amazement, 26-year-old Princess Adelaide of Saxe-Meiningen willingly accepted his offer of marriage.

While William was always meant for the navy, his younger brother, Edward Duke of Kent had always been intended to be a soldier. But not just any soldier. He was meant to be a *German* soldier, and at any early age, he was sent off to Hanover for training. Even in his late adolescence, Edward had developed habits of wild extravagance so when he arrived in Hanover, the punishing discipline of German military life came as a rude shock to the English prince. But despite all the expected difficulties with the rigorous training, five years later Edward was given the command of a regiment and was posted to Gibraltar, much to the consternation of his commanders. This reluctance was mainly due to the fact that they understood the difference between being a good soldier and being a good commander. The two scenarios were totally different but Edward seemed oblivious to the distinction. He had excelled in his training and it had turned him into a good soldier but what it had also done was to bring out a rather nasty, mean streak in his character.

Edward arrived with enthusiasm and bravado at his new position. He revelled in drills and inspections much like all previous officers but his troops soon found a very different side to his nature surfacing. At the beginning, he would silently watch his men stand on the parade ground for hours on end but slowly a tyrant appeared who was completely and utterly severe with them. Even the smallest infringement was met with merciless floggings. His men detested him and his commanding officers back home all agreed that to avoid a mutiny, he had to be sent away to Quebec in Canada. What they should have realised was that being in a different country doesn't change a person's personality.

Perhaps Edward was miffed at the slur on his character by people he saw as beneath him or perhaps he just saw Canada as a remote and barbarian country. Perhaps it was simply that it had connections to the hated French. Whatever the reason, and much to his troops horror, they found the brutal

Gibraltar pattern continuing. In fact, it worsened. He was even crueller to his men than he had been in Gibraltar and the barrack's grounds echoed with the screams of his men being flogged daily. One French deserter was tracked down unrelentingly and when brought back was given the maximum sentence of 999 lashes.

If Edward had hoped for some sort of reaction, he certainly got one. But I'm sure it wasn't the reaction he expected. As he stood silently watching the punishment being delivered, the deserter did not so much as whimper. When the punishment was over, he staggered determinedly up to Edward, blood running down his back, and told him that no whip could cower a Frenchman.

It was while Edward was stationed in Canada that he met Therese-Bernadine Montgenet, the daughter of a respectable engineer, who for some reason he affectionately called Julie. Despite the fact that she'd had at least two previous aristocratic French lovers before him, Edward had no hesitation in stepping in as the third candidate and taking her as his mistress. For the next two and a half decades, they lived in relative happiness while Edward continued his military career.

Had Charlotte not died, there is every chance that they would have lived happily ever after, despite always scratching around for money. But one morning, while the sun shone gloriously and while Edward was quietly eating his breakfast, Julie opened the mail and fished out the *Morning Chronicle*. Charlotte's death was all over the papers and the headlines jumped off the page. Princess Charlotte, heiress to the British throne, was dead.

Perhaps she had some idea that her relationship with Edward was over because the news exploded like a bomb at the breakfast table and she fainted. It turned out she was right to be concerned. After hasty messages to his brothers, Edward learned that they were doing their utmost to discard their mistresses and pursue brides of childbearing age. Edward had no intention of being left out of the baby race so he packed his bags and left Julie high and dry after 28 years, armed with letters of introduction for Charlotte's widower, Leopold, to woo his sister Marie Luise Victoria, the pretty widow of Emich Carl, Prince of Leiningen. Ah, romance.

Marie Luise, known as Victoire, came with two children of her own and together they lived in the Principality of Leiningen that had been impoverished since the Thirty Years War in the seventeenth century. Napoleon's army had left both her native land of Saxe-Coburg-Saalfeld and Leiningen desolate and by the time Victoire's father had died, Napoleon had formally brought the region to an end and her people were actually starving when she became the duchess. They had never seen more wretched times.

Victoire had known the hazards of being royal where the monarchy could be reduced to ruins, or killed, at the whims of fate. The plump, rosy-cheeked woman with brown ringlets lived in a state of abject poverty (acting as regent for her son until he came of age) and had a profound sympathy for anyone else who lived the same horror. At 32 years of age when she met Edward Duke of Kent, she was penniless with no prospects outside the chance of marriage and unfortunately for Edward, he was not that far in front of her. In fact, she was swapping life as a penniless widow in an impoverished country to marry a virtual pauper. Still, taking all of this into account, she believed she'd landed on her feet in clover. The challenge for Victoire was to produce a child before anyone else in the family did.

By then, the race for a royal heir was in full swing. William was still eyeing off the heiress in Brighton. Ernest's wife, who had lost her first baby minutes after his birth, was pregnant again and Adolphus was on the point of marrying Princess Augusta of Helle-Cassell. As for Edward, his eldest brother George, acting as Regent for his mentally-ill father, gave Edward permission to marry Victoire and Parliament increased his income to £6,000. With huge gambling debts hanging over his head, he had been hoping and praying for the same amount of £25,000 that his elder brother Frederick had been offered (the large amount had been offered to Frederick by Parliament to bring his German wife back from the countryside) but sadly for Edward, he was told that times were tough and he'd have to make do with the initial offer despite Frederick's determination to leave Frederica stashed permanently away in the countryside no matter how much money he was offered. It wasn't what Edward wanted to hear and he made a lot of noise about it but with all four brothers lining up at the starting gate there was very little time available to quibble over the money issue. Grudgingly he agreed, realising it was too nail-bitingly close to nit-pick.

Edward and Victoire settled into a fond companionship, quietly thrilled with each other, and left Britain to be married in a beautiful baroque Schloss in her native Coburg, which her brother Leopold had only just finished refurbishing. With that out of the way, they turned around and headed back to England where they went through another marriage ceremony according to the rites of the Church of England. Beside Edward and Victoire at the altar, stood his older brother William who was marrying Princess Adelaide of Saxe-Meiningen in a double ceremony. After the ceremony, the two brothers parted ways.

No one believed for a second that the weddings were anything but ones of convenience. What Edward *did* have was plans. On his first visit to Coburg for the initial wedding ceremony, Edward had seen the Schloss after the refurbishment but it was certainly not up to scratch, not by a long shot. With grandiose ideas and £10,000 of borrowed money, the happy couple returned to Germany, where her 15-year-old son Carl Friedrich had been ruling in her absence, ready to beautify the Schloss. With them, they brought English workmen to install stoves, plant gardens and build stables.

It was during his frenzy of refurbishment that Victoire told Edward she was pregnant. Since William's wife had miscarried again, Edward realised that he had actually beaten his brothers to the royal nursery and he began making jubilant plans. Victoire would have the best of care in the early stages of her pregnancy and after a quiet winter in Germany, they would return to England in her last trimester with the future monarch of Britain nestled safely in Victoire's womb, ready for the birth.

You'd have thought that a six-month warning would have been sufficient to make travel arrangements. Instead, they set out for England when Victoire was eight months pregnant, ready to travel over 430 miles at a time when there was no such thing as a tarmac road in Europe. Edward was desperate to get his heavily pregnant wife to Britain in time to give birth to a baby he hoped would one day sit on the throne. He wanted his child's first bawl to be on English soil but when he looked down at his wife's pale face, her hand rubbing her swollen tummy where tiny feet kicked, he must have realised it was going to be a close call.

If the journey weren't so desperate, the entourage would have been comical. Since money was again tight and they had no money to pay a coachman, Edward drove the two-seated cart himself, pulled by two horses with no covering top to shade Victoire sitting in discomfort beside him. Behind them came a carriage carrying Victoire's favourite caged birds, cats and dogs. After them came English maids, two cooks, a retired naval surgeon, an obstetrician and a skilled midwife. As personal attendants, they not only brought maids and a valet but also Victoire's lady-in-waiting whom she had kept after the death of her first husband. Following all of them was Edward's personal officer, a handsome Irishman by the name of John Conroy, a staff officer in the Royal Horse Artillery, to attend to his horses.

At this stage, John Conroy was almost certainly unknown to the players in the melodrama. It was only after the baby was born that he would become a villain. It's also worth knowing that in time, gossipers would whisper rumours that he had been Victoire's lover and some even suggested that he was the father of the child. Of course, no evidence exists of such a thing and at birth, Victoria's resemblance to George III was remarkable and unmistakable.

For many years, Conroy's obsession with the Royal Family was mysterious. Long before Victoria was born, strange ideas were buzzing around in his head. In fact, Conroy believed that his wife Elizabeth was Edward's daughter, born after he was sent to Canada to keep him out of any more trouble in Gibraltar. In actual fact, it was impossible since she was born in 1790 when Edward was still stationed in Gibraltar as one of the most detested officers in the British Army, dishing out horrendous and merciless punishments to his troops.

It's not clear how Conroy formed this obsession, and not even if Elizabeth was aware of it after bearing him six children, but he was unable to stop thinking the delicious thoughts and very soon his contemplations snowballed to thoughts of royal bastardry. What if there had actually been a clandestine marriage between Elizabeth's mother and Edward? What if there was a marriage certificate accompanying Elizabeth's birth? Wouldn't the subsequent marriage between Edward and Victoire be classed as invalid? Shouldn't *his* wife be the one wearing the British crown instead of the rosy-cheeked baby bawling in the cradle? Wouldn't that mean that John Conroy's rightful title was Prince Consort to Queen Elizabeth II of England? Surely that's what it meant. It was a wonderful dream and he just couldn't let it go.

Sorry, back to Edward and Victoire.

Onwards the noisy caravan bounced, first through Frankfurt, bumping and rumbling over slippery cobblestones, until finally, they reached the seaside port of Calais on 18th April right in the middle of a storm. The blustery wind was howling and the waves were breaking mercilessly on the shore and as the wind buffeted their clothes, Edward must have been feeling more than a little nervous. With the unpredictability of the English Channel, it was unthinkable for a heavily pregnant woman to cross the channel for any reason whatsoever. A week passed and the storm abated, but by then, there was little choice of what they should do. If Edward wanted the baby to be born on English soil, they needed to set sail immediately, no matter how choppy the seas. It had become urgent.

The three-hour sea journey must have been almost unbearable for Victoire as she rocked and swayed on the waves, her arms wound protectively around the baby kicking restlessly in her tummy. But when they finally arrived on a beautiful spring day, with the meadows full of glorious colour, they must have realised they had miraculously beaten the odds because Victoire had not gone into labour. They headed straight to Kensington Palace where George, in one of his rare benevolent moods, had offered them the use of two floors of rooms in the south-west corner known as Apartment I where his deceased wife had lived, above his brother Augustus Frederick Duke of Sussex and next to their near-blind sister Sophia who was showing signs of senility.

Kensington Palace was originally a two-storey Jacobean mansion purchased by 1st Earl of Nottingham in 1619 and called Nottingham House but it began life as a King's playground a hundred years before that. The gardens were part of Hyde Park and hosted Henry VIII's huge deer chase. When William and Mary came to the throne, they bought the mansion from 2nd Earl of Nottingham and instructed Sir Christopher Wren to begin immediate expansion of the palace in 1689 as well as creating a separate park. Mary commissioned a palace garden of formal flower beds and box hedges and Queen Anne had followed on and created an English-style garden making it the perfect venue for fashionable court entertaining away from the chaos of town. Even George I had spent lavishly on new royal apartments, creating new state rooms, the Cupola Room and the Withdrawing Room. The last reigning monarch to use Kensington Palace was George II who left the running of the palace to his wife. After her death, George neglected many of the rooms and the palace fell into disrepair. By the time their father George III took the throne in 1760, Kensington Palace was only used for minor royalty.

What George had forgotten when he offered the apartments to Edward was that in a rather vindictive moment, he had stripped the apartments of furniture to make it unbearable and impossible for Caroline to live there and never felt the need to replace them after her death. When Edward and Victoire arrived, the apartments were empty and had neither been aired nor heated. To top it off, the larder was unusable because water constantly dripped from the ceiling.

Luckily, Edward had a knack for home-improvements so he borrowed yet another £2,000 from somewhere to refurbish his new abode. In the coming two weeks, the rooms were repainted, furniture was purchased, a desk was placed in the library and the windows and bed in Victoire's bedroom were decorated. A mahogany crib was waiting on new carpet and on 23rd May at 10.30 in the evening, Victoire went into labour. Even by today's standards, it was incredibly tight.

After a relatively short labour of six hours, a roaring, plump baby daughter was born at 4.15 in the morning. Within moments, the room was crowded with politicians, clergymen and chancellors, all pressing their ruddy faces close to the bawling baby girl to attest that the child was in fact Victoire's. No one wanted the same scandal that James II and his second wife Mary of Modena had suffered. She had delivered a thriving baby boy without the necessary witnesses being present at the birth so the majority of the public (mainly Protestants who disliked her Catholic husband) believed that she had in fact miscarried yet again and that a live baby had been smuggled into her room in a warming pan to replace the dead child. At that stage, James had been desperate for a male child to succeed him since Mary and Anne were his only surviving children from his first marriage. It was one of the factors that led to the revolution that knocked James II of his throne so Edward was very particular that history wasn't about to repeat itself with his child.

As they stared at the vocal child, no one in the room had any idea that in two decades, they would be bowing to this plump baby and that she would be commanding armies, appointing prime ministers and selecting archbishops. From the moment of her birth, because she was an important child fifth in line to the throne, she would never be alone and every morsel of food would be tested before it reached her lips.

As the sky lightened, her mother lay exhausted in her bed and the tiny child grizzled. The duchess had endured the presence of the men as they peered at the child before they shuffled out of the room murmuring their congratulations to the father and mother. Her father was full of pride at both producing a legitimate child when his brothers seemed to be struggling to do so and for his wife's 'patience and sweetness' during labour. Despite the unromantic beginnings, they had succeeded when others around them had failed.

Although there was a brief moment when Edward was disappointed at not having a son, the duchess was instantly smitten with her daughter, opting to breastfeed for the first six months while most aristocratic women employed wet nurses. Her peers raised eyebrows but she continued nursing and Edward watched his stout, pretty daughter grow miraculously.

The 19th century was a dangerous time to be born. Out of every thousand infants, about 150 died at birth and the prevalence of measles, whooping cough, scarlet fever and cholera meant that a child might only survive to the age of five. It was also a common practice to give infants laudanum to stop their crying, colic and coughs.

Laudanum was basically an opiate largely unknown until the 1660s but had grown popular as a general remedy to aid sleep, ease pain, stop diarrhoea (commonly bought on by cholera or dysentery), curb menstrual cramps and flatulence, dull labour pains and soothe earache, toothache and sore throats.

While innumerable women were prescribed the drug, mixed with everything imaginable from herbs, opium, distilled water, belladonna, whisky, gin and cayenne pepper, nurses had begun spoon-feeding noisy crying infants, readily using it as a cure for a bad cough or restless and teething babies. It became widespread amongst working-class families with little money to feed their children due to its ability to stop hungry babies from crying and at only a penny for twenty to twenty-five drops, it was being overused.

One Manchester druggist admitted to selling between five and six gallons of 'Mrs Winslow's Soothing Syrup' every week. That's 24 pints. Unfortunately, they would find that opium caused infant mortality to rise through starvation rather than overdose. One doctor stated that infants were kept in a state of continued 'narcotism' and thereby were disinclined to eat although extremely undernourished. Coroners recorded the cause of their deaths as 'starvation'.

But Victoria blossomed without the use of laudanum, soothed with German lullabies and her father boasted that his chubby daughter with her enormously fat legs was *"a pocket Hercules"*. While Edward crowed with happiness, his brothers were not so happy. His eldest brother George, who had lost his only child Charlotte and grandchild on the same day, hated Edward with a passion.

We have a long series of 'ifs' to consider with regards to Victoria. We have *if* Charlotte and her baby hadn't died and *if* the baby race hadn't happened after their deaths, and again *if* Edward hadn't married Victoire and produced Victoria, it would be a very different history we'd be looking at right now. Instead of Victoria, it could very well have been another extremely unpopular brother, Ernest Duke of Cumberland, who succeeded William. Ernest was a scar-faced brute who was widely believed to have murdered his valet and married a woman who was rumoured to have killed her two previous husbands and had Victoria not been born, he may have become the next king and Britain may well have gone down the same path they had when Oliver Cromwell took over.

One month after the birth, a gold font was brought from the Tower of London to the top floor of Kensington Palace, along with crimson velvet curtains from the chapel of St James, ready for the christening. Despite it being a rather small gathering, there was no question that this was a royal christening worthy of a future monarch.

It was a small gathering mainly because Prince George, Edward's eldest brother and currently the Regent while their father George III was once again incapacitated, was seriously miffed at his brother for outdoing him by producing an heir. Make that furious. Of all his brothers, George despised Edward the most.

George's disagreeable temperament was not helped by that fact that he was dependant on Laudanum to ease the pain in his swollen, gouty legs. He had hated the wife his father had chosen for him and he was an obese 57-year-old playboy who was waiting not so patiently for his father to die so he could step up to the throne as King of England. Things were not looking good for George. As such, he was not going to let Edward have his time in the sun. The ceremony, he insisted, was not to be elaborate one and no one was permitted to dress up in uniforms. And he would have the final say on a name for the child.

Their original choice for a name was to be Victoire Georgiana Alexandrina Charlotte Augusta and they had dutifully sent word to George of their choice. It was a mouthful by any accounts but it ticked all the right boxes. It combined the names of all the Georges, Queen Anne and her godfather, the Russian Tsar, with the added bonus of the child's mother's name. Word came back immediately that George would not permit the name Georgiana because he did not believe that a derivative of his own name should be placed before the derivative of the Tsar of Russia's name, out of respect for the Tsar. He would let them know at the ceremony of his choice of name.

It was a surprising show of reverence, especially coming from George who had never shown the characteristic before, but there was absolutely nothing Edward could do.

At the christening, as the Archbishop of Canterbury held the plump baby, he asked *'By what name does it please Your Highness to call this child?'* George firmly said, *'Alexandrina'* which is when Edward quickly offered up Charlotte as a second name, then Augusta. George shook his head to both. Next Edward suggested Elizabeth which George also rejected because he did not wish this baby, a rival to the throne, to inherit such a historic name from a past British royal family. At which time Victoire burst into tears.

Heaven knows George was used to displays of emotion, although temper tantrums were his own personal forte. But in the chapel of St James, in front of the Archbishop of Canterbury who was shuffling his feet nervously while the restless infant grizzled in his arms, surrounded by embarrassed dignitaries and nobility, even George must have felt out of his depth. To the sound of heart-breaking sobs from his sister-in-law reverberating around the chapel, he finally and reluctantly conceded, *'Give her the mother's name also then, but it cannot precede that of the emperor.'* Without further speaking to his brother, George turned and stormed out. From that day, she was Alexandrina Victoria, and Drina for short.

Three months later, as Victoria was successfully being vaccinated for smallpox, news arrived of another birth. In the summer palace of Rosenau, four miles from Coburg, Victoire's sister-in-law, Luise Duchess of Saxe-Coburg-Saalfeld, had given birth to a son whose name would be Albert. Something to tuck away for later.

For all the celebrations of royal births, England was in a bad way. Four years previously, the Napoleonic Wars had finally ended but as damaging as they had been to the English economy, they were nothing compared to the chronic unemployment, famine and economic depression that followed. By the beginning of 1819, something had to be done to address the industrial unrest spreading through the North and a well-known radical orator by the name of Henry Hunt was just the man to do it.

Monday 16th August 1819 dawned with the promise of being one of those glorious summer's day when nobody wanted to be cooped up inside. With not a cloud in sight, the beautiful weather served to increase the size of the crowd marching from outer townships and by 10.30 am, St Peter's Field in Manchester had been cleared ready for a larger than usual assembly. As expected, crowds of men, women and children gathered, numbering around 60,000, in their Sunday best, disciplined and orderly. Each village and town had been given a time and place to meet and from there the members were instructed to proceed to assembly points from larger towns before heading on to Manchester. Everything was methodical and organised with no sign of unrest or conflict.

A local landowner and chairman of the magistrates, by the name of William Hulton, watched the growing crowd from a house on the edge of St Peter's Field. What he saw terrified him. Thousands of enthusiastic people, standing so close their hats seemed to be touching, were cheering Hunt as he arrived in his carriage shortly after 1pm, making his way to the stand. Frightened by the prospect of riots, the militia was summoned and arrest warrants were hurriedly issued for Henry Hunt and three of his main supporters. The warrants were then handed to two horsemen standing by with instructions to make haste and take the notes to the Manchester and Salford Yeomanry stationed a short distance away. The two enthusiastic troopers immediately drew their swords and galloped away but unfortunately one trooper, in a frantic effort to keep up with his companion, knocked down a woman, causing the death of her son when he was thrown from her arms. It was the catalyst that started the mayhem.

As the pandemonium was building at the meeting, sixty cavalrymen of the Manchester and Salford Yeomanry, led by a local factory owner by the name of Captain Hugh Hornby Birley, arrived at the house of the magistrates ready to accept orders.

Sixty men sitting around for hours with nothing to do but drink and chat meant that when the urgent call to arms came, most were in such a drunken state they were unfit for duty must less capable of sensibly controlling the angry crowd.

Hindsight is a wonderful thing and given the choice, considering future circumstances, I'm sure Hulton would have preferred he'd sent Birley and his inebriated men back to the station for replacements. But there were no replacements and with one part of the crowd cheering loudly as Hunt stepped onto the stand and another part calling for action against the trooper who had knocked the woman down, time was of an essence. Birley was hurriedly instructed to take his cavalry to the meeting and remove Hunt and the other three ringleaders.

The route to the St Peter's Fields was narrow and already packed with people so as the cavalry pushed forward, they became stuck in the midst of the crowd. It was at this point that Birley lost control of his men. In the chaos, his men drew their sabres and frantically hacked indiscriminately at anyone who appeared to be obstructing them. People screamed and horses reared and kicked as everyone tried desperately to get out of the way.

From his vantage point, Hunt saw the assault unfolding below him but instead of trying to calm the situation, he bellowed *"Disperse the meeting!"*, spurring them on even more. Eventually Hunt was arrested and dragged from the stand but it didn't stop the Yeoman. They were in a frenzy, shredding and destroying the banners and flags on the stand, trampling on the dead and the injured and turning the countryside into a bloody battlefield.

The exact number of those killed and injured at the 'Peterloo Massacre' has never been established with certainty. Sources claim 15 were killed and around 600 trampled and injured. A particular feature of the meeting was the number of women present, dressed in white and carrying their own flags. Of the 600 injured, at least 168 were women, four of whom died as a result of their wounds. As a consequence, meetings were called all over the country as the working class declared war.

With George's lack of military acumen, it was Edward who stepped in with his reputation for being a fierce army officer, intent on strict discipline. As we know, reprimanding this sort of behaviour was right up his alley. He actually revelled in it. But perhaps he had mellowed with marriage and fatherhood because he reacted less brutally than the Edward of old. While authorities believed the country was heading towards armed rebellion, they were ready to introduce legislation to suppress radical meetings and place every significant working-class radical reformer in jail. But for once in his life, Edward was thinking outside the box. What if England could meet the working-class halfway? What if the monarchy gave them enough leeway to mollify them? He envisaged an England with the working-class people as a sturdy base and sitting high and dry at the apex was the monarchy but to do that, the monarchy had to get the workers onside. Over the course of autumn, he made plans to visit Lanarkshire after Christmas to set his ideas into action.

Fate had other ideas.

Edward had been accumulating enormous debts again in the short time since coming back to England. He was overspending, gambling and living the good life, much like in his bachelor days, so with little money available, he decided to winter modestly away from society beside the seaside in Devon. As an added bonus, doctors had discovered the healing powers of the sea and saltwater baths were highly recommended for nursing mothers. Once again, he borrowed money and the family set off in early December, staying for a short time in Salisbury before arriving on Christmas Eve at Woolbrook Cottage in Devon. Time passed quietly with lazy days idly playing with his daughter, until a rather disconcerting and ominous incident made Edward stop in his tracks. A fortune-teller told him that two members of the Royal Family would die soon and of course Edward was unnerved. It's not that he took the words of the gypsy *too* seriously, but with the child mortality rate so high, he was unwilling to take any chances when it came to his precious daughter. Precautions were taken and Victoria was bundled up warmly and cosseted even more than usual. By then Victoria was 8 months old but was the size of a 1-year-old with two teeth that had cut through her gums without her even flinching.

As it turned out, it was Edward who caught the cold and in the weeks after Christmas, it worsened. After a fall of heavy snow, Edward and John Conroy took a long walk on the cliffs for some fresh air and Edward returned complaining that the cold made his bones ache. But still there was no cause for alarm.

By 18th January however, his condition had worsened and on the 20th, he took to his bed. Fever and delirium had set in and of course the doctors took over with their gruesome medical treatments. Blistering, bleeding and leeches were administered but not surprisingly, everything failed. During a short respite on 22nd, Edward made a hurried will, making sure that his beloved daughter Drina would be entrusted to the care of her mother.

By evening, a small group had gathered around his bed. He looked at his wife and said, *'Do not forget me'* and sank once more into delirium. By then, Victoire was anxiously pacing the room and had not changed her clothes or slept much for several days. She would not sleep at all for the next 24 hours. At 10 o'clock in the morning of 23rd January, Edward died.

Victoire's world changed overnight. Only a month before she had been a happy wife and mother and all of a sudden, she was a penniless widow for the second time in her life, living in a country where she could barely speak the language among people who thoroughly disliked her. Still in a state of shock, Victoire decided to return to Kensington with her daughter to grieve and with the help of her brother Leopold, all three set off.

Before the month was over, the gypsy was proven correct. The old king, George III, blind and suffering from recurring madness, had spoken non-stop for fifty-eight consecutive hours, almost without drawing breath, and had died six days after his son Edward. Victoria's Uncle George was now the king and Britain turned its nose up in disgust.

George had always been an embarrassment for the British but he was about to excel himself as his coronation approached. His estranged wife Caroline had been in France making plans to return to Italy when she heard of her father-in-law's death and the news stopped her in her tracks. Suddenly everything changed. Her husband, even though they'd been separated for the last 25 years, was now the king and since they were still officially married, she intended to take full advantage of her new improved status. With her head full of delicious thoughts, she sent news to England that she would be returning as soon as possible to attend George's coronation as his Queen.

When the reply arrived, she was shocked. Instead of the expected greetings, she was told that the date of the coronation had not been set as yet but in any case, she was not welcome and not to bother attending the ceremony.

It was like waving a red flag in front of a bull. Gone were the visions of jewels adorning her hair. Gone were the dreams of attending glittering balls and parties, despite the fact that she had to share the excitement with her grossly overweight, obnoxious, philandering husband. Instead, she was being rudely pushed aside, as if she hadn't suffered enough already. Furious at the insult and unwilling to give up her rights without a fight, she was determined that she would return to Britain for the ceremony anyway.

Of course, George knew exactly what Caroline would do. They'd been at each other's throats every day of their marriage and she'd gone against everything he'd said over the years, more out of perverseness than anything else. He'd put up with her public insults and he'd put up with her slurs over those years and he'd even tried unsuccessfully to divorce her. But it was all going to end. He'd been waiting for his coronation day for a very long time and he wasn't about to let her spoil it for him. George informed his ministers that if she turned up, they were to get rid of her in any way possible, and then he continued happily with his plans for the exorbitant ceremony that he would make sure outshone Napoleon's coronation.

After watching the pair at loggerheads over the years, the last thing Parliament wanted was a public fracas on the day of the coronation. As much as they disliked their future king, it would be a total disgrace for England if the world saw anything except a glittering occasion to welcome George as their monarch. Rather than run the risk and with plenty of time up their sleeves, (the ceremony would not be scheduled until the next year), they offered Caroline an increased annuity of £50,000 if she simply stayed away. Caroline replied that she would be pressing ahead with plans to attend and once again, she was told not to. Still the advice fell on deaf ears.

Eighteen months after George III's death, all plans were finalised and the coronation date was set for 19th July. During the wait, George kept himself busy. Costumes were selected for all the participants inspired by Tudor styles. His robe of crimson velvet costing £24,000 was commissioned with gold stars and ermine trim and a train stretching for 27 feet. He had rejected the traditional crown, St Edward's crown, and commissioned a new one adorned with 12,314 rented diamonds at a cost of £6,525 - a rate of 10% of their actual value - allowing light to enter through the open back of the setting. He also acquired a large blue diamond in the possession of a diamond merchant, originally looted from the French crown jewels in 1792 that had turned up in England as a pre-cut stone after the statute of limitations for the theft had run out in 1812. This diamond would become known as the Hope Diamond.

George was half an hour late to the ceremony due to a piece of clothing having torn while he tried to squeeze in but once that was fixed, the procession to Westminster Abbey proceeded. George's herb woman and her six young attendants dressed in white strewed the way with herbs and flowers in accordance with centuries-old tradition that was a precaution against the Plague. Next came the officers of state with the crown, the orb, the sceptre and the sword of state. Then followed three bishops carrying respectively a paten, a chalice and a Bible. Next came George in his sumptuous robe wearing a brown wig with a black Spanish hat surmounted by sprays of ostrich feathers and a heron's plume. Twenty-seven pages walked behind carrying the 27-foot long train embroidered in gold followed by the peers in their state robes and coronet marching in order of seniority. Waiting at the entry to the East Cloister was Caroline.

She had been warned not to attend. Twice, in fact. So when she was refused entry, she remained undaunted and moved to the West Cloister, only to be refused again. Still determined, she made her way to the entry via Westminster Hall, where many guests were gathered before the service began. She was greeted by prize fighters dressed as pages holding bayonets under her chin and the Lord Chamberlain slamming the doors in her face.

While Caroline fumed outside the abbey to the open stares of the guests, George was having his own problems. The day had turned hot and still and during the five-hour ceremony, dressed in his heavy robes and wig, George was physically distressed, almost to fainting, and had to be revived with Salvital. Invigorated, George continued to the banquet gallery filled with guests competing with each other in their magnificent clothes, literally ablaze with diamonds.

That night as the revellers partied, Caroline fell ill. She took a large dose of milk of magnesia and a physician prescribed laudanum for the pain in her abdomen. You'll remember that laudanum was a magic drug, widely used as a general remedy to aid sleep, ease pain, curb menstrual cramps and flatulence, treat hysteria and insanity and help with 'fatigue and depression'. Still the pain continued.

One month after the ceremony, Caroline was dead and rumours abounded that she had been poisoned. The upside for George was he was finally free.

While Victoria's Uncle George settled into his throne, her Uncle William's wife delivered a daughter almost six weeks premature they named Elizabeth Georgiana Adelaide. Unfortunately for Victoria, William was older than her father had been, which meant *his* child was in front of Victoria in the royal queue to the throne. It looked like she had been not only deprived of a father but also of her chance of becoming the future Queen of England.

Unfortunately for William, Elizabeth lived for only three short months and after her death, William's wife would suffer three more stillbirths. With each death, Victoria's position became more certain.

Victoria's first memories of life in Kensington Palace was being told to keep quiet so as not to disturb her frightening uncle Augustus living in the apartment below them with his vast collection of books. By then she hated sitting still, hated taking medicine and hated being told what to do. In short, she was a bad-tempered and defiant little girl who liked getting her own way.

Augustus had become a figure of dread to her with his funny wig lopsidedly covering his own hair and his own frightening bouts of temper where he threatened severe punishments if she made any noise. Her uncle Frederick was the most popular of her 'wicked uncles' and regarded his niece as a ray of sunshine. The childless duke looked forward to her frequent visits and he even bought her a donkey to ride on as well as arranging Punch and Judy shows for her in his garden.

It has often been wondered why, in melancholy times later on in her life, Victoria would recall her childhood as being unhappy. A capacity for dramatisation and self-pity has been considered since her childhood, at least her early years, would never be seen as 'unhappy'. By any standard, she was treated with pure indulgence and very much cosseted. She was very well fed and housed. She had dedicated nurses and a devoted mother who supplied her with countless toys and amusements. She was encouraged to study hard and was provided with tutors to make sure she spoke English without an accent and her beautiful bell-like voice could be heard singing throughout Kensington Palace. She also had a German tutor, a Lutheran clergyman for religious study, another who taught her arithmetic, at which she excelled, as well as historical and geographical studies. She had horses to ride and took regular trips to the seaside with attendants who doted on her. She couldn't even say her mother had neglected her. Victoire left letters on her pillow in tiny pink envelopes telling her how much she loved her and that nobody in the world loved her more. So considering everything, it's quite the opposite of her adult 'memories' and not conductive of an emotionally deprived childhood at all. She even frequently shared a room with her elder half-sister

Feodora, Victoire's daughter by her first husband, who would be her lifelong friend.

By the time she reached 7 years of age, her Uncle George had become a huge, gouty man but not weakened enough that he hadn't been beguiled by the plump little blue-eyed girl. Or more to the point, her elder half-sister Feodora.

People love to gossip and George's self-absorption and appearance gave everyone plenty to gossip about. Rumours bubbled to the surface as people began to notice that an animated George had been seen way too often in Feodora's company and he was paying an awful lot of attention to the pretty 18-year-old. One thing led to another and before anyone knew it, rumours had George re-entering the baby stakes with the intention of providing Britain with another heir by marrying Feodora and having a child with her.

Tongues began to wag even more when Victoria and Feodora visited George just prior to his planned trip to Edinburgh. By then, he was ruling a Britain that was semi-detached from Scotland and he was savvy enough to understand that being the first Hanoverian monarch to visit Scotland since the 1745 rising, when the Scottish Highlanders had supported Bonnie Prince Charlie's claims to the throne, was a definite plus for him. Unfortunately, he also felt the need to dress in Highland dress and it was often noted that he was so fat that his belly dangled *below* the hem of his kilt.

Ghastly visions of the dangling tummy below his kilt comes to my mind and it must have been a horrid shock for the pretty 18-year-old when she realised there was a possibility she had been chosen to carry the child of the bewigged, powdered and obese 64-year-old man.

Thankfully for her, George's mistress Lady Conyngham had also heard the rumours and she put a stop to any such romance by promptly sending Victoire, Victoria and Feodora back home to Kensington Palace, well away from George and his flirtations. Lady Conyngham had no intention of losing her benefits or her standing as far as George was concerned.

It's another of those weird twists of fate. If Lady Conyngham hadn't jealously stepped in and sent them home, and if George had in fact married Feodora and had a child, Victoria would never have sat on the throne. She would probably have been married off to some duke or other and her name would only have been a footnote in history. Her grandchildren would never have been born and perhaps the worst family squabble in history, resulting in the death of millions of innocent people, would never have occurred.

While all this was going on, John Conroy stood by in the shadows, watching the family closely and keeping things well and truly under his control. He still privately believed that his wife was the late Edward Duke of Kent's daughter and that her rightful place was heir to the throne ahead of Victoria. While he watched, he was busy devising a plan he called the 'Kensington System'.

The plan basically isolated Victoria from the English court and from her uncles while making Victoria and her mother utterly dependent on him in their apartment in Kensington Palace. The one exclusion to this isolation was Victoria's unmarried aunt, Princess Sophia, and all four would sit down and have dinner together two or three times a week. By then, Conroy had inserted himself well and truly into the family life and was controlling not only the finances of Victoire but of Sophia as well.

With a wife and six children of his own, and no savings in the bank to speak of, money was always short for Conroy. It will come of no surprise that he was squirrelling away a nice, tidy little nest egg for himself as well as paying for an estate in Montgomeryshire worth £18,000 (in today's money that is the equivalent to £1.2 million) with no one being any the wiser. If nothing ever came of his belief that his wife was the heir to the throne, he had this scheme as a backup and it was working quite well for him.

While the system helped Conroy to feather his own nest, it actually had its merits. Victoria's uncle on her mother's side, Prince Leopold, could only agree with Conroy that it was unwise for Victoria to see too much of the rakish life of her uncle King George or her dysfunctional family in Coburg. Every day it seemed there were disturbing reminders from the continent that kings could be made and unmade almost overnight. News filtered in that King Charles X of France had been cast out by his general, Louis-Philippe, who had taken the throne for himself and in Brussels the Belgians had stated they did not want to be under Dutch control anymore. They were demanding that they be made an independent kingdom and their candidate to govern them was Louis-Philippe's son.

The prize, however, was finally offered to Leopold, because of his diplomatic connections with royal houses across Europe. Not only that, he was seen as a British-backed candidate who was not affiliated to other powers, such as France.

Leopold had already turned down the throne of Greece, believing it to be too precarious, but Belgium, well that was another story. Not only could he turn Belgium into a modern, constitutional monarchy but the juicy carrot was that he could leave the predominantly female household consisting of Victoire, Victoria, Feodora and their governess behind in Kensington Palace. Better still, he would still be sufficiently close to London to maintain his influence.

While that was all well and good, his departure had other far reaching consequences. It left the dominant male figure of John Conroy in his place, and in Leopold's absence, Conroy's dominance grew. And as his power grew, the rumour mill worked overtime again.

This time heads were turning as they noticed that Victoire was relying on Conroy more and more and suspicious whispers were being spread throughout court about their ... closeness. People were putting two and two together, looking at dates and doing the math, and soon many were making snide remarks that he could very well be Victoria's father since Conroy had been with Victoire and Edward even before the child was born.

Despite the rumours, there can be no disputing the fact that George III was Victoria's grandfather. She had the same hooded, protuberant eyes, the same bird-like nose and the resemblance couldn't be disputed. She was a pure Hanover in every way down to her furious temper tantrums and discordant emotional behaviour and many ministers feared that she was showing the same signs of mental instability that George III had. She was known to have even thrown a pair of scissors at her governess at one time.

English ministers knew all about the Hanoverians and their fiery tempers. They'd watched George I jealously fight with his popular son and in turn, George II had rowed publicly with *his* son. They'd watched as George III's children grew up and they'd witnessed first-hand the near-murderous arguments between the brothers and their father. They'd seen Edward as a soldier trying to physically knock discipline into his troops on Gibraltar, almost provoking a mutiny with his rages, and they'd seen his savagery when he refused his troops a drink after standing in the hot, scorching sun for hours. One Christmas Day, he even had three men shot by a firing squad while other mutineers were being lashed. And as if it was at all possible, his brother Ernest Duke of Cumberland was an even harsher disciplinarian. As a Colonel of the 15th Dragoons, he had caused a scandal when he thrashed, not a private, but a fellow officer with his cane. You can be sure Victoria's ministers were very well aware of Victoria's Hanoverian genes and although she could certainly be lovable when she chose to be, learning to live with her furious, unreasonable, sudden temper tantrums was a challenging exercise.

By watching Victoria and George closely, it was becoming increasingly clear that the king was dying. His younger brother Frederick Duke of York was already dead which meant the next in line to be king was 65-year-old William Duke of Clarence and for the middle-class workers, the future looked grim. William was violently against reform and as far as they were concerned, he was the one standing firmly in the way of progress and their freedom. You didn't need a crystal ball to see where this was going.

And sure enough, when George died, William's accession to the throne was greeted with ugly mob scenes. He and his brother Ernest were pelted with stones and abuse and hooted at on many occasions and at one time, a stone even hit William on the head. In the end, it was either risk death or listen to what the people were saying.

For many years, the people had criticised the unfair electoral system and for many years George had disregarded their protests. There were constituencies, they argued, that only had a handful of voters who elected two MPs to Parliament. With few voters and no secret ballot, it was easy for candidates to buy votes. While they had been busy doing exactly that, towns like Manchester had no MPs to represent them despite having grown over the previous 80 years.

While the House of Commons passed a Reform Bill and the House of Lords defeated it, riots popped up in London, Birmingham, Derby, Nottingham, Leicester, Exeter and Bristol. The riots in Bristol were so savage that public buildings were set on fire with more than £300,000 worth of damage done as well as twelve lives lost. Of 102 people arrested and tried, 31 were sentenced to death and Lieutenant-Colonel Brereton, the commander of the army in Bristol, was court-martialled.

The fear in the government was that unless there was some sort of reform, there might very well be a revolution. You didn't have to be a genius to understand that what was happening in England was the exact same thing that had happened in Europe. In July 1830, there had been a revolution in France, which had resulted in the abdication of King Charles X and the initialising of a constitutional monarchy and standing firmly in the way of any reform in England was William.

Eventually, and reluctantly, all William could do was agree to accept the Great Reform Bill. With the flick of a quill, 'rotten boroughs' were removed and new towns were given the right to elect MPs even though there was a caveat that only men who owned property worth at least £10 could vote. It was still a long way from silencing all protests since it still effectively cut out most of the working classes with only men who could afford to pay to stand for election could be MPs. But with his signature on the bill, Britain was on its way to becoming a full parliamentary system although it was still a long way from being a democracy.

While most of his family were seen as violent and aggressive, William was seen as a buffoon, although a somewhat amiable one. But he tried, he really did. He hosted a feast on one of his birthdays for over 3,000 poor people and attended several musical charities. One even raised the enormous sum of £7,600 (around £500,000 by today's standards) and there was scarcely a hospital that had not applied successfully for help. He even gave £1,000 to house indigent Irish Protestant clergymen in London and another £3,000 to rebuild a church at Kew while his wife Adelaide was one of the most generous benefactors in history, giving away around £40,000 per annum out of an income of £100,000.

If the public loved Adelaide, Victoire (now being called the Duchess of Kent) did not receive the same sentiment. The two women shared a frosty relationship and although Victoire and Victoria were invited to attend William's coronation, neither of them appeared. Victoire was meant to carry Adelaide's coronet at the ceremony but instead of seeing it as an honour, she saw it as humiliating and under no circumstance would she be so belittled. She was after all the mother of the future Queen of England.

It was not Victoire who sent the letter to Adelaide stating that they would not be able to attend. It was John Conroy and the snub did not go down well. In fact, it only served to inflame resentment even more.

In the interests of training Victoria for the role of Queen during her teenage years, William and Victoire tried to overlook their mutual antagonism towards each other, but for Victoire, it was difficult. She was alone, she was foreign and she had a very imperfect grasp of English and their way of life. With the departure of her brother Leopold for the throne of Belgium, and then the death of her mother, she felt terribly isolated.

As such, Victoria entered puberty with the sharp sense of bad blood between her mother and her uncle and in this environment, it was easy for people who had an influence over her to take advantage of the situation and perhaps make it even worse. Meaning John Conroy. As she grew older, it became more obvious that her mother was in no position to control the situation.

History paints Conroy as a calculating villain, and there is no doubt that he had many faults. But there are always two sides to a story. Sure, he was ambitious for power but he was no different from thousands of others who were seriously intent on social climbing. Not just that, he proved to be a good friend to Victoire, even though he'd had his hand in the cookie jar for most of that time. It was Conroy who stood by her and it was Conroy who helped her when no one else would and it would also be purely sentimental not to see that Victoria herself could be self-willed and very difficult. With her Uncle William ageing, a strong person was needed to keep the wilful young princess's feet firmly planted on the ground.

Over the previous year, William had stated that he was going to live long enough to see Victoria sit on the throne at 18 years of age at any cost but it was obvious to all that his health was failing. Fully aware of this, his main priority became his 17-year-old niece's marriage and he threw himself into the plans, mainly due to his complete lack of trust in Victoria's mother to choose a worthy husband. Despite knowing the problems associated with close familial marriages, a husband from the German family gene pool was seriously considered. Either that or one of the Princes of Orange. But Victoria's mother was just as determined that her daughter would do no such thing. She and her brother Leopold had other ideas. As Victoria's husband, the successful candidate would have incredible power as her consort and they wanted that power to stay securely in the Saxe-Coburg-Saalfeld family. With Leopold standing silently but firmly behind his sister, William and Victoire locked horns yet again.

There never seemed to be a time when Victoire and William saw eye to eye on anything and no one knows for sure if she argued with William because she didn't like him or because she honestly didn't think the Prince of Orange was suitable for her daughter. All we know is they argued and bickered bitterly and despite William being the king, she stood her ground. *That* match, she stated, just wasn't going to happen.

Furious at being challenged yet again by Victoire, William went ahead and held a lavish ball for the arrival of Prince of Orange at Windsor Castle, ready to introduce Victoria to him. At the same time, and unbeknownst to William, Victoire held one of her own events and invited her two nephews, her brother Ernst's boys from Saxe-Coburg-Gotha, to join her at Kensington Palace to do the exact same thing. The gauntlet was thrown.

Victoire's eldest nephew, Ernst of Coburg, was not the handsomest or smartest of her two nephews. He was rather large for his age and most people agreed that his flashing black eyes, full of spirit and energy, were his only good feature. But he was the eldest of the two nephews by 14 months and as such he became Victoire's preferred choice. With Ernst, the House of Coburg and Hanover would combine and simply continue as they were with the added bonus of the throne of England from Victoria.

But fate has a nasty way of stepping in when you least expect it. Accompanying Ernst was his handsome 16-year-old brother Albert, and with that one addition to the guest list, England's fate was sealed forever.

Prince Albert of Saxe-Coburg-Gotha was Victoria's first cousin, delivered within months of each other by the same midwife. Much like Victoria, Albert came from a totally dysfunctional family of his own. Born in Coburg, the second son of Duke Ernest, the ruler of the two minor German states of Coburg and Gotha, he was very much a poor relation. Albert's father had married Princess Louise of Saxe-Gotha-Altenburg, a beautiful 16-year-old girl, when he failed to win the hand of a Russian grand duchess. Though not quite the most romantic of stories, I'm sure the innocent girl had dreams of being swept off her feet by the handsome duke and living happily ever after. What Louise had no way of knowing at the time was that the marriage would be a very unhappy one nor did she know that they would separate when she was only 24 years old.

All fingers of blame cannot be pointed solely at Ernest since Louise was no angel herself. The ducal court was alive with spicy scandals and wild stories mainly because both husband and wife were promiscuous. It all came to an unhappy end when Albert's parents were divorced when he was barely 5 years old with both boys remaining with their father. Seven months later, his mother secretly married one of her lovers only to die five years later of cancer when she was only 31 years old.

Albert's father waited one year after his wife's death before he began searching for a new bride but due to his age and his terrible reputation, he found his choices very limited. He finally settled for his 33-year-old niece, Duchess Marie of Wurttemberg, his sister Antoinette's daughter, and despite the uncle-niece relationship being frowned upon among European royalty, the marriage went ahead. This effectively made her Albert's first cousin as well as his stepmother.

Being motherless and rather neglected by his father, Albert's life and career was shaped by his uncle Leopold, the widower of Princess Charlotte who died in childbirth, and he had never forgotten how he had been cheated of his chance to rule as king consort of England. Since 1831, Leopold had been King of Belgium but England was never too far from his thoughts and ambitions. Which is where his nephew Albert fitted in nicely with his plans. He sent Albert to the University of Bonn to receive an education in law, finance, public administration and history and Albert never disappointed him. He rose each morning at 6 am to study, shunned social invitations, drank only water and retired to bed at nine every night. Of women, he had no experience and very little emotional knowledge. Despite this, his uncle judged him ready for his destiny. Victoria.

They had met only once before when he had fallen asleep after dinner and had suffered from a bilious attack. Even then, Victoria had warned her relations to expect no engagement in the future because of her *'great repugnance to change my present position'*. But when Albert arrived at Windsor that day, late and travel-stained from a bad crossing but still incredibly handsome, the short, plump 17-year-old with protruding teeth watched him from the head of the staircase, and well, it was a *fait accompli*. She wrote to her uncle to thank him *'for the prospect of great happiness'* and although there was no formal engagement, both parties assumed the match would take place in the near future.

As her uncle William had hoped, he lived long enough to witness Victoria's 18th birthday. But only by a whisker. By 4th June, two weeks after her birthday, William's lungs contained blood, a valve in his heart was closed and his liver and spleen were swollen to twice their size. Barely one month after Victoria's birthday on 20th June, William died and Victoria moved out of her mother's bedroom and into the still unfinished Buckingham Palace, far away from her mother with whom she was barely on speaking terms.

Being incredibly protected by her mother all her life did not leave Victoria shy. On the contrary. She had always known she was meant for the throne of England - there simply wasn't anyone else - and knowing that piece of information gave her a certain awareness of her entitlement. It made her self-reliant, impulsive, volatile and it gave her a steely conviction in her own judgement. And of course, she had a Hanoverian temper to go with it that no one had ever thought to teach her to control. As a result, she never learned to accept other authority figures because *she* was the supreme authority.

Victoria depended on the workings of two Houses of Parliament as well as the efficiency of the army, the navy and trade. Members of the House of Commons were not being elected by the people but by a small number of men who owned a lot of property. Checking and approving what the House of Commons did was the function of the House of Lords, some hundred or more rich men who owned most of the land, and who let Britain know in no uncertain terms *they* were the ones really running the country. Unlike France, there had not been a revolution to overthrow these arrangements but it was definitely being monitored closely. They liked to tell one another that the monarch was simply a figurehead, kept in place by the Whigs, but that was far from the truth. The monarch still occupied a position of real power in Britain, even though they had exercised that power recklessly, and the monarchy in turn depended on the peerage for economic prosperity. The powers were all delicately balanced in trade, law and the church and it was essential for Victoria's future that all these institutions continued to support the monarchy and that she should maintain the status quo. There was no room for failure. For this timid 18-year-old, it was an incredibly daunting prospect.

But the dramatic events of her accession left Victoria feeling very isolated and desperately lonely and this is where Albert stepped back into the picture.

Victoria had been wise not to choose Albert's elder brother Ernest. In later years, he would become a philanderer like his father, suffering from syphilis in his late teens and early twenties most likely due to their father taking Ernest to *'sample the pleasures'* of Paris and Berlin. Albert was entirely different. He was gentle, almost effeminate, intelligent, an art lover, a scholar and a workaholic in a family full of lusty barbarians. He was so unlike his brother it was rumoured he was the son of the court chamberlain, the Jewish Baron Ferdinand von Meyern, fathered during a time when Albert's mother was avenging herself on her unfaithful husband by taking lovers of her own. Nothing was ever proven because the only person who could tell the truth was his mother and she wasn't talking.

Victoria's wedding took place in February the following year in the Chapel Royal, six months after her coronation at St James's. But there were mixed feelings from the public. Their Queen had the right to call herself the most eligible woman in the world and for a modest prince like Albert from Saxe-Coburg, sometimes seen as a priggish, pompous and humourless German from a rather obscure place in a small German duchy, the public regarded the match with trepidation. In the back of their minds was a distrust of the monarchy (looking at Victoria's vile uncles) and an intense dislike for Albert who they thought had arrived in order to exploit the wealth and the dignity of Britain by marrying their Queen.

But at a time when the lower class of England desperately needed a diversion from their everyday poverty and hardship, they softened when watching the tiny bride glow with love. It actually had the makings of the greatest story ever told.

Despite torrents of rain, violent gusts of wind and extreme cold, people pushed and shoved each other to get a good view of the 5-foot bride, dressed beautifully in white satin and lace, a diamond necklace around her neck and glittering diamond earrings in each ear as well as a magnificent sapphire brooch that Albert had given her to adorn her wedding dress. Behind her were twelve train-bearers wearing white dresses adorned with white roses watched on by 300 aristocrats. Beside her walked her cranky old uncle Augustus Duke of Sussex, who gave her away, smiling for once on her wedding day.

Like most marriages, there was a settling in period and there were times when the relationship gears didn't quite mesh. She loved to stay out late and dance until early in the morning but Albert had not been raised that way. He didn't like dancing late and he wanted to be in bed by 10 pm. More so than in most marriages, there was a thunderous clash of personalities full of terrible rows, slamming doors and fits of shouting echoing through the halls of Buckingham Palace. But after every bitter argument were the heart-felt makeups and in Victoria's case her love was almost palpably impassioned.

There was no disputing their intense feelings towards each other but the start to the marriage was tempestuous and passionate with neither wanting to surrender their own personal independence and personality. If she was difficult to live with, I think Albert was actually a bit difficult in his own way as well. He could be rather school-masterly, treating Victoria rather like an errant child, which of course she was, and that was like adding fuel to the fire.

But above all else, Albert and Victoria truly and genuinely loved each other and when they were functioning well, they were an amazing pair to behold. Albert came with a lot of emotional baggage because of his family's dysfunctional history and all he wanted was to be the model husband that his own father wasn't. To achieve that, they needed to create a fresh image of family values to the expanding middle class. But it came at a price. Albert was more than a little daunted by his role as Consort to his feisty queen and from the very first day, even though she was besotted with her handsome husband, she would not concede any political power to him.

For Victoria, the unfortunate by-product of her obsession with Albert was the arrival of children. And she proved to be a healthy fertile woman. Within weeks of the marriage, she was pregnant. Almost nine months to the day, their first daughter was born and named Victoria, (nicknamed Vicky after her mother) and only months after giving birth, she was furious to discover she was pregnant with a second child because pregnancy meant enforced abstinence from nights of married bliss with her *'angel'* Albert. Because of their vigorous sex life, Albert, Alice, Alfred, Helena, Louise and Arthur soon followed over the space of seven years. Leopold and Beatrice would both be born later in the coming years and with each addition to the growing family, Britain's memory of her notorious philandering uncles was being purged. But as much as Britain loved Victoria, they saw it as a little odd that she was not the ideal model of motherhood, overheard saying that children were smelly and awkward, with a *'terrible frog-like action'* and not fit to handle until they were at least 6 months old. She not only found her babies repulsive, she also refused to breastfeed them, having a totally insurmountable disgust for the process. You see, for Victoria, her total attention was focused on Albert.

But for all their sexual harmony, they were locked in a struggle for dominance. Albert had married a queen and Victoria was not shy about reminding him who was in charge. She clung to her power but due to the pregnancies, she was uneasily aware of her inadequacy. As for Albert, he knew exactly what he wanted. He had a desperate need to put his own stamp on British history instead of meekly fitting in with the traditions of the English Royal House and living in the palaces of his wife's quarrelsome predecessors. He not only wanted control of the royal family but also the royal household and if he was being honest, even the monarchy itself. In his male-dominated childhood, he had little faith in a woman's ability to rule.

Morally upright in the extreme, Albert was everything his amoral father hadn't been. He was totally loyal to his wife and he was a hands-on father, scolding them when he felt it was necessary and punishing them at times rather severely. As a result, the children were in awe of their father and just a little scared of their mother and her fierce tempers. Albert was deeply troubled by Victoria's fierce temper. Always in the back of his mind was the reminder of a particular royal legacy: insanity. And in particular, her grandfather George III. Where most men might confront his wife about her temper, Albert chose the safe ground and walked on eggshells around her, especially during her pregnancies, although sometimes this just made things worse.

It wasn't only Albert who was nervous that she had inherited the Hanoverian insanity. Watching Victoria's temper tantrums, her doctors were concerned as well. Any mention of the madness of her grandfather was suppressed largely because Victoria herself was sensitive about the subject. But you can believe her doctors were very well aware of it. It had also ruined the lives of George III's daughters. Most were prevented from marrying and confined to a so-called nunnery at Windsor but for those who did marry, none produced any children. And we all know the story about his sons.

But was it madness or was it another case of porphyria? Most of George III's children were afflicted by some of the symptoms of porphyria and his son, the Prince Regent, was laid low by bouts of acute illness and episodes of mental confusion. Even the medical history of Victoria's father includes attacks of abdominal pain, rheumatism and acute sensitivity to sunlight. All are symptoms of porphyria.

Porphyria is a dominant gene, which means that each child of a carrier has a 50% chance of inheriting the disease. However, one of the peculiarities of the illness is that in 90% of those with the faulty gene, it remains latent and they show no symptoms of the illness. The gene can thus appear to skip generations and then resurface. So, when looking at her grandfather and all his peculiarities and fits of temper, to say the doctors were keeping a close eye on Victoria is perhaps a huge understatement.

Victoria's terrible rages was not the only problem in the family. Behind the façade of a model family was a hornet's nest of hostilities with Victoria feeling trapped in her perpetual cycle of pregnancy and children arriving with monotonous regularity. With each new pregnancy, she was forced to relinquish more and more of her political duties to Albert and of course, since he was also trying to be the role-model husband and father, he struggled to balance work and family. He loved his children but he was on his self-created treadmill of work, work, work and duties. And the more Albert worked, the more he was absent, not only from his children, but also from his needy wife. Which created more tension and more rows. Instead of the chocolate box of gorgeousness that everybody was led to believe existed, behind closed doors it was a place riddled with conflict and a cauldron of simmering tension and huge resentments.

Albert was finding his enormous workload exhausting which in turn was affecting his health. He was plagued with neuralgia, fits of shivering, toothache and insomnia. But despite Victoria's proclaimed adoration for her husband, she had very little sympathy for him. Having given birth to nine children, she thought Albert was just being weak with the inability to endure pain. What she needed was someone *she* could depend on, not the other way around. And she wasn't shy about telling him.

Tension over power and politics was never far away from the couple and her hatred for her repeated pregnancies clouded Victoria's very existence. To soothe things between them, Albert took his wife on repeated holidays together, leaving the growing brood in the capable hands of governesses. But at the end of each holiday, when they came home to Buckingham Palace, Victoria complained it was unsuitable for a royal personage. With an expanding number of children, even though during George IV's time £500,000 of alterations had taken place, a new residence was needed.

Ever the dutiful husband who disliked confrontations, Albert took the safe ground once again and packed them all up and moved to Windsor while the Isle of Wight was decided upon as the family retreat. This idyllic spot in the south of England with its gentle, natural coves framing the sea became the home for his growing family where the children would grow up in a lush environment. There the children could hunt butterflies and play on Osborne Beach and they could learn important life lessons and learn to cook and grow vegetables. As the children were left to find their own amusements, Victoria seemed to calm down, although she never let Albert forget that she was the one ruling the roost.

But even with these new concessions, Albert's relations with his wife had reached crisis point.

By early 1856, Victoria's doctor expressed concern about her mental state and warned that another pregnancy could endanger her mind. Albert should avoid confrontation when she was angry, he was told, or it could cause long-term damage to her mental state. By July however, Victoria was pregnant again, this time with Beatrice, and Albert was tiptoeing nervously around her, petrified that she would start screaming again. By then, her intense rages were astounding him.

Albert was a very intelligent man. He knew the past reputation of his wife's family and if anyone was looking for the model of a happy family, they were never going to pick the Hanovers. But then again, his wasn't much better. To try and remedy that ill feeling, he was determined to present a happy family image to the world, determined that they would make it better this time. In a sense, he was trying to heal their own childhoods by doing it right with their own children. Like most of us, it's a common impulse to try and put it right with the next generation. But to do that, they needed to find a fresh way to relate to their subjects. With the danger of revolution still looming in Europe and many other European countries, not to mention dynasties feeling threatened, Albert knew he needed to connect to the middle class and show them that their family was a close knit and loving one. And his children were vital to that plan.

The first publicly-shown photograph of the Royal Family was taken at Osborne in 1857, of Victoria, Albert and all nine children and the public lapped up these nuggets of Royal intimacy. For the first time, the monarchy was something the people could relate to. The Queen became a person. The children became real. The family tenderness became genuine.

And then Albert went one step further. He wanted their children to marry into various European dynasties, cementing England's place in the world, and he believed the best place to start his plan was with Germany. Isn't hindsight a wondrous thing?

Prussia was the largest state in Germany and it was the obvious choice for Albert. It was an out-of-the-way place that had a fine education system, a fast-growing industry in the Rhineland and it had been one of the first to emancipate Jews. And they had been forward-thinking enough to pull together and fight Napoleon. But they were still stuck in the dark ages. Autocratic landowners, with a reputation for being tough, incorruptible and piously Protestant, dominated the ruling system. And time and time again, history showed that war really did pay off.

Although Germany had lost almost half of its population to famine and disease during the 17th century, it had benefited territorially. In the 18th century, King Frederick had doubled Prussia's size. Their intervention in the Napoleonic wars had doubled it yet again, making it the most prominent state in Germany although it came at a huge price - Prussia had been humiliated while the French and the Russians had become good friends. The ruling dynasties of Hohezollern and Romanov had even intermarried and had developed solid friendships. Since then, Prussia had been hostile towards France but carefully respectful towards Russia. And Germany stood uncertainly in the middle between England and Russia.

Albert could see the potential in a stronger bond with Germany. Under the right circumstances, a royal marriage between Britain and Prussia might just nudge Germany in the right direction towards unification and that in turn would produce a safe haven for his family. It could bring an alliance with Britain, which would ultimately become the foundation for peace in a Europe that hadn't seen it for centuries.

It was a wonderful dream and the cornerstone of this dream was his eldest and cleverest daughter, Vicky. She had to marry the eventual heir of Prussia and by doing that, she would rescue it from the extravagances of a growing German military. It was Vicky's job to make sure that this new Germany was a liberal pro-British constitutional monarchy and if she pulled it off, there would be a liberal Prussia and a liberal Germany and both would be friends with Britain.

Frederick William Hohenzollern, or Fritz as he was called, was ten years older than Vicky but dashingly handsome and charismatic and he was next in line to the German throne after his 62-year old father, William I of Prussia. William's age and ill health meant Vicky and Fritz shouldn't have to wait very long to become rulers. Well, that was the plan anyway. With no way of knowing the horrific consequences of his decision in the future, plans went into full swing.

The meeting at Balmoral between Fritz and Vicky was supposed to be entirely secret, away from the press and away from the eyes of the public. But no sooner had the meeting occurred than the news leaked out. People at court had been listening, picking up titbits, and in no time at all, someone had spilled the beans to the press. Instead of celebrating the news, the British public were horrified. Hadn't Prussia refused to unite with Britain in the Crimean War just a few years earlier?

Albert was very aware of how the Royal Family were written up and how the arranged marriage was perceived. But more important than his popularity with the public was his belief that unity between England and Germany was something the nation desperately needed. He was convinced that her marriage was for the greater good, a vital part of his dynastic plan, and it would lead to liberalism in Germany. The best laid plans....

Vicky was 17 years old when she married 27-year-old Fritz in January of 1858. Not the youngest bride in history by any means, but a sheltered child nonetheless. She was precocious and intelligent and very unlike her younger brother, Albert Edward. She could read and write before the age of 5, had learnt science, literature, Latin and history as well as politics and philosophy. She could speak French and German and she was carefully trained by her mother and father to understand the importance of the task set before her. It was a huge burden to place on the shoulders of a 17-year-old girl.

The marriage looked incredible on paper: the heir to the rising powerful German state marrying the daughter of the richest, most stable power in Europe. It looked like a match made in heaven. But the most amazing added bonus was, that unlike most arranged royal marriages, it actually worked. Fritz adored his clever British bride and she adored him in return. Soon the couple were expecting their first child.

What Albert hadn't realised was that because of his prolonged absence from Germany, he was out of touch with the aggressive rising power of Otto Von Bismarck, the acting Prussian Prime Minister. And things went wrong rather quickly. Bismarck was suspicious of Vicky's Englishness and Vicky disliked him intensely in return. But what became a huge problem was that Fritz's father turned out to be astonishingly long-lived and he appointed Otto von Bismarck as his chief minister.

What bothered Bismarck more than anything was that Vicky was a little too bright for his liking. Everyone knew that Prussian wives were supposed to be silent and submissive. They did *not* host parties and they certainly did *not* mix with non-royals, artists and intellectuals, common or not. And here she was, this young slip of a girl, intelligent and educated, sweeping in with high ideals, dominating her husband Fritz and rocking the boat. She complained about the rigid, deathly dull Prussian court with their threadbare carpets, dirty floors and lack of baths and toilets but worse still, she was heard to say on many occasions that everything was so much better in England than in Prussia. Her complaints spread through the Prussian court in angry whispers and very soon there wasn't one person who would give her the time of day.

It was just homesickness and loneliness talking, but it wasn't a good start. To top it off, her in-laws were very unsympathetic to her needs and Vicky had no idea what to do or who to talk to. In her sadness, she wrote endless letters back home to her mother complaining bitterly of the wicked minister Bismarck.

Back home in England, her mother was shockingly unsympathetic. Hundreds of letters passed backwards and forwards between mother and daughter, showing both a mutual love but also Victoria's obsessive demanding manner as she poured out her mind. *"your answers yesterday by telegram are not quite satisfactory", "and you wouldn't say whether your cold is better or not", "I really hope you are not getting fat again", "do avoid eating soft, pappy things or drinking too much – you know how that fattens", "I wish you for the future to adopt the plan of beginning your letters with the following sort of headings – yesterday, or day before, we did so and so, dined here and there and then where you spent the evening".*

They were small picky directives from Victoria but to Vicky who was 800 miles away from Windsor and terribly lonely and homesick, they were not the supportive letters she would have hoped her mother would send. When a pregnant Vicky fell down the stairs and badly sprained her ankle, her mother wrote… *"I fear you exaggerate as you so often used to do. Others who do not know your disposition think you are really ill, which you are not."*

Vicky replied, *"Don't be angry, dear Mama. It is very painful to think I have annoyed you or displeased you."* and all went back to normal.

As it turned out, Bismarck was just a hiccup for Vicky. The first of her real problems was looming on the horizon and just about to materialise. At the end of a happy, rather uneventful pregnancy except for the sprained ankle incident, she gave birth to a son she and Fritz called Wilhelm.

Wilhelm's problems began on the night he was born. His birth had been terrible. He was breech and no matter what the doctors did, he was coming out bottom first. His legs were over his chest and his arms were behind his head and by the time the doctors realised it, it was too late. They somehow brought his legs down but they had to use considerable force to do it.

When you think about it now, the eleven hours of labour must have been excruciating for the 18-year-old girl who had been too embarrassed to allow her physicians to examine her beforehand. Thoughts of Princess Charlotte's death and her stillborn baby would have laid heavily on everyone's mind and they'd just about given up any hope of a happy outcome when the baby finally appeared.

It was in those early moments of life that Wilhelm's personality was formed. The baby arrived pale and limp, badly bruised and not breathing. His left arm was wound around his neck and it would be three days before anyone noticed that it was of little use. He couldn't lift it and it just wasn't working properly.

When Vicky eventually realised, she was devastated. The thought that her first-born son, the future of Germany and the first grandchild of Queen Victoria, would be permanently regarded as a cripple was something she did not even want to think about. When Wilhelm's grandfather, Fritz's father, saw his first grandson, everyone held their breath. He turned to his son and asked if he expected to be congratulated on the birth of a defective child.

It was everything that Vicky had feared. She had failed in her main mission in life.

They say that the most important years of a person's life are the ones before the age of five. These years build character and shape personality. If this is true, then Wilhelm's destiny was already doomed.

During the first few years of his life, Wilhelm was subjected to a series of desperate treatments for his disability. From 6 months old, he underwent strange treatments to mend the arm. He was sprayed with seawater, massaged weekly and given 'animal baths' in which he was placed inside the warm carcass of a freshly killed hare – an experience Vicky noted that Wilhelm seemed to like very much.

If all of those seem medieval, the next treatment had a more lasting impact on the little boy. His good right arm was strapped to his body to force him to use his damaged left arm and it resulted in many painful falls on the endless marble corridors of their palace in Berlin. As you can imagine, this strapping only compounded his problem because he had nothing to balance himself with when he walked. To make matter worse, by 4 years old, Wilhelm's head had begun to twist to one side as a result of the imbalance in his neck muscles. The right side of his neck had contracted; lifting his shoulder and making him look crooked. To treat this, he was then strapped into a body-length machine to stretch the muscles. In the end, he was subjected to electric shocks and had two small operations performed to sever the tendons that were distorting his body. His incredible torture continued until he was 10 years old.

Despite the suffering he endured, he seemed to be a boisterous affectionate little boy, although somewhat unpredictable. One day, he could be interesting and charming, clever and amusing and then the next, he was aggressive and difficult, hitting out at his nurses.

Seeing his visibly distraught mother only made things worse for Wilhelm. He could see that she was finding it impossible to accept his disability and as a result, he felt more isolated and rejected. Her subliminal message to him was clear. He was her greatest failure. When more siblings arrived, all perfectly healthy, things couldn't have been worse for Wilhelm.

Things were changing across the sea in London as well. Although Victoria was robust, Albert was suffering from Crohn's Disease. His teeth and gums had deteriorated and they were in an appalling condition. With the news from Europe getting worse by the day, worry left him weak and miserable and as the conflict accelerated, it made every symptom seem just that little bit worse. Issues at home with his eldest son Albert Edward, nicknamed Bertie, did not help either.

From an early age, Bertie refused to conform to Albert's strict regime of education, both in the classroom and at court. Unlike his sisters, Bertie found it hard to concentrate. His mind was always wandering, which made learning difficult for him, until many were looking at each other and wondering if perhaps he was a little ... well ... *slow*, if you know what I mean.

But despite everything his tutors said, Bertie was far from stupid. He could speak three languages and when he could be bothered to try, he had an excellent memory. His problem was that he was frivolous, selfish and he could not bear to be alone or unoccupied for a minute. So to cover for his difficulty in the classroom, he would fly into terrifying rages where one minute he was affectionate, courteous, charming and tactful and the next, he would be screaming, throwing his pencils, pulling his sister's hair and being downright rude to his tutors. He would even rant over such banal things as a spot of food on his shirt. His normally unappealing, pale, hooded Hanoverian eyes would be popping out of his head in fury. While his tutors were proclaiming him an absolute nightmare, he was in fact, acting just like his mother and being very Hanoverian.

For most of his life, Bertie fought his mother with sullen resistance and hysterical tantrums, which got him nowhere. Victoria was strong-willed herself and with every subject in Britain jumping to attention at her every command, she wasn't about to let a mere child get the better of her. It was a battle of defiance and wills but it was a battle Victoria was very determined to win. So instead of giving in to him, Victoria put more pressure on him and she dealt out more severe punishments. They were on a collision course and the vicious circle left him feeling more rebellious as his mother bemoaned at his frivolity and his failure to be like his wonderful father.

As a result, it was a rebellious 18-year-old who emerged with an appetite for clothes, smoking, gambling, food and women. And like most of his ancestors, he especially loved the food and women part. Keeping that in mind, Victoria and Albert thought he might learn a few lessons in discipline with the Grenadier Guards at an army base in Curragh in Ireland during the summer of 1861. It was a decision Victoria would regret for the rest of her life because it was there that his friends would organise a surprise for him that had the potential to ruin the family's reputation that his father had tried so very hard to build.

No one knows for sure where Nellie Clifden came from. Some said Connemara while others said Waterford. What everyone was sure of was that Nellie was just one of a group of sixty women, aged between 17 and 25, the soldiers called 'wrens'. These women had turned to prostitution and made their way to the biggest army barracks in Ireland called Curragh Camp where 12,000 Grenadier Guards were stationed and most nights soldiers could pick and choose between the women all huddled together with blankets wrapped around their rain-soaked shoulders.

Nellie's story was no different from most of them. She was vivacious, pretty and delightfully promiscuous and had been orphaned during the Great Famine, which had desecrated Ireland during her childhood years. As a result, she had turned to prostitution as a reasonable livelihood. With the vast number of men in Curragh, life was preferable to the alternative horrors of the workhouse in Naas.

The story goes that one night, two soldiers drew up outside Nellie's door and of course, she ushered them through her ramshackle corrugated door held up by two splintery posts. As the soldiers stood in the doorway, they would have looked around and seen very little in the way of luxuries. There would have been a shelf with a cup and teapot, a couple of saucepans beside a turf fire that spewed smoke languorously out the front door and a pile of straw beside hollowed-out ground where Nellie and her fellow wrens had their beds. On that wet afternoon near the end of summer, the wind was howling when they made their proposal to her. When they finished talking, Nellie's contagious laugh was heard throughout the small 'nest'.

It was that evening that Nellie dressed in her freshly laundered corset, her starched petticoat and stiff crinoline dress, put her stockinged feet into wooden clogs and exited her nest with her bonnet firmly secured to her head. Nellie Clifden was off on a lark and she was about to become an extremely well-known person.

The mess party was in full flow when Nellie sashayed her way through the barracks to the officer's quarters. From there, she made her way to a separate house where a somewhat bigger bedroom than most was situated and as instructed, she sat on the bed and waited. The 20-something-year-old man who came to the bedroom was tall, bearded and a little bit drunk and to Nellie's experienced eye, he was a 'first timer'. The officer was Edward, Prince of Wales, eldest son to Queen Victoria and Prince Albert and his destiny was to become King Edward VII on the death of his mother.

Nellie had clearly impressed the fun-loving young man because three nights later, she was summoned back for a second visit, then later again for a third. Before she knew it, the officers, who were not all prone to silence, were calling her the 'Princess of Wales'.

Bad news always travels fast and news of Bertie's 'disreputable liaison' with a 'good-time girl' quickly became the talk of gentlemen's clubs across Britain and Ireland. For posterity, her career was recorded as 'actress' but there was little doubt that Nellie was one of the higher-class Curragh wrens.

When Bertie's father heard a somewhat edited version of the story, instead of smiling indulgently as most fathers would have done, trying to keep it in perspective, Albert had a meltdown. Here he was, in the process of proving that his family were people Britain could look up to and admire and there was Bertie running around town with an 'actress'.

Albert broke an even further watered-down version to Victoria, sparing her the disgusting details, and Bertie was quickly plucked away from Curragh and shipped back to Cambridge.

Albert's plan to bury the memory of the debauched House of Hanover who had been ruling Britain for generations before Victoria turned out to be just a romantic fantasy. The dream where his sons, Bertie, Affie, Arthur and Leopold would be standard bearers for the new honourable life of the monarchy, better than any monarchy in the past, wobbled tenuously because instead of holding that moralistic banner high for the world to see, Bertie had let the team down.

It was obvious that Bertie had an old-fashioned autocratic idea of sex. Get as much as you could with whoever you could and don't get caught doing it. And his younger brother Affie wasn't much better. By the time Affie was 20, he would have a reputation as a drinker and a womaniser as well.

Bertie's misconduct came at a bad time for Albert. He had never been a strong man but he hadn't been feeling well for quite some time. He complained of a 'weak stomach' and gastric attacks and they were becoming progressively worse. He'd also taken a fall the previous autumn in Coburg when his carriage horses had bolted, flinging him out, and although he'd only received cuts and bruises, he was badly shaken by the incident. He was already depressed and anxious and he broke down and let it all out to his brother during his stay. He returned to England suffering diarrhoea and cramps.

At only 42, he looked pale, paunchy, balding and perpetually exhausted.

Crohn's disease, stress and overwork made him vulnerable and add that to the fact he was probably a very lonely man with few friends, he was heading for more serious health issues. But he still couldn't set Bertie's indiscretions aside.

The disgraceful jaunts of his errant sons couldn't have come at a worse time for him. Albert wrote hysterical and furious letters to Bertie telling him it was not the done thing for the future King of England to be seen gallivanting around gentlemen's clubs at all hours with 'women of the night'. Albert was terrified Nellie would go to the papers or worse still, she would end up pregnant with all kinds of financial demands being made and Bertie would be dragged endlessly through the courts in paternity suits. And let's not even mention venereal disease. What Bertie clearly needed was a wife.

Having trawled through the German gene pool unsuccessfully, Albert came up with Princess Alexandra, the daughter of the soon-to-be Danish king. Alexandra was the daughter of Prince Christian, a captain of the Danish Royal Guard, who was the godchild of the King of Denmark, named as the king's heir ten years previously. They were a close-knit, down-to-earth bunch, although known for being informal, uncultured and unsophisticated. Weighing up the situation, Albert was certain that he had found the perfect match for Bertie. Married to the beautiful Alexandra, there would no longer be the threat of him disgracing the family name.

Feeling weaker and weaker by the day, Albert paced up and down at night and wore himself out even more. He was far from the romantic version of the 1840s prince who had arrived full of health to meet Victoria. He was ageing fast and his reserves of strength were evaporating fast and his virility had waned. He was irritable and Victoria was becoming alarmed at how ill and 'fagged' he looked. Not long before, Albert had complained of 'violent sickness and shivering' in the confines of his room at night. His attacks were severe but as usual, he concealed them from his family. He had more important things on his mind.

Bertie's misdemeanour had upset Albert so much, he felt anxious and shaken most of the time. Finally, Albert decided it was his duty to go to Cambridge and speak to his son, man to man. With his dream for perfect children failing and his dynastic dream at stake, it was time for him to take action.

It was on a wet and stormy day on 25th November 1861 when Albert insisted on going for a walk away from prying eyes and eavesdroppers. Despite the appalling weather, the subject matter was not one to be discussed indoors where hopeful ears could be pressed against the walls eagerly listening for a little bit of gossip to circulate. So father and son paced around outside through a chilly downpour, squelching in mud puddles and getting thoroughly soaked. The pair were out for longer than they expected and by the time they returned, Albert was soaked through to the skin with racking pains in his legs and back. Even though he'd complained of sleeplessness over the past fortnight, he stayed up talking to Bertie until the early hours of the morning. Eventually Bertie promised to behave and Albert spent the night in Maddingly Hall, sleepless and shivering. In his weakened state and within days, the niggling cold Albert already had turned into something like influenza and by the time he returned to Windsor, he was a seriously sick man. He complained to Victoria that his 'shattered state' was due to worry but asked her not to ask questions. All he wanted to do was go to bed and rest.

While Albert shivered, miserably sick inside his warm coats, he paced restlessly around Windsor's bedrooms worrying that Bertie was spending far too much of his time with Natty Rothschild and his hounds. By 7th December, Albert had worried himself so sick and had become so desperately ill, he was confined to his bed. Still day by day, his health worsened.

Sending for Bertie to be at his father's bedside was the last thing on Victoria's mind. She was still seething from his misdemeanour that summoning him was so far down the list of priorities, it was almost nonexistent. It was her daughter Alice who had the foresight to send Bertie a telegram asking him to return to Windsor as soon as possible. The wording had been casual so Bertie had no idea how sick his father really was. Rather unconcernedly, he left the next day at 11 am, arriving at Windsor at 3 pm, talking cheerfully. It was only when he arrived that he discovered how ill his father actually was.

On the 11th December Albert could only eat a little broth and his hands shook. Even then, his doctors said he was doing well. They gave him ammonia to help his rapid respiration and brandy was being administered every half hour. Still his doctors told Victoria they had seen infinitely worse cases and that she should not worry. On the 13th, they moved Albert into the Blue Room, the same room in which both George IV and William

IV had died. Still the doctors told Victoria that things were looking hopeful.

When Victoria saw Albert the next morning, he seemed over the worst of it. Sure, his weight had dropped, but he looked almost as young as when she had first met him. Relieved, she walked out on the balcony with her daughter Alice and they both held each other tightly and cried with relief. But when Victoria walked back in to see him a short time later, she thought he had a 'dusky hue'. By 10.50 pm, her husband, the man who had actually been the one running the country and making the political decisions for her, was dead and Victoria collapsed.

In her pain, she would have been remembering the last Christmas she'd shared with Albert. It had been the coldest Christmas for fifty years and a bitter winter had followed on the heels of a chilly and sunless summer. It was so cold that people talked of birds frozen to the tress and thrushes dying in the thousands. It was so cold that waterfowl were stuck to the ice of lakes and ponds. Londoners had the worst of it with thirteen inches of ice on the Serpentine in Hyde Park, providing a welcome Christmastime recreation for hundreds of skaters. At Windsor, twenty-one miles west of London, a heavy frost had descended. Barely one week before the royal family had transferred from Buckingham Palace to their private apartments in preparation for the festive season.

Usually Windsor Castle came into its own at Christmas. The silence of the Grand Corridor, where noise was muffled by the red carpets and damask curtains, was broken by the happy laughter of children's voices. Games of hide and seek in the towers and staircases ensued and fires blazed with beech logs in all the reception rooms.

Albert had never been happier than having his family around him and that year, there was more to celebrate. Despite his favourite child, Vicky, resigned to spending Christmas in Germany, isolated from her family, Bertie had just returned from an official tour where he had acquitted himself well, thankfully. Alice had met her future husband and all the children were delirious with excitement at the festive season.

It was the last Christmas any of them would remember with happiness.

The public outpouring of grief at Albert's death in the days immediately afterwards bears many parallels. The last time the nation had mourned the loss of a member of the royal family in similar circumstances had been back in 1817 when Princess Charlotte died shortly after the birth of her stillborn baby boy. This time, the loss was made equally poignant by the presence of two of Albert's young sons, Bertie (aged 20) and Arthur (aged 11) walking gravely behind the coffin. The whole country was swathed in black. Shops were shuttered, blinds drawn, flags at half-mast, theatre performances and concerts cancelled. In the future, a century later in 1997, the same grief would follow after the death of Princess Diana as her two grief-stricken sons, William and Harry, followed their mother's coffin stoically.

Once the initial shock of Albert's death had receded, the far more pressing question in everyone's minds, particularly the government, was what would be the impact of Albert's death on Victoria. How would the queen bear it? How would she cope with her onerous duties without Albert by her side?

Nothing could console Victoria. Albert had been everything to her: husband, friend, confidant, counsel, and unofficial secretary. There was not a single aspect of her life on which she had not deferred to his advice and wisdom. She was so reliant on his opinion that she would even consult him on what bonnet to wear. With Victoria continually sidelined by pregnancy, Albert had become all-powerful, performing the functions of king without the title and driving himself relentlessly through a schedule of official duties.

Victoria descended into a crippling state of unrelenting grief. She found herself making lists of all the things Albert had been good at: his construction of the beautiful new dairy at Windsor, the laying out of the superb kitchen gardens, his brilliance at the piano, his musical compositions, the building up for the royal art collection, the Great Exhibition of 1851, the creation of the Royal Horticultural Garden, the Kensington Museums, the foundation of Wellington College. This was not to mention his productive work as Chancellor of the University of Cambridge, his programmes of social housing in Kennington, his fascination with scientific discovery and his wide reading in contemporary literature and in philosophy.

In her intense grief, Victoria withdrew from the public eye and lost interest in all political matters. She could barely function as a human being let alone as a monarch. Where once her palaces were places of laughter and happiness, they had turned into mausoleums. Every morning, she continued to lay out his clothes and shaving gear and she clung desperately to her children, especially her youngest daughter Beatrice. Not only did Beatrice cosset her mother emotionally, she took over politically as well and in many photos taken of her at the time, Beatrice's haunted eyes showed the stress she was under.

It wasn't just Beatrice whose life had changed for the worse. Helena's did as well. She was the plainest of Victoria's children and she also wrestled with her weight, not unusual in Victoria's family. Victoria herself frequently weighed almost 12 stone, despite being only 4 feet 11. But poor Helena bore the brunt of her mother's criticisms for being *"so very large that it quite spoils her looks"*. For a full year after Albert's death, Victoria refused to let either of them leave her. They lived like grieving prisoners in the vaults of Windsor castle, attending to their mother's consuming needs. Although still teenagers, just at an age when they were ready to marry, their lives were put on hold to look after their mother.

No one found life more claustrophobic than the second youngest daughter Louise, still a teenager when her father died. She had always been a bit of a rebel, chafing against her mother's unyielding grip, and at an age when she thought her world and her horizons should miraculously widen, she found they were suddenly and considerably narrowed. She was watched and cosseted to the point that it became stifling and at a time when she should have been making friendships, she was forbidden because *"girl friendships and intimacies are very bad and often lead to great mischief"*. At the age of 17, when she should have had her coming out dance as every other girl of her age was having, Victoria refused because she had not opened the ballroom at Buckingham Palace since Albert had been alive and she wasn't going to do it for any dance for Louise.

Desperate to break away from her over-bearing mother, Louise had the confidence to take up sculpture in her own studio to which she could escape, despite her mother's stern advice that it was unnatural and not ladylike.

By choosing sculpture, Louise had pushed the boundaries, trying to see how far she could go. And her determination paid off. She was allowed to attend the National Art Training School, although her attendance at the school was limited because she was needed to stay at home to help with her mother's large private correspondence.

But Louise was much more enterprising than her mother thought. With her lovely blue eyes, fair curly hair and curvaceous figure, her looks were wreaking havoc at the school. At 21, she had caught the eye of a dashing sculptor by the name of Sir Joseph Edgar Boehm much to the disgust of her mother. After a stormy argument, Victoria decided the only solution was to find a husband for her errant daughter and with a desperate shortage of acceptable princes available for Louise except for Prussian ones, the whole family became involved, each favouring a different candidate, much to Louise's despair. She stated she did not want to marry a foreign prince, particularly a Prussian since most of them *"smelt bad and had an appalling sense of humour"*.

With Louise determined not to marry a foreign prince, they resorted to a reference book called Burke's Peerage for a home born aristocrat. And they came up with a rather romantic-looking figure with thick, luxurious, fair hair and piercing blue eyes by the name of John, Marquess of Lorne, the heir to the Dukedom of Argyll. He wrote articles and dabbled in writing poetry and Louise was hooked. And for once Victoria and Louise agreed.

Perhaps they should have looked a little closer because when you try to research the Marquess of Lorne, you come up with a lot of allegedly, possibly's and maybe's. There's a great deal shrouded in mystery but it all relates to the fact that he was gay. There is a delicious story where Louise, while living in Kensington Palace with her husband, had the French windows in their apartments bricked up so that she could stop her husband getting out at night and cruising soldiers in the park. As you may suspect, the marriage was not a happy one. Years later, there would be a scandal where the sculptor Sir Joseph Boehm, while 'entertaining' Louise in his studio, collapsed and died in her arms, in flagrante.

Their elder sister, Alice, had been the lucky one. Six months after her father's death, Alice escaped her mother's grasp and married. On the day of her wedding, she was allowed to wear white but eventually when she left England, her trousseau was laid out, as per her mother's instructions, and it would be totally black. Photos of the day show an unsmiling couple standing behind a stern Victoria who sat before them staring grimly at a picture of her dead husband. It was more like a wake than a wedding.

Living in Germany, Vicky was feeling unfulfilled. She was able and clever, groomed by Albert to be a force of change in Prussia, but in reality, she had no influence at all. Without a role, she threw herself into the role of matchmaker for her siblings. First was Helena, now aged 19. She found a match in her German friend Prince Christian of Schleswig-Holstein and amazingly, Victoria approved. He was penniless and homeless but she was thrilled with her un-prepossessing future son-in-law because by marrying Helena, they would be forced to settle in Britain and live with her at Windsor. Poor Christian ended up with a rather absurd role living on the estate at Windsor, managing Frogmore, where it was his job to do things like make sure there weren't too many frogs hopping around. His resolution was to import more ducks into the estate who would then eat the frogspawn, reducing the numbers of frogs. Instead of managing the reunification of Germany, he was worrying about vermin on the estate.

However happy everyone else seemed with the marriage, Alice was furious. She saw it as a cynical ploy to keep Helena at home (which is was) and it was the beginning of a rift between Victoria and Alice that would never heal.

By 1872, Beatrice, the baby of the family who Victoria clung to for comfort after Albert's death, was her only unmarried daughter. And she was determined it was going to stay that way. Beatrice was her constant companion who occupied a central position in Victoria's emotional life but the consequence of that was she seemed to age prematurely. There is a sense in which Beatrice and Victoria became almost the same age, with Beatrice taking on the characteristics of a much older person. She suffered from extreme rheumatism, her figure filled out and she became rather portly.

All that changed in 1884 when Beatrice made a bid for freedom at the age of 28. She'd met and fallen in love with Prince Henry of Battenberg and desperate to escape, she announced that she wanted to marry him. And of course, Victoria flatly refused. For the next six months, Victoria would not so much as talk to Beatrice, only communicating with little notes passed to her daughter with averted eyes. Eventually Victoria gave way, but on one condition: Beatrice and Prince Henry should always remain with her at Windsor.

While Victoria battled with her daughters, Bertie went from bad to worse. He'd always been difficult but after the death of his father, he was not just a disappointment, he was a disgrace. He continued to visit gentlemen's clubs and always on his arm was a different woman smiling seductively up into his eyes. He increased his gambling and drinking habits and his grades at Cambridge began to suffer. He was getting a disastrous reputation and Victoria lamented that he was nothing like his father, her beloved Albert.

But if Victoria was honest with herself, she would have realised that while hoping that Bertie would inherit his father' personality, he had actually inherited *her* Hanoverian genes with all of the implications.

The only solution was for him to be respectably married as soon as possible.

Victoria was more than happy to get Bertie out of her sight. After all, she had no doubt who was to blame for the loss of her dear husband. If Bertie had behaved himself, Albert would never have decided to leave Windsor and go to Cambridge to talk to him. He would never have caught the cold, his illness would never have happened and he would still be with her. But choosing a wife for Bertie was going to take some considered thinking. Not just anyone was going to turn Bertie's head and keep it turned. Bertie's wife had to have special qualities.

Of course Albert had been right, she decided. At the time when they were looking for someone of royal blood to settle their wayward son down, Alexandra of Denmark had looked perfect. And the closer she looked now at her credentials, the more she became certain that Alexandra had the potential to be the type of daughter-in-law she could control and mould into the future queen she believed Britain needed.

Alexandra Caroline Marie Charlotte Louise Julia was the daughter of Prince Christian of Schleswig-Holstein-Sonderburg-Glucksburg, (phew), and although her family lived a comparatively normal life and were certainly not wealthy, they had all the right ingredients.

Alexandra's story is quite an amazing one. Four years after her birth, the current king of Denmark, King Christian VIII, died leaving his only son Frederick to ascend the throne as Frederick VII. Producing children to carry on the family name is always uppermost on every monarch's mind and Frederick was no different from any other. But after two brides, Frederick had still not produced any children and he had moved on to a third wife in the hope of remedying the situation. When no children arrived from this marriage either, the common consensus was Frederick was infertile, certainly not an unfamiliar story in royal history, and as always, on everyone's lips was *'but who will be the heir?'*

Growing up as a prince of Schleswig-Holstein-Sonderburg-Glucksburg, a junior branch of the House of Oldenburg and the House of Hesse, Alexandra's father was not in the immediate line of succession. In front of the queue was his half-second cousin and wife, Louise of Hesse-Kassel, niece of the deceased Christian VIII and aunt of Frederick VII. But since Holstein was predominantly German, the law held that no female could inherit the throne.

Christian had quite a few things in his favour. He was descended from a first cousin of King Frederick VI, was brought up as a Dane by his great-aunt Queen Marie Sophie and he never bore arms for German interests against Denmark. From a Danish viewpoint, this made him a relatively attractive royal candidate for the throne. The thorny question was whether this was enough. After a lengthy conference in London to decide his eligibility for the role, it was decided that since he was married to Louise anyway, he was streaks ahead of any other candidate.

Christian's family barely existed in a rent-free house on an army wage of about £800 per year so. With this new windfall, Christian, Louise and their six children (the eldest daughter being Alexandra) moved into a new official residence, Bernstorff Palace. Unfortunately for the family, their income remained maddeningly the same for quite some time and because of this, Alexandra and her sister Dagma shared a draughty attic bedroom, made their own clothes and waited on her parents' table.

As fate would have it, Bertie was bowled over by Alexandra's beauty. And it wasn't just Bertie. The British public loved her as well. She was the Princess Diana of her day and they crowded excitedly outside St George's Chapel in Windsor on March 10th, 1863, to catch a glimpse of her as she walked towards the entrance dressed in her wedding gown of white silk and satin trimmed with lace and puffs of tulle, trailed by a 21-foot silver moiré train. As she walked towards the entrance behind her eight bridesmaids, the scent of orange blossoms, myrtle, white rosebuds, orchids and lily of the valley would have wafted headily over the crowd from her bouquet. Held back behind barriers, they gaped in awe at the pearl necklace, earrings and brooch given to her by Bertie and the opal and diamond bracelet given to her by Victoria. They would have come dressed in their own finest for the occasion and the cheering would have been almost deafening.

But while the wedding was a glorious occasion, the Danes were surprised and dismayed because only Alexandra's closest relations had been invited to the wedding. Victoria had insisted that the wedding be lavish but small and since the court was still in mourning for her beloved Albert, ladies were restricted to wearing only grey, lilac or mauve. In the wedding photos, Victoria herself was depicted as a black-clothed figure standing in her box, her face and widow's cap bathed in light.

But the wedding would also be remembered for another reason. It was the first public appearance of Queen Victoria's 4-year-old grandson, Wilhelm, by her eldest daughter Vicky and Fritz, the future German Kaiser. Dressed in a kilt and a sporran, Wilhelm wriggled restlessly between his British uncles, scratching and pinching them on the legs and throwing his sporran into the choir. After being scolded, he bit Leopold.

It was a big year for Alexandra. Within a year of the marriage, her father had ascended the throne of Denmark, her 17-year-old brother had become King of Greece, Dagma was betrothed to the heir of the Russian throne and Alexandra had given birth to a tiny son they named Albert, born two months prematurely. It was an auspicious start to her new life but it would also be the beginning of a long and tortured relationship between Alexandra's Danish family and her Prussian in-laws. No sooner had her father taken the throne of Denmark, Prussia invaded Denmark over the possession of Schleswig and Holstein, two provinces in Denmark's south the Prussians regarded as theirs, and as you can imagine, the effect of this aggression set up open hostility between the two countries. A Peace Conference eventually broke it up and concluded that Schleswig should be incorporated into Prussia and Holstein incorporated into Austria.

The attack on Denmark had been Bismarck's idea and it had the desired effect of strengthening his clutch of power. It resulted in a series of smaller wars to crush other smaller independent German states and from Prussia, he moved on to Austria to take Holstein. The war lasted seven weeks (the Prussians called it a *Blitzkrieg* or 'lightning war') and at the end, Prussia occupied Schleswig, Holstein, Frankfurt, Hanover, Hesse-Kassel and Nassau. By 1871, he had transformed the map of Europe and he was well on his way to achieving his dream of a larger unified Germany. With the increase in population and power, his dream was that Germany could one day dominate the entire continent.

While Germany climbed up the totem pole, Britain was already at the top in the world's financial and economic climate and they were feeling pretty pleased with themselves. They produced two thirds of the world's coal, half the world's iron, steel and cotton and traded 40% of the products to the world. London was the world's centre of banking, insurance and commodity dealing and her navy was the most powerful in the world. Victoria's empire was around 9.5 million square miles, with the highest wages and cheapest food in Europe and despite areas of miserable poverty in the East End of London and the new industrialised towns in the North, Britain was the envy of the rest of Europe. As well as that, Britain declared that she was both a monarchy and a democracy, even though over the past 200 years the monarchy had been pretty much stripped of their powers and left more symbolic and figurative. Unsurprisingly, for a woman like Victoria who loved to have her finger in every pie, she didn't much like the idea of being purely decorative. She pushed and manoeuvred her royal rights as much as she could and she exploited any advantage she could.

But despite her increasing powerlessness when it came to government, Victoria's dynasty was the world's most prestigious royal family (if you forgot that with her throne came madness, sex scandals, financial extravagance and general mismanagement). With Albert's careful investment and exploitation (and despite Bertie and Affie's philandering), Victoria's dynasty had almost restored the British monarchy to irreproachable dignity and morality after only 25 years. Her jewels were as good, if not better, than the wealthy Romanov's famous diamonds. Her art was perhaps better than the Hapsburgs, and her palaces, although she did not have as many, were more comfortable. She demanded, and received, copies of every treaty and discussed every line of them exhaustively. Also up her sleeve was the fact that she was a woman and a widow, which made her seem unthreatening, when in actual fact, she took full advantage of the situation and was very much on the ball.

It was a haven for any royal child to grow up in and Alexandra proved not only to be very fertile, she was also a dedicated mother. Within four years, she had produced another healthy son and a beautiful daughter. The second robust son, George, was born six years after Vicky's son Wilhelm in Germany, and George's idyllic childhood was a sharp contrast to little Wilhelm's life in Germany.

George was born 18 months after his brother Albert Victor, nicknamed Eddy, and as such was not intended for the throne. It meant that George could live happily in the shadow of his elder brother and be spared the hothouse education inflicted on his German cousin. So while Wilhelm was determined to be the first in everything and felt the need to be assertive, George was more than happy to remain unremarkable and live in mediocrity in his elder brother's shadow.

Having children inevitably slowed Alexandra down. Three more siblings arrived over the next five years: two daughters and another son, who unfortunately died the day after his birth. Through it all, Bertie remained a notorious philanderer. Although fond of his wife, slowing down was not for Bertie. His appetite for women was as undiminished as ever and within a year of George's birth, rumours put Bertie in the bed of an actress called Hortense Schneider and later Harriett Mordaunt. With the vast majority of the population firmly on Alexandra's side, Bertie found himself hissed and booed wherever he went and the acknowledged Republican party were hell-bent on ending the monarchy after Victoria's death due to his unpopularity.

For all Alexandra's seeming acceptance of Bertie's unfaithfulness, his behaviour had come as a terrible shock to her. Whether she loved her husband or not, she must have felt she had been deprived of the life she had been promised when she married him. Not for a minute would she have imagined that he would wander the bedrooms all over Britain and Europe while hers was still available at home.

But the next scandal that arose wasn't anything to do with Victoria's wayward son. Rumours had arisen of a more toxic relationship than any Bertie had partaken in. Fresh rumours were concerning Victoria and her relationship with her Highland servant, John Brown.

Victoria never fully recovered from the terrible shock of Albert's death and at a time when she needed someone to lean on, John Brown was her loyal servant who stood by her side and became a stalwart friend who faithfully supported her. As such, he soon became her favourite. In return for his support, she gave him gifts and created two medals for him, the Faithful Servant Medal and the Devoted Service Medal.

He was a fine man physically, with eyes that would have reminded Victoria of Albert's. Some said that when she gazed into Brown's eyes, she would have been reminded of how passionately in love she had been with her dead husband and perhaps she had believed that the Prince's spirit had passed into Brown. It was four years since her widowhood and she was still very unhappy and heartbroken. Brown had a strength she missed and his loyal support would have won the grieving widow over to his side. It could well be the reason she gave Brown so many privileges.

Inevitably, stories began circulating that something 'improper' was going on since they slept in adjoining rooms whenever she visited Balmoral. Some even called him *'The Queen's Stallion'* and even went so far as to call her *'Mrs Brown'*.

For a Queen, and a widow, to have a rumour of sexual relations with anyone, let alone a servant, was unthinkable. But throughout her life she had depended totally on Albert and now, filling the gap in her life, was a Scotsmen who openly called her 'wumman' at times.

While Victoria was obviously smitten by Brown, most people knew him to be a drunkard and a bully who terrorised the household and to say that her children and ministers resented him is somewhat of an understatement. His cruelty to Victoria's sons, in particular Prince Leopold who had been diagnosed as a haemophiliac, is well documented with him hitting Leopold, scolding him from morning to night and keeping him in isolation. The family hated Brown intensely, especially Bertie, but through all the controversy and the open hostility from the family, Brown reigned supreme.

By then she had become entrenched in her long-unchecked self-indulgence and despite her workload consisting only of short notes, Victoria complained vehemently that she was overworked and more than happy to let John Brown take the burden from her. She was reluctant to let her family take the pressure off her, preferring instead to depend on John Brown to guide her.

A deeply insecure man and irritated by his mother's attitude to servants, Bertie was blisteringly offended and humiliated that his mother should consider a servant to have finer qualities than himself and take Brown's side during quarrels. Having been on the receiving end of her tirade at his *'indiscreet alliances'*, he was shocked at her own impropriety that was visible to the world. Despite his own serial adultery, Bertie was stung by the rumours that persisted for decades about his mother and John Brown. There is a saying that goes, *"Revenge is a dish best served cold"* and it could have been written for Bertie because he would have his revenge in the future.

As for Victoria, she was well aware of the scandalous rumours that circulated. She had been brought up in a world full of sexual tittle-tattle in her own mother's entourage. As a child, hadn't she even glimpsed the tender whispers, the touched hands, the arm around the waist that had suggested intimacy between her mother and John Conroy? And then there was the horrid gossip abounding her randy Hanoverian uncles. Perhaps by then, she was immune to gossip.

Because Victoria's life was largely hidden from the public, it is hardly surprising that a whole range of myths about her were given undue credibility. When looking at Elizabeth I and her intense attempt at privacy, it's understandable how gossip circulates. Myths still abound about Elizabeth ranging from her having illegitimate children hidden away to perhaps Elizabeth was not even Elizabeth at all, but a young replacement, The Bisley Boy. If Bram stoker is to be believed, Kat Ashley and Tom Parry had secretly replaced the dead 14-year-old princess with a look alike to avoid Henry VIII's wrath when an imminent visit was due. The elaborate plan had worked but they knew without a doubt that they couldn't admit what they'd done. The king's fury would be infinite. So the deception became permanent, which is the reason Elizabeth had never married.

Victoria was not immune to the same court gossip. Several rumours in particular, as alive today as they were in her lifetime, were given regular airings. The first was that Victoria and John Brown were secretly married. Secondly, that a child had been born to the Queen and John Brown and thirdly, that Brown was a medium who helped Victoria keep in touch with her beloved Albert. The rumours only served to add fuel to Bertie's fire.

Incensed at his mother, and almost out of spite, Bertie took solace in the arms of mistress after mistress while Alexandra cocooned herself and her children away in the loving folds of her family in Denmark, leaving Bertie to his not-so-private jaunts.

Although comparatively impoverished, the Danish royal family had succeeded in marrying into various European dynasties. Cousins, uncles and aunts from across the continent would all meet at the Danish summer home outside Copenhagen and the atmosphere was always relaxed and happy. Among them were the Russian royal family. It was here that George first met his Russian cousin, Nicholas, the future Tsar Nicholas II.

* * *

Nicholas' father, Tsar Alexander III of Russia, was a larger than life personality and his mother Dagma was Alexandra's sister. The closeness of Dagma and Alexandra was well known and what they wanted more than anything was to bring the families even closer by gathering the family together every year for reunions.

Nicholas's family, the Romanovs, had ruled Russia since 1613 but it was only after the Napoleonic Wars that Russia came into its own. Up until then it had been a collection of eighty or so nationalities from Poles to Uzbeks, all of whom had little in common with Britain. Five-sixths of the Russian population consisted of peasants and almost 80% were illiterate by the end of the 19th century compared to 5% of Britons. Foreign wars had nearly brought the county to bankruptcy and it was no wonder that Europe had regarded the country as backward and corrupt. So it was a proud Tsar Alexander II, Nicholas' grandfather, who rode down the Champs-Elysees after defeating Napoleon.

Theoretically, the Tsar's power was unlimited and the Romanovs regarded Russia as their own empire. And they were determined to keep it that way. This meant that anyone attempting to make a change could expect a trip to Siberia to cool off. Alexander II appointed and sacked at will and the law came explicitly from him and him alone. There were no representative assemblies of any kind and anyone who had ever read a newspaper knew how brutal Russians could be. Ask the Jews.

But while his son, Alexander III, was determined to follow in his father's wake and keep the country under Romanov control, Russia was falling behind commercially and industrially. Russia was locked in a near feudal hierarchy where everyone was registered to a particular social estate and your estate dictated your dress, your education, your occupation, where you could travel, how much tax you paid and what you were entitled to. It's not surprising that artists and writers were from aristocratic families.

What the government feared most was that Russia would fall too far behind the rest of Europe. They wanted to modernise it and industrialise it and the question of whether the tsar would allow it was on everyone lips. What was becoming apparent to Nicholas' father, Alexander III, was that the government was prepared to do it, with or without him.

Tsar Alexander III was a mountain of a man. He stood well over six feet tall and was famous for being able to break iron pokers with his bare hands.

But unlike his ancestor, Peter the Great, Alexander disapproved of Westernisation, believing that as a true Russian should be rough in his manner and have a touch of brutality in his personality. Alexander had no interest in culture, art, cuisine or good wine: he did however love his country.

Alexander had not always been the heir to the Russian throne. That was reserved for his elder brother Nicholas who, for most of his life, had seemed in robust shape. He was betrothed to Princess Dagma of Denmark and a happy and prosperous future seemed inevitable. That is until 1865 when Nicholas showed signs of ill health, initially diagnosed as rheumatism. He had back pain and a stiff neck as well as sensitivity to noise and light. Even then, the notion that he might be seriously ill never entered anyone's head.

As Nicholas made a tour of Italy, his health worsened and everything changed. He was sent to Nice in Southern France to rest but the move made no improvement to his rapidly worsening condition. It was eventually determined that he was suffering from cerebrospinal meningitis, thought to have been brought on by an accident in a wrestling match where he had been thrown down. That spring, at the age of 21, Nicholas continued to decline and by April that year he was dead.

A romantic legend has it that on his deathbed, Nicholas expressed the wish that his fiancée become the bride of his younger brother Alexander, now the future heir to the Russian throne as Alexander III. The beautiful story fails when we hear that Alexander's own fiancée was banished abroad and Alexander was virtually frogmarched to Copenhagen by his father to propose to his dead brother's fiancée, like it or not. Inevitably, one year later, the couple were married, Dagma converted to Russian Orthodox and changed her name to Maria Feodorovna.

Dagma seemed the opposite of her new husband. She was tiny and pretty, although not as pretty or as charming has her elder sister Alexandra in England. She did however love beautiful clothes, lavish jewellery and she loved parties. Two years after the wedding, their first son, named Nicholas after his dead uncle, was born on 6th May 1868 and over the coming years, two more boys and two girls would follow.

There is no doubt that Alexander loved his family. On one occasion, when their train had derailed in 1888, Alexander had single-handedly lifted the roof of the carriage where his family was trapped and saved them. To the shy, withdrawn Nicholas, his massive father and his loud booming voice seemed almost superhuman and so utterly without hesitation about anything. Even when he spoke, Alexander seemed on the verge of attacking and it left little Nicholas somewhat in awe of his father.

Childhood for the Romanov children was idyllic. They grew up in a series of snow-covered palaces in the isolated regions of northern Russia in a very similar domestic household as their English cousins. Nicholas, nicknamed Nicky, and his siblings spent their first years surrounded by English nurses and nannies sent over by Alexandra who constantly reminded Dagma about her sister-in-law Vicky and Wilhelm's difficult birth in Prussia. With a father and grandfather who had an intense distrust of almost everyone outside their family, it seemed the perfect home for the Romanovs although everything about the remoteness of their home left Nicky innocent and naïve. It denied him the experience of high society in St Petersburg and it denied him culture and company since contact with anyone except his family and servants was very rare.

Being the Russian royal family, you can imagine that nothing the Romanovs did was on a small scale. The number of servants across the palaces was around 15,000 and the palace in St Petersburg had 900 rooms. One year, at Anichkov Palace, where the family spent the early months of the year, Nicky would watch his mother dressing each evening with five maids and a Mistress of the Wardrobe in attendance as she stepped into a heavy silver brocade dress with ten rows of pearls around her neck. Spring was spent in the Gulf of Finland in one of the family villas and summer was spent on the royal yacht with a trip to Denmark at the end.

Every trip the family took was a logistical nightmare. Accompanying the family would be twenty railway trucks of baggage and an entourage of a hundred, to say nothing of the security around them to protect his family from what Alexander saw as the harsh outside world. And he was right to be protective.

It was Sunday 13th March 1881 and as usual, Nicky's grandfather Tsar Alexander II was on his way to Mikhailovsky Manege in St Petersburg for the military roll call. He always travelled in a closed carriage accompanied by five Cossacks, a Polish noble with a sixth Cossack sitting on the coachman's left. Following the carriage was the Chief of Police and the Chief of the Emperor's Guards. As it turned out, it wasn't enough security to prevent disaster.

In hindsight, using the same route via Catherine Canal and over the Pevchesky Bridge every Sunday was a huge mistake. It left the way open for members of the Narodnaya Volya (the People's Will) to plan an assassination attempt.

Narrow pavements bordered the street for the public to watch the Tsar, but also waiting in the crowd were two assailants. As the carriage drew alongside one of them, he stepped forward with a small white package wrapped in a handkerchief and threw it under the horses' hooves.

The explosion killed one of the Cossacks and seriously wounded the driver and even though it had only damaged the bulletproof carriage, it was understandably a shaken but unhurt Alexander II who stepped out of the carriage. That's when the second assailant threw another package at the Tsar's feet.

The explosion was deafening. Through the smoke, debris, blood and snow, Alexander's weak voice could be heard crying for help. It was only when a guard ran to help him that he noticed the Tsar's legs were shattered, his stomach was torn open and his face was mutilated. Fifteen horrendous minutes later, the Tsar died.

Witnessing the assassination first-hand was his son, the future Alexander III, and his grandson, 13-year-old Nicholas.

By the time Alexander II died, he and his son had been estranged for years, mainly due to his son's resentment towards his father's long-standing relationship with Catherine Dolgorokov (with whom he had several illegitimate children) while his mother was suffering from chronic ill health. The anger only increased when Alexander II married Catherine a mere month after his wife's death in 1880.

Alexander III's policies were very different from his father's as well. On the morning of the assassination, his father had signed an order to set up a commission to advise the monarchy but the day after his father's death, Alexander III tore it up and gave fresh orders. The Russian language would be made mandatory, even to his German, Polish and other Russian subjects and *his* Russia would be composed of a single nationality, language, and religion. If Catholics, Muslims and Protestants didn't like it, they knew what they could do. As for Jews who decided to stay, they were banned from inhabiting rural areas and their occupations were severely restricted.

Forever the peacemaker, Alexander III was trying hard to keep Russia together but all he managed to do was create a breeding ground for furious revolutionaries. By 1890s, the exclusion of peasant communities created even more resentment causing furious separatist movements to take root across the empire. As much as Alexander hated it, Russia was slowly and painfully changing. There was no way he was going to be able to put this genie back in the bottle.

Russia shared a long border with Germany but they also shared a complex dynastic history as well. Like the British royals, the Russian tsars found Germany to be a handy source of wives and both British and Russians royal houses were more German than any other nationality. There was so much intermarrying with Germans that three of the junior branches of the Romanov family were naturalised Germans and the government had welcomed large numbers of clever, ambitious Germans into senior government offices.

The relationship was even more delicately balanced as Russia became more vulnerable to German financial muscle. Germany was Russia's main source of borrowed money and the chief market for Russian wheat. So in Germany, Otto Von Bismarck knew if he raised grain tariffs or closed the money markets, Russia would be in deep trouble.

Alexander's accession to the throne after his father's assassination pushed the royal family further into retreat away from St Petersburg to the country. Gatchina, a huge, cold empty castle, 25 miles south west of the city surrounded by soldiers, seemed perfect. Visits to St Petersburg became rare and it is no surprise that the yearly summer visits to Denmark were welcomed as parties with the Danish king and queen felt like a release from prison. In Denmark, the Romanovs felt at peace, as they never did at home, surrounded by other royal children and family members.

Every year and for many years, there were crowds of royal families holidaying in Copenhagen. There were Danish cousins as well as the heirs to the throne of Hanover. Dagma and her family came and Alexandra's brother, King George of Greece, joined them with his wife who was Alexander's favourite cousin. Then there was Alexandra, sometimes Bertie, who brought their own children as well. Every year, screams of happiness could be heard as Alexander took the children off to catch tadpoles or steal apples. He'd let them ride on his knee and tug at his beard and once turned the garden hose on the King of Sweden, *'whom we all disliked.'* George, so intimidated by his own grandmother, Queen Victoria, referred to Alexander as *'dear old fatty.'*

From the first day they met, the cousins George and Nicky found they had a lot in common and they became firm friends. Both loved the outdoors, both were shy and young for their age, both had a passion for practical jokes and both had possessive mothers and powerful fathers. They even looked uncannily alike.

But in all of this insane happiness, there was one royal cousin who was never invited to the family parties: Vicky's son Wilhelm, the future Kaiser of Germany. Because of Prussia's humiliating defeat of Denmark and because of Dagma and Alexandra's intense hatred for Prussia due of this, Wilhelm was never welcome. Many of the guests were from numerous minor German houses that were also defeated in Bismarck's wars of unification so they were no keener than their Danish hosts to admit Germany to the festivities.

The holidays had a clear political purpose. Both sisters were trying to strengthen Anglo-Russia by trying to draw their husbands away from Germany and in that respect, they were very successful. And no doubt about it, it would have been an uphill battle to achieve that if Bertie's sister Vicky and her German family had been hovering in close proximity.

Heads together, the two sisters came up with a marriage plan between Bertie's loutish younger brother Alfred and Tsar Alexander III's only sister, the Grand Duchess Maria Alexandrovna, reputed to be the wealthiest woman in the world. And amazingly, the plan worked. In March 1874, the couple were married at the Winter Palace in St Petersburg and they soon made an entrance into London society.

But as idyllic as the plan had seemed from the sisters' point of view, for the British, especially Victoria, the match was definitely not made in heaven. Russia had always been a traditional enemy and having Alfred Duke of Edinburgh married to the haughty Russian aristocrat sent shock waves through the country, especially when Grand Duchess Maria showed surprise that she would have to take second preference to their own beloved Alexandra Princess of Wales.

Throughout the 19th century, most British people looked at Russia with fear. They were a neighbouring country that threatened India, the jewel in the British crown, and of course, they were also descendants of the Mongol barbarians. Needless to say, Russia and Britain were archenemies. Even

Victoria called them *'detestable Russians who were horrible, deceitful and cruel'* and who could never be trusted. The Russians were not very fond of the British either. They resented British presence in India, Africa and central Asia, and they regarded Britain as hypocritical and a nuisance who blocked Russia in all sorts of ways. British feelings of superiority also stuck in their throats.

From the late 1870s, Britain and Russia, along with Germany, had launched themselves into a violent phase of territorial acquisition, carving up Europe into colonies. Everyone wanted to exploit weaker territories because they needed more raw materials and new places to put their money so if punching their competitors out of the way was the only way around the problem, then so be it.

The frantic territory grab got into full gear after 1882 when Britain took over Egypt. As everyone watched, Europe began to realise that if they didn't join in the scramble, Britain would snap up the whole of Africa and of course, France was the first to step in. No sooner were centuries old Anglo-French hostilities revived than one empire after another began competing with each other in an endless stream of nasty little regional conflicts. No one wanted to be left out.

From the start, Russia saw themselves as different from Britain. Their expansion had never been about trade. Theirs had been more about the love of conquests. And even though their country was already a sweeping mass that had absorbed the Crimea, much of Poland, Finland, Mongolia and all of Siberia, the fever still gripped Russia as strongly as ever. Instantly, the two ruling dynasty's conflicts turned personal and Russia began to turn away from Britain and look to Germany for support.

Bismarck was ecstatic at the turn of events. He had been working hard to cultivate good relations with Russia because in the back of his mind, he was always fearful of an alliance between France and Russia. If that alliance happened, he was sure that eventually it would leave Germany totally encircled by their enemies and totally vulnerable to attack on all sides. So as part of his encouragement of Russian support, he sent a delegation to Russia to celebrate Nicholas' *'coming of age'*.

It was a good plan and it had the potential to work. The only hitch with the plan was Bismarck's choice of representation. As a delegate, he chose Nicholas' German cousin Wilhelm and as incredibly flattering as it was for

Wilhelm, it was a terrible slight to his father Fritz who had always worked hard to become involved in political events. And he was seriously miffed.

* * *

With everything his parents had subjected him to in his life, Wilhelm's heart had hardened towards them and he had become fiercely hostile to everything they stood for. Wilhelm knew exactly how his father would react to Bismarck's invitation. He'd watched his father over the years as he tried to manipulate his way into politics by offering to act as a figurehead with suggestions and advice, all of which Bismarck disregarded. In the background, Wilhelm smouldered. So when the offer came from Bismarck for Wilhelm to represent Germany instead of his father, Wilhelm jumped at the amazing opportunity to lord it over him.

Of course, it only made things worse. His father was hopping mad and his mother sent more and more letters to her mother in England telling her of Wilhelm's chauvinistic and loud-mouthed attitude and his ignorance of anything foreign. He would do anything, Vicky said, to annoy his parents, even changing from liberal to conservative, which is what Bismarck encouraged as well. The tension between Wilhelm and his mother was only exacerbated by Vicky's ferocious attachment to Britain. She was still saying how good England was and how rubbish Germany was in comparison.

When Wilhelm arrived in St Petersburg, he was absolutely enthralled. 12,000 soldiers were lining the railway tracks, waving and cheering him as he went past, and the feeling of self-importance was so overwhelming, he wholeheartedly waved back. It was nothing like his experience with his distant parents and he never wanted the feeling to stop. In his euphoria, he saw Alexander as a demiGod who lived in a glamorous, extravagant palace and wielded unlimited power and he was thoroughly intoxicated.

He returned excitedly to Germany from his trip and instantly began a private, and rather alarming, correspondence with the Tsar in which it was clear his hostility to his mother now extended to the whole of the British family.

Wilhelm's relationship with his mother mirrored his relationship with Britain in all its complexity. He was pulled in all sorts of directions. He was fascinated by Britain and he desperately craved to be noticed by them, but because they ignored him, he hated them. He did, however, love his grandmother who had always been the one who actually listened to him. But behind everything he did was his insecurity. In his heart, he never felt quite good enough.

It all came to a head in 1887 at Victoria's Golden Jubilee. It was three years after Nicky's coming out party and Wilhelm, far fonder of his English grandmother than his own mother, had persuaded his German grandfather to send him to the ceremony as the German representative, rather than his parents.

It was a brazen thing to ask and I don't understand how he thought he could pull it off. After all, the celebration was for Vicky's mother and of course Vicky wanted to be included and represented at her own mother's ceremony.

As it turned out, Vicky should not have worried. Victoria knew exactly what Wilhelm was up to. She'd read every letter from her daughter and as always, Victoria kept herself very well informed on everything that was going on. There was very little, if anything, that got past her. And she wasn't stupid. She was well aware that Wilhelm had basically invited himself, bypassing his parents by going to his grandfather. In a show of support for Vicky, Victoria disinvited Wilhelm as the representative and asked her daughter instead. He could come if he wanted to, she stated, but it would be his parents who would have pride of place, not him.

It was yet another slight for Wilhelm. His grandmother had been the only one who'd ever listened to him and there she was, insulting him and ignoring him, just like his parents. But regardless of how 'put out' he felt, there was no way he was going to miss the celebrations. So he bit his tongue and kept his pride in check and made the trip with them.

The Golden Jubilee celebrations marked a limited return to public view following Victoria's near total isolation after Albert's death 26 years ago. Wearing the Order of the Garter and the Star of India, she was led to Westminster Abbey by an escort of Indian cavalry and true to her word, as the grand procession wound its way through the streets of London, Wilhelm had to make do with a paltry role towards the rear of the parade. Later, in formal pictures of the family gathering, Wilhelm stood to the back of the room near a window, behind everyone else where Victoria had relegated him, staring sulkily at the group while his mother sat beside her mother in pride of place.

The slight from his grandmother made his hatred for Britain even more intense and a few months later, as Europe gathered once again, this time for the funeral of Wilhelm's 90-year-old grandfather, the memory of his deep humiliation resurfaced.

It had taken 30 years for Vicky to become the wife of a German Emperor and it's another of those great 'what ifs' in history. If Fritz's father hadn't lived so long and if Fritz had taken over sooner, Germany may have evolved in a very different way. Fritz had been a staunch liberal and he wanted Germany to become a constitutional country. Wilhelm, however, only wanted to oppose his father in absolutely anything.

As it turned out, Fritz's elevation to Emperor was not to be a lengthy, joyful celebration. Fritz was soon to find that he was dying of throat cancer. It had taken ages for the diagnosis to come in and by the time it did, it was too late. He'd already had a tracheotomy and couldn't speak and no one expected him to live long after the operation. He scribbled orders on bits of paper but mostly they were simply ignored and he lacked the energy to pursue them. He became Kaiser in March 1888 but by then, he only had a few months to live.

Once again, Vicky wrote constantly to her mother telling her that she and Fritz were just passing shadows, soon to be replaced by her angry, erratic son Wilhelm when Fritz died. Fritz was too weak to do anything and everything he had worked for and planned for Germany over the previous years was just not going to happen. It was all very grave.

While his mother fretted, Wilhelm on the other hand was only too eager to get started as Emperor. He'd honed his whole personality to be the charismatic, can-do-anything-soldier-king from his purposeful stance to his deliberately fierce expression, and while Wilhelm puffed and beat his chest, many watched his dangerous behaviour with fear.

Ninety-nine days after ascending to the throne, Fritz died and 25-year-old Wilhelm became the Kaiser of one of the most powerful countries in the world where ultimate power still rested with the monarch.

As it turned out, people were right to fear Wilhelm. His first official act was to surround, isolate and search the palace, combing for every piece of paper that related to Fritz's short time on the throne.

It was a monstrous aggressive act aimed primarily at his mother in the attempt to stop her from smuggling letters out of the country to England. But he was too late. As Fritz lay dying, she outsmarted Wilhelm by sending everything she could find in boxes to England via the British Embassy.

When he found out, Wilhelm was in a state of apoplectic fury. He declared his father would be buried three days later without the traditional 'lying in state' period due to a monarch, and to top it off, no foreign dignitaries were invited to the funeral. Even Bismarck was to stay away.

In England, when Bertie heard what his nephew had done, he sent a letter telling him of his outrage at his impertinence. As if Wilhelm cared what his pompous British uncle thought. It was Bertie by the way who had insulted him during the Golden Jubilee celebration only a couple of years before and he wasn't about to forget that little issue.

Wilhelm started his reign with a catastrophic bang. A visit to St Petersburg was meant to seal a conservative alliance with his hero, Tsar Alexander III, but instead Alexander, a devoted family man, was deeply offended and appalled by Wilhelm's lack of grief at his father's death just a few short weeks before. To Alexander, Wilhelm came across as a scoundrel who threw his weight around and thought way too much of himself. As for Wilhelm, he thought he was just showing off his diplomatic abilities.

Wilhelm moved happily around the public stage in a blur of activity, constantly travelling with a need to be seen and photographed. One day he was in front of immaculate German soldiers, the next he was at a factory, devoutly surrounded by his six tall healthy sons, none deformed in any way. His speeches were reported constantly in the papers and though the reports were not always flattering, he was always full of confidence, determined to control German foreign policy himself. But within months, the German alliance with Russia disintegrated and Russia had signed an alliance with France. It was the first stage of the encirclement that Bismarck had dreaded and he fully blamed Wilhelm.

Wilhelm was determined his reign would be lavish and extravagant and to prove the point, he and his wife Dona and their children moved into a staggering 650 room Berlin Schloss. Millions of marks were spent on renovations, extensions, heating lights and bathrooms were installed. He bought eleven gilded carriages, one big enough to contain a table setting for twenty-four people and a new cream and gold yacht he named the *Hohenzollern*.

By then, the erratic young Kaiser was veering wildly back and forth in opposite directions between Russia and Britain. Suddenly, Wilhelm sent a request to his grandmother for him to attend the regatta at Cowes. This famous regatta takes place once a year in August on the Isle of Wight and is a gathering place for the richest people in Europe to gather and show off their wealth. And Wilhelm desperately wanted to be invited.

There are several reasons for the Wilhelm's change of heart towards Britain. Firstly, Bismarck was again feeling uncomfortably sandwiched between Russia and France and the Russian press was in the grip of a new wave of anti-Germanism. But probably more to the point was the fact that Wilhelm's mother had packed up and moved to Frankfurt and overnight his ill feelings towards Britain disappeared. When she left, so did his animosity towards England. It would seem that he cursed everything English purely to annoy his mother.

As you can imagine, after everything that had been happening, Victoria did not want him to attend. Only months before, Wilhelm had insulted his uncle Bertie in Vienna and Wilhelm had refused to apologise to him. Of course, Wilhelm's insult had been out of envy, although he would never admit it. Bertie was popular, Wilhelm felt despised. Even fashionable young men in Berlin wanted to copy Bertie's suits and Wilhelm wanted desperately to have the kind of approval that Bertie seemed to attract effortlessly. To top it off, Bertie was an attractive man who loved life and had lots of friends. And there was Wilhelm, always feeling that someone was laughing at him behind his back and not being taken seriously.

Wilhelm tried to throw his weight around to make people like him but of course, that just made them dislike him even more. He was masterful and had authority but what he wanted more than anything was Bertie's ease of nature. Wilhelm's emotions were all tied up with his confused feelings of inferiority and anger. Slights, imagined or not, touched a nerve with him and set him on to a path of retaliation. What he actually longed for was his uncle to show him approval and respect and in Bertie's utter dislike for his nephew, it was the one thing that Bertie struggled to do.

With the family squabble getting out of hand, Victoria's Prime Minister persuaded her that Britain needed to show themselves to be at least *friendly* with the Germans. Watching the growing tensions in Europe, Victoria could only agree with her Prime Minister and reluctantly she sent an invitation to

Wilhelm to attend the regatta. But with the invitation came one condition. He was to write and say how happy he was to be meeting again with his Uncle Bertie and he was to say how sorry he was about the misunderstanding in Vienna. If he did that, she in turn would make him an honorary admiral of the Royal Navy, complete with a white and gold uniform.

Wilhelm arrived at Cowes on 2nd August 1889 on his yacht the *Hohenzollern* in a fabulous mood and in his new admiral's outfit. Arriving on your own private yacht was like arriving in your own Lear jet and most royal families had two yachts. Instead, escorting Wilhelm, were twelve German battleships.

Despite his staggering and disconcerting entourage, the British family were courteous and gracious to Wilhelm. Bertie met him accompanied by his sons Eddy, who was at Cambridge, and George, who had just become a captain in the navy after six years of duty. Neither boy had seen Wilhelm since the Jubilee celebration of 1887 and before that, in the 1880s. As for Victoria, she assured her daughter Vicky that she was going to be chilly to her grandson and that she would not speak to anyone in Wilhelm's entourage who had been horrible to her daughter.

It was a difficult promise to keep since Wilhelm had handpicked every member of his party because of their dislike for his mother.

As it turned out, Wilhelm behaved himself and outshone everyone. He attended a naval parade with Bertie and inspected the warships, even offering suggestions on how they could improve their guns. He watched the yacht races and Bertie put him up for membership at the Royal Yacht Squadron. Wilhelm in turn invested his cousins with the Order of the Black Eagle and told everyone how fond he was of his Uncle Bertie as he presented a portrait of himself, complete with a pointed Prussian helmet on his head, to his grandmother.

In his gracious presence, Victoria thawed as he kissed her affectionately and joined her for breakfast and dinner every day, whatever the weather. It gave Wilhelm the opportunity to rub shoulders with everyone who had shunned him before and prove that he was someone of worth after all. As Wilhelm looked around the smiling family group, disagreements seemed a thing of the past.

When Wilhelm arrived back home in Germany, it was not a happy Bismarck who greeted him. Wilhelm was seized with a new and vociferous attachment for Britain once more and Bismarck commented that Wilhelm seemed enslaved by the shiny new British admiral's uniform his grandmother had given him.

It was the fly in Wilhelm's ointment. His thought was that he, as Admiral of the Fleet, had a say in English naval affairs and as such could give his grandmother, the Queen of England, his expert advice. And he had no qualms in letting Bismarck realise that little point.

You can imagine Bismarck's mocking laugh. An honorary title, he scoffed, was only a flashy trinket given as a sign of friendship. It meant your picture would go up in the mess and they had a drink to celebrate your birthday each year. Nothing more. No one took him seriously and Wilhelm was naive if he thought any different.

But Wilhelm *had* taken it all seriously and he was furious at Bismarck's rebuff. To prove his point, and worth, he set off to the Greek coast on his yacht for the wedding of his sister Sophie to Prince Constantine, the heir to the Greek throne, and Alexandra's nephew.

I can only imagine the welcome he received. After all the years that Alexandra and Dagma had spent criticising the Prussians and their invasion of Denmark, ostracising Wilhelm and his family from get-togethers and generally badmouthing the German side of the family, here was their nephew totally ignoring everything they'd said over the years by marrying a Prussian and worst of all, Wilhelm's sister. Oh to be a fly on the wall.

Seemingly undeterred, Wilhelm put on his shiny new admiral's uniform, flew the pennant of a British navy admiral, and invited himself to inspect the British squadron that was anchored there. And of course, he had some 'helpful suggestions' that, in his opinion, might improve the fleet. Two of the many guests who looked on in amazement were his cousins George and Nicky. As it turned out, the wedding would be one of only two occasions in their lives when Wilhelm, George and Nicky would be in the same place at the same time.

It's hard to know what Wilhelm was thinking by offering his presumptuous advice. He seemed certainly capable of two different wishes at the same time: a desire to be politically close to England and a desire to see England at war with France. We already know that he was arrogant and full of his own importance. And there's no doubt that he had a sense of entitlement and unlimited power. But put all that together with his hatred of criticism and a proneness to envy, plus his disappointing lack of empathy, you could be forgiven for believing that he had an egotistical personality. But he wasn't the only one. Plenty of royals shared the same narcissistic attributes.

I suppose being a royal had certain compensations. You could be selfish and eccentric and get away with it. After all, plenty of royals were eccentric. Look at the Hapsburg family. They had their fair share of oddballs, although this could have been through both inbreeding and syphilis. One archduke killed himself by drinking water from the river Jordan in a religious obsession and several others were enthusiastic cross-dressers. Empress Elizabeth, sister of mad King Ludwig of Bavaria, devoted her entire life to the maintenance of her eighteen-inch waist with a regime of obsessive exercise, leather corsets and a diet of raw steak and milk. She even had herself sewn into her clothes rather than bear the imperfection of creases. When looking at these eccentricities of the royal production line, it's easy to think that Wilhelm's problems may have surfaced during his youth after suffering the terrible 'treatments' he endured to improve his looks and hide his physical faults.

Victoria listened with gritted teeth to his cheery suggestions and in the future read his persistent letters, constantly reminded by Parliament that things were much better than they had been in the past. He was a changed man from the one only twelve months ago and if it only took a shiny admiral's uniform and a forced smile to do it, then Britain was in front by a long shot.

Bismarck, however, was not pleased at all with Wilhelm's sudden passion for England, especially when it was accompanied with a fresh wave of hostility towards Russia. Since Wilhelm's visit to Russia for Nicky's coming out party in St Petersburg in 1888, Alexander had shown no inclination to visit Berlin whatsoever. In his opinion, Wilhelm was a German pipsqueak who threw his weight around and thought too highly of himself. And of course, with Alexander's refusal to visit Berlin, Wilhelm felt spurned. It put him back in the anti-Russian camp, see-sawing from one relative to the other.

But Britain was not the only thorn in Bismarck's paw. He and Wilhelm were also arguing about domestic politics as well. Neither wanted to give an inch and when it finally came down to it, the issue at stake was who was in charge issuing the orders and who should be receiving those orders and upholding them. As the Emperor, Wilhelm was determined to rule by himself but Bismarck had been the unofficial master of Germany for nearly thirty years and he wasn't about to give up without a serious fight.

In October 1889, Alexander finally, and reluctantly, relented and visited Berlin. Wilhelm assured the tsar that Germany had no desire for conflict with Russia and in reply, the Tsar gave his word of honour that Russia would not attack Germany. All seemed back on track again until December when the relationship between the 75-year-old Bismarck and Wilhelm disintegrated completely. By March, Wilhelm had demanded Bismarck's resignation just as his cousin and uncle, George and Bertie, arrived in Berlin for a state visit.

Dressed in his admiral's uniform with a radiant smile on his face, Wilhelm arranged celebrations on a grand scale with banquets and military inspections. As Wilhelm danced attendance to the British royals, the rest of Europe watched on in alarm at Bismarck's fall from grace. None more so than Russia. Suddenly, Russia was asking for the 'Reinsurance Treaty' to be renewed quickly to safeguard their confidence in both Wilhelm and his policies. Two months later, Germany let the treaty lapse.

Bismarck had not bothered to explain the policy to Wilhelm and gratified by Alexander's apparent desperation to be his friend, Wilhelm couldn't see the point of it anyway. No one seemed to understand the huge symbolic significance of the treaty for the Russians. It was a sign of the German government's fundamental goodwill towards them and with the lapse, suspicions and doubts rose once more to the surface.

Not that Wilhelm noticed. He was feeling too buoyant with his new status and he planned a full state visit to Britain to celebrate. And when he arrived in London, things couldn't have looked better for him. The streets of London were decked out with garlands and crowds gathered outside Buckingham Palace to catch a glimpse of the young Kaiser and his famous moustache and pointy hat. It was a visit that held promise and hope for the future and he was determined to be on his best behaviour.

At a speech, he stood before the crowds like a true Prussian soldier and told a cheering audience that he felt at home in their lovely country as the grandson of Queen Victoria. He bestowed a blessing on England and commented that the same blood that ran through the British monarch's veins, ran through his as well. He finished by saying that it was in his power to maintain the historical friendship between the two nations and that his aim, above all, was the maintenance of peace.

His eyes were bright and clear and at that time in his life, he probably meant every word he spoke.

In Frankfurt, his mother Vicky was not so sure.

* * *

THE RELATIONSHIP between Wilhelm and his mother Vicky was dramatically different from Alexandra and George's relationship where Alexandra absolutely doted on George, sending him endless letters of encouragement and support. It was also obvious that Alexandra's loathing for Germany had not diminished over the years and it was never more evident than at a ceremony where George was made honorary colonel in a Prussian dragoon during a visit to Germany. His father Bertie squeezed himself into a rather tight uniform for the occasion while George kept a low profile in the background as a sign of respect for his mother, who was making it plainly obvious of her hatred for Germany.

As the second son of Bertie and Alexandra, George had always been behind his brother Eddy in line for the throne. He had always been intended for a role in the English navy and as such, he was extraordinarily badly educated, not even able to speak a foreign language. Not that George cared too much. He'd never been particularly outgoing. He was content with his role as the 'spare' to the throne and happy with his position in the navy. He liked the discipline, the order and it suited him nicely to sit in the background and let others do the work.

Then in 1892, everything changed. Alexandra had just taken their three daughters on a holiday to Denmark and had refused to come home after a particularly awful scandal regarding Bertie and a former mistress had become public. While she was away, George contracted typhoid and Alexandra was forced to rush back home despite her reticence. Bertie himself had suffered badly from it in 1872 and everyone was preparing for the worst.

As it turned out, George survived and by the end of December, he was well enough to return to Sandringham for New Year's celebrations after a rather joyous time for the family that Christmas. George was well again, Eddy had just become engaged to a wonderful young lady by the name of

Princess Mary of Teck and the tension had eased a little between Alexandra and Bertie during the festive season. Then in the second week of January, Eddy came down with a bad dose of influenza. The flu swiftly turned into pneumonia and one harrowing and distressing week later, Eddy was dead.

This wasn't the first time in history that a strong, young prince had succumbed to an illness when it was least expected and it wasn't the first time that the parents were devastated and unable to function through grief. Heartbroken, Bertie and Alexandra were inconsolable, refusing to even step back inside their home because Eddy had died there.

On the day his elder brother died, George's world changed overnight. Even while he was grieving, he was suddenly landed with all the responsibilities that he had never anticipated, wanted or prepared for. It was a terrifying prospect for him.

So while Bertie and Alexandra grieved, Victoria took George under her wing and as usual, her first thought was to find a suitable wife for him, just as she had for Eddy. She made him Duke of York and was determined to have him married as soon as possible. She'd spent a lot of time and energy reviewing suitable brides for Eddy and she saw no reason why those efforts should be wasted. She briskly turned to the Eddy's fiancée, Princess Mary of Teck, known as May, as the perfect bride, exactly as Alexander II of Russia had done when his eldest son had died.

George may still have been in a daze after his brother's death but he could see what his grandmother was doing. He told his grandmother he didn't want to think about it at all and found the idea of marrying his dead brother's fiancée quite upsetting. As usual, Victoria was relentless. George needed a wife and May was going to be the one. That was final.

No one except Victoria saw May as a suitable bride for George. She was only a minor member of the British Royal Family: the daughter of Francis Duke of Teck, of German extraction, and Princess Mary Adelaide of Cambridge, the granddaughter of King George III through his youngest son Adolphus and Charlotte of Mecklenburg-Strelitz. The couple had nothing in common except for the fact that they were both painfully introverted. She wasn't beautiful, rich or sufficiently royal and if you asked anyone for their opinion, they'd have told you that her family was actually quite embarrassing. May's father had humiliating public temper tantrums and her mother was selfish, loud, 17 stone and known as 'Fat Mary'. On top of all that, both parents were extravagant and had fled their country to escape creditors when May was in her teens. No doubt because of her parent's indiscretions, 24-year-old May was a model of quiet dignity, simply delighted to be part of the British monarchy regardless of which brother she married.

It would seem George and Nicky had a lot in common. Firstly, there was their remarkable physical resemblance. Secondly, each of them were extremely shy with doting mothers who, by the way, were sisters. And lastly, just as Nicky's father had been forced to marry his dead brother's fiancée, George was being forced to do the exact same thing by marrying May. It was extraordinary that the two immensely prominent figures, both introverted young men who would be kings of their own countries in the future, shared so many coincidences as well. A sense of shared destiny drew George more than ever to his Russian cousin Nicky.

But there was one key difference between the two royal cousins. Where George dutifully married his death brother's fiancée and moved into York Cottage on the Sandringham Estate in Norfolk to start his family, Nicky's marriage would be an epic tale of romance and disastrous drama, one that would alter the course of Russian History.

* * *

IT WAS during a family visit in 1889 to St Petersburg that Nicky was to meet and fall deeply in love with his German cousin, (a granddaughter of Victoria), Princess Alexandra Viktoria Helene Luise Beatrix of Hesse. Alexandra, nicknamed Alix, was the daughter of Victoria's second daughter Alice who had married a German duke, Louis of Hesse-Darmstadt, from a small German duchy best know for the arts.

Alice had died when an outbreak of diphtheria had swept through the Grand Ducal House of Hesse when Alix was only 6 years old. Alix, her three sisters and her brother Ernest, as well as her father, all fell ill at the same time, while Alix's sister Elisabeth, nicknamed Ella, had been sent to visit her paternal grandmother and as such had escaped the outbreak.

At 6 years of age, Alix didn't care much about looks but she knew her adored elder sister Ella was beautiful and different. Even her name was different, uncommon in a family full of Victorias and Alberts. She'd been named after her father's mother and she cared about everyone from the lowliest servant and was even careful of hurting the feelings of their bombastic cousin Wilhelm.

Alix's mother nursed the sick children herself rather than abandon them to doctors and it's not surprising that she herself fell ill as all but the youngest child survived. From the day Alice died, Victoria surprised everyone by taking her daughter's six motherless children under her wing. She found them tutors and governesses and every autumn, they came to stay with her at Windsor Castle, allowing them a light-heartedness that she never showed her other grandchildren. Alix soon became Victoria's favourite with her fair hair and good looks and she in turn instantly demanded to be regarded as English rather than German, refusing to do anything except speak and write in English.

Although clearly loved by her grandmother, Alix had a solitary childhood. Her siblings were all much older than her and her father was often away in the army. As a result, she grew up mistrustful of anyone outside her immediate circle although most of the family excused her self-absorption and melancholy given the fact that there was no one of her own age to communicate with except her busy, self-absorbed grandmother.

Nicky and Alix first met in 1884 at Ella's wedding to Nicky's enigmatic uncle, Grand Duke Sergei. Ella and Sergei's marriage is barely documented and a great deal of controversy surrounds Sergei, based on the nature of his personal life and character. He was shy by nature and dreaded personal contact with anyone but in contrast, his harsh manners made him appear arrogant, obstinate, humourless and disagreeable. Conjecture about the unhappy nature of their marriage has abounded and some contemporary reports have gone so far as to suggest that Sergei was homosexual. Contrary to this belief, the marriage appeared happy in its own way, although no children were born from the marriage.

To say it was an unusual wedding is an understatement but it was there that Alix felt the first flutters of love. She was 12 years old, pretty but terribly sad, while Nicky was a shy and reserved 16-year-old. She responded to Nicky's gentle nature immediately and Nicky was fascinated by her intensity. It would have been like a torture to them both as they agonisingly stumbled over words while family members watched on from a distance in the background. Four years later, they met again when Ella brought Alix to St Petersburg with the conscious intention of snapping up a good match for her younger sister. And who better than the heir to the Russian throne? By the end of the trip, Nicky was well and truly hooked.

There were, however, serious obstacles. We know that Victoria took a particular interest in Alice's children and in particular, her favourite granddaughter and her marital prospects. The thought of her marrying the Russian prince revived all of her fears and suspicions of anything Russian, even though Alix's great-aunt Dagma had married Tsar Alexander II. At the time, Victoria's choice for Alix had been one of her first cousins, either Eddy or even George.

The second obstacle was Nicky's family. They had no qualms about stating that they disliked Alix. She had a gloomy personality, and they were certain she was not suitable enough to be a tsarina. They had other choices in mind. Nicky's father was angling for a bigger catch for his son than the melancholy British princess and that catch was Princess Helene, the tall dark-haired daughter of Philippe Comte de Paris, the pretender to the throne of France. When Nicky was told of his father's preference for an arranged marriage to Helene, he uncharacteristically made a stand. His heart was set on Alix, he stated.

Fortunately for Nicky, Helene also resisted. She was a Roman Catholic and her father refused to allow her to become Russian Orthodox. On those grounds, even the Pope refused to give permission.

The next consideration became Princess Margaret of Prussia, another sister of Wilhelm's, and like Alix, also a granddaughter of Victoria. This time Nicky was more adamant in his refusal with the prospect of Wilhelm as a future brother-in-law. He flatly declared that he would rather become a monk than marry the boring, and rather plain Margaret who was the sister of his loud-mouthed, egocentric cousin Wilhelm.

It was a stalemate. Nicky refused any of his father's suggestions and his father declared that as long as he was alive and well, he would not give permission for his son to marry Alix. Not a person to be put off lightly, Alix's sister Ella continued to work hard at the match.

Alexander's statement that there would be no permission to marry Alix as long as he was alive and well, did not seem overly ominous at the time. It was just a push and shove situation between a father and a son who were both refusing to give in. However, four years later, with his words still hanging in the air, Nicky's father became seriously ill and those same words began to have a more worrying implication. With Nicky still resisting any suggestions for a bride and his father feeling very mortal, Nicky's father finally and reluctantly granted permission for Nicky to marry Alix. And Nicky decided to ask Alix to marry him at his cousin George's wedding in July.

George's wedding was the biggest royal event since his grandmother's Jubilee in 1887 and May was radiant in white satin embroidered with silver roses, shamrocks and thistles. Anyone who was someone was invited, including the Romanov family.

Nicky and George spent his last bachelor evening chatting until late into the night and during the day, Bertie had crammed every spare moment organising tailors, boot makers and hatters for his nephew. He was taken to a game of polo, made an honorary member of the Marlborough Club, shown George's new rooms then taken out to dinner. Nicky staggered in the heat and marvelled at the 1,500 wedding presents – including a cow – and loved every minute of it. At a garden party, George was even asked how he liked London compared to Russia and Nicky was congratulated on his forthcoming wedding.

Age had not diminished Victoria's intense dislike of Russia and the two countries were arguing yet again. This time it was over the mountains bordering Afghanistan, of all places. She arranged for Nicky to meet her at the bottom of a staircase in Windsor where she could stage her own entrance, proceeding slowly down the stairs and demonstrating that she could keep *anyone* waiting, even a Russian prince, if she chose to do so.

To everyone's surprise, even to herself, Victoria was won-over with Nicky. He wasn't quite what she had expected. He was polite, unassertive and keen to win over Alix's imposing grandmother at any cost. He spoke English without a fault and listened attentively to every word she spoke. Later, he would comment that she looked like a *'big round ball on wobbly legs'* but during his visit, he charmed her and she melted. With his heart soaring, he then proposed to Alix.

What he hadn't expected was for Alix to turn him down. Tail between his legs, he returned home.

One year later, they met again in Coburn in Germany when the royalty of Europe gathered for the wedding of Alix's brother, Ernest of Hesse-Darmstadt, to Princess Victoria Melita of Saxe-Coburg and Gotha, (nicknamed Ducky), the younger daughter of Victoria's second son Alfred, (nicknamed Affie). Ducky had inherited a duchy from a childless uncle and Marie of Russia, and after the windfall, she was being regarded as something of a catch. Once again, both were Victoria's grandchildren and among the guests were Wilhelm and his mother Vicky.

No one was happy about the marriage except Victoria who had bullied the couple endlessly. Ernest needed an heir, as his grandmother constantly reminded him, and Ducky was young and rich and they were first cousins, which was seen as a bonus.

Very much like his sister Alix, Ernest was a rather forlorn man. They'd grown up in a loving household with parents who demonstrated their affection for their children and as such he grew very attached to his parents and siblings. It was his terrible misfortune to witness several of their deaths during his childhood. When he was five, he and his only brother, 2-year-old Friedrich, had been playing a game when the younger boy, who suffered from haemophilia, fell through a window onto the balcony twenty feet below. Needless to say he died and Ernest was inconsolable. Five years later, when he was 10 years old, an epidemic of diphtheria swept through their home and his mother cared resolutely for her family. In November that year, his youngest sister Marie died from the disease and one month later, his mother, Alice, followed.

Whether it was because of his sadness or because the marriage was a prearranged one, the marriage was a terribly unhappy one. She was enthusiastic about the entertaining part of her role but less so with fulfilling her other duties. She avoided answering letters, put visits off to elderly relations, and talked to people at official functions who amused her while ignoring the people whom she found boring, regardless of their social or official standing. Her inattention to her duties provoked hideous quarrels with Ernest and the young couple had furious arguments, which sometimes turned physical. She would throw tea trays, smash china against walls and throw anything at hand at Ernest. They held off from a divorce until 1901 mainly because of their daughter Elisabeth, whom they both adored. Not too long after, Ernest found a suitable bride for himself and Ducky married one of Nicky's cousins.

Sorry... back to the wedding.

Everyone knew about the drama that was happening between Nicky and

Alix. They knew Alix had rejected Nicky and everyone was itching to see what would happen this time when they met. With no one taking the slightest notice of Ducky at her own wedding, all eyes were turned to Alix, willing her to say yes. As Wilhelm watched the drama unfolding, his practical mind was hoping for the wonderful opportunity to improve Russian-German relations. Such a romantic.

With the death of her father only two years before, Alix was sullen and upset at the prospect of losing her brother as well. Over the next few days, when they managed to get time alone, Nicky spoke quietly to her. She was heard crying and whispering *'No, I cannot.'* After everything Nicky had done to gain his parent's permission, his whole plan was failing anyway.

It shouldn't have come as such a big shock that one of Alix's main objections was due to religion. Like the other candidates, marriage to Nicky depended on their conversion to Russian orthodox, and as we know, no one was prepared, or even allowed, to do that. Alix herself was deeply religious and loath to abandon her Lutheran faith. She admitted that she was in love with Nicky and would readily have married him ... if he hadn't been Russian, and if he wasn't Orthodox.

Nicky was still reeling from her second rejection when Wilhelm cornered him to have a chat. Since the Reinsurance Treaty had lapsed, things had been chilly between Russia and Germany, in both trade and family, and Wilhelm complained that Nicky's father, Alexander, was snubbing him and gathering forces along the German border. Worse still, only months before, Russia had done the unthinkable and made an alliance with France, leaving Germany sandwiched between two potential enemies. It was exactly what Bismarck had been trying to avoid for decades.

Nicky nodded a lot and made a good attempt at being charming and agreeable, but politics was the last thing on his mind. All he wanted was to go home after being crushed by Alix's second refusal.

Family members gathered around Alix to listen and everyone tried to convince her that a conversion to Russian Orthodox was just a formality and that it really didn't mean anything in the scheme of things. But it wasn't just religion that was weighing heavily on Alix's conscience. There was another problem more difficult to overcome.

The ominous shadow was the disease haemophilia, hovering like a silent threat between them. This dreaded disease prevents the blood from clotting and primarily affects men, although it is passed through the women. It had entered the royal family through Victoria and had become a terrible reality in Alix's bloodline. Memory of her young brother's grisly death at 2 years old surfaced again. The disease had been passed on to Friedrich from Alix's mother so she was only too aware of the consequences. No one could really deny the fact that it was in her family and possibly lying dormant in her blood.

Of Victoria's nine children, three were affected by the condition. Of course, Victoria absolutely refused to admit the condition came from *her* since for the last seventeen generations before her, there had been no mention, or record through the British Royal Family, of any instances of haemophilia and her half-sibling had not suffered from the genetic disorder either. But what she couldn't deny was that her son Leopold was diagnosed with the disease when he was 6 years old and had died at the age of 30.

Although his death was mourned terribly, it came as no surprise. No one had expected him to live as long as he had, despite being mollycoddled and cosseted by his mother. Knowing full well the hazards and extent of his affliction, Leopold was determined to escape the constraints of his dominating mother in the attempt to live a normal, if somewhat careful, life. Her grandmother Victoria was just as determined otherwise. He was her most intellectual and artistic son who, in his determination to live life to the fullest, had even married and produced two children. Every precaution had been taken but in the end, the inevitable had happened when he fell and bumped his knee and hit his head. In the early hours of the next morning, he began having convulsions and soon after, he died of a cerebral haemorrhage.

Alix had every right to feel anxious. Even though Leopold was the only child of Victoria to have actually inherited the disease, in the future it would become a fact that two of her daughters were carriers and they in turn would pass the gene on to some of their sons. From Victoria, the disease would flow into the Royal bloodlines of Europe, afflicting the monarchies of Spain, Germany and Russia.

In the 1890's, doctors understood it was an inherited gene. But are you going to tell the formidable English Queen or the Russian Tsar that their children's future generations were going to be compromised because they may just be carrying haemophilia? After all, the whole business of royalty is about heredity. You have to have healthy children to produce more healthy children in order to prolong the dynasty.

Nowadays, statisticians have calculated that a woman who is a carrier has a 50/50 chance of developing the condition and there is a 1 in 25,000 to 100,000 chance of developing the disease as the result of a mutation in the mother's ovary if the father is of an advanced age. If a mutation *did* occur, it has been seen likely that it occurred with Victoria's father, Edward Duke of Kent and not with Victoria's mother. This theory is the dominant one especially when you consider that Edward and his French mistress did not have children after 24 years and no children born in the British Royal Family before then had suffered from haemophilia.

The Russian royal family, related through the Danish royal family, were at this stage free of the disease, so the fear that Alix might be a carrier of the dreaded disease would have been uppermost in everyone's minds. Everyone was fully aware that if she passed the disease on, it could have tragic consequences on the Romanov dynasty. Considering all of this, Nicky still persisted. He had loved Alix from the first day he met her and he was not going to change his mind *in case* she was affected.

On the last day before leaving Germany, with Nicky's uncles and Wilhelm in the next room waiting, the couple sat down together again. And Nicky pleaded once more.

Finally, Alix relented.

The engagement came at a very fortunate time. It was becoming obvious that Nicky's father was dying of kidney failure and he had been moved to his estate by the Black Sea in the hope that the mild climate in Crimea would revive him. The best German doctors were called but there was nothing they could do. He was almost blind and so weak he could hardly talk and Nicky and Alix were urgently summoned. Alexander's wife, Dagma, sent a telegram to her sister Alexandra to come quickly and she and Bertie left Britain immediately.

Bertie and Alexandra arrived to find the family in a state of shock. Two days before they arrived, 49-year-old Alexander III had died in horrible pain and everyone was dressed in black. Dagma had locked herself in her room, refusing to come out and sitting alone, rocking gently back and forwards, a terrified Nicky was repeating over and over that he did not want to be the tsar.

For all his frivolous ways, it was Bertie who was to be Nicky's rock. While Alexandra comforted Dagma, Bertie took over the funeral arrangements and tirelessly questioned ministers. Days later, the body made its 17-day journey to Kazan Cathedral in St Petersburg, through endless overheated palaces on an interminably slow ritual as tens of thousands of soldiers and crowds of sobbing peasants lined the railway tracks. Behind the procession, Bertie and the family followed. On each day, the tsar's family knelt for hours during services, kissing the icon held in the corpse's hands.

By the end of the journey, the corpse had begun to decompose and by the time Alexander was buried, his face had begun to rot. Worse still, ritual decreed it could not be covered.

Witnessing the decay were sixty-one European royals including George, summoned by his father, to be a pallbearer. It took four hours for the funeral cortege to reach the Cathedral and in the vast overheated church, where there were no pews to sit on, three ladies fainted. Throughout it all, Bertie stood stoically beside Nicky and along with the Romanovs, he kissed the rotting lips of the dead monarch.

A week later on his mother's birthday, Nicky, pale and drawn, married Alix, who seemed pinned to the ground by the weight of her traditional silver brocade and cloth of gold, diamond-encrusted, ermine-lined, Romanov wedding dress. It took eight pages to simply lift the train and in photos, Alix looked thin-lipped and frowning. In the streets, 40,000 soldiers took their hats off simultaneously as they drove off in their carriage to Nicky's quarters in Anichkov Palace.

At 26 years old, Nicky was totally unprepared to be the tsar and had never really wanted to be the head of the country anyway. He'd never even played an active role in government. What he loved was the army. He loved the happy crowd of healthy young men gathering in the officers' mess discussing horses, art and French songs. He loved the order and the routine, almost as much as he liked the lie-ins, the skating with fellow officers, lunch with one of his grand duke uncles, afternoon teas with his aunts, the balls and the trips to the ballet. In the barracks, dinner involved getting fashionably drunk on champagne and port, then rushing out into the snow, stripped naked, and howling like wolves. In 1891, he had even acquired the aristocratic accoutrement, a ballerina mistress, a fact he told Alix before the wedding. He had started collecting honorary titles from foreign regiments and he had a passion for uniforms that cost millions of roubles. He loved being a soldier.

For all the Romanov's opinion that Alix was not suitable material to be tsarina, Nicky's beautiful young wife was already on hand to offer support, devotion and steely resolve at a time when he desperately needed it. But like most people who convert to another religion, they often overdo it. In her attempt to be the perfect wife for Nicky, she underwent an enormous emotional struggle to convert to Russian orthodox and eventually became more Russian orthodox than the Russians themselves. She infused her husband with the idea that if you were God's representative on earth then you couldn't be told to do anything by anyone else. Nicky, always easily led, readily agreed with his wife. It was the Divine Right of Kings all over again.

Adrift and uncertain again, Wilhelm thoroughly approved and agreed with his young cousin's anti-democratic instincts and the two men met again on their royal yachts while sailing on the Baltic.

For Wilhelm, it was a fresh start in German relations with Russia but for Nicky, who had witnessed Wilhelm's trapeze act between relations, found him difficult, manipulative and as pushy as ever. The visit for him ended up more as an ordeal than enjoyment.

* * *

As part of the anti-Prussian club in support of her Danish mother-in-law Dagma, as well as her Danish aunt Alexandra in England, Alix could not warm to her cousin Wilhelm either. Though Wilhelm took the credit for bringing them together, Alix made no attempt to hide her contempt for him. Throughout her life, he had always been the cousin that no one wanted to play with and hence, she sat firmly in the anti-Wilhelm club.

On the face of it, Wilhelm had good reason to feel slighted by Britain. It's not like he had anything to do with the invasion of Denmark. That had been Bismarck. Wilhelm was only 4 years old at the time, still being stretched and pulled on a rack to make him appear acceptable in the eyes of the world. For Wilhelm, his continued exclusion from the Copenhagen holidays was a conspiracy between the Russians and the British and he firmly believed that all of the funny little Prussian principalities were ganging up against him, laughing and talking about him behind his back.

His obsession worsened when it became clear to him that Nicky's wedding and his ascension to the throne, had led to a softening of relations, not with Germany, but with Britain. Then, on top of it all was the colony rush in Africa.

For Germany, the problem with coming late to the game meant everyone else had already taken more than their fair share. The way Wilhelm saw it he had two options. Draw back and resign Germany to just a few minor colonies or press on and ignite conflict with Britain. And in his present frame of mind, he much preferred Option B.

Both options fell by the wayside however when a major gold field was discovered at an outcrop on a large ridge sixty kilometres south of the capital at Pretoria in the Transvaal region. All of a sudden, the Transvaal was so much more appealing to Wilhelm and as it turned out, the Dutch farmers, calling themselves Boers, actually liked him.

The British, needless to say, hated the idea of Wilhelm taking a share of their prize and the warning of *'serious consequences'* was mentioned if Wilhelm continued. Quick to reply, Wilhelm asked if Britain was threatening him yet again. On the last day of 1895, Wilhelm had his answer. Six hundred armed men, some of whom were officers of the British army, crossed the border into the Transvaal in an attempt to overthrow the Boer government.

To say Wilhelm was furious is an understatement. He wrote a letter to Nicky in Russia telling him of his outrage and the next day Wilhelm strode into a meeting with his ministers demanding invasion forces and warships. Someone had to teach Britain a lesson and he was just the one to do it.

Wilhelm's ministers were just as angry as he was but they managed to calm Wilhelm and talk him down. Finally, it was decided that he should send a telegram of support to Paul Kruger, the Boer leader, for the outrage committed.

By today's standards, the telegram was mild and very ordinary. It was worded politely and was simply meant to assure the Boers that Germany had no hand in the attack. But in Britain, at a time when they regarded Germany as a country who was flexing its muscles, it brought a surge of violent and hysterical anger. And their anger was focused on Wilhelm who found himself denounced, not only in the press, but also in gentlemen's clubs. Even women were sending him poison-pen letters and German shopkeepers had their windows smashed. Everyone expected such goings on by the French, but not the Germans.

It wasn't just the English people who were angry. Victoria was outraged as well. She sent Wilhelm a scathing letter, followed by one from Bertie, who also gave full vent to his dislike of Wilhelm. In his scathing letter, he referred to the Kruger telegram as a sign of Wilhelm's true feeling regarding Britain. Even George spoke out against his cousin. To punch home the message of Wilhelm's slight to his English relatives, George informed Wilhelm that unlike his usual practice of coming to Cowes for the regatta every year, this year Wilhelm could forget about it. He was absolutely not welcome.

Wilhelm was completely stunned at the ferocity of British reaction and he crumbled immediately. He sent a pleading reply, blaming his ministers for the telegram but Victoria would have none of it, saying that was illogical. However, when her ministers reminded her that some of what was said about the war was actually true, she backed down a little although she was still seriously miffed. In South Africa, Kruger told the German ambassador scathingly, *'the old woman just sneezed and you ran away.'*

The weird thing is that in Germany, Wilhelm had become exactly what he always wanted to be. He had become a hero. The raid had prompted a very anti-British feeling, focused on Victoria who they said was an unworthy sovereign, and Wilhelm was the man of the hour who had told her so.

As Wilhelm basked in the warm glow of German approval, Victoria turned her charm towards Nicky again, who was preparing for his coronation. George was quite excited at the prospect of seeing his Russian cousin again and had fully expected to attend. Much to his annoyance, Victoria decided to send his younger brother Arthur instead. It turned out to be a blessing in disguise for George. The coronation would be a disaster.

* * *

TRADITIONALLY ON THE day of the ceremony, the tsar would give an open-air feast and Nicky's uncle and brother-in-law Sergei, who was married to Alix's sister Ella, was given charge of the preparations. A feast was something that Nicky's starving people were not about to miss out on and half a million people turned up happily for the festivities. It turned out that Sergei had greatly underestimated the numbers and as a result, had under-catered.

As people scurried to attend the ceremony, food disappeared fast. In the rush, as the crowd stampeded towards the remaining morsels, thousands of people were crushed and killed. There had been a police presence but in the chaos, they were unable to do anything to stop the bedlam.

The severity of the disaster was hidden from Nicky who seemed oblivious of everything even though it was said that bodies had been shovelled under the very grandstand where he stood, so he could not see them. To make matters worse, on the night of the disaster, as Nicky attended a ball at the French embassy where he was seen drinking champagne, people were mourning and crying over the mangled bodies lying in the fields of Khodynka.

Sergei had always been a bully. He was a mean man and as mean men do, he stood over Nicky. On the other hand, Nicky was more than happy to let someone else shoulder a lot of the burdens that he felt he was not able to handle. So instead of ordering an enquiry into Sergei's role in the disaster, Nicky rather stupidly promoted Sergei to Commander-in-Chief in Moscow. And the slow festering anger that had been rising towards their corrupt government rose even more.

To show her support for Nicky, Victoria invited Nicky and Alix to visit her at Balmoral.

There was no more remote a place in the Scottish Highlands than Balmoral and Victoria loved it. She felt free and alive in the wilderness and she would put on a Scottish accent as soon as she crossed the border into Scotland. She even decided she was actually Scottish.

It was a remarkable turnaround for Victoria. Although born in England, she had always declared that she felt more German than English since she was three-quarters German. But that was before Wilhelm was born and it was before the Scotsman by the name of John Brown began standing staunchly by her side.

Most of the adults besides Victoria hated Balmoral. They hated its remoteness, its dullness and they hated the freezing cold stone corridors since Victoria never felt the cold and forbade fires. They even hated the tartan wallpaper with thistle designs and the inedible traditional Scottish fare. Most of the family referred to it as Siberia and of course, most of them hated John Brown with a passion.

The Russian couple arrived wet and sodden on 22nd September with their first child, Olga, after having driven through Edinburgh in an open carriage in the pouring rain. Everyone was nauseous after the long train ride but Victoria greeted them all enthusiastically with open bonfires. Along with their entourage of several hundred, including plain-clothed secret servicemen, Nicky and Alix arrived travel-worn and pale. Beside a beaming Victoria stood Bertie, dressed in his best Russian uniform complete with astrakhan hat, knickerbockers, Norfolk jacket and red greatcoat, all too snug and much too tight due to his increasing girth.

Not everyone was overjoyed as Victoria to see the Russians. Her household called the visit *'the Russian occupation'* because of the huge number in the entourage. Balmoral maids had to sleep four to a bed and because of the vast number of Russian servants, George and May had to be boarded up the road since there was simply no room for them at Balmoral.

Once again, Nicky enchanted Victoria. Head to head they chatted. She warned him about his German cousin and Wilhelm's worrying propensity to create conflict where it wasn't wanted and Nicky listened intently. As an aside to him, she told him not to worry because she was keeping close tabs on it all.

Nicky totally agreed with her that Wilhelm was playing a dangerous game. All Russia wanted, he confirmed, was to be left alone and to develop their position in the world. As he opened up, the bond between them grew and gradually became a slow-motion reversal of the traditional power relationship in Europe. Victoria was drawing Britain closer to her former enemy Russia and further away from her traditional ally, Germany. It was an extraordinary thing for her to do, considering her lifelong dislike towards Russia and her intense sense of kinship with Germany. By including Nicky in her thoughts, it meant Wilhelm had worn her down.

At first, the Balmoral household found the Russian pair a bit standoffish. Beyond Victoria, her family, the court and government, Nicky met virtually no one. But when they eventually left, Nicky left a breathtaking £1000 tip while Alix left a trail of diamond and pearl brooches among the ladies-in-waiting.

Nicky and Alix had decided to return home via Paris and everywhere the Russian couple went, Wilhelm watched their progress, injured and hurt, as they were mobbed and cheered. He was fully aware that they had spent time with his British relatives while he had not been invited and it wounded him more than he cared to admit. Not only that, his grandmother had welcomed her lifelong enemy, Russia.

In the end, his tangled relationship with his British relatives played a key part in the eventual disintegration between the two nations. Almost a year after the Kruger incident, Victoria's Diamond Jubilee, organised to celebrate her 60 years on the throne, loomed on the horizon and Wilhelm sent a hopeful letter to his grandmother asking about the plans for the celebration. He was fishing for an invitation but Victoria's answer was straight to the point. He was not invited. Her Jubilee was to be celebrated within the *empire* and no foreign crowned heads were invited. Instead, she told him his younger brother Heinrich could come in his place. Forlorn at the rebuke, he sent a letter back begging her to reconsider. But she would not relent. Her Jubilee was to be a statement. Britain occupied 25% of the world's landmass and encompassed 444 million people and they didn't need anyone else to help her celebrate, thank you very much. It would be splendid enough without him.

It wasn't just Wilhelm that Victoria was having serious issues with. Her government and family were in a state of meltdown. And it was all because of her relationship with an Indian servant by the name of Abdul Karim.

In June 1887, a tall handsome stranger walked into Victoria's life and 14 years of trouble began. When she saw this gorgeous man with his sash and turban bend low and kiss her feet, she was smitten. Her companion John Brown had died 4 years before from a severe form of the skin complaint called erysipelas, an acute infection causing fevers, chills, fatigue, vomiting and headaches due to a Group A streptococci. His death had been painful and she was left devastated and once again alone. Enter Abdul Karim.

24-year-old Abdul was one of two Indian servants who had arrived as gifts from her Indian Empire. When he proceeded to tell her stories of an exotic India, she was hooked. As Empress of India, she had long since wished to visit the country but found it impossible. Now Abdul brought the country to her and she was enthralled. He told her wonderful stories of mysterious spices, of saris and colourful peacocks and he didn't just spice up her romantic images of India, within a couple of weeks he was adding spice to her food in the kitchens in the form of authentic curries. But Abdul had more ambitions than just being a chef. He had his eye on a serious promotion.

Victoria had always been a needy person who was emotionally hungry. She grew up without a father and a mother whom she believed did not love her, despite all reports that would indicate exact opposite. She believed she did not have a happy childhood so in later life what she needed was someone to give her unconditional attention.

At 68 years of age, Victoria was a figure of great authority but her private life was marred by tragedy. She had never fully recovered from the death of Albert but for two decades, John Brown had been her most intimate male companion. After his death, she had been left bereft, until Abdul arrived on the scene. She soon found Abdul was more than willing to step in and replace him.

Just weeks after his arrival, Victoria made a startling announcement. The 24-year-old kitchen boy was to be known as her teacher of Hindustani, the official language of her Indian subjects. She had made him her undisputed favourite and she didn't care who knew it.

But not everyone was as smitten with Abdul as she was. He had landed in a country governed by strict codes of protocol and the idea that someone who was a servant and an outsider with no pedigree or social standing, could suddenly leap frog into a position of great importance to the queen was something they found not only threatening but wrong. The palace simmered with quiet rage over the servant who didn't know his place and who was catapulting his way further and further into the limelight.

Things went from bad to worse. By Christmas, he had become her private secretary and had been elevated into the top rank of the palace hierarchy. And they were not amused. But while Abdul was turning over the establishment in the royal household, he was about to fall out with the most powerful man in the Empire: The Viceroy of India himself. And it all started with a simple Christmas card.

Just prior to Christmas, the Viceroy was opening his mail when he came across a card from Windsor. Surprised, he opened it and all hell broke loose. The card was wishing him a very Merry Christmas and the signature stated it was Abdul Karim from Windsor Castle.

Despite his anger by returning the card with an appropriate response, he was shocked to find that Victoria defended Abdul. It set a string of events into motion. Fritz Ponsonby, the son of the Secretary, would head off to

Abdul's home town in Agra on a mission: to investigate Abdul's family credentials. And he came up with some powerful ammunition.

Abdul had given the impression that his father was a high-flying surgeon in the Indian army. In fact, he was a low-ranking orderly cum doctor at a jail in Agra and not nearly as prestigious as Abdul had inferred. When news reached the British court, feathers began to fly.

But as the hostility rose, once again Victoria took a surprising view. The more the attacks arrived the more enraged she became and defended him. And Abdul prospered even more. Victoria gave him three houses: one in Balmoral, one at Windsor and one at the grounds at Osborn.

Like Brown, Abdul was universally despised. He was a pompous, conceited and manipulative man who continually pushed himself forward to get more and more. And it wasn't just the aristocrats who loathed him. The other Indian servants hated him just as much because he was domineering and unkind to them. When travelling on a train, he was even known to demand the entire carriage for himself.

But it was his elevation to private secretary that shocked her government. In this position, he had access to secret documents on vital matters of foreign policy regarding Russia, the Middle East and Afghanistan. And no one knew what to do.

By 1897, as her Diamond Jubilee approached, she had become totally dependent on him to the exclusion of her staff and family. It was then that Victoria and Abdul dropped a bombshell over the Jubilee honours: Abdul Karim would be knighted.

You can imagine the shock that reverberated through the palace. He already had a chest full of prestigious medals. He had The Star of India and the Companion of the Indian Empire from Victoria and he also wore the Order of the Red Eagle he had received from Wilhelm. But the prospect of Sir Abdul Karim was one step too far.

Bertie had finally had enough. After four discussions with Victoria's physician, Sir James Reid, the pair came up with a plan. The following day, Reid visited Victoria with a letter in his hand. The letter stated that the only charitable explanation for her incredible behaviour was that she was not sane and the time was approaching when she would be forced to save her reputation by coming forward and saying so. And her son Bertie was backing him up since it was affecting the realm.

To stand up to Victoria was a remarkable feat on its own. But amazingly the plan worked. The threat to have her declared officially insane hit home and for once in her life, she admitted defeat. But there would be a caveat. Abdul would remain Mr Karim but he would remain by her side mingling with Indian princes and European monarchy during her Jubilee celebrations.

On 21st June 1897, the palace opened its gates to celebrate Victoria's 60 years on the throne and a long glittering parade of soldiers from all over the empire followed Victoria's carriage through London to St Pauls Cathedral to the sound of deafening cheers. True to her word, Wilhelm was not among the guests.

But while Britain celebrated Victoria's Jubilee, the newspapers were not so supportive. India was in the grip of a horrifying famine and photographs of the hideously starved people, courtesy of new Kodak cameras, were sent around the world, though they were markedly absent from British papers. As Empress of India, what was she doing about it? At the same time, the newspapers reported the British government in South Africa was quietly importing Chinese labourers, effectively making them slaves,to work in the mines in order to reduce wages. As scathing as the accounts were, the overwhelmingly expensive celebrations continued.

* * *

WHILE BRITAIN PARTIED, Nicky and Alix moved to a new house fifteen miles east of St Petersburg to Alexander Palace in Tsarskoe Selo. Nicky had inherited his father's suspicions of anyone outside the family and he and Alix had developed a healthy dislike for St Petersburg. With that dislike increasing over the years, they became almost reclusive.

The elegant provincial town of Tsarskoe Selo, built originally by Catherine the Great, was perfect for the Romanov family. It was a strange place, almost like a theme park, with two royal palaces and holiday homes for the highest aristocracy set in 800 acres of perfectly manicured lawns, gardens and hedges. Surrounding it was a high fence with Cossack guards and thousands of servants. Inside the boundary was the only town-wide electrical system in the country, the first railway and the most advanced water and sewage system in all of Russia. Unfortunately for them, the move created a vicious circle.

To most Russians, Nicky and Alix were an enigma. Despite have a personal suite of 200 ladies in waiting to call upon, Alix confined herself to her family and a small group of women she believed she could trust. As for Nicky, he was happy to follow Alix's lead. He loved his privacy, his wife and he loved his family.

Because of their self-imposed segregation, his contact with other classes became minimal and he became oblivious to his people's suffering. While they liked to think they were bourgeois and lived in moderation, they really had no idea what life was like outside their palace. Their household consisted of 16,500 people, mainly servants, hundreds of court officials, 103 stewards, 40 gentlemen of the bedchamber, hundreds of officers and four 'Ethiopians' dressed in gold-embroidered jackets, slippers curved at the toe, standing outside Nicky's study ready to open the doors silently when needed. Both of them claimed to be bored with court etiquette but they loved the ability to live well apart from everyone else. Then there were the other palaces and the yachts, one of which had a gold strip down the sides and a gold double eagle on the stern.

The truth was Nicky had no idea, and actually didn't want to know, how much Russia was changing. He did not want to know that the old class distinctions were breaking down and that serfs were becoming merchants and tradesmen's children were becoming teachers, engineers and doctors. He didn't realise that peasant life meant living in crisis and misery and he didn't understand that all they wanted was a better future for their children. He just didn't see why things simply couldn't stay as they had always been. Instead, he had chosen to live in his fairyland at Tsarskoe Selo, slumbering peacefully on the brink of an abyss, lulled by his starving population as they softly sang 'God Save the Tsar.' His preoccupation with his family meant his court had become little more than a huge extended domestic household full of people obsessively polishing gold braid and silverware.

Nicky hung on tenaciously to his belief in the Divine Right of Kings. The moment the crown hit his head, and under Alix's quiet insistence, God's purpose was magically transferred to him and he knew better than any of his ministers in what Russia wanted and needed. As the years passed, this sense of entitlement counterbalanced his lack of confidence. He became increasingly resentful of what he regarded as infringes on his authority and despite mountains of paperwork, he refused to have even one secretary in his employ who might contradict him. Russia was his private estate and he wanted to run it like a landowner. He would listen, of course, to what was being said to him. He would even smile and nod sometimes. Then he would do something else entirely. He knew that there was a growing agricultural crisis and a financial situation but instead he encouraged extravagant spending on his Russian fleet and spent huge sums of money on taking over parts of China.

* * *

WHILE NICKY LOCKED himself and his family away in seclusion in Russia, it was much the same in England for his grandmother. By then, Victoria was almost 80 years old and would disappear into her apartments for days at a time, leaving courtiers to hang around in corridors bored and unable to leave the building until she did, which was rare. George on the other hand was only too happy to keep himself as far from public scrutiny as possible in his quiet domestic life in York Cottage on the Sandringham estate. He felt safe on the 30,000-acre estate where he could shoot to his heart's content. For George, it was his haven.

George and Nicky had a lot more in common than just their looks. They were both shy men who loved the life of a country gentleman, no happier than when they were massacring a few thousand birds a week. Both preferred their families to court society and both were addicted to routine. Nicky would arrive for tea at the precise time every day and George had to know exactly what he was doing every single moment of the day and hated any disruption. Every clock was put a half hour in advance so that he would not be late for anything. Both had an intense dislike for change of any sort and both felt deeply anxious about their role in the world.

To everyone else, York Cottage was dark and gloomy, architecturally repulsive in a higgledy-piggledy sort of way and always full of the smell of cooking. It had fake Tudor beams and sat in eternal shadow amongst the trees overlooking a dark pond in which stood a leaden pelican silently watching the water lilies and bamboo. During the day, while George sat quietly in his library indulging in his hobby of stamp collecting, the house would be bursting at the seams with assorted nurses, housemaids, governesses, nannies, footmen, wine butlers, a valet and a chef. Later he would retire to the sitting room, big enough really for only two adults, although later it would also be crammed with six children after tea.

But despite all efforts to dislodge him elsewhere, George refused to move into a bigger house. For George, York Cottage reminded him of his early life on board a ship and he had no want to leave that part of his life behind. He loved his life as a Norfolk gentleman, a rich one mind you, with an income of £100,000 a year (£40,000 from Parliament and £60,000 from the duchy of Cornwall). He loved his Savile Row suits and he loved his guns with cartridges engraved with little red crowns and from his estate in Sandringham, he could retreat with no need to engage in the outside world. Although he was related to all twenty of the reigning monarchs in Western Europe, he hated the thought of going abroad because travelling made him homesick and seasick and due to his inability to speak any foreign language, making speeches was a nightmare.

After George left the navy, there were no obligations hanging over his head, apart from the occasional public engagement. For seventeen years, he had nothing to do except hunt animals on the estate and stick stamps in albums. Even his father's staff ran the estate. He would spend several afternoons a week arranging and re-arranging stamps, poring over catalogues, occasionally bidding vast sums of money on rare issues, unbeknownst to his father. By the end of his life, he had amassed 325 albums, the largest collection in the world and when he became king, he only collected stamps with his own face on them.

Like so many of the habits of the British aristocracy, shooting was the signifier of a leisurely life. When he went shooting, he had thousands of available animals secluded in the bushes, plus beaters to dislodge them, someone to carry the guns and someone to carry lunch. George could bring down the obscene number of 1,000 peasants in one day and feel happy about his accomplishment.

Although Victoria had arranged his marriage to May, it was hailed as a great success. Within a year, May had produced an heir, Edward Albert Christian George Andrew Patrick David (nicknamed David), and they quickly became a beacon of respectability and domesticity. On paper, the marriage was perfect.

But George and May had a complicated marriage. Perhaps he cared for her in his own way but always on the fringe of his domestic life were his sisters and his mother. His mother Alexandra made a point of demonstrating her power over him by turning up at the house unannounced whenever she felt like it, moving furniture around and quick to point out anything that May did which could be construed as neglect of her *"Georgie"*.

Although she couldn't actually say she liked George's mother, May disliked her father-in-law Bertie intensely. She disapproved of Bertie's joking, his rakish lifestyle and his many mistresses but above all, she disliked the hold he had over George. George even consulted his father on everything down to what colour livery his footmen should wear.

Despite everything, May never complained and committed herself entirely to accommodating her husband and her submissiveness fortified George to treat her rather badly in the true Hanoverian style: quick to anger with a terrible temper. After being shouted at, May would often leave the table when he was openly rude to her in front of the children and they in turn would get up and follow her out. To his children, he was a strict, bullying and impatient father who found it hard to show them tenderness, just as he found it difficult to show love to his wife. They were dominated by his fierce personality and his strict discipline as he set ridiculous standards. Like his own father, George frightened his children. For them, dirty hands, making a noise or even wriggling in church was horrifying.

But it wasn't just George's personality that affected the children. Their mother had detached herself as well. As a young woman, she cultivated a reserve to cover up for her shyness but it made her a less than an ideal mother. It was as if she went through life wearing a psychological suit of armour, which prevented her from showing real warmth.

The harshness of life at home with their ferocious father and distant mother, who after two years of marriage could only convey their feelings for each other in the form of letters, would have serious consequences in the future. Looking back on his life, his eldest son, David, would describe his childhood as wretched. George's second son Albert would be subjected to having his legs secured in metal stints to correct his knock-knees and although he was left-handed, he was forced to use his right. And then there was his stutter. Life at home had became so traumatic that he developed a serious stammer, which did not improve his father's temper as he began shouting *'Get it out boy!'* when the small boy struggled to speak. His third son Henry would cocoon himself in the army and seem hell-bent on breaking all the rules while the youngest son George would be labelled as bisexual and a drug addict. The only son who seemed to have escaped was John who had been sent to another household, separated from his family because of his epilepsy.

To give George a little bit of leeway, his coldness could perhaps be put down to the fact that he was like Nicky in a lot of ways. He was afraid of the future when one day, he would be king and he felt totally unprepared for it. But for May, who saw how George's indifference affected his children, there was no excuse for her coolness towards her children.

Perhaps it was because she received so little love from her husband or perhaps it was as simple as she had never imagined herself married to George in the first place. Like Victoria, she hated being pregnant. She bundled the children off to nursemaids and nannies and it took May three years to realise that one nanny was routinely abusing her two eldest boys.

But for both parents, the youngest son John was an embarrassment. At the age of 4, people began to observe that John was 'slow'. That same year, he suffered his first epileptic seizure and was later diagnosed as having some form of intellectual disability. By the age of 11, his seizures had become more frequent and severe and he was sent to live separately with his own staff in a cottage on the Sandringham estate out of the public eye and away from his brothers and sisters because it upset them so much.

John died in his sleep at the age of 13 and for a long time, his name did not appear on the Windsor family tree. Although he may have been an embarrassment to his family, his lonely life would have been far better than his siblings who still lived with parents who could barely stand to talk to each other.

* * *

FOR BOTH GEORGE AND NICKY, the world was encroaching on the walls that they had built around themselves, but Wilhelm liked to think that unlike his cousins, he was immune to public opinion. All over Europe newspapers couldn't get enough of the drama surrounding the royal family and they were becoming much more aggressive with what they printed. Wilhelm tried to dismiss the increasing power of the press nonchalantly but in fact, he was obsessed with it. A critical story would send him into a frenzy of fury and a flattering one, rare as they were, would bring forth a burst of love for 'dear old England'.

For most people in England, the hostility with Germany was reversible; after all, they were family. But gradually with reports of Wilhelm's behaviour forever in the paper, a feeling of uncertainty was growing and no one was sure if Germany could be trusted anymore. There had been a tangible shift towards hostility concerning Britain in the highest quarters of the German government, but it was not entirely due to Wilhelm. People were pointing their fingers at Wilhelm's new favourite and secretary of state for foreign affairs, Bernhard von Burlow and his new head of the Naval Ministry, Admiral Alfred von Tirpitz. With their appointments came a marked shift of hostility towards Britain and it was obvious that both men regarded Britain as the chief obstacle to Germany's glorious destiny.

Burlow was a smart man. He knew he needed Wilhelm on his side and away from Britain and he knew exactly how to do it: through Wilhelm's ego. By the end of 1897, Burlow had convinced Wilhelm that an honest, trustworthy Anglo-German alliance was no longer possible. He was saying that Britain was looking down their nose at both him and Germany with indifference, sometimes with contempt and arrogance, and as far as Germany was concerned, England was the most dangerous of enemies. And of course Wilhelm listened to him.

Slowly Wilhelm began to lean towards Russia again, believing that it made no sense to get too close to Britain and lose Russia's friendship. Besides, Russia was of much more use to Germany than England was. This won Wilhelm more cheers from the right-wing parties that he needed to cultivate in the Reichstag but while Wilhelm glowed with pride at his growing popularity at home, Victoria wasn't too pleased with him, yet again. It wasn't just his going behind her back. It was his weak attempt to set Britain against Russia. It all came to a nasty head when Wilhelm showed no sign of sympathy at all when his 24-year old cousin Alfred Duke of Saxe-Coburg and Gotha shot himself in January 1899.

The exact circumstance of young Alfred's death is not known for sure and varying accounts have been published. His sister Marie's memoirs say he 'broke down' after a scandal surfaced regarding his mistress while other writers say he had *'consumption'*. *The Times* published an account saying he died of a tumour while the *Complete Peerage* simply stated he *'shot himself'*. But what is known is that by 1898, Alfred had begun showing severe symptoms of tertiary syphilis in which mental peculiarities are a major symptom and a frequent cause for institutionalisation in insane asylums. On the night of his parent's 25th wedding anniversary, while the rest of the family gathered to celebrate at the Schloss Friedenstein in Gotha, Alfred took a revolver outside into the cool night air and shot himself.

For all Wilhelm's postulations to be regarded as part of his British family, his total lack of concern for his cousin's death was the final straw for Victoria. While she publicly grieved, she let Wilhelm know in no uncertain terms of her anger at his coldness. No one knew that just one year later, the squabble would reach a new high with another close death.

Victoria's son Affie had inherited the title of Duke of Saxe-Coburg and Gotha when his uncle (his father Albert's brother) Ernest II, had died in 1893. As the heir apparent to the British throne, Bertie, then Prince of Wales, had renounced his right to the Duchy and the title had then passed on to his younger brother Affie. Affie promptly left the navy and moved to Gotha as the reigning duke, surrendering his British allowance and his seats in the House of Lords as well as the Privy Council.

One year after young Alfred's suicide, Affie would be diagnosed with throat cancer and by July 1900, he would be dead as well. With both Affie and young Alfred dead, the big question on Victoria's mind was, who would inherit the Duchy of Coburg?

While in obvious distress at the death of her son Affie, the inheritance of the Duchy of Coburg was a major issue that Victoria needed to resolve. And as always, she had ideas. For much of Ernest's reign, the heir presumptive to Saxe-Coburg and Gotha was his only sibling, Albert, Victoria's beloved husband. After him, the title would be passed on to Albert's descendants, namely Affie and then Affie's son Alfred. This meant that the Duchy belonged in *her* family and she meant to let the world know that she wanted the estate to pass on to her third son Arthur, Duke of Connaught and Strathearn, who in turn would then pass it on to *his* son.

But Wilhelm had ideas of his own too. Since Coburg was in Germany and he was the Kaiser of Germany, his idea was that *he* should inherit the duchy. He even threatened to make it a law that no *'foreigner'* could inherit a

German duchy at all and he went so far as to send a scathing nine-page letter to Victoria accusing her Prime Minister, Lord Salisbury, of high-handed treatment.

Once again, Victoria and Wilhelm clashed terribly over the matter. Both had strong personalities, both were determined to win the issue and neither of them were prepared to back down. With all of the backwards and forwards anger, a fresh geyser of resentment and suspicion grew between the two. But Victoria was used to having her own way and letting her grandson lord it over her was just *not* going to happen. Without further ado, she confidently gave the duchy to Arthur.

But for all of the fighting and the battle of wits with Wilhelm, what Victoria had never imagined was that Arthur would go against her wishes and renounce his rights to the succession. Not only that, he renounced the rights for his own son as well. For Arthur, accepting the duchy would have meant leaving the British Army and uprooting his family to take the reins of government in Coburg while leaving his British life behind. And he had no desire to do any such thing. England was his home and that's the way he wanted it to stay. Without the use of a crystal ball, that one fateful decision may just have saved the lives of both him and his family.

So like musical chairs, the duchy was up for grabs again.

The next in line for the duchy was 16-year-old Charles Edward George, son of Prince Leopold who had died earlier of haemophilia. Charles Edward was attending school at Eton with another cousin and rumour has it that the cousin threatened to beat him if he did not accept the duchy. Add that to the fact that Charles Edward's mother had drummed into him the importance of duty and obligation and with such strong influences from his mother and his grandmother, Charles accepted the offer since refusal would mean that the seat of Coburg would become extinct.

Surprisingly, Wilhelm was somewhat mollified by the choice. The boy had been a somewhat favourite of Wilhelm's during Charles Edward's youth and some had even called him the Emperor's 7th son. At 16 years of age, Charles Edward was still under age so a regency was needed until he came of age. And never missing an opportunity, Wilhelm stepped in to keep a strict eye on everything. In five years' time, when Charles Edward reached 21, Wilhelm would choose his wife's niece to be Charles Edward's bride, a choice that would have far reaching consequences on future events.

Despite the relatively good outcome for both parties, Victoria and Wilhelm still fumed at each other and in the end, she retaliated by not inviting him to her 81st birthday party in May.

Wilhelm probably would have liked to remain cool about the rejection and give him his due, he held back for about two weeks. When he couldn't hold his anger in any longer, he summoned the British attaché and demanded he do something. The attaché calmly told him the matter was out of his hands. Wilhelm was just not invited to the party.

This latest rejection was just the last in a long line of rejections. He'd never been invited to the Spring holidays in Copenhagen purely because he was German. He'd been refused an invite to his grandmother's Jubilee celebration and his cousin George had informed him that Wilhelm was absolutely not welcome to Cowes for the regattas any more. Painful memories bubbled to the surface clouding every instance of Wilhelm's perception of mistreatment.

His reply is one that will be remembered forever in history. He replied, *'One day, England will be sorry.'*

It was a threatening thing to say and in light of what would happen in the future, it was an ominous prediction. It was also unprecedented for one monarch to attack another monarch in such a threatening manner.

Victoria rallied herself but she was feeling her age. She was almost blind, completely lame, increasingly tired and she had been withdrawing more and more from public affairs. She just couldn't bear to argue anymore. But the one thing she *could* do better than anyone else was to remain obstinate. Wilhelm was just not invited to her party.

Victoria's anger hurt Wilhelm more than he would admit and he seemed constantly on the edge of hysteria, bullying his entourage and flying into rages. Months later, he gave a farewell speech to his troops who were leaving to crush the Box Rebellion in China and the world suddenly saw the rawness of his emotions. Despite being very pleased with himself, his speech sounded out of control and his rhetoric was the epitome of a brash, arrogant military leader who knew he was heading a very powerful army. By giving his overconfident, aggressive speech, Wilhelm had done the exact opposite of what he actually wanted. His speech forced Britain to do what they really didn't like doing. They had to make allies during times of peace. And what do you do when you have an enemy? You look for your enemy's enemy. So they chose France.

Towards the end of 1900, after Affie's death in July, news came that Vicky also had cancer and it was entering its final virulent phase. Victoria tried to keep up a positive persona but as time passed, she became more and more morose. Sitting alone in her rooms, she started to compile an album for the dead but very quickly abandoned it because she said it made her too sad.

By December, she was totally blind and feeble and by the New Year of 1901, it was obvious she was dying. She had rheumatism in her legs that rendered her lame and cataracts clouded her eyesight. She was feeling weaker, dazed and confused and by 22nd January, at the age of 81, she finally gave up.

In Berlin, Wilhelm was in the midst of celebrating the 200th anniversary of the Prussian crown but when he heard that his grandmother was seriously ill, he dropped everything and prepared to rush to her side.

Of course, no one in the German government wanted him to go. His departure, they warned, would certainly affect the German people's opinion of him. But it fell on deaf ears. He was determined to be by her side.

As you can imagine, after everything that had happened in the past, his eminent arrival in England upset the British family. Each member of the family had just a few precious minutes alone with her and Wilhelm's arrival meant they had even less time. When it was his turn, Wilhelm was shocked at her frailness. He knelt by her bedside and held her for two and a half hours without moving, shortening even more the British relatives' time with her. As she died, he held her tenderly as she gently passed away. He then helped to lay her out beneath the portrait of her German husband Prince Albert, along with her written instructions regarding her burial. In her coffin, along with Albert's dressing gown and a plaster cast of his hand, she was to be buried with a lock of John Brown's hair, his photograph and a ring worn by Brown's mother, given to her by Brown himself, as well as several of his letters. His photograph, wrapped in white tissue paper, was to be placed in her left hand, with flowers arranged to hide it from view. She wanted the ring placed on the third finger of her right hand.

Everyone present knew that Victoria's passing meant the end of an era. The grandmother of Europe, who held the extended royal family together, was dead and no one knew who could possibly take over that job now. For hundreds of thousands of people throughout the world, Queen Victoria had become something more than simply a caustic, selfish old lady in a bonnet. Sure they knew she could be dismissive, obstinate and prone to self-pity. And yes, millions died of starvation and disease during her reign and she seemed blind to their plight. She could be demanding, rude and frequently fled public duties for the peace and solitude of Scotland. She even formed attachments to her servants that were so strong they were considered peculiar and even suspect.

But she had loved fiercely, despised racial and religious prejudice and had survived six assignation attempts. She had surpassed autocracy and had become the role model for all future successful constitutional monarchs, as well as a beloved figurehead. Under her reign, England had achieved a greatness it had never known before. This queen with the stern profile, clothed in her reams of black mourning cloth, would forever be associated with growth, might and democracy. Her legacy was enormous: an empire, nine children, forty-two grandchildren and the longest-reigning monarch in English history to date. She safeguarded the British people as they took steps towards democracy in a century full of unrest. She may have done it as a mother, who followed her husband from room to room while they fought, storming, yelling and crying, and she may have done it while she tried to resolve her depression and overwhelming, prolonged grief. But she had done it. Her story was one of a tiny, strong woman at the heart of an empire and without her, a chilly uncertain new century was dawning.

Two days after her death, Wilhelm rode side by side with his old sailing rival, now King Edward VII, behind Victoria's coffin: uncle and nephew united in grief.

In Germany, there were howls of fury.

EDWARD VII

Born 1841
Reign 1901 – 1910

𝒜 story circulated just after Victoria died that Alexandra had knelt before her husband and kissed his hand, murmuring *'Sire'*. It brings to mind colourful visions of yesteryear. Of beautiful women in flowing colourful dresses bowing courteously and reverentially as their dresses dust the floor. Of courtiers whispering quietly in halls, humbly lowering their heads to the sad news of a monarch who has passed. Of rising princes who sorrowfully raised their heads high in reverent esteem as they paid their last respects to a revered monarch. The visions disappear when we hear 59-year-old Bertie's reply. *'It has come too late. I would have liked it 20 years ago.'*

Late it may have come but one thing was certain: Bertie could now take joy in a certain type of revenge. And as we know, vengeance is best served cold.

The longest memories that endure far beyond the happy ones are always the most painful ones. Bertie's next actions may have been petulant and undignified but I'm sure they were immensely satisfying for him.

In the months that followed his mother's death, Bertie, now Edward VII, had one thing on his mind: the obliteration of all the artefacts, busts and statues of John Brown. On the very morning of her death, shepherds on the hills above Balmoral noticed that the cairn of stones the Queen had raised to the memory of John Brown had been flattened and the stones scattered and spread around. The utter desecration was too severe for the gales on the slopes, no matter how violent, and all who viewed the site had a fair idea who had given the order to destroy the site.

At Windsor, the Keeper of the Royal Pictures received an unequivocal order as well. A life size portrait of John Brown in a black coat, dark brown tweed kilt and brown horsehair sporran, commissioned by Queen Victoria two months after Brown's death in 1883, was to be removed from its place of honour, deleted from the inventory at Windsor Castle and set gratis to John Brown's brother, William at Crathie, in Scotland. Hammers smashed plaster busts, scissors rent keepsakes and photographs buckled and sizzled on bonfires, reducing them to ashes. No one in the inner royal circle had any doubt about the reasons for the new sovereign's fury against Brown. He was erasing the memories of being smacked on the backside as a young prince, of being criticised and humiliated as an adult and he was trying to erase the pain and insult as his mother chose the overconfident Scotsman over him.

It wasn't just John Brown who was on Bertie's hit list. Abdul Karim was not forgotten either. Days after Victoria's death, Abdul received a visit from several ministers whose orders were to seize any documents with the royal seal and destroy them. With that out of the way, he was then to be turned out of his house, return all other property to the realm and be banished to the estates in India that Victoria had so generously given him.

Whether it was an eradication of past injustices or just the cleansing of the slate, Bertie was making it pretty clear that it was *his* turn now. There must have been a contented sigh at the end of his tirade as the bubbling cauldron of his emotions finally came to a head.

When his mother died, Bertie was actually in a bad way. He was in the throes of depression, a product, he said, of his childhood, much like his temper. He was still recovering from a bout of pleurisy, his bronchitis was becoming chronic and a broken kneecap was making it hard for him to walk. Along with his mother's death, he was still mourning for his brother Affie from the year before and his favourite sister Vicky was in the last painful descent of cancer. The Boer War was a mess, morale was fragile and the British army, under the influence of Lord Kitchener, had become ruthless in its attempt to flush out the last Boer guerrilla fighters. The army burned farms, shot prisoners and imprisoned women and children, Boer or black, in concentration camps. In the appalling conditions, prisoners died in huge numbers of famine, thirst and cholera.

No one seemed especially pleased that Bertie was the king. He was the heir who had been waiting around for 40 years to take the throne (since his father's death and his mother's withdrawal from her family and her court) and in that time he'd had plenty of time to lose the little appeal he may have had. In Bertie's case, Britain had lost their powerful queen and instead they had a 59-year-old lecherous playboy who was growing fatter by the day and still showing signs of being spoilt, self-indulgent and obsessed with clothes. To the world, he was a man who was immoral, lavish and feudal and someone who found his amusement at someone else's expense. He was impatient, restless and hated boredom and even though he liked to travel incognito, he threw a wobbler if he was kept waiting in a restaurant or hotel. He smoked twenty cigarettes and twelve cigars a day and then there was his colossal appetite. He ate five mountainous meals every day and dinner consisted typically of twelve courses including oysters, caviar, pheasant stuffed with truffles, quails stuffed with foie gras and frog's legs in jelly. In later life, he was known to take a whole chicken to bed with him. No wonder he could barely climb a flight of stairs. He was, in fact, a true Hanoverian in every respect.

Everyone in the world seemed hostile towards Britain and Bertie had no idea what he was supposed to do about it. His mother had been so insistent on doing everything herself and as such, Victoria had deprived Bertie of any sort of formal experience of government.

Despite this, he seemed to instinctively adapt to the role. The womanising *almost* came to a stop and after the long years of waiting for his mother to die so he could take over the role as king, there was an abrupt shift from the party-going Prince of Wales to a conscientious workaholic king.

As a young man, it was hard to warm to Bertie who blatantly cheated on his wife and ruthlessly discarded mistress after mistress, although some may find an explanation in the unhappiness and loneliness of his loveless childhood. However, as he reached middle age, he changed subtly and it was hard to actually put a finger on the reason. He continued to be unfaithful but the pattern of the relationships transformed somehow. His later love affairs actually mattered to him.

In Bertie's youth, at the centre of his life or close to it, were his parents, their relationship so passionate that it blinded them of the needs of their children. His mother seems to have deeply resented her children both as rivals for her beloved Albert's attention and as unwelcome interruptions in her relationship with him. Her letters and diaries portray a lushly romantic woman with intense physical needs who was swept off her feet the moment she met her husband. But not so much as to forget that *she* was the queen. This side of her differs sharply from the plump, severe, almost forbidding queen with a frown on her face and a crown on her head.

Her opinion of her son was well known. *'The poor country,"* she once wrote, *"with such a terribly unfit, totally unreflecting successor!...He does nothing!...Bertie (I grieve to say) shows more and more how totally unfit he is for ever becoming King."*

It seems his greatest sin was that he was nothing like his father and he learned early on in life that nothing he did would ever earn her approval. And let's not forget he was blamed for his father's untimely and early death due to his scandalous behaviour.

Bertie's father had not been much better than his mother. He was stiff and demanding, delegating Bertie's education to unsuitable tutors with the result that the prince excelled at nothing except French and German. It was fortunate that he did have a fluency in these languages because they would play a huge part in his success as a diplomat in the future.

If Bertie felt ignored by his father, the same could not be said for his elder sister Vicky. His father doted on the 3-year-old who could already speak and read French and the arrival of Bertie did not change his devotion as it often does, especially since the new child was a male and the heir to the throne. On the contrary, his father made no attempt to conceal his preference for Vicky. By comparison, Bertie seemed backward.

It was at the age of 3 that furious stamping and throwing tantrums began and as he grew older, so did the intensity of the tantrums. By 3½, he was refusing to do his lessons, throwing his books across the room and he had developed a stammer. What they could not see, or would not see, was that his naughtiness was just a cry for attention, typical of a less loved second child because Bertie knew he could not possibly do better than his elder sister. His reaction was to rebel and refuse to do anything at all.

The dynamics of the nursery changed with the arrival of the third child Alice, a quiet, pretty addition to the family. Eighteen months younger than Bertie, the two became the greatest of friends, always playing together.

Despite Vicky's popularity with her father, Albert knew that Bertie's education was vitally important. He was after all the heir to the throne and no matter how unbecoming his behaviour was, he still needed a rounded off education if he was expected to take over one day. Keeping that in mind, Albert decided his son would have the same counsellor he'd had as a child because he followed the typical German model of princely education that had succeeded so well with Albert. When the tutor arrived and heard of Bertie's behaviour, it was decided that Bertie would be educated in seclusion and by a strict time-table of lessons between the hours of 8am and 6pm consisting of French, German, geography, reading, writing and also dancing, history and poetry.

I'm sure this latest regime of education was meant to be a form of treatment for the special needs of an essentially nervous and excitable child but it soon became apparent that the system was a complete failure. At 6 years old, he was only reading the same book as his younger sister Alice who was neither studious nor clever and by seven he was totally uncontrollable. A firmer tutor was seen as the only remedy.

Next on the scene was a good looking 30-year-old Eton master by the name of Birch with a string of Cambridge prizes to flaunt. Birch was soon hired and installed next door to Bertie's room but instead of an improvement in Bertie's behaviour, the first few weeks were disastrous.

Bertie had always been rude, disobedient and rebellious but he reached a new high with Birch. He refused to get out of bed until late in the morning, he lost his temper whenever he attempted anything difficult and he was cruel and offensive to his brothers and sisters. By then, other siblings had appeared on the scene.

So Bertie took his lessons alone. He saw no one except Birch apart from 15 mins a day at 9 am, which he spent with his parents, and once again before he went to bed. And his mother made sure to keep a disgusted distance from him except for those few paltry minutes a day. Surprisingly, after a year, Bertie began to improve slightly although by this time his father was beginning to have less faith in Birch and was still looking for other reasons behind his son's dreadful behaviour.

A phrenologist, specialising in the mind and the brain, was called in and after studying Bertie closely, it was pronounced that Bertie's brain was feeble and abnormal. The anterior lobe devoted to intellect was deficient in size while the organs of combativeness, destructiveness and self-esteem were overdeveloped. This irregularity, he declared, was what made him highly excitable and prone to vehement fits of opposition, self-will and obstinacy and instead of punishing Bertie, the treatment should be a 'soothing system' of kindness since any unnecessary irritation would only make the brain feebler. By punishing him and speaking harshly to him Albert was only aggravating his condition.

Albert was not convinced by the specialist's opinion that kindness was needed. Not when he saw Bertie throwing books across the room and screeching at his siblings on a daily basis. He was sure his son's Anglo-Saxon, obnoxious brain could only have descended from the odious Stuarts since both he and Victoria had strong German blood coursing through their veins. A second look at Victoria's incredible tantrums would perhaps have made him think again. As for the specialist, he was certainly not convinced by Albert's conclusions concerning Bertie's Stuart heritage. He firmly believed Bertie had actually inherited his tendencies from the Hanover gene pool, more particularly, George III. And everyone knew about George's issues with insanity.

Unfortunately, while Albert was searching for excuses for Bertie's obnoxious behaviour and dishing out blame, he had failed to recognise that there had in fact been a slight improvement in Bertie's conduct and no matter how small the improvement was, it was possibly due to the fact that Birch was giving his son precisely what he craved. Attention. And Bertie was thriving on it.

But because the improvement had been so slight, Albert was oblivious to the change. This time it was Birch who was to blame and he had to go.

Bertie was 9½ when Birch was sent away. But before he left, Birch made one final entry in Bertie's book. *"He has a keen perception of right and wrong and a good memory...and for a year and a half I saw numerous traits of a very amiable and affectionate disposition."* Birch firmly believed Bertie's father had exacerbated his problems by restricting his contact with boys his own age and he wrote, *"There is every reason to hope that the Prince of Wales will eventually turn out a good and, in my humble opinion, a great man."*

But there was no telling Albert. Birch was out and the search for another replacement began.

The arrival of the next tutor meant Bertie's school agenda escalated to six hourly lesson periods a day between 8am and 7 pm, six days a week. Not surprisingly, Bertie rebelled with uncontrollable fits of temper. The more the tutor tightened the screw, the worse Bertie became, yelling, *"other children are not always good. Why should I always be good? Nobody is always good."* Photographs from this time show a small boy hanging his head, looking sulkily down at his feet. In my humble opinion, Bertie's solitary lessons were abject cruelty and it's not difficult for anyone to feel just a little bit sorry for the lonely little boy.

While the schoolroom for his siblings moved with the royal family to Buckingham Palace, Balmoral and Osborne on the Isle of Wight against a background of luxury and opulence, home for Bertie was an enclosed world at Windsor, consisting of towers and battlements above the River Thames, less a castle than a prison. Bertie was however allowed to join the family most summers in Osborne where Victoria and Albert could play at domesticity and from Osborne in the summer, the family moved to Balmoral in the autumn to the mountain solitude of the Scottish Highlands. But while everyone else took a holiday, Albert forbade Bertie to join in. Bertie's routine was to stay the same and his lessons would continue as normal. And while Bertie suffered and ached, Albert busied himself designing a Balmoral tartan in grey and purple and ordered chairs to be covered in the tartan, curtains to be made of the same tartan material and even the linoleum was to be tartan. As for Victoria, she was so emotionally dependent on Albert that she only wanted him and him alone. Children, especially disobedient, rebellious ones, were a necessary evil she was happy for Albert to handle.

As we know, during her life, Victoria restricted Bertie's access to government, referring to him as *"the boy"*. But behind the scenes, while Victoria ruled autocratically, 12-year-old Bertie became fascinated by international politics, like a child staring longingly out of the window. Bertie watched his mother pin medals on to the soldiers of returning soldiers from the Crimean War and he watched as she allowed wounded men into the garden at Buckingham Palace where they walked about or sat on benches. While his mother seemed relaxed and at ease, his father, however, was wearing himself out.

The first visit to Paris by a British monarchy since Henry VI was a ten-day revelation for Bertie. His mother was in a state of euphoria, welcomed by rapturous French crowds, while his father's ego was soothed with equal applause. Released from his schoolroom temporarily, Bertie was in heaven, winning the heart of the French crowds by his proficiency with the language when he was allowed to speak. In fact, Bertie was every bit as smart as Birch had written. From the shadows, Bertie had watched the proceedings and he had taken notes. He had seen the transformation in his mother and the contentment of his father and he knew they were somewhat mollified by his surprisingly good behaviour. It was about this time that things began to change again.

Almost overnight, Bertie was no longer rebellious but had turned miraculously into a disciplined, almost tame child. But that was in front of his parents. Behind the scenes, it was something else. He and Alice (who he adored) played dreadful private pranks on their tutor while the younger Affie eventually joined in. At 14 years old, Bertie was becoming a chameleon.

His mother was quietly thrilled to hear of his about-face, but a few months later, when Bertie and Affie were caught smoking, all hell broke loose.

There could have been much worse things to get caught doing but by now Albert had had enough. Both boys were given three days solitary confinement and after that, they were to be separated. Affie would be sent to separate housing at Royal Lodge in Windsor Park with an officer of the royal Engineers as his sole companion. Bertie was to be kept at home under his father's watchful eye. And Bertie sobbed bitterly.

In his isolation, Bertie reverted yet again to being the rebellious child of old and something in his pain and anger must have communicated itself to his parents because a note of panic began to creep into their dealings with him. Bertie's erratic behaviour was having a profound effect on them, especially his mother, who was well aware that as the eldest child Bertie was the obvious successor to the throne when she died.

To say that his behaviour was alarming is perhaps an understatement and Victoria's decision to give Albert the title of Prince Consort was a direct result of that concern. By doing this, Victoria was giving Albert precedence over their son, Prince of Wales, in the event that anything happened to her. This meant that Albert himself, and not their son, would become second to the Queen in the event of her death. In Albert's mind, this issue had become urgent because of the fear that *"wicked people might succeed in bringing up the Prince of Wales against his father."*

Did he have an inkling that he may have been a tad too harsh with regards to his chastisement of Bertie? Was he was seeing his eldest son, still in his teens, as a potential adversary in the future?

At 16 years old, Bertie was alone in a world of excruciating pain. It was the year when his elder sister Vicky would marry Prince Frederick William of Prussia, (nicknamed Fritz), 11 years her senior, and she would leave to start a life of her own in Germany. It was the year that his parent's attention was transferred from Bertie to the fate of their eldest child, thankfully taking the pressure off him.

Despite the age difference, Fritz was a typical prince from a Walt Disney movie with his glittering blue eyes and mane of blond hair. But it wasn't Fritz's good looks that had interested Albert for his daughter. It was the possibility of an incredible dynastic match and the cornerstone to his project for creating a liberal Germany under Prussia. The down side to achieve that goal meant Vicky had to leave England for good. On the day Vicky left for Germany, she buried her head in her father's breast and sobbed while Victoria, annoyed at her daughter's weakness, told her she should be grateful.

As Vicky sailed away to start her new life in Prussia, the family dynamics changed yet again and Victoria turned her attention back to Bertie. From the shadows Bertie had enjoyed a certain degree of anonymity while his parent's concentrated on Vicky's future but with her departure, Victoria was dedicated to raining all her annoyance once again on him.

As Vicky tried desperately to settle in to her new home, Victoria bemoaned Bertie's shortcomings in letters to her. Bertie was lazy. Bertie was weak. Bertie was dull. *"Handsome I cannot think him, with that painfully small and narrow head, those immense features and total want of chin".*

Bertie was maturing fast but at 17, he was still producing dismal reports on his progress. Becoming a good man and a thorough gentleman became the top of the list of priorities and the only way they saw those ideals becoming anywhere near possible was to have him receive the Order of the

Garter, enlist him at the rank of Colonel and assign him a governor. The governor chosen was Colonel (later General) Robert Bruce, a strict disciplinarian who could be trusted to rule the prince as if he were an unruly colony.

Bertie was thrilled with the new uniform although not so thrilled that he was made a Colonel straight away. He felt that he was merely playing soldier; a tailor's dummy in a sparkling new uniform, preferring to work his way up the ranks instead. It was the stirring of maturity in Bertie that was typically overlooked because regardless of what he thought, he was suited up and packed off to Oxford.

Instead of the distance between them (giving Bertie a bit of leeway) his mother could have been feet away, not hundreds of miles. She still sent stinging letters to him, regarding his clothes, his weight, the way he combed his hair and his physical appearance. *"The nose"* wrote the doting mother to Bertie, *"is becoming the true Coburg nose and begins to hang a little, but there remains unfortunately the want of chin which with that very large nose and very large lips is not so well in profile."* A letter in return from Bertie simply said, *"I hope that you will excuse that I have not written before, but as I had no news of any sort to give you, my letter would have been very dull. I have nothing of any interest to communicate to you."*

Although Bertie hated the constant monitoring of his movements, he was able to make one good friend, although an extremely unsuitable one. Sir Frederick Johnstone was exactly the type of man that Albert was anxious for Bertie to avoid. He was a heavy drinker, a member of Bullingdon Club devoted to gambling, horse racing and womanising and in the end, he was the one who led Bertie astray. Under his direction, Bertie hired a first-rate chef, took up fox hunting (much to his mother's horror) and Bertie's name was soon found in the ledgers of a Savile Road tailor along with his measurements of 33¾ inch chest and 29¼ inch waist.

There's no doubt Bertie was stung by his mother's continuous scathing criticisms but long (and sometimes inappropriate) letters from his favourite sister Alice helped to soothe him. *"I think it would be better dear Bertie,"* she wrote, *"if when she makes such remarks, and gives you such advice, that you should not only thank her for it, but tell her you will follow it."*

Victoria and Albert had firmly believed that by sending Bertie away to Oxford, the strong discipline would make Bertie knuckle down and start toeing the line. What actually happened was Bertie began to find himself. When Bertie headed the procession of dons at the Christ Church ball at the end of the first term, an audience of rowdy undergraduates gave three hearty cheers for him and the attention was intoxicating. Fame, it seemed, was stimulating and being famous, just because of who he was, was terribly invigorating. It gave Bertie a newfound confidence and self-esteem and he never once looked back.

Next on his father's program for his son was a year at Cambridge. In hindsight, I'm sure they regretted that decision more than any other decision they'd made for him in his life.

For the first time in his life Bertie was in his element. He sucked on strong cigars and took up drag hunting, a form of equestrian sport where mounted riders hunt the trail of an artificially laid scent with hounds. But while Bertie was relishing the beginnings of his new freedom away from home, his father was beginning a new file of marriage prospects for his son, sure in the fact that Bertie must marry soon, despite being only 18 years old.

The name of a beautiful, slender, blue-eyed 16-year-old from Denmark appeared on the list. Alexandra Caroline Marie Charlotte Louise Julia was the daughter of Prince Christian of Schleswig-Holstein-Sonderburg-Glucksburg, who had been proclaimed the heir to the Danish throne after the current childless king, Frederick VII, died.

Alexandra's father had grown up as an obscure and impoverished princeling with nothing remarkable about him except his name. But the juicy part of the story isn't about the lucky dip Christian and his family received. The interesting bit is Alexandra's heritage.

Through both her parents, Alexandra could trace her family's lineage back to 1013 AD. Alexandra's ancestor was King Sweyn II of Denmark, grandson of Sweyn Forkbeard and the nephew of Canute the Great, the first Viking King of England. Bertie and Alexandra's children would share her bloodline, passed down through the generations, linking each of them to the first Vikings who plundered and ransacked Britain in the mid 980s. It was a complete circle of blood.

As we all know, none of Alexandra's early relatives were saints. By 1013, they'd raped and pillaged their way through the north of England while King Ethelred struggled to keep them out. Sweyn was not one for mercy and he burned women alive, impaled children on lances and even murdered men by suspending them by their private parts. And Canute's children were no better. They were crude, brutal Vikings who were hell-bent on retaining the thrones in both England and Denmark, despite whatever Magnus I, the King of Norway, had to say about it. And they had managed to hold on to the throne of England for a short while, until William the Conqueror threw his hat into the ring. Amazingly, William was a descendant of another Viking, Rollo the Walker, who was given a plot of land for his support and allegiance to the French. With that plot of dirt, he became the first Duke of Normandy and an ancestor of William the Conqueror.

It was an amazing inheritance to have. No one in their wildest dreams would have believed that Sweyn, the tall, powerful, ruthless warrior who walked with a limp nineteen centuries ago, would produce children who would carry his legacy through to the present day. Once again, the Vikings would return to rule England through Alexandra and her marriage to Bertie, the future King of England, as Edward VII.

Prince Christian's elevation to heir made very little impact on his family's of life. The family barely existed in a rent-free house on an army wage of about £800 per year since neither he nor Princess Louise had any personal fortune. Their home, pompously named the Yellow Palace, had been no more than a large town house while Bernsdorff, their country palace, had been merely lent to them by King Frederick while their income remained maddeningly the same.

The more Victoria and Albert delved, the better Alexandra looked. She had bearing, she was relaxed and graceful and her manner was both charming and gentle. Sure, her family had very little money but she dressed with a quiet elegance that belied that minor detail. She spoke English and German and whether she was clever or not was of no consequence since Bertie was certainly no intellectual himself.

But that was where her suitability ended. Both Victoria and Albert had serious reservations where Prince Christian's daughter was concerned because what they were basically looking for was a German princess. Backing this up was the fact that Denmark had been on unfriendly terms with Prussia, locked in a quarrel over the disputed territories of Schleswig and Holstein and relations were severely strained. If she was to sanction a marriage between her heir and a Danish princess, she would appear to be siding with Denmark against Prussia which was the very last impression she wanted to create. Apart from that, the very thought of Alexandra's frivolous, gossipy, mischief making, anti-Prussian Hesse-Cassel relatives was enough to send shivers down her spine.

But if she ruled out the Danish princess, who else was there? No one it seemed. For what her idle, feckless, incompetent son needed more than anything was a princess with *"good looks, health, education and a good disposition"*. She also knew that *"good looks"* was high on her list of necessary qualities because Bertie would happily dispense with education, character and intellect in his bride, but he would never settle for plainness. Where else was such a paragon to be found?

It wasn't just Victoria and Albert who were searching. Victoria had entrusted Vicky as well to find her brother a suitable bride and try as she might, Vicky wrote to her mother that she was continually drawn back to the beautiful Alexandra. On seeing a photograph of Alexandra for the first time, Victoria sighed *"what a pity she is who she is!"*

Victoria was bombarded with letters from her enraptured daughter in Germany, imploring her to reconsider. Alexandra was lovely, bewitching, ladylike, natural, unaffected and aristocratic in every way and this jewel must be secured for her brother at all cost. Already suitors were lining up. Succumbing to her daughter's pleading letters, 19-year-old Bertie was packed off to the Rhineland for a 'chance' meeting with Alexandra while visiting his sister.

From all accounts, Alexandra knew nothing of the negotiations. Her parents, more particularly her quick-thinking mother, were agog at the prospect and had kept Alexandra in complete ignorance. It was while on a holiday in the Rhineland that Alexandra accompanied her parents on a visit to Speyer Cathedral in Strelitz and as if by chance, they came face to face with Fritz and Vicky who just so happened to have Bertie Prince of Wales with them.

If Alexandra's looks were impressive in a photograph, in the flesh they were overwhelming. In the cool half-light of the Cathedral, as the small group of royals chatted in hushed voices, Vicky was being impressed by Prince Christian's gentlemanly bearing while Bertie was warming to Alexandra's good looks and charming manners.

There was nothing it seemed to stand in the way of taking the next step. In Albert's precise and meticulous plans, Bertie had one simple role to play:

he must fall in love with the *"Danish pearl"*. And by the looks of it, there could not possibly be an obstacle.

But to Albert and Victoria's utter shock, Bertie refused, saying he was in no hurry to wed.

The statement fell like a lead balloon at the feet of his astonished parents. What they were unaware of was with his newfound freedom, this new Bertie had emerged with an appetite for clothes, smoking, gambling, food and women. And Bertie especially loved the food and women part.

It was during that fateful summer of 1861 when Victoria and Albert decided that Bertie should spend time at an army base in Curragh in Ireland where he might learn a few lessons in discipline with the Grenadier Guards and it was a decision that Victoria would regret for the rest of her life. It was that summer in Curragh that Bertie met the 'wren' Nellie Clifden and it was the catalyst that produced a meltdown on the Vesuvius scale for Albert because it allowed a string of raw memories to surface from his humiliating childhood. He was emotionally scarred by his father's sleazy exploits and his mother's resulting adultery, that despite the 1860s being a decade of sexual liberation, Albert could not imagine his son sinking any lower.

It was on a wet and stormy day on 25th November when Albert insisted on going for a walk with Bertie around the grounds of Cambridge away from prying eyes and eavesdroppers, squelching in the mud and getting thoroughly wet. It was the day his father caught a cold and in his weakened state, he deteriorated quickly until eventually he was confined to his bed, seriously ill.

It was his sister Alice who had the foresight to send Bertie a telegram asking him to return to Windsor as soon as possible. The wording had been casual so Bertie had no idea how sick his father really was. Rather unconcernedly, he left the next day at 11 am, arriving at Windsor at 3 pm, talking cheerfully. It was only when he arrived that he discovered how ill his father actually was.

His father briefly recognised Bertie the next morning but his breathing was rapid, his tongue was swollen and blackened and he could barely speak. He rambled incoherently and by late afternoon, it was plain to everyone that Albert was sinking fast. As evening wore on, his breathing became more painful and he became bathed in sweat. Sitting beside him, his mother held his hand and watched on in mild panic. By quarter to eleven the next night, the man who had actually been the one running the country and making the political decisions for his mother, took a few gentle breaths, and died.

In the first few days, Bertie stayed close to his mother who was heavily sedated. But it wasn't just Victoria who was in a state of shock. Bertie was as well. The queasy fact was, if Alice hadn't telegrammed him, he wouldn't have been present at his father's death at all and it came as a huge blow to him. A further blow would soon come with his mother blaming him for his father's death and as his mother retreated more and more into mourning, she refused to have anything to do with him. At the time, the diagnosis was pneumonia weakened by his stomach illness but it's widely believed that he was actually suffering from a progressive inflammation of the gut causing abdominal pain, vomiting and diarrhoea. There had been anguish and depression as well as exposure to intense cold on two occasions and his fatigue hadn't helped things for him either. And it was all Bertie's fault.

His mother's grief was all consuming. She had depended on Albert for everything and as she wailed and cried, Bertie could only watch in horror as his hysterical mother was crippled with grief. Still she refused to let Bertie handle any state affairs. She woke weeping and crying every morning at 4 am insisting on performing the business of monarchy herself.

Bertie had not only lost a father, he was made to feel that he was responsible for his death and the deep compassion he had originally felt for his mother soon turned to resentful anger as he grieved in private. Yet again, his mother had pushed him aside.

While Victoria mourned demonstratively, Bertie went from bad to worse. He'd always been difficult but after the death of his father, he seemed to throw all care into the wind. He continued visiting gentlemen's clubs and always on his arm was a different woman smiling seductively up into his eyes. He increased his gambling and drinking habits, his grades at Cambridge began to suffer and he was getting a disastrous reputation.

As the stories flooded in to Victoria, she sent letters of sin and redemption to Bertie but by then, his replies had become devoid of feeling and emotion. He was doing what his sister Alice had suggested and had become somewhat like an actor in a play. All he did was learn the lines his mother wanted to hear and then perform them on cue. For Bertie, communicating with his mother was like negotiating with a hostile power.

Victoria was more than happy to have Bertie away from her and out of her sight. After all, she had no doubt who was to blame the loss of her dead husband. If Bertie had behaved himself, Albert would never have decided to leave Windsor and go to Cambridge to talk to him. Albert's illness would not have worsened and he would still be with her to that day. But through her anguish, Victoria forged on with plans for Bertie's marriage. Albert's last wishes had been that Bertie should marry Alexandra of Denmark, and marry her he would. But to be fair, she wondered if she should warn Alexandra's parents about Bertie's true character.

Alexandra's mother had already heard the rumours and unlike Victoria, was totally unaffected by them. The idea of a prince losing his virginity before marriage, to a prostitute or otherwise, was neither shocking nor novel. In fact, it would have been more disturbing if he *hadn't* lost it. That would have led to worse insinuations than simply being a philanderer. Her own father and mother may have led virtuous lives but the same couldn't be said for her various relatives. The twice-divorced Danish king Frederick VII had lived openly with his mistress for years and *her* relatives were reputed to be highly immoral.

Like most women of the day, Alexandra probably accepted this code of behaviour before marriage and I don't believe she was exactly ignorant of the plot and the ramifications. That she would marry Bertie was never in doubt. Alexandra's mother, Princess Louise was an ambitious matchmaker, anxious that her two daughters should marry into the best European royalty despite being almost impoverished. She and Prince Christian owned no estates, and their income had only just increased from a mere £800 to £2000. It was still far from being enough for them. Their daughters' beauty were the only real assets they had and they guarded them jealously.

All that was left was for Victoria to meet Alexandra. Tactfully wearing a simple black dress and no jewellery, Alexandra embraced Victoria shyly, and Victoria was enchanted although she noticed Alexandra's 22 inch waist and 32 inch chest. Compared to Victoria's full-bodied figure, Alexandra hardly seemed built for child-bearing and that was the bottom line for the monarchy.

Satisfied that Alexandra was the right choice, Victoria journeyed to Coburg to visit the scenes of Albert's youth, leaving Bertie to propose. This he did on 9th September and of course, Alexandra accepted immediately. Victoria then stepped in to make all the arrangements.

The wedding was set for Lent, more precisely 10th March the next year, and would take place at St George's Chapel in Windsor, as was Albert's wish. The court were to remain in mourning for her dear departed husband Albert, the dress code was half-mourning colours of grey, silver and lilac. She herself would wear black and watch the ceremony from a gallery overlooking the altar instead of taking part in the ceremony. Only Alexandra's immediate family circle would be invited to the wedding because not for the world would she invite the disreputable Danish king, Frederick VII, and his detestable mistress. And she hadn't forgotten that relations between Denmark and the German Confederation was deteriorating at an alarming rate.

The chapel was packed to the rafters on the morning of the wedding. Victoria, dressed in new widow's weeds, had invited her entire household and few seats were left for Bertie's friends. Of the four friends he *was* allowed to invite, one was his friend Carrington from Oxford and another was an adventurer by the name of Disraeli. Bertie entered pale and nervous flanked by his brother-in-law Fritz and his uncle Ernest of Saxe-Coburg. He bowed stiffly to his mother in the gallery then waited fifteen minutes for Alexandra to arrive trembling and red-eyed, having cried all morning at leaving her mother. Standing tall and straight in his uniform, Prince Christian of Denmark watched his daughter walk towards the heir to the British throne.

Beautiful and glamorous, Alexandra was the Princess Diana of her day, already wildly popular with the British public. But the wedding would also be remembered for another reason. It was the first public appearance of the Victoria's 4-year-old grandson, Wilhelm, by her daughter Vicky and her husband Fritz, the future German Kaiser. Dressed in a kilt and a sporran, Wilhelm wriggled restlessly between his British uncles, scratching and pinching them on the legs and throwing his sporran into the choir for attention. After being scolded by Leopold and told to sit still, Wilhelm bit him.

Neither Bertie or Alexandra wrote accounts of the wedding but one photograph in particular says it all. Bertie and Alexandra's wedding seemed almost immaterial to the drama of his mother's grief. In prominent position, photographed sitting in front of the tight-faced couple in her mourning dress, Victoria's sharply focused face was in profile as she gazed theatrically up at a bust of Albert, his chiselled features dissolving into a blur. Bertie stood behind his mother, clean-shaven for once, puffy-eyed, plump and looking a little seedy and bulging out of his too-tight black coat. Alexandra looked neither at her husband nor her mother-in-law but skittishly over her shoulder as the photographers had told her to do.

After the ceremony, and after the wedding guests had partied then departed in an undignified rush from Windsor station, the happy couple then left for their honeymoon in Osborne, before moving into their new house in Sandringham. Rather like an omen, the countryside was bleak with a chilly wind blowing wildly.

Sandringham was undoubtedly impressive and so very different from the Yellow Palace where Alexandra's family lived. Her Danish home had been a modest townhouse with a front door that opened directly into the street where she shared a bedroom with Dagma to whom she wrote long homesick letters too. But if she thought Sandringham was impressive, she was about to be astounded.

In London, they were installed at Marlborough House, modernised and renovated at a cost of £60,000, originally given to Sarah Duchess of Marlborough by Queen Anne as a token of her gratitude before Sarah's spectacular falling out and eviction from the inner circle. Already an impressive building, Bertie had it enlarged to accommodate the whole of London society at one single ball. The house was lavish with state drawing rooms, dining rooms and he was allowed to decide on such details as lighting. No sooner had they unpacked than the London season began. Night after night the couple hosted dinner parties, attended banquets and attended the opera. Through it all, Alexandra curtseyed continuously and looked exhausted while Bertie beamed happily, obviously in his element.

The year 1866 was a big year for Alexandra. Within a year of the marriage, her handsome unpretentious 17-year-old brother, still a naval cadet and regarded as an amiable buffoon, had astonishingly become King of Greece, her 45-year-old father had finally ascended the throne of Denmark as King Christian IX and her sister Dagma was betrothed to the heir of the Russian throne, the future Alexander III. For both the Danish princesses, it was like something out of a fairy tale, brought up very simply but each one managing to snare two of the most eligible princes in Europe.

But trouble was not too far away for the Danish royal family. As soon as Alexandra's father has assumed the throne, a crisis concerning the duchies of

Schleswig and Holstein, one Dutch and one German, raised its ugly head and the long-smouldering feud flared up once more. The Danish parliament insisted that Christian sign a new constitution incorporating both duchies into the Danish territories despite Holstein being German, and even though Christian knew it would anger Germany, he had little choice but to do as his parliament insisted. And he had been right to be concerned. As he'd expected, Germany were outraged and Victoria, feeling more German than British, totally agreed with the Germans.

While everyone was intent on picking sides, in Prussia Otto von Bismarck was silently doing something far worse. He was preparing for war against Denmark.

Christmas 1863 was a dismal time for the royal family. Bertie and Alexandra were staying at Osborne with Victoria when news came through that German troops were occupying Holstein. Alexandra was at this stage heavily pregnant and broke down into tears insisting that the duchies belonged to her papa. Victoria stared stonily at her daughter-in-law and told her that if war ensued, she would be under no obligation at all to rush to the assistance of Denmark.

The couple left immediately and returned to Windsor where on the morning of 8th January, Alexandra complained of pains while she watched Bertie playing ice hockey. By the afternoon, the pains had increased and the physician was called. At 8.50 Alexandra gave birth to a tiny boy weighing only 3¾ pounds.

The couple had always openly affectionate and tender towards each other but with the attack on Denmark and with the birth of his son, named Albert after his father, Bertie seemed to change. He would find Alexandra crying nightly over the tremendous humiliation her parents were suffering at the hands of his family in Germany and in a show of support for her and her family, Bertie stood stoically by her, although it meant cutting himself off from his mother and sister Vicky in Germany.

Considering the aggressiveness of the attack, it was disappointing that Victoria took Prussia's side. But then again, from her own personal point of view, she considered herself pretty much completely German, although she had been born in England. Her mother was German, her maternal grandmother was German as were their parents. Even her father's family were German. So when she ordered Bertie to remember that his connection to

Denmark was purely through marriage and that he was from a family of Germans, half German himself, not too many people were surprised. Disappointed, yes. Surprised, no.

Being the daughter-in-law of someone as strong-willed as Victoria meant Alexandra had to mind what she said, especially when it came to voicing her opinion about the marauding Germans, knowing where Victoria's sympathy lay. But in her heart, she was determined to support her Danish homeland, despite what her domineering mother-in-law said. She may have been the wife of the future British king and the mother of yet another one, but be damned if she was going to forget, or forgive, the Prussians for what they had done to her homeland.

As Alexandra bit her tongue, her sister Dagma was preparing for her marriage in St Petersburg to the heir to the Russian throne. Now this is a rather interesting story.

Dagma was exceptional with her velvety eyes, her wide flashing smile and her slender figure and her fiancé Nicholas was worth a second look as well. At 21 years old, the eldest son of Tsar Alexander II was quite different from his five hulking brothers. He was slim, handsome and graceful and to a young and unsophisticated Danish princess like Dagma, he was the most romantic of all figures. The marriage was arranged for the spring of the following year and the future looked promising.

Then it all started to unravel. Nicholas had always been delicate, prone to colds and flus, so the attack of bronchitis he suffered the winter before the wedding did not take anyone by surprise. He was young and no one was too concerned, not at this stage anyway. His doctors said all he needed was a healthy dose of warm sunshine away from the bite of a chilly Russian winter so he was packed off to Nice in the South of France to recuperate. Weeks turned into months with no change in his condition and benevolent smiles slowly turned into concerned looks. By March 1865, it was clear he was dangerously ill. Dagmar was summoned and accompanied by her mother Queen Louise and her eldest brother Prince Frederick she hurried down to the South of France to be with her fiancé and the entire Russian imperial family.

The story goes that Nicholas knew he was dying and had already sent for his brother Alexander. He assured the weeping Dagma that his brother would make a better husband than he would have done and he put

Dagmar's tiny hands into Alexander's enormous ones, linking the couple's future. With that final gesture, Nicholas died.

It's a touching story but one suspects that it was invented to mask the indecent haste with which Dagmar was handed over to the younger brother. The man she found herself bequeathed to was very different from his dead brother. This brother was huge, broad-shouldered, slow moving, heavily jowled and he had none of his brother's refinement and elegance. And since Alexander had been second in line of succession, not much attention had been paid to his education. But he was essentially a man of duty and he agreed to marry his dead brother's fiancé.

Two months after the death of Dagma's fiancé, and eighteen months after Albert's birth, Alexandra gave birth to another son they named George. Being the second in line after his brother (nicknamed Eddy) George was never intended for the throne. It meant George could live happily in the shadow of his elder brother and be spared the hothouse education inflicted on his German cousin Wilhelm, who was assertive and determined to be first in everything. George was more than happy to remain unremarkable and live in mediocrity in his brother's shadow.

Having children inevitably slowed Alexandra down. Bertie however, was spending more and more time away from Alexandra. Although fond of his wife, slowing down was not for Bertie. His appetite for women was as undiminished as ever and rumours put Bertie in the bed of an actress called Hortense Schneider although he was still spending time at home with Alexandra. By June 1866, within a year of George's birth, Alexandra found she was pregnant with her third child, almost at the same time that Dagma announced her wedding date.

Six months pregnant and not feeling well enough to travel to Russia for her sister's wedding, Alexandra was forced to stay behind while Bertie went on alone. As it turned out, Bertie was entertained splendidly. Not only did he attend a ball and dance in his kilt, Bertie noticed that Dagma's father-in-law, the Russian Tsar, lived openly with his mistress while his wife lay upstairs slowly dying of tuberculosis. Pretty soon, rumours reached the ears of everyone back home that Bertie was perhaps enjoying himself a little *too* much, flirting and entertaining the pretty women of St Petersburg.

For all Alexandra's seeming acceptance of Bertie's philandering, his unfaithfulness had come as a terrible shock to her. Whether she loved her husband or not is irrelevant. What she did feel was that she had been deprived of the life she had been promised when she married him. Not for a minute had she imagined that he would wander the bedrooms all over Britain and Europe, both squalid and imperial, while waited for him at home. And hand in hand with his philandering was the fact that Bertie liked the races a little too much and money seemed to slip through his fingers like water.

By the end of the 1880s, Bertie's finances had reached a crisis point. Moneylenders continually pestered him despite his annuity from Parliament set at £39,000 and his income from the Duchy of Cornwall at £64,500. But Bertie knew if he asked Parliament for an increase in his allowance, a scrutiny of his affairs was bound to happen and he had no intention of opening up that Pandora's box. He also knew that Parliament would ask, *"What exactly does the prince's work consist of?"* On a typical day, he unveiled a statue, dined at the Mansion House, witnessed part of Figaro at Covent Garden and held a reception at his home. It was hardly a full days work in need of a pay increase.

Just before the birth of their third child, Alexandra came down with a mystery illness and for several days, things looked pretty grim as she writhed in pain. Bertie, out at the races, had to be summoned three times before he finally assented to come to her sickbed. Her doctors had no idea what the problem was but of course, suspicious ladies-in-waiting spread quiet rumours and pointed their fingers at Bertie.

The word 'syphilis' was a word no one wanted to mention. It was an epidemic in the brothels of mid-nineteenth century Europe and Bertie had not bothered to hide the fact that he frequented them. His 'fall' led to the rumours that the prostitutes he saw had caused him to be infected with the syphilis organism and he could hardly fail to pass it on to Alexandra since sufferers were infectious for two years. The early stages were unpleasant enough with genital soreness, ulcers and rashes. 40% of sufferers showed signs of heart problems, loss of hearing and sometimes produced symptoms of madness. But no one was really sure if it was syphilis since Bertie was not suffering any symptoms at all.

Finally, Rheumatic fever was diagnosed, the frightening disease triggered by streptococcal infection in the throat which can also permanently damage the heart. Remember this was pre-penicillin days so treatment of the disease was restricted to reducing inflammation. Then, after months of recovery, Alexandra had the onset of deafness and tongues began to wag even more furiously about syphilis. But she was also complaining of severe pain and swelling in her knees and not sure of what the problem was, her doctors diagnosed septic arthritis caused by some bacterium. All she could do was weather it out.

Deafness was a crippling handicap for a woman in Alexandra's position, not to mention the beastly cage around her leg, so she withdrew into her family more and more while Bertie moved on to a string of public scandals since his wife was heavily pregnant again. Weeks later, she delivered a girl she named Louise after her own mother (much to Victoria's annoyance) while Bertie plunged himself headlong into a bachelor's life of drinking and 'amusements'. Interspersed with obligations such as cutting ribbons, opening bazaars and planting trees, he was spending more and more time with a string of different mistresses and more and more time away from home.

For three years Bertie and Alexandra spent little time at Sandringham while it was being refurbished. It was on their return that she found out she was pregnant for the sixth time. But this pregnancy was different from all the others. She suffered from irregular bleeding (for a while she was unsure if she was even pregnant at all) and at the six months mark, she was listless and depressed and barely showing at all. Then she fell heavily while out skating on ice and she crashed down on her bad knee. At seven months pregnant, she fell again tumbling out of her carriage while on the way to the wedding of Bertie's younger sister Louise.

The fall was just one more circumstance of Alexandra's fragility and after she arrived back at Sandringham, she woke soon after complaining of labour pains. Later that day, a tiny baby, even smaller than Eddy had been, arrived into the world six weeks too early with cold hands and a weak cry. By 8 pm he was sinking fast and a clergyman was summoned for baptism, christening him John. Twenty-four hours later, while Alexandra sobbed softly at his crib, John died.

Alexandra's lifestyle was already one of isolation due to her deafness but the death of her last child made her withdraw even more. She was only 26 years old but after six pregnancies in eight years, she was worn out, ill, spitting blood and in a deep depression. In her seclusion, as Bertie absented himself more and more from the family, Alexandra overcompensated and poured all of her time and affection into her children, creating a home in Sandringham full of endless romps and a child-centred environment. The children grew up simply and informally surrounded by nature, servants, a menagerie of dogs, monkeys, parrots, horses, cattle and sheep, totally unaware of their father's rakish lifestyle and the large debts he was accumulating.

But during the early part of 1888, other disturbing news had reached Victoria's attention. While Alexandra was being understanding, dignified and charming and Bertie continued philandering, in the impoverished district of Whitechapel a serial killer was on the loose, strangling his victims, cutting their throats, slashing their stomachs and finally eviscerating them.

Even from a distance of 130 years, the nightmarish facts of the Jack the Ripper killings make for unsettling reading. But for the residents of the Victorian capital, the case was far more visceral. Jack the Ripper was not the first serial killer in history but his notoriety is well remembered because he was never caught.

The name 'Jack the Ripper' had originated in a letter sent to a newspaper and was signed by someone claiming to be the murderer of female prostitutes working in the London slums. Although the threat affected only a very small section of the community, the murders had a huge impact on society as a whole.

There were eleven separate murders, starting from 25th February 1888, but only five murders, known as the 'canonical five' are widely believed to be the work of Jack the Ripper. Of the other six, Annie Millwood could have been the first but I'll let you make your own assumptions.

Annie was a 38-year-old widow who was admitted to the Whitechapel Workhouse Infirmary suffering from stab wounds to her legs and lower abdomen. She stated a man with a clasp knife had attacked her but other than that, nothing else was noted, despite the savagery of the attack. She was sent home but died the next day.

On 3rd April, Emma Smith was sexually assaulted with a blunt object brutally inserted into her vagina, rupturing her peritoneum. She developed peritonitis and also died the next day but before she did, she stated *two* men attacked her. At the time, it was attributed to gang violence and her file was placed alongside other unsolved murders. Martha Tabram was not so lucky.

She died on 7th August after suffering 39 stab wounds in Whitechapel and once again, her file was placed with other unsolved murders. If it was the same man (or men) committing the murders, he (they) had apparently grown more violent and confident after each attack.

Anyone who has ever watched reruns of CSI will know that it is rare for a serial killer to just emerge suddenly and embark upon a killing spree. There is often a pattern whereby the killer graduates from attacks and assaults to full-blown murder and this is when his distinctive 'modus operandi' is established as the work of a particular murderer. There is a high probability that he would have committed earlier crimes such as assaults on women or even murder. Ask Michael Connelly. But having said that, one of the first things to become apparent from trawling through the vast amount of information dedicated to crime in this era is that violent assaults on women were disturbingly commonplace. As such, it's difficult to point the finger of blame at Jack the Ripper for the handful of cases in those past few months, despite bearing similarities.

Then shortly before 4 am on 31st August, a cart driver found the body of a woman in Buck's Row close to Bethnal Green. She was on her back with her skirt pulled up around her waist and her throat had been slashed so deeply she had nearly been decapitated. Her name was Mary Ann Nichols and she was the first *official* victim of the Whitechapel murders attributed to Jack the Ripper.

Just over a week later on 8th September, the body of Annie Chapman was found with similar injuries to those of Mary Nichols. This time however the find was grizzly. Some of her internal organs had been removed and her small intestine lay by her right shoulder.

On 30th September a double event occurred. Elizabeth Stride was found with injuries not as severe as the previous two victims and the general consensus was that the Ripper had been disturbed but had quickly found another victim, Catherine Eddowes, killed not too far from Elizabeth Stride. Catherine was not as lucky as Elizabeth. Her intestines had been savagely ripped out and the killer had taken her left kidney and uterus.

Barely two weeks later, the body of Mary Kelly was found on a bed in a shabby lodging house and this time, the killer took his time. Mary's body was brutally mutilated. Her breasts were cut off, one left under her head and the other by her right foot, her face was hacked beyond recognition while the whole surface of the abdomen and thighs were removed and the abdominal cavity emptied of its viscera and left on a table beside the bed. Her liver rested between her feet and her heart had been removed and taken.

Although Whitechapel was an impoverished area and violence was common, these murders were linked together through a distinguishing modus operandi. All the murders took place within the distance of a few streets, late at night or in the early hours of the morning, and all the victims were women whose throats were cut and bodies mutilated. The removal of internal organs from three of the victims led to contemporary proposals that *'considerable anatomical knowledge was displayed by the murderer indicating his occupation was that of a butcher or a surgeon'.* Who could do such a thing?

Given the sheer brutality of the crimes, it was perhaps inevitable that many Britons concluded that they must be the work of an evil person that had entered Victorian society from the outside. From 1882, Britain had been experiencing an influx of Irish immigrants who swelled the population in the East End of London, as well as Jewish refugees from Russia who had survived horrific massacres. As a consequence, Whitechapel was severely overcrowded and submerged in poverty. Work and housing conditions worsened with the influx and a significant economic underclass had developed. Robbery, violence and alcohol dependency were common in the area and the widespread poverty eventually drove many women like a magnet to the only occupation they knew: prostitution. When Jack the Ripper started his short killing spree, it was estimated that there were 62 brothels and 1,200 women working as prostitutes in Whitechapel alone.

The East End was a vast, densely inhabited working-class district full of dark, narrow courts and alleyways with many lodging houses, small workshops and moist, foggy wharfs. It was packed with street urchin and prostitutes living in reeking, damp dwellings while men in top hats and cloaks meandered the gas-lit alleyways. Even before the brutal murders, a spotlight had been thrown on the abject poverty of east London. Employment in the nearby docks and markets were often casual and seasonal where thousands of men, women and children were ruthlessly exploited, toiling away for long hours for little pay.

The police and newspapers received anonymous letters, supposedly sent by the killer dubbed 'Jack the Ripper', but most were dismissed. However the letter signed 'From Hell' was treated more seriously because with it was a small box containing half of a preserved human kidney.

There is little doubt that his reign of terror struck fear into the hearts of all Londoners. There was someone out there wandering silently amongst them in search of prostitutes to butcher and the thought horrified them all. Despite having had only five certain victims, and a further six suspected victims over a period of time that lasted for a mere twelve or so weeks, it was undoubtedly a period of time when society was already fighting a daily battle against poverty and starvation. This added horror was something they could definitely live without.

In the labyrinth-like area of Whitechapel, the police used every method they could to try and track down the killer before he could kill again. Their main problem was that in the tiny passageways and alleyways, few of them were lit at night and of course, the detectives hunting down the killer were hampered by the fact that the art of forensics was very much in its infancy.

Extensive newspaper coverage only increased the notoriety of the Ripper but still no one was charged, and there was a cast of thousands including butchers, physicians and surgeons being investigated. And then, to Victoria's anxiety, the name of her 24-year-old grandson, Eddy, appeared on the list.

By most reports, Eddy was a 'slow' child who grew up to be a rather backward self-indulgent adult who had a reputation for being a 'ladies' man' (rumours had made their way around the Palace that he had been involved in many a scandal that had been immediately hushed up). Despite the secrecy, the newspapers had picked up on the gossip at the Palace.

SOURCE: Evening Post, Volume XXXII, Issue 136, 23 October 1886, Page 1

"The growing unpopularity of Prince Albert Victor is giving both the Queen and the Prince of Wales serious anxiety. The young man will take no pains to propitiate people. He is dense, apathetic, short-tempered, and sulky. The Marlborough House set made him their butt. His father alternately scolds or exhorts, whilst his mother pets and protects him. The young Princesses of Wales openly deride Victor's "stolidity," and even "Brother George" must feel a certain amount of contempt for his elder's lack of savoir faire. The Queen alone

treats the heir-presumptive with consideration. At Windsor or Balmoral the young Prince is always sure of a cordial welcome, though her Majesty makes no secret of her disappointment at his repeated failures in public. Considering how well most of the Royal Family deliver common-place speeches, Albert Victor's utter inability to string together half-a-dozen sentences coherently seems inexplicable. For years past the chief work of his life with Canon Dalton has been studying this very art, yet he has not even mastered the ABC of public speaking. Even if it is merely a case of returning thanks after dinner, the speech has to be written out for him. When he repeats it he does so like a parrot, without feeling or expression, and then, plumping down in his chair, takes no further interest in the proceedings, whatever they may be."

As with all unsolved horrific crimes, theories pop up, and the Ripper crimes had more melodrama to offer than most. This is where the theory commonly dubbed the 'Royal Conspiracy' came to light in 1962 and as far as theories go, it had, and still has, all the main ingredients to be totally believable and juicy. The Annie Crook theory is an incredible one (although to be truthful, it has little corroborative documentary evidence to support it, hence the word 'theory') but it has become accepted among certain historians as the explanation.

Annie Crook was a rather plain Catholic girl, working in a 'shop' on Cleveland Street notorious for its brothels. As a quick aside, Charles Dickens is known to have lived nearby as a child at what is now 22 Cleveland Street and then again as a teenager ten years later. His residence in the street has led to the suggestion that a nearby workhouse was probably the inspiration for *Oliver Twist*. Anyway, Annie stated that she had made a clandestine marriage to 23-year-old Eddy and together they produced a daughter. When Victoria heard the story she was horrified at the possibility of yet another scandal involving Eddy and blackmail was always uppermost in her mind. She appealed to her Prime Minister Lord Salisbury to put an end to the liaison and Salisbury ordered a raid on Cleveland Street to apprehend Annie and silence the whole affair.

However, they were just a tad too late. It seems embarrassing matters hadn't been hidden at all. Annie's friend, Mary Kelly, was spreading the story far and wide, telling the romantic tale of Annie and the Prince and how Annie had been dragged away to hush up the marriage and the birth of little Alice.

With the gossip spreading like wildfire, Salisbury had panicked and enlisted the help of the royal physician, Sir William Gull, to 'eliminate' all Mary Kelly's friends who may have listened to the story. Those friends were Mary Nichols, Annie Chapman, Elizabeth Stride: all Ripper victims. It's believed that Catherine Eddowes was just at the wrong place at the wrong time when the Ripper had been disturbed in the process of killing Elizabeth Stride. Finally, Mary Kelly herself had to be eliminated. And rather damningly, once Dr Gull had successfully completed his assignment, the killings miraculously ceased. It *does* explain one of the puzzles of why the Ripper stopped but where is the evidence to prove it?

Very little is known about Annie Crook. There *was* an Annie Crook who worked in Cleveland Street and she *did* give birth to a daughter Alice Margaret Crook. The child's father was not named at the time and whether that father was Eddy is not substantiated, despite the fact that he was known to frequent those very same brothels in that very same street and recognised by those very same Ripper victims. The theory falls apart, despite all the necessary ingredients of madness, sex and prostitutes, because rather fortuitously (perhaps *too* fortuitously) Eddy was reported to have been in Balmoral in Scotland on the day *after* the murders.

But while some are pointing their fingers at Victoria's physician, other Ripperologists have a different idea. Many believe that Jack the Ripper was not an impoverished Jew or an Irish immigrant. Nor was it Eddy. The name that keeps popping up is James K. Stephen; Eddy's tutor at Cambridge, a first cousin of Virginia Woolf and the son of a prominent lawyer, judge and writer, Sir James FitzJames Stephen, 1st Baronet. The two men remained in touch through correspondence and through their mutual acquaintances long after their ... um ... 'close' association at Cambridge when Stephen's mission was to try and bring Eddy's intelligence up to acceptable levels since according to one former tutor, Eddy's mind was *"abnormally dormant"*.

The relationship with Stephen supposedly ended in May 1885, although the pair stayed closely in touch, but two years later, Eddy was once again in the limelight over his preference for the *"gaieties of London society"* and an obsession with a young lady by the name of Lady Churchill. The girl was given an interview with Victoria and the next thing we hear is Eddy was awarded an honorary degree by the university and detached from the 'Prince of Wales' Own' (10th Hussars) and ordered to the 16th Rifles in Malta under the guardianship of Colonel Greville after being lectured severely by his grandmother, his father and his mother. This is probably the time to add that letters dated 1885 and 1886 had surfaced, written from Eddy to his doctor, with details of medicine he was taking for gonorrhoea.

It was the first time Eddy had been sent off on a foreign duty, evidently as a severe course of discipline, but strangely enough, at the exact same time that Eddy was cooling his heels in Malta after the Lady Churchill affair, Stephen reportedly had a rather bizarre accident where the horse he was riding shied and backed him into a moving vane of a windmill.

In a book written by Peter Harrison on the life of The Duke of Clarence, (Eddy) the suggestion is that Stephen and Eddy had indeed been lovers at Cambridge but when the affair ended, Stephen became morose and depressed. Then when Eddy appeared to have moved on with Lady Churchill, Stephen became unhinged and distraught.

Although he appeared to have made a complete recovery after his 'accident', it was later discovered that he became a patient of Victoria's physician, Sir William Gull, in 1888, who declared Stephen's brain had been permanently damaged in the accident and he was slowly going mad.

Now researching this story, and joining all the dots together, bells are clanging madly in my head along with loads of questions. Is there a veiled hint of a cover up here? Why would the royal physician, Sir William Gull, have anything to do with Stephen and this rather odd accident? Had there even been an accident with the windmill vane or had Stephen simply had a meltdown when he heard of his friend's association with Lady Churchill and begun...let's say...killing prostitutes? And knowing that both Stephen and Eddy were 'close' for years at Cambridge, is it possible that both men could have contracted gonorrhoea, perhaps even syphilis? Is it possible that Eddy was also slowly going mad? And if so, was he 'mad', perhaps 'deranged' enough, to commit the Ripper murders? Remember, one of the first victims, Emma Smith, stated that *two* men had attacked her. Is it too impossible to imagine a cover up and fabricated reports that Eddy was in Balmoral at the time of the murders? Or was it actually Stephen who had been the Ripper, killing women in areas he knew Eddy was known to frequent?

So was it Eddy, or Stephen or Sir William Gill acting on Victoria's behalf? Or was it someone entirely different?

Nothing will ever be proven and as we know, Jack the Ripper suddenly disappeared without a trace after Mary Kelly's murder and was never found or heard of again. But for many months afterwards, Eddy was secreted away from the public eye and somewhat miraculously - and suspiciously - the killings ceased.

One year later, things had just begun to settle down and the press had stopped rehashing the grisly details. Then like a bad penny, Eddy's name popped up again in July 1889 but this time during a raid on a male brothel at 19 Cleveland Street, coincidentally the same street that Annie had once lived. At the time, all homosexual acts between men were illegal, and clients were facing social ostracism, prosecution, and at the worst, two years' imprisonment with hard labour. The scandal implicated high-ranking figures in British Society and top of the list was Eddy's name once again.

Whether Eddy had actually visited the brothel with his friends or whether he was homosexual or more than likely, bisexual, is beside the point. The point was Eddy had already been implicated in the Ripper murders and now he was implicated in a homosexual brothel in the same area that the murders had taken place. He had become a huge problem to the royal family.

Bertie and Alexandra were inundated with anonymous letters until Bertie intervened and swept it all under the royal carpet, although suspicious whispers still persisted. It wasn't just his son's sexual preferences that Bertie was concerned about. His son Eddy had become a chain-smoking, aimless layabout and something had to be done. Two months later, Eddy was sent away on a seven-month tour of British India, although court officials stated that the time had already been planned months before.

Strangely enough, Bertie was living through a very similar version of his father's dilemma and Bertie's remedy was exactly the same as his fathers had been. What Eddy needed was a wife.

Eddy seemed blissfully unaware that the scandal was breaking news in London. He was writing a letter to his cousin Lord Battenberg pouring out his heart that he was totally in love with his first cousin Alexandra (Alix) of Hesse and his desire to marry her. Then out of the blue, he received a letter from her. She could not possibly marry Eddy as she had set her mind on marrying someone else: his cousin Nicky, the heir to the Russian throne.

The choice of a bride for Eddy was very limited. Alexandra ruled out his first cousin Margaret (whose mother was his aunt Vicky in Germany) not only because Margaret was a despised Prussian but also because the marriage to yet another German would not have been at all palatable to the English.

What they should have been concentrating on, in my humble opinion, was yet another marriage between first cousins. Eddy was by no means an intellectual gladiator to begin with, so what would be the prediction for his future children? Had they forgotten all about George III? Nevertheless, his family continued to sift through the German gene pool for a bride, but while they looked, Eddy was doing some searching of his own. He had met Princess Helene d'Orléans and he declared he had fallen in love with her.

The 19-year-old Helene was the daughter of Prince Philippe Count of Paris and Infanta Maria Isabel of Spain and the two had met through Eddy's sister Louise while he was visiting her in Scotland. With the encouragement of both mothers, Eddy obtained permission to meet alone with his grandmother at Balmoral Castle and with him was Helene, who he intended to introduce.

Eddy had overlooked one major detail when he set his sights on Helene. She was a devout Roman Catholic and as such a marriage to her would have meant a constitutional forfeiture of Eddy's claim to the British throne under the Act of Settlement passed by William and Mary in 1701. And his grandmother told him in no uncertain terms that *that* was not going to happen.

It all got a little messy and somewhat desperate sounding when Helene tearfully offered to become an Anglican and Eddy offered to renounce his succession. But it was Helene's father who had the final say. He would not allow her to convert. In any case, the Prime Minister, Lord Salisbury, had serious objections to the alliance as well and even if the father had agreed, the proposed marriage seemed doomed from the outset.

Helene should have been counting her lucky stars because while Eddy was sprouting undying love to her only weeks after having told Alix that he was hopelessly in love with her, Eddy was being treated yet again by several doctors for *"a form of venereal disease"* while sending eye-popping graphic letters to Lydia Miller, a former chorus girl from the Gaiety Theatre. Meanwhile he was appealing to his solicitor to help him pay off two other ladies who were demanding money for the return of explicit letters he had also sent to them. It was sounding all too reminiscent of Bertie's behaviour.

The next name on the list was Princess Mary of Teck, a daughter of Victoria's first cousin Princess Mary Adelaide of Cambridge, the granddaughter of King George III through his youngest son Adolphus and Charlotte of Mecklenburg-Strelitz. Victoria's father Edward and Adolphus had been brothers and when the baby race was in full swing after the death of their elder brother's only child and heir, Charlotte, during childbirth, Edward had beaten his brothers to both the altar and the nursery.

Eddy and Mary, who chose to be called May, had nothing in common. She wasn't beautiful, rich or sufficiently royal and if you asked anyone for their opinion, they'd have told you that her family was actually quite embarrassing. May's father Prince Francis of Teck had humiliating public temper tantrums and her mother was selfish, loud, seventeen stone and known as 'Fat Mary'. And Mary Adelaide had expensive tastes, choosing the high life of parties, holidays abroad, expensive clothes and loads of food. Hence the name 'Fat Mary' I imagine. What Mary Adelaide didn't have was a rich husband.

By the age of 30, Mary Adelaide was an unmarried woman with an expanding girth who had been unable to find anyone of royal blood who wished to marry her. Her cousin Victoria took pity on her and came up with the suitable candidate in Wurttemberg of Prince Francis of Teck. He was of lower rank than Mary, had little income and had no succession rights to the throne of Wurttemberg, but he was at least of royal blood and he had a princely title. Plus he was unmarried. With no other options available, Mary Adelaide consented to marry him. The ceremony went ahead in June 1866 in Surrey and they took up residence in apartments in Kensington Palace, thanks to Victoria, with a £5,000 per annum annuity from Parliament. Eleven months later, their first child May was born.

With her husband's modest income and Mary Adelaide's love of the good life, the Tecks found it impossible living within their means. They ran up huge debts and were relentlessly pursued by creditors, and eventually, after auctioning off their possessions, they were forced to flee to Europe when May was in her teens. They spent two years in Florence before finances became tight once again so they moved in with relatives in Germany and Austria. Initially they travelled incognito under the names of Count and

Countess von Hohenstein but since Mary Adelaide liked attention and better service than a lowly count could expect to receive, they reverted back to their royal titles of Prince and Princess and travelled more in style.

At the same time that May and Eddy were getting to know one another, the newspapers came alive again with another story about a Ripper murder in Whitechapel. At 2.15 am on Friday 13th November 1891, the body of Frances Coles was discovered, with her throat slashed from ear to ear. A policeman had passed the spot 15 minutes before and was adamant that the body hadn't been there then. Returning at 2.15 am, he heard a man's urgent footsteps running away and shining his torch into the dim archway, he noticed a figure lying on the ground in a pool of blood. The consensus was that once again the Ripper had been disturbed before he could complete the grizzly crime.

Eddy and May's engagement early December took everyone by surprise. On his grandmother's strong recommendation, Eddy proposed to May, who of course readily accepted, and for the first time in a very long while, things looked like they had turned around for the better. Eddy would have a beautiful wife by his side and with the marriage date set for a rather hasty two months' time on 27th February, he would be appointed Viceroy of Ireland.

Other suspicious facts to add to the bubbling cauldron is that while the engagement notice was being published in the newspapers, Lydia Miller (the Gaiety Theatre showgirl) had committed suicide by drinking carbolic acid.

Quietly in the shadows, while plans progressed for Eddy's wedding, Eddy's younger brother George had fallen in love as well. His intention was to marry his 17-year-old first cousin Princess Marie, the daughter of his uncle, Prince Alfred Duke of Edinburgh, but things were not going smoothly. Intricate family squabbles surfaced when Marie's mother, the only daughter of Tsar Alexander II of Russia, resented the fact that, as wife of the younger son of the British sovereign, her daughter would have to yield precedence to George's mother Alexandra, whose father after all had only been a minor prince before being called unexpectedly (and let's face it luckily) to the throne of Denmark. With her mother so adamantly opposed to the marriage, there was not much Marie could do except turn George down when he proposed to her. Instead, she would marry Ferdinand, the future King of Romania, and the marriage was all set to go ahead on 10th January. And George was crushed.

While George licked his wounds, plans were made for 8th January to celebrate both Eddy's 28th birthday and his engagement with a shooting party at Sandringham organised for the 6th January to precede the birthday party two days later. I can't imagine George would have felt much like celebrating either events since Marie would be walking down the aisle on 10th, two days after the birthday party.

The weather had been bleak and partway during the day, Eddy felt ill and walked back to the house after lunch. It was the year when influenza was rampant and newspaper reports outlined the progress of the pandemic as millions of people died all over the world. On the morning of his birthday, Eddy struggled downstairs to see his presents but felt too ill to appear at his birthday party that night. The next day the doctors were called.

Within days, Eddy's condition had worsened and newspaper reporters saw Bertie anxiously pacing up and down in the softly falling snow at Sandringham as he fretted. Shortly afterwards George appeared but by then Eddy was delirious with fever and did not recognise anyone. His fingernails and lips had turned a vivid blue, and he was raving 'Helene! Helene!' By 14th January, he was dead.

I'm sorry, but I have to make another side track. This story is too good not to mention.

SOURCE: West Coast Times, Issue 9601, 14 August 1893, Page 4.

"A very strange story is being whispered about the clubs, but has not as yet got into print. I have heard it twice, and in each case the narrator explained that he learnt it from his wife, who was told the tale by one of the royal trades folk (presumably a dress maker), who got it – of course in strictest confidence – from the upper servant (the dresser or superiors lady's maid to the Princess of Wales she said) at Sandringham. The narrative has to do with poor Prince Eddie's death, which, it alleges, was not the result of natural causes. His Royal Highness, the story goes, had certainly the influenza, as given out, but he was getting over it nicely, when, in a fit of low spirits, he drank some of the carbolic disinfectant placed in the sick room. The doctors stomach-pumped him and did all they could to bring the young man round, but the influenza and the poison combined proved too much for a by no means robust constitution, and he ultimately sank and died, much as described in the newspapers. The yarn

goes on that within a few hours of the Prince succumbing, the Princess of Wales, who was in the deepest distress, summoned the women folk of the household, and, besides entreating them as a suffering woman, laid her royal commands on them, one and all, that there should be no gossip either in or outside the house, concerning the duke's death. Her Royal Highness gave no reason for or explanation of this strange request, which was also, it is said, made by the Prince to the men servant. Amongst the household it was no secret that Prince Eddie had been in wretched spirits for some time previously; ever since, indeed, the suicide of the Gaiety girl with whom the tongue of scandal connected his name. Whether there was or was not any truth in that rumour the servants don't know. They say, however, that about the same date a violent quarrel took place between the duke and his father at Marlborough House. The two men were locked in the Prince's sanctum together, and their voices were raised so high in anger that the Princess grew alarmed, and, regardless of the expose, summoned servants to assist her in interrupting them. From that day, Prince Eddie was dull and depressed. I can hardly imagine anybody deliberately or malevolently inventing a tale of this sort, so that I think it must have some foundation. Moreover, one instantly recalls the extraordinary precautions adopted to keep all strangers, especially reporters, outside Sandringham during the days immediately following the Prince's decease."

OKAY, back to the story... Eddy was raving 'Helene! Helene!' By 14th January, he was dead.

I wonder what Marie was thinking when she heard the news of Eddy's death four days after her wedding to Ferdinand? Was she angry that her mother had forced her to marry her second choice? And what was her mother thinking? Was she regretting her ... yes I'm going to say it ... haughty decision not to let her daughter marry George? If Marie had gone with her heart, she would be the one marrying George and she would certainly not be 'yielding precedence' to Alexandra as her mother had so snootily pointed out. It seems a dreadfully sad twist of fate that Marie would spend the next few years of her marriage in wretched unhappiness, struggling to adjust to life in Romania.

As the terrible news of Eddy's death was being published in every newspaper in the country, Stephen was reportedly starving himself to death in the asylum. By 3rd February, he was dead.

With Eddy's death, George's marriage became a matter of urgency. The press were clamouring for George to marry May, as was May's father, who kept muttering to himself about George's aunt Dagma who had been engaged to Nicholas, the heir to the Russian throne, when he'd died suddenly of meningitis. Dagma's engagement had been transferred to his younger brother Alexander, so why couldn't they do the same with May? No one felt inclined to mention Henry VIII who had married his dead brother's widow Catherine of Aragon and the major fiasco that had followed on from that.

No doubt because of her parent's indiscretions, 24-year-old May was a model of quiet dignity, simply delighted to be part of the British monarchy regardless of which brother she married.

Six months later, George visited his sister Louise at Sheen Lodge in Scotland where May had been invited from nearby White Lodge and he was pushed by his sister into the garden to propose. And of course, May accepted.

I have to do it. By now, you know how much I love a conspiracy theory. So here is one more piece in this puzzle.

In 1970, a surgeon by the name of Dr Thomas Stowell, wrote an article in the Criminology Journal.

Source: **Watertown Daily Times, Watertown, N.Y., Tuesday Nov. 3, 1970, page 9**

LONDON (UPI) – Citing as evidence an article published today about Jack the Ripper, a London newspaper has suggested London's 1888's sex killer was the grandson of Queen Victoria and heir to the throne of England.

The Sunday Times raised the name of Duke of Clarence, Prince Albert Victor, grandson of Queen Victoria, brother to George V and heir to the throne on the strength of an article in the journal Criminology by surgeon Dr Thomas Stowell.

"All the points of Dr Stowell's odd story fit this man," the newspaper said in an article on the still-unidentified killer of at least five prostitutes in London's East End.

"The evidence suggests that the murderer was a man so senior in the hierarchy of the land, of so noble a family that the police, when they realised who was involved, were forced to conceal his identity," the criminology article said.

Stowell said he knew who the killer was but refused to identify him. "I would never dream of doing harm to a family whom I love and admire," he wrote. But he supplied a detailed series of clues.

"Jack the Ripper, he said, "was" the heir to power and wealth. His family, for 50 years, had earned the love and admiration of large numbers of people by its devotion to public service."

"His grandmother, who outlived him, was very much the stern, Victorian matriarch, widely and deeply respected. His father, to whose title he was the heir, was a gay cosmopolitan and did much to improve the status of England internationally," Stowell said.

Stowell referred to his suspect as "S", who at the age of 16 went on a world tour during which he contracted syphilis. The disease gradually began to dominate his life, Stowell added. The Sunday Times said the suspect resigned his commission at age 24 after a raid on a homosexual brothel, the name of which had been linked to a member of the royal family. Sir William Gull, the royal doctor, treated "S", Stowell said. Gull's daughter, Caroline Acland, a friend of Stowell, who is now in his 80's, described an 1889 entry in her father's diary to him which said "informed blank that his son was dying of syphilis of the brain."

According to Stowell, Gull realised his patient was Jack the Ripper and asked commissioner of police Sir Charles Warren to keep the name secret. For that reason, he contended, many of the clues of the killer's identity were destroyed, including at least one message by Warren himself. Police vigilance relaxed in November 1888, because the police knew the killer had been restrained in a mental home, Stowell said.

Prince Albert Victor, first child of King Edward VII, who was the eldest son of Queen Victoria, was born in 1864 and was on a world tour from 1879 to 1882. He died early in 1892, at the age of 28, outlived by his grandmother, Queen Victoria who died in 1901.

I BELIEVE the Watertown Daily News got it wrong. Dr Stowell was not implicating Eddy because his initial could not be confused with the letter

'S'. But James Stephen did have that initial, his father and grandfather had both devoted themselves to public service, his strict grandmother Mary Cunningham did outlive him, he was treated for *'a form of venereal disease'* at the same time as Eddy was being treated, his name was indeed linked to the royal family through Eddy and he died in a mental institution from madness, perhaps as a result of advanced syphilis. It would seem that the person Dr Stowell believed to be the Ripper was in fact James Stephen.

Sorry again...back to George and May. And more importantly, Bertie.

The wedding took place on a hot day in July and between the wedding breakfast and a family dinner, Bertie somehow managed to squeeze in a 'visit' to a married friend, Daisy, who claimed descent from Charles II's mistress Nell Gwyn. Not too far in the future, Daisy would become Countess of Warwick when her husband succeeded as Earl of Warwick, inheriting Warwick Castle.

At 56 years old, Bertie was ageing rather badly. He was overweight, threatened with heart problems and possibly diabetes. He was also using the new wonder therapy of the day, electric shocks, administered for impotence.

So much is known about Bertie's daily life but what went on in his thoughts and behind his mask was carefully concealed. His mother was 77 years old and she had been sitting on the throne for longer than any English monarch in history, even beating her grandfather George III's record of 59 years. She was lame, almost deaf and nearly blind with cataracts and relied heavily on her daughter Beatrice, especially after the death of Beatrice's husband Prince Henry of Battenberg. Still she hung on, always reluctant to share work with Bertie.

The morning of her Diamond Jubilee dawned warm and dull with the sun only appearing once through the clouds. By then, Victoria was too lame to dismount from her coach to the open-air celebration outside the west front of St. Paul's Cathedral. As the procession crawled toward St. Paul's, the cheering was deafening and as she approached the cathedral, the crowd burst out singing 'God Save the Queen.'

Despite being put down and rejected by his mother for as many years as he could remember, Bertie played the role of dutiful son to perfection, like any true chameleon. The most enjoyable part of the day for him was that his despised nephew, Wilhelm, had been refused an invitation to attend.

Wilhelm's father by then had died, making him the ruler of Germany, and he was making sure everyone knew it.

The year 1900 held both good and bad for Bertie. His horse Diamond Jubilee won the Derby and later that year, he also won the Grand National with Ambush II. But soon after, terrible news arrived that his 55-year-old brother Affie had died.

The exact circumstances of Affie's death are unknown. Affie had begun showing severe symptoms of tertiary syphilis in which mental peculiarities are a major symptom and a frequent cause for institutionalisation in insane asylums. On the night of his parent's 25th wedding anniversary, while the rest of the family gathered to celebrate at the Schloss Friedenstein in Gotha, Affie took a revolver outside into the cool night air and shot himself.

But as saddened as Bertie was, the health of his elder sister Vicky was more devastating. Bertie knew Vicky had been suffering from breast cancer for almost two years and of late she had been complaining of lumbago as the cancer metastasised to her spine. By then, morphine was only dulling the pain for ten minutes at a time.

Bertie wrote her endless letters updating her on matters at home, one of which was their mother's health. Victoria was complaining of insomnia, lack of appetite, upset digestion and depression and most of the time she was drowsy, incoherent and confused. She no longer raged at everyone and things that had once irritated her, she now accepted. His sister Helena telegraphed every day with reports that she was cheerful and that there was no need for Bertie to come – something Bertie was only too willing to believe.

The pretence went on until 19th January when Bertie received an enraged phone call from Victoria's physicians saying the Queen might die at any time. He left for Osborne that morning and in the evening Bertie was sitting quietly by his mother's side.

At 82 years of age, it was obvious to all that Victoria had given up and was dying. The rest of the family was summoned and among the family members stood Wilhelm, upset to think his indomitable, stubborn grandmother was actually dying. Beatrice whispered the names of the people in the room to her mother, but rather pointedly the only name she left out was Wilhelm, standing right by her side. By 6.30 that night, she died and Bertie, now almost 60 years old, was finally king.

The nation was hardly thrilled by Bertie's accession and everyone had something to say about it. None seemed too impressed and few kings in history have come to the throne with lower expectations from his subjects. He was a 59-year-old philanderer, a poor talker and a worse letter writer. He was not witty or clever and had always been easily bored. Even his Prime Minister, Lord Salisbury, had virtually no respect for Bertie at all, perhaps because he'd had to extricate Bertie from some extremely embarrassing mucky situations. He pointed out that if Bertie wanted to make a difference and take control, he had to address the conditions of the poor in what was the richest country in the world. And he had to address their life expectancy.

Salisbury had a good point. At the time of Bertie's ascent, life expectancy among the bottom third of the population was 45 years old. For dockers, it was lower at 35. One in three children died in infancy and another third of those ended up in the poorhouse. In the slums of major cities, even the air you breathed made you feel sick. Salisbury pointed out to Bertie that he was one of the aristocrats who owned some of the vilest slums in the country and made £60,000 a year out of them.

A Hanoverian he may have been, with all of the resulting foibles, but Bertie had a few useful qualities up his sleeve that most of his ancestors had not possessed. Bertie was a charmer. And with that charm, he became a great networker with an eye for cultivating the right people when he needed to. He realised he had this rare quality, awkwardly absent in his Hanoverian royal family, and he knew how to perform in public. If you had to put in one word what best-described Bertie's quality, that word would be 'charisma'.

The aristocracy in the late 19th century have been dubbed 'the great ornamentals', and if that is true, Bertie was the greatest ornament of all. He created a persona for himself of geniality and affability and he was determined to be visible, which was a direct contrast to his almost reclusive mother. He allowed himself to be photographed with his grandchildren and he gained a reputation for himself for speaking off the cuff in public and in three languages, no less. Unlike both his nephews, Nicky and Wilhelm, he understood the power of the press and what it could do for him and he had some ideas of his own about how to work it.

All of a sudden, Bertie's talent for publicity opened up the world for him and he revelled in his new role. He wanted to impress on everyone that instead of conflict, Britain needed to compromise. What he really wanted to do was make a difference.

In the past, the public had been shocked at his scandalous behaviour and on more than one occasion, he had marginally avoided the divorce court as a co-respondent. But what came as a big surprise to Bertie was that most of Britain actually loved reading about his wild behaviour. They loved to read about his horse racing, his yachts, his theatre going and even his stylish women. Behind the shocked expressions were a hidden smile and an amused shake of the head at Bertie's wild goings on. But while Bertie revelled in the limelight and made eloquent speeches, his son George took virtually no interest in government whatsoever. Instead, he took up golf, cycling, bridge, cars and luxury living.

Bertie had learnt a valuable lesson from his mother's lack of instruction and he did not want his son George to experience the same confusion he had suffered when coming to the throne. George was about to take lessons in what was expected of him as a monarch and he was about to take them immediately. George, as the new Prince of Wales, was placed at a desk near to his own to ensure his son had the understanding and experience in government that had been unfortunately denied him.

This was Bertie's settling in period and for the first time in his life, he had a full-time job. Day after day he would clump around the rooms in Windsor, followed by a dog, wearing a hat and swinging a walking stick. He had furniture moved, pictures were taken down of John Brown and bonfires were made at his home, Frogmore Cottage, to burn his mother's letters to her Indian servant. Even his widowed sister Beatrice, who had lived at Windsor was asked politely to remove her furniture as soon as possible.

Parliament saw a new side to Bertie. For the first time in forty years, a monarch drove to Parliament. Bertie would sit towering above the crowds in the tall glass state coach, dressed in a crimson robe and the Imperial State Crown drawn by eight cream horses as it lumbered and swayed on leather springs. Beside him, Alexandra wore a black mourning dress accessorised by the Koh-I-Nor diamond and Queen Victoria's small diamond crown as she clasped Bertie's hand tightly. By projecting the monarchy as tradition, Bertie believed he was reforming it instead of deserting it as his mother had done. Not only should a monarch work, he should be *seen* to work.

In a little over a year after succeeding to the throne, Bertie had made himself the most glamorous monarch in Europe and he relished his newfound reputation. After having had no training at all in how to be a monarch, his on-the-job-training made him look effective and successful. When his country needed a front man, he stepped up to the mark perfectly and did the only thing he knew how to do. He charmed the crowds. And it worked brilliantly.

What Bertie was actually doing was bringing the monarchy back from seclusion. His mother had withdrawn from the public and retreated into obscurity and invisibility as she abandoned her duties. She had been an old woman and a recluse who had given up a long time ago but still hung on to the throne, depriving Bertie the best years of his life as the monarch. Yet behind the scenes she clung tenaciously and obstinately to her authority, much like a tyrant.

What alarmed Alexandra was that as his ego ballooned, so did his figure. He bolted down everything and anything, hardly bothering to chew. She complained that his appetite was appalling, his waist had swelled to 48 inches and his chest and abdomen had swelled so alarmingly, he no longer allowed himself to be weighed. Even his uniforms were too tight. But still he ignored her.

But while Bertie settled into his role as king, he made it clear from the beginning he would not be dropping his lady friends although Alexandra should be styled as Queen and treated with full dignity.

It had been 64 years since England had had a king and no one could remember what a Queen was supposed to do, much less Alexandra who had willingly withdrawn from society years before. She observed Bertie happily assume court duties while she was told to *'stand by, mute and still'* and she soon realised that he was as jealous of his entitlements as his mother had been. Being silent suited her just fine since she was plagued, not just by deafness, but by tinnitus as well. Quietly, in the growing uncertainty of what was expected of her, she withdrew even more.

Parliament rapidly became aware that Bertie's style of monarchy was going to cost money, after all, he told them, he had Balmoral, Osborne and Sandringham to run. £500,000 should do it. When looking around at the shocked expressions, he grudgingly agreed to pay income tax on the money, something he instantly regretted. Nonetheless, six years later, his debts were gradually paid off.

The £500,000 from Parliament was barely enough for Bertie's needs. Cuts had to be made if the money was going to cover everything. Household officials had to take a salary cut and the Royal Buckhounds were abolished. Next he gave up his share of Osborne, shared with all of his brothers and sisters which Victoria left to all of her children, and then promptly gave it to the nation, much to his sister Beatrice's shrill outburst, because she had recently relocated there when removed from Windsor.

Bertie's sister Vicky was too ill to attend her mother's funeral so in his first year, Bertie visited Germany twice: firstly to see his dying sister, terribly swollen and wracked by nausea and vomiting and then again after she died. Both times, he was greeted with boos and hisses in the streets but he stoically refused to show his annoyance. And he controlled his irritation with Wilhelm, which had always been an effort for him every time they met.

The two men had a complicated relationship. Wilhelm thought Bertie had never liked him, and Bertie thought Wilhelm was tiresome and loudmouthed. And he wasn't the only one. Wilhelm seemed to have a way about him that alienated many royal families. One time, he slapped Ferdinand of Bulgaria on the bottom during a state visit and behind his back he called him 'Fernando naso' because of his large beaky nose. He also called the small Italian King, Umberto I, 'the dwarf' in the presence of his entourage. Even the Greek royal family hated him.

Despite the personal friction between Bertie and Wilhelm, Bertie made a conscious effort to stay on good terms with his nephew. He sent a Christmas gift with a message stressing how much he wanted goodwill with Germany for the sake of peace and all mankind. Wilhelm's reply to his uncle however was not quite so friendly. He admitted the press were awful but he wanted Bertie not to place him in the spot of choosing a course, which could be a *'misfortune to both'*. The ominous undertones were obvious. Needless to say, George's visit to Berlin the following year was strained.

The bombshell that Bertie dropped a few days after George's return, put Britain's name on everyone's lips. Britain was signing a defensive alliance with Japan and the world, especially Wilhelm and Nicky, were shocked and rattled.

Seven years before, Russia had occupied the Liaodong Peninsula in China, built the Port Arthur fortress and based the Russian Pacific Fleet in the port. It was basically an anti-British move to counter the British occupation of Wei-Hai-Wei in Shandong Province but in Japan it was seen as an anti-Japanese move along with Germany occupying Jiao Zhou Bay and building their fortress in Tsingtao. With Port Arthur occupied, Russia began building the Chinese Eastern Railway in Manchuria and sent 177,000 Russian troops in to protect the railways.

It was like waving a red flag in front of a bull. Anti-colonial, anti-foreign and anti-Christian sentiment was rampant and serious discontent in north China was growing mainly due to missionary activity. The combination of a drought followed by floods in Shandong province in 1897 had forced farmers to flee to cities to seek food and two years later, the Boxer Rebellion was in full swing.

The Japanese were well aware that they had no hope in evicting the Russians so as a compromise, they proposed giving Russia control over Manchuria in exchange for Japanese control of northern Korea. It was in this atmosphere that Bertie signed the Anglo-Japanese Alliance in 1902. Basically it meant that if any nation allied itself with Russia during any war against Japan, Britain would enter the war on Japan's side. It also meant that Russia could no longer count on receiving help from either Germany or France without the involvement of Britain. With such an alliance, Japan were free to commence hostilities, if necessary.

Knowing full well what the treaty meant, Nicky immediately began evacuating troops out of Manchuria at the same time that Wilhelm began sending supportive letters telling him that it was in Russia's power to save the *"entire white race"* from the *"Yellow Peril"* if they so wanted, which in turn would deal a deadly blow to their common antagonist, Britain.

Nicky had no want to start a war with anyone. It was the last thing he wanted considering he had no money in his bank. He replied to Wilhelm stating all he wanted was peace and he was prepared to compromise with Japan if that's what it took. Wilhelm could hardly believe what he was reading. It started a flurry of letter sending backwards and forwards but while Nicky and Wilhelm were bickering, Bertie was busy taking steps towards peace by grinding the Boer War to a halt. The cost of the war had been enormous, both monetary and politically. They had spent a fortune and goodwill had been forfeited while Britain's reputation for good had been blown out of the water with an estimation of 75,000 British soldiers, Boer soldiers and Boer civilians dead. Somewhere in the terrible figures, between 14,000 and 20,000 non-combatant black Africans had died as well. As a means of compensation and reconstruction, he handed over the massive amount of £3 million.

With the end of the war, it was assumed that Germany and Britain would once again be on good terms. They still had trading ties and of course, there were the strong blood ties as well. But in the right-wing press, a new Germany was surfacing. As Germany's population increased and its shipbuilding began to outstrip Britain for the first time in history, seeds of concern had begun to germinate in several British government departments.

Through it all, Wilhelm and Bertie went on demonstrating a certain degree of civility in public, even though Wilhelm was shocked at the new strain of hostility towards him in the British papers. The suddenly expanding German navy was a serious issue for Britain and an intelligence unit reported that German army intelligence had recently started to gather information on British coastal defences. Feeling threatened, Britain sent a flotilla of warships to blockade the coast of Venezuela and the papers were full of anti-Germanism statements.

As relations with Britain became shakier and shakier, Wilhelm seesawed back again to Russia after four years of frostiness on Nicky's part. The thaw had come not from his relations with Britain but from a financial viewpoint by Nicky's new foreign minister, Count Vladimir Lamsdorff.

Wilhelm's Secretary of State for Foreign Affairs, Bernard von Bulow, was delighted with the new state of affairs. He'd been angling for the cousins to make up for years and to demonstrate his goodwill with the new arrangement, Wilhelm rode across the Russian border to a small village, which had recently experienced a devastating fire. In the town square, he distributed purses of money to the mostly Jewish population and gave a speech to them in German (which by the way, no one could understand) and from then on, their relationship seemed to go ahead in leaps and bounds.

After eight years of being tsar, Nicky was feeling comfortable enough in his role to ignore his senior ministers. For a man who had no idea what was worth more, 25 roubles or a gold watch, Nicky closed all Russian-controlled ports to foreign trade and took control of all diplomatic administration out of Lamsdorff's hands. And then, for some unknown reason, he suddenly stopped evacuating his troops out of Manchuria.

It was a decision that was the beginning of the end for Nicky. It did nothing but eat away at Russian finances, already in serious danger, and it pushed the Japanese Taro cabinet to vote to go to war against Russia. Two months later, they recalled their minister from Russia and severed all diplomatic relations. Already an unpopular ruler, his popularity dwindled even more.

In England, it was a totally different story. Bertie's cheeriness was winning over the British public and feeling quite buoyant about it all; he decided it was time to show Europe a new side of Britain. He set off on a five-week cruise to the Mediterranean with an all-male crew accompanied by eight battleships, four cruises and four destroyers. His first stop was Italy with a last minute decision to visit Paris as well.

From the very start, it was obvious to the Italians that Bertie had charisma. He walked among the crowds and refused police protection and everywhere he went the crowds went wild. He stood good-naturedly for hours and when called upon, he remembered every single person's name. It was the first time a British monarch had visited the country since the Middle Ages and little gestures, like taking his hat off when he went through the Porta Pia and when he met the Pope, brought the house down. Next on the agenda was Paris.

Paris was a place where Bertie had spent many pleasurable hours. But this time, he was determined to use his charm in the service of his country instead of his...um...personal enjoyment. Anything regarding foreign policies, he would leave to his new foreign minister, Sir Edward Grey.

To his surprise, when he arrived in Paris it was to serious boos and jeers and it took Bertie back a bit. It was as if every quarrel since the Middle Ages was being remembered. But steadfastly, Bertie turned in a faultless and confident performance and within three days, he had converted the boos into cheers. He walked into the crowds, spoke fluent French about how much he loved the city and how he felt totally at home there. Everywhere he went he looked constantly delighted. By the time he left, the French were eating out of his hands, allowing the governments to sit around the table and lay the grounds for a treaty to be signed the following year.

Combined with the Franco-Russian defence pact signed a decade before, the new intended agreement between Britain and France meant that it was the Germans who would be isolated. It was Wilhelm's worst nightmare come true and once more, he turned anxiously to Nicky.

Nicky was on his annual visit to Hesse when Wilhelm waylaid him. His concern, he explained to Nicky, was about the Anglo-French relations. Once the two countries signed the agreement, it would finish over a thousand years of rivalry and if the two countries were now united, it meant that neither of them could be trusted anymore. He was desperately trying to drive any wedge he could in the new Anglo-French relationship by having Russia and Germany standing side by side as allies.

Bertie knew exactly what Wilhelm was trying to do and he was conspicuous by his silence as he continued his tour to Vienna to meet Emperor Franz Joseph. Although he admired the Austrian emperor, it was a little more difficult for Bertie since neither man had anything in common. Franz Joseph was a man of routine. He was known to rise at 4 am, eat his lunch at twelve and his dinner at five and be in bed by seven, ready to start the same routine the next day. Bertie had barely had his first cup of coffee by ten in the morning. But still, the visit was a resounding success.

Understandably, the only city Bertie did not visit was Berlin. His excuse was that he was far too busy when in fact, his good humour just didn't quite stretch as far as his German nephew. This, on top of everything else, sent Wilhelm into a palpable fury at being sidelined yet again. As Bertie progressed happily from country to country, Wilhelm watched with seething resentment, sure that his uncle was playing a game with him. Refusing to be ignored, Wilhelm decided to play back. Within days of Bertie's departure from Rome, Wilhelm arrived and announced that he too had come to see the Pope. And when Bertie left Vienna, Wilhelm turned up to see his old friend Franz Joseph as well.

In Russia, his uncle's progress was the furthermost thing from Nicky's mind. He was having problems of his own without worrying about Wilhelm's nervous theories. By then, he had fully expected to be finished with the Japanese, or *"little short-tailed monkeys"* as he called them. Instead, when Japan unexpectedly sent torpedo boats into Port Arthur, sinking two of the most modern Russian ships, Nicky knew he was in serious trouble.

The attack was a shocking surprise to the Russians and they were completely unprepared. Defeat followed defeat and at every turn, the conflict exposed astonishing incompetence in the Russian army. For such a major world power, it was obvious that their war-planning had been virtually non-existent with the average age of a Russian general being 69 years old. They were spending more time infighting than actually fighting wars.

The conflict with Japan cost over 2 billion roubles and left Russia unable to even give her soldiers a hot breakfast or gunpowder for their guns. And of course, someone had to be blamed. Suddenly, Nicky began to see what Wilhelm had been trying to tell him about British duplicity. In the back of his mind was the memory of Bertie signing a defensive agreement with Japan and as a result, an increase of anger toward the British bubbled to the surface. It became all too easy to blame the Russian catastrophe on Britain's support of their enemy.

While Nicky openly fumed at what he saw as British help to mobilise the dreaded 'monkeys' against his country, Wilhelm was only too happy to help his Russian cousin. It was the bond Wilhelm was hoping for, praying for, and he rushed to offer Nicky the use of German coaling stations, saying that the British were telling him not to do it. Wilhelm was playing a dangerous game in his haste to undermine England.

Bertie could see where it was all going and his government urgently advised him to do something to alleviate the powder keg situation. In an attempt to reassure Nicky of his goodwill, Bertie offered to act as a mediator with Japan on the Russian's behalf (which Nicky angrily turned down) while Wilhelm sulked in Germany because Bertie seemed to want an alliance with everyone else, except him. Unlike the rest of Europe, nothing Bertie did seemed to please either of his nephews.

Finally, and reluctantly, Bertie agreed to attend the Kiel Regatta in June 1904.

With the news that Bertie would be attending, Wilhelm went into full swing in his effort to impress his uncle. His finger was in every pie and every one of his sons were ordered to attend the Guard of Honour. He was so excited, he was dressed in his parade uniform hours in advance, pacing the deck of the *Hohenzollern*.

When Bertie arrived, his serenity was unmistakable. He looked like a man who knew every move of the game and he was comfortable with it all. Wilhelm, on the other hand, looked agitated and jittery. In the tenseness, things went downhill rather quickly as soon as they sat down to talk. Don't forget, Bertie saw himself as someone who was sitting with an unruly nephew, and one he disliked intensely.

Bertie had a great deal of confidence in both himself and with his new role as diplomat. He knew what was required of him and it was up to him to try and talk rationally to Wilhelm. In the back of his mind however he knew Wilhelm was anything but rational.

Bertie started out by talking about peace and his desire to reduce friction between them all. But even as he spoke, everyone could see the amicability was forced. At one time, the veneer of cheer cracked when they disagreed volubly about the Russian-Japanese war. Wilhelm talked about crushing the *"Yellow Peril"* and Bertie said there was no such thing. He stated that Japan had been in the right since Nicky had rejected their diplomatic approaches in the first place. And the Japanese had done brilliantly. They were just as civilised as Europeans and it had nothing to do with the colour of their skin.

It was a serious rap over the knuckles to Wilhelm who couldn't resist the urge to retaliate. The night before the naval review, and despite being told to play down how much the German navy had expanded, Wilhelm instructed his cabinet to send out everything they had, down to the smallest boat, to impress his uncle.

Of course, the reaction was not what Wilhelm had anticipated. The new German navy certainly impressed Bertie but instead of the expected adulation, Bertie was seriously alarmed. He went home with a feeling that the Germans were only building up their navy in order to *"fall on"* Britain as soon as it was strong enough.

As Bertie became more suspicious of Wilhelm, bad feeling increased even more between Britain and Russia. But it was about to get far worse.

The small flotilla of boats had only been fishing off Kingston upon Hull near Yorkshire. It was the middle of the night on 21/22 October 1904, their nets were down and all was calm and peaceful. Unbeknownst to them, Russian warships had been navigating a non-existent minefield and had sailed into the North Sea. They were on full alert because earlier on in the night, a Russian supply ship had mistaken a Swedish ship for a Japanese torpedo boat and radioed that he was being attacked. So when the Russian warships sighted the fishing boats through the thick fog, they illuminated the trawlers with their searchlights and opened fire.

The British trawler *Crane* was the first to sink but four other trawlers were severely damaged. In the pandemonium of screaming and dying men, and because they could only see vague shapes, the Russians started shooting at each other. Several Russian ships even signalled that torpedoes had hit them and they were about to be boarded by the Japanese, despite being more than 20,000 miles from Japan. One warship reportedly fired more than 500 shells without hitting anything while crews donned life vests and drew cutlasses. After twenty minutes', the surviving fishermen saw a blue light on one of the warships signal a ceasefire.

When the smoke cleared, the Russian admiral looked around. It was only then he realised what his warships had done. And he panicked. He left without picking up any survivors or even informing the Russian government of what had happened.

Bertie was at the Newmarket Races when he heard the news but he left immediately to send an urgent, and furious telegram to Nicky. The reply that returned was unrepentant. Nicky backed his navy by saying that St Petersburg was in the grip of a Japanese spy scare and with Japanese torpedo boats shadowing the Baltic fleet, his warships were sadly trigger-happy. Even George, always happy to sit quietly in the background and watch, commented that if the Russians couldn't tell the difference between fishermen and Japanese destroyers, they must have been drunk. Or maybe they were just incompetent.

For five days, the English were at boiling point. 28 battleships were ordered to raise steam and prepare for action, while British cruiser squadrons shadowed the Russian fleet as it made its way through the Bay of Biscay and down the coast of Portugal on its way to Tangiers in Morocco. Later on, as the fleet left Tangiers, one ship accidentally severed the city's underwater telegraph cable with her anchor, preventing communications with Europe for four days.

All Nicky could do was back down and in the aftermath, he agreed to pay £66,000 in damages to the fishermen. Money, by the way, that Russia simply could not afford. But the gesture had the desired effect and Bertie calmed down.

Not so Nicky. It was yet another incident where the English had lorded it over him and he wrote furious letters to Wilhelm who was, of course, terribly sympathetic. In one letter, Nicky wrote that it was high time to put a stop to it all and Germany, Russia and France should unite in an agreement to abolish Anglo-Japanese arrogance.

Wilhelm didn't need to be told twice. He immediately sent Nicky a draft of a treaty. It stated that the Hull fishing fleet *had* been foreign vessels and that his proposed treaty was purely defensive, meant for one another to come to each other's aid if necessary.

Wilhelm had left one major question unanswered in the wording of his treaty. What if France attacked Germany?

All of a sudden, Wilhelm was hesitating about including France. Nicky wanted to show the treaty to the French before he signed it to see what their reaction would be, but Wilhelm was adamant that they shouldn't. No one could trust the French, he reasoned.

By Christmas, after both monarchs had repeatedly exchanged assurances of their loyalty to each other, the treaty was dead in the water (excuse the pun) and Russia was in the grip of more crises. Port Arthur had surrendered to the Japanese after a 156-day siege and weeks later the Russian imperial guard had fired shots into a largely peaceful demonstration of workers as they'd gathered in front of the Winter Palace. The workers had only been delivering a petition begging the tsar to help them but the guards had overreacted and killed 1,000 defenceless people.

The massacre was the moment in Russian history when the loyalty of the people began to break down irretrievably for Nicky. It was an occasion when even Bertie did not send a message of support. Wilhelm, who had fallen into a paranoid grip, sure that Britain were about to attack Germany now that they knew the size of his new navy, did however send his support. He could not afford *not* to.

Nicky met with a small delegation of workers and told them they had been duped by enemies of the county and to have patience. Of course, no one listened. They'd already been patient, they cried. They had shouted out for help and in return, every single one of them had lost family members and friends in the massacre. Patience was out of the question now.

It was February 1905 and 400,000 workers were on strike in St Petersburg when yet another disaster struck, this time closer to home. Nicky's uncle, Grand Duke Sergei, was in a particularly good mood after receiving a miniature portrait of Alexander III from Nicky. The portrait was surrounded with gold laurel leaves and showed a personal mark of favour from Nicky to his uncle. After having lunch, Sergei left for the Governor's mansion in his recognisable carriage drawn by a pair of horses, fully intending to finish off some work that needed to be done. What he didn't know was a terrorist was waiting for him in the Kremlin with a nitro-glycerine bomb wrapped in newspapers.

The carriage passed through the gate and turned the corner into Senatskaya Square when a member of the Socialist-Revolutionary Party stepped forward and threw the bomb directly into Sergei's lap. The explosion disintegrated the carriage and over the bloodstained snow lay pieces of scorched cloth, fur and leather.

With the bomb sitting in his lap, there was nothing much left of Sergei except splintered bone although some of his fingers, still adorned with rings, were found on the roof of a nearby building. In the chaos, the carriage horses bolted towards the Nikolsky Gate, dragging with them the front wheels and coach-box as well as the semi-conscious and badly burned driver, whose back had been riddled with bits of bomb and stone.

The bomb blast shook the palace and rattled the windows and Sergei's second wife rushed to the scene of the explosion. In shock and kneeling in the snow, she helped to gather up Sergei's remains – part of a skull, a hand fragment, a still booted foot – and placed them on a stretcher covered by an army great coat.

In seclusion in his palace at Tsarskoe Selo as his country progressed into full revolution, Nicky had no idea what to do except protect himself and his family. The fences around the palace were raised higher and ten-foot high barbed wire with spiked railings was installed. Behind his walls, Nicky felt utterly confused and powerless as he detached himself even more.

But there was another reason why Nicky was isolating himself. After the birth of four girls, Alix had finally given birth to a boy they named Alexei. The excitement of the birth of Nicky's only male heir gave way to the terrible realisation that Alix had been correct to fear the possibility of faulty genes. The little boy, the precious heir to the Russian throne that Nicky and Alix had so longed for, had haemophilia. Small knocks and tumbles produced ugly dark blue swellings on the boy's body, causing terrible pain. Their worst nightmare had come true.

The realisation couldn't have come at a worst time. There was no doubt that the Japanese War had been a total disaster for Russia. It had brought humiliating defeat, incredible debt and all-out revolution. The trains stopped, factories stopped producing and riots broke out. His government was losing control.

In the chaos, the couple decided to keep Alexei's illness a secret. Their instinct was to keep the world out, forbidding the discussion of their son's health problems and not revealing the problem. They had made the same decision that George and May had made when the British couple were told that their youngest son John was epileptic and perhaps autistic. Both couples had decided to hide the disabilities and keep up appearances.

Safe in her cocoon, there was nothing that Alix missed about the outside world. She spent her days surrounded by her children, walking in the garden and nursing her fragile child. But Alexei's birth had aged her and her own health had become delicate. She was always exhausted and complained of shortness of breath as her lips turned blue at an alarming rate. No one knew what was wrong and even her doctor called it hysteria. Still there was no doubt that her mental and physical health was deteriorating.

It wasn't just Alix who was under stress. Nicky was feeling the strain as well. His younger brother had fallen in love with a commoner and he had been forced to have them both arrested as they attempted to leave the country to get married. He had already exiled two of his first cousins for making what he saw as unsuitable marriages. While Nicky stressed over issues, Alix made a mistake that would change their lives forever.

All Alix wanted was to alleviate her son's distress because nothing she did seemed to be helping. Just by being a protective mother who only wanted to save her small child from pain, she made the biggest mistake of her life. In her anxiety, she placed her trust in a peasant from Siberia who was a self-proclaimed faith healer while seemingly ineffectual doctors were told they were no longer needed. The faith healer's name was Grigori Rasputin and his hypnotic pale blue eyes promised miracles. Alix was instantly snared.

The amazing part of the story is, whatever it was that Rasputin did, Alexei responded. Suddenly his agonising swellings subsided and his internal bleeding stopped. Rasputin's magnetism was so profound that even Nicky felt at peace around him.

Alix had no idea that away from the royal family, Rasputin was a totally different person - manipulative, coarse and bullying. As Rasputin's influence grew in Tsarskoe Setoe, trouble was brewing in Austria.

The year was 1908 and it was a year that no one would ever forget. Austria announced to the world that it was formally seizing the small

Ottoman-owned Balkan state of Bosnia-Herzegovina, since they had been administering the state for the past thirty years.

It wasn't that Russia was against seizing other countries for themselves. They'd done the same thing by seizing Siberia. Bulgaria had already declared independence and Greece had claimed the island of Crete as their own. But Austria's grab of Bosnia sent angry ripples through Russia. Russia had seen themselves as the protectors of Bosnia and despite admitting that Serbia was the most aggressive of all states, Bosnia was Russia's closest Balkan ally.

Russia immediately voiced outrage at Austria's seizure of Bosnia, and Serbia declared that if Austria didn't withdraw, it would mobilise its army. In return, Austria told Serbia that they were a cancer undermining their empire.

They were strong words and they lit the fuse leading to imminent war. And of course, Russia began to panic. With the war against Japan still vivid in their minds, the Russian foreign minister Alexander Izvolsky begged Britain to support a conference between the two countries and although the British Foreign Secretary Sir Edward Grey was less than enthusiastic about being brought into the conflict, he reluctantly agreed.

It was all for nothing. Austria refused to cooperate and of course Germany backed Austria.

At that precise time, Wilhelm did something remarkable. He announced that he could no longer cope and would have to abdicate. He literally collapsed in a heap. His entourage picked him off the floor and put him to bed where he lay for two weeks in utter exhaustion. As he lay in quarantine, Serbia and Austria continued to swap threats while in Russia, the press were demanding action against Austria more and more insistently.

The problem was that the government was painfully aware that it simply couldn't afford to offer Serbia any military support. By late December, Nicky wrote a desperate letter to Wilhelm asking him to use his influence with his friend Franz Joseph in Austria to resolve the crisis once and for all.

Still unwell in his bed, Wilhelm refused.

While Russia and Germany remained at loggerheads, Sir Edward Grey was insisting that Bertie and Alexandra should not delay their planned visit to Berlin any longer. With the state of affairs in Europe, he did not want any more conflict with Germany than there already was. He pointed out that German papers were calling Bertie a *"20th century Napoleon"* after his last visit to Emperor Franz Joseph and Berlin was full of rumours that Bertie was scheming to detach Austria from Germany as well. Rumours like that had to be squashed before they got out of hand.

Bertie was not in good physical shape himself. He was 69, obese with chronic bronchitis and his striking energy of the past few years had all but disappeared. Terribly upset at what he saw as Franz Joseph's dishonesty, Bertie asked that all speeches be given before breakfast rather than impromptu ones as in the past. He was dreading that Wilhelm might slip in another horror that he would have to deal with.

With news of Bertie's planned visit, Wilhelm bounced back remarkably well from his recent collapse.

Bertie's visit to Berlin was a disaster from the beginning, with an almost 'keystone cop' routine. When the train rolled in at the Berlin station, Bertie and the German-hating Alexandra were up front in the queen's carriage while Wilhelm, his wife Dona and their entourage had to scuttle humiliatingly down the platform to greet them. Then, the horses drawing Alexandra and Dona's carriage in the procession refused to move and two cavalrymen were thrown off their horses. Later, when Wilhelm and Bertie arrived at the Berlin Schloss, it was to find that there was no one behind them.

Outwardly, the visit was going well. Bertie melted the unfriendly Berlin crowd by an impromptu speech in German, giving thanks to the little girl who presented him with a golden goblet of Rhine wine as Alexandra smiled serenely beside him. But Bertie was far from well. Climbing stairs left him breathless and at the first dinner, Bertie sat down on a sofa with a cigar and began to cough horribly before passing out with the cigar popping out of his fingers on to the carpet. Alexandra scrabbled to loosen his ever-tightening clothes and Bertie's doctor ran in ordering everyone out. Bertie appeared later insisting that everything was fine and had recovered and instantly lit another huge cigar.

But Wilhelm's nose was out of joint with what he saw as a snub from Bertie's entourage. On February 14th, Wilhelm stiffly escorted Bertie and Alexandra back to the Berlin station where the two men awkwardly embraced before Bertie and his entourage boarded the train again.

The two men would never see each other again.

As the Austrian army was mobilising to attack Serbia, Russia was massing soldiers on the Austrian border and Bertie was commanding his government in London to increase British shipbuilding to stay ahead of the German navy. But it was an ailing Bertie who was doing the commanding.

Bertie left Buckingham Palace after dinner on March 6, 1910 in a closed carriage on his way to Victoria Station. He waved happily to the crowds watching him walk across the crimson-carpeted platform to the royal train that would take him to Paris by the following afternoon and it would be while he was attending a play that night with a mistress that he caught a chill. From Paris he left for Biarritz where his health finally broke.

Bertie knew he was ill. The chill had turned into a severe cold, possibly bronchitis, and he wasn't able to even leave the house. He had a fever, his breathing was fast and he was coughing so badly he had to sit up all night while a nurse cared for him. As he struggled for breath, he must have known that he was fighting for his life. That he might die in a hotel room in Biarritz with only a mistress at his side must have been a terrifying scenario for him.

Luckily for Bertie, he turned the corner a week later and was well enough to send good news back to England and light up another big cigar. Seemingly without a care in the world, he continued with his rather extraordinary life filled with motor drives and dinner parties with different mistresses. Alexandra urged him to leave Biarritz and join her at Genoa on a Mediterranean cruise but he refused. It wasn't until 26th April, that he returned home looking tired and pale ready to attend a private viewing at the Royal Academy. Two days later he boarded a train on his way to Sandringham. Despite saying the breakfast on the train had upset his stomach, he walked about the grounds inspecting new planting and at dinner he was his usual self, telling stories and playing bridge.

Monday dawned wet and cold but Bertie insisted on traveling back to London in the afternoon. He wasn't in a very talkative mood but still went to his usual bridge game with a mistress, despite continuing to cough. The next night he was still coughing but now he was unable to eat, opting instead to smoke a cigar to soothe him. By Wednesday, as he struggled to put on his clothes in front of a mirror, the face staring back at him had large black circles under his eyes.

None of us need to be told now that if you have a persistent cough, smoking is the worst thing you can do, and I'm sure Bertie was told time and time again of the consequences. But it wasn't until Thursday morning when Bertie woke after another bad night's sleep, bluish in the face, that a nurse administered oxygen from a huge metal cylinder and his doctor gave him an injection of strychnine to stimulate his heart.

From Calais, Alexandra had no idea how ill Bertie was. The first ominous sign was when he was not present to meet her at Victoria Station when she arrived back in London. By the time she reached Buckingham Palace, Bertie was in a bad way. He looked grey and sunken and unable to sit upright in his chair so she issued an announcement that said the King was suffering from a severe bronchial attack. Everyone knew he was severely overweight and smoked too much but he'd only been on the throne for nine years and looking at the age of Victoria, who had been overweight for many of the last years of her life, no one expected that he wouldn't rule for many more years to come. Still everybody looked at each other in consternation.

Bertie remained stoic, if not annoyed. *'I am feeling better'* he complained that night when he refused to go to bed, still fighting for his breath. The next morning, he insisted on getting dressed, angry at the doctors for forbidding him to have a bath. By 5pm that night, he had fainted and was falling in and out of consciousness.

The last authentically recorded words of Bertie on 6th May 1910 were *'I am so glad'* spoken to his son George when he told him his horse, Witch of the Air, had won the 4:15 at Kempton Park. He then suffered a heart attack and fell into a coma. Archbishop Davidson was called at 11.30 pm and fifteen minutes later, Bertie was dead from emphysema and heart failure.

Bertie had lived on borrowed time for the past three years, spending winters abroad in the sun but still smoking continually. Now it was his son George, who would be pulled from his relaxed world and placed firmly on the throne of England, while a cousin in Russia and another in Germany watched on angrily, leaving him bewildered and alarmed.

GEORGE V

Born 1865
Reign 1910 - 1936

It was a dull, grey morning on 19th May 1910 and the streets below Windsor Castle were crowded, waiting to catch sight of the silk covered coffin drawn by black horses as it completed its journey to St George's Chapel. Every window, every rooftop, every available space was taken up by pale pinched faces. Many had not eaten or slept since the day before and 1,600 required medical attention. An iron wall of soldiers lined the processional route, many of them mounted on horses, so the crowd would have seen very little of the procession.

The crowd was eerily silent as they stood shoulder to shoulder, some waiting twelve hours in torrential rain along the processional route, but none pushed or shoved. Bareheaded, black coated, and hushed, the people quietly mourned. Thousands had already passed his body soundlessly as it lay in Westminster Hall but the streets were the last chance for a glimpse of their king who was to be buried in royal splendour. Their lives had never crossed Bertie's but still his death awoke powerful emotions of loyalty in them.

Victoria would perhaps have been shocked at the turnout for Bertie's funeral because the crowds were even bigger than at her funeral only nine years before. The number who paid their respects was estimated at around 400,000 or more and many were visibly and profoundly stricken. Perhaps she would have been surprised at that sorrow because he was the son she never had a kind word for and because their distress seemed deeper for him, despite their love for her. Bertie, the rakish, self-indulgent Prince of Wales, had somehow magically transformed himself into the beloved father of the nation.

The dazzling group not only included the immediate British royalty but the extended family of the German Emperor, cousins of the Russian dynasty, uncles and aunts who married into the royal houses of Norway, Greece, Spain, Denmark, Romania, Portugal, Bulgaria and many smaller dynasties. To the poor people on the street, it was mind-boggling. These virtual strangers were celebrities who held the absolute power of Europe and they had come to pay their solemn respects to their king, to the sound of rolling drums and brass playing Beethoven's Funeral March.

At 10 am, the glittering procession clattered out on to the streets led by his son George, now King George V, who was obviously devastated by his father's death. Following his glittering plumed head rode his cousin Wilhelm on his white horse. The kings had donned their uniforms, waxed their beards and moustaches and posed for photographs, dressed in all of the necessary embroidery, as if the past few years had never happened. Once again in the streets of London, people were cheering Wilhelm, showing they wanted the tensions in Europe to go away. And who wouldn't cheer Wilhelm on that day? He looked forceful in his spiked helmet, yet distressed as he clasped George's hand across the coffin. Family sticks together, right? At that moment, he had no idea that back in Germany, half the country was howling in outrage.

Walking behind the two cousins was a cobweb of family members. Bertie's son-in-law King Haakon VII of Norway, his brothers-in-law George I of Greece and Frederick VIII of Denmark, his nephew-in-law King Alfonso XIII of Spain. King Albert I of Belgium, King Manual II of Portugal and Tsar Ferdinand of Bulgaria all followed solemnly behind.

Behind them were 30 more of Europe's princes, including Bertie's nephew Prince Charles Edward, Duke of Saxe-Coburg, Nicky's brother Misha and their mother Dagma. Also among them was the doomed heir to the Austro-Hungarian throne, Archduke Franz Ferdinand, whose death plays an important role in the near future. Representing the United States was Theodore Roosevelt who had recently and reluctantly stepped down from the presidency. Conspicuous in his absence was Nicky who did not attend.

It was a glittering procession and it wound its way up the hill into the courtyard and slowly filled the chapel. None of the mourners could know as they took their seats that history was in the making. This was the high tide of royal power and it was about to ebb dramatically.

Unbeknownst to anyone, the lives of many of the dignitaries lined up in the carved wooden pews were poised on the threshold of an earth-shattering change. No one had any idea that the words ringing across the chapel were just a terrible premonition that all would eventually *"come to dust"*. Within a few short years, most would be divided by war and revolution, four empires would be destroyed and several royal houses would be uprooted from their kingdoms. Manual II of Portugal would be exiled from his country very soon, as well as Alfonso XIII of Spain in another decade. Even Wilhelm was oblivious to the fact that in the near future he would be forced to abdicate his throne and his cousin Nicky and his wife Alix, their tiny son and four beautiful daughters would be roused from their sleep and brutally butchered in the early hours of a cold, grey morning.

The starting gun that started the horrible events was fired at the assassination of Archduke Franz Ferdinand in June 1914 and with it, the 'Great War' began. It's somehow shocking that one careless action can destroy so much. Most would vow that there would never be another war like that one in Europe ever again. Sadly, they would be wrong.

By the size of the attendance, it's easy to understand how important Britain was in 1910. It was the largest empire in the world covering 11 million square miles and spanning almost a quarter of the surface of the planet. Britain had 400 million subjects scattered over India, Africa, Canada, Australia and even coral islands speckled across the Pacific Ocean. Britain's navy spanned the globe and her steel, textiles and cotton fuelled the abounding success of the country.

There is no doubt that George's feelings of loss for his father was incredible. But underneath all the pain came terror. His relaxed world had changed dramatically with the death of his father and as well as being heart-broken and overwhelmed with grief, his new world left him bewildered and alarmed. He found strikes and union rallies all too confusing and incomprehensible, not to mention the unrest in Europe with his cousins constantly banging heads. Above all else, George felt utterly unready to rule. The only place he felt comfortable was at home among the shooting aristocracy at Sandringham. *That* was the one place where he had some semblance of control. At home, he felt insulated from public attention and the messy world of politics.

From the start, it was clear that George was not planning to have an active role in government the way his father and grandmother had. He was well aware of the fact he did not have their drive and imagination nor did he ooze charm like his father. But while Parliament regarded George as a ruler who could not distinguish between the trivial and the important, George believed his ministers were browbeating him and taking advantage of his inexperience. So instead of turning to them for advice, to their mortification George found it easier to take his concerns to his wife May, now being called Mary. She in turn was giddily signing documents.

As tempers escalated, George saw it as the perfect opportunity for he and Mary to set off to India for the Delhi Durbar where he would present himself as the Emperor and Empress of India to Indian dignitaries.

The Delhi 'Durbar', meaning Court of Delhi, had been held three times in history at the height of the British Empire. Queen Victoria attended in 1877, Edward VII attended in 1903 and now it was George's turn to mark his succession as Emperor of India. Although not a popular occasion with the Indian people, it was an official event attended by Viceroys, Maharajas, gentry and Indian intellectuals. It was the culmination of control from the British East India Company to the Crown and George desperately wanted to be a part of it.

Although the public had little forewarning of the event, 100,000 people came to the durbar and watched as George and Mary sat under a golden dome on silver thrones in glittering coronation robes. 40,000 tents were pitched on the hills around to accommodate the throng who had come to see him and even a feature film was made to celebrate the occasion.

It was a curious thing to do, considering the spectacular extravagance of the event during a time of terrible unrest in Europe, economic problems in England and shocking famines in India where hundreds of thousands were dying of starvation. But throughout it, George seemed oblivious to it all. He smiled benignly as bejewelled Indian maharajahs came to offer respect and he wore a new crown made for the event, covered in 6,170 exquisitely cut diamonds, sapphires, emeralds and rubies with a cap weighting 965g (34.05 ounces). As for Mary, there was a magnificent tiara and a necklace presented to her by the Maharanee of Patiala on behalf of the Ladies of India. Although at the time, the design was Mary's suggestion to match her other emerald jewellery, one year later Garrard jewellers in London were commissioned to slightly alter it by making the emerald pendant detachable and adding a second detachable diamond pendant, one of nine stones cut from the Cullinan Diamond. This stone weighed 8.8 carats on its own.

From Delhi, George and Mary departed for Nepal on a two-week holiday with a local Maharajah and accompanying George were 600 elephants and 1,400 bearers. During the holiday, he personally shot 21 tigers, 8 rhinos and a bear and at the end of his visit, he seemed convinced that the trip had made a big difference. He was however a little shocked and taken back when Maharajah Sayajirao III left his presence with only a simple bow then turned his back on them when leaving.

It took a while for England to get the hang of George with his melancholy stare and the white gardenia constantly in his buttonhole. He was unflashy, forever wearing old-fashioned clothes but from what they could see, he had old-fashioned values that were refreshingly different from his father's values.

While George was settling in, stories filtering in from Russia became increasingly unnerving. In 1912, tsarist soldiers had shot dead 500 striking miners and wounded hundreds of others at the goldfields in Siberia where conditions had been horrendous. Not only was the accident rate 700 per 1,000 workers, men worked fifteen to sixteen hour days and the food that was brought in from the outside was often rotten or insufficient. Not surprising, the strikers were demanding eight-hour days and a 30% wage increase with an improvement in food supplies and Russia was struggling to keep the miners under control. And then there was Rasputin.

Alix was trusting Rasputin more and more and had drawn him into the heart of the family, strangely even allowing him to watch her daughters get ready for bed. She was asking for his advice more often and even told Nicky to comb his hair with Rasputin's comb before making any difficult decisions. Secure in the royal family's favour, Rasputin exploited his position. Scandalous rumours began to mushroom about his appetite for sex and booze and at one time, when he started a drunken brawl at a Moscow restaurant, he took out his penis, laid it on the table and said he could do what he liked with the 'old girl'. Nicky and Alix were repeatedly warned about him but they simply refused to listen. By then, they were ignoring everything they didn't want to hear. They were sleepwalking towards revolution.

May 1913 was a happy time for Wilhelm. It was the wedding of his youngest child and only daughter, Victoria Luise, and it was meant to be a happy solution to the old dispute over Prussia's swallowing up of Hanover in 1866. Victoria was marrying the wealthy heir, Prince Ernest August Duke of Cumberland, both Alexandra and Dagma's nephew, and the grandson of Queen Victoria's cousin, the King of Hanover. It was set for 24th May, his beloved grandmother's birthday, and it was being hailed in the press as the end of the rift between the House of Hanover and the House of Hohenzollern and a union akin to *Romeo and Juliet,* but with a happier ending. It also meant Wilhelm could show off to his two cousins, Nicky and George, who had both surprisingly agreed to attend the celebration in Berlin.

On that day, George, Wilhelm and Nicky, the three cousins who ruled half of the world's population, stood side by side staring up at the sky as a Zeppelin sailed majestically overhead. Unbeknownst to them as they watched, the future of the Royal families loomed silently on the horizon and Europe was staggering into a bloody conflict. The world was poised at the starting gate of a tragedy full of uncertainty and betrayal, marking the day their worlds, full of royal pomp and ceremony, would begin to unravel.

Wilhelm, overdressed in one of his grand uniforms, was in his element hosting the extravagant event. Using the reception as his own personal launch pad for a diplomatic event, he was still torn between delight at the attention given him and jealousy of his two cousins' friendship, although if he'd looked closer, he would have seen a feigned amount of camaraderie between the men when they were together. With all of his insecurities raging inside him, he had made it clear to George that he was *not* welcome at the train station when he went to meet Nicky and he was equally determined that his two cousins would *not* be left alone together just in case they whispered about him behind his back.

The line had been drawn in the sand but it was only a matter of time until someone stepped over it.

If you were a fly on the wall at the beautiful ceremony, you could have been forgiven for thinking it was like watching a charade. There was a pretence that they were all a loving family but somehow the atmosphere crackled with tension and everything seemed a little off kilter. If you had looked around, you would have seen nervous glances from 57-year-old Prince Louis of Battenberg, a British citizen since he was 14 years old and married to Alix's elder sister, Princess Victoria of Hesse. He was First Sea Lord in the British Navy but still a German prince and as such there had been many suspicious whispers regarding his loyalty if tension in Europe increased.

On the other side of the room, you would have seen Wilhelm talking earnestly to Nicky who, as usual, was doing nothing but listening. No doubt he would have been telling Nicky that Russia should never fight Germany and perhaps he would even have asked Nicky what he would do if hostilities began. The reality was Nicky wanted to be away from the whole event and back with Alix and his own family in Russia. He would have preferred to be hunting for mushrooms on the grounds of Tsarskoye Selo and looking after his little Alexei who had not yet recovered from a bleeding episode the previous winter. You would have seen all six of Wilhelm's tall sons gathered around the drinks table since none of them were averse to getting drunk on any occasion. Talking to George would have been his youngest sister Beatrice and her three handsome boys; two of whom were afflicted with haemophilia and would never marry. Perhaps you would have noticed that everyone was smiling a little too brightly as they danced, glancing just a little nervously around the room. It was almost as if the air fizzed with the unspoken word... war. As family members finally left for home, Wilhelm was sure his cousins, who had actually restrained themselves from talking politics, had been plotting against him all the time at the wedding.

After that beautiful spring day in Berlin, the three cousins would never meet again. Not too far in the future, the magnificent cavalrymen who had led the happy parade down the streets of Berlin would swap their dancing horses and feather hats for the mud and blood in the trenches and no one would be cheering.

One year later in Germany, talk of war just wouldn't go away. Russia and Germany were once again trading threats and Russian attempts to lure Britain into an alliance continued to fail. France and Russia were preparing for a decisive struggle with Germany and Austria had voiced their intention to strike at the first opportunity. Things were hurtling downhill fast and there didn't seem any way to put a stop to it. Woodrow Wilson, the current president of The United States, was certainly not stupid. He could see where Europe was headed and his primary objective was to keep America out of the war that was brewing.

On 27th June 1914, an American special convoy, which had come to Europe to try to broker a pact between the United States, Germany and Britain to prevent a major war, met with Sir Edward Grey in London. His thoughts were that Germany would strike quickly when she had the opportunity but still, in the back of his mind, he couldn't quite believe that the Kaiser himself wanted war, despite his military forces seemingly prepared for it at any time.

The next day, everyone's nightmare became a reality. And once again, Austria was at the heart of it all.

The heir to the Austrian empire Archduke Franz Ferdinand and his wife Sophie were visiting Sarajevo, the capital of the Austro-Hungarian province when a grenade was thrown at their car. The bomb detonated behind them, hurting the occupants of the following car, but both Franz and his wife were safe. They were badly shaken by the time they arrived at the Governor's residence but after a short rest, the couple insisted on seeing all those who had been injured by the bomb at the local hospital.

The decision to visit the hospital is one of those 'if only' situations in history. 'If only' they had continued on with their planned itinerary, they would not have been waylaid en route to the hospital. 'If only' the drivers had been informed that the itinerary had changed, they would not have had to back the car down the street onto a side street where Gavrilo Princip, aged 19 at the time and a member of an organisation called the Black Hand, was sitting at a nearby café.

I think it's pretty safe to say that most Serbs still had vivid memories of being called *a cancer undermining their empire* by the Austrians in 1908 when they had seized Bosnia. And seeing Archduke Franz Ferdinand sitting in one of the stalled cars in front of him would have made Princip sit up and taken notice. It only took a few seconds for him to come to a fateful decision. He reached into his pocket for the pistol given to him by a Serbian Army Colonel and walked calmly across the street, only coming to a stop when he saw the royal couple through the window.

Princip's first shot hit Sophie in the abdomen and his next hit Franz Ferdinand in the neck. Franz, still alive and bleeding profusely, leaned over his crying wife and uttered his dying words, *'Don't die darling, live for our children'* before sagging down unconscious. Despite several doctors' frantic efforts, Sophie died from internal bleeding and Franz died shortly after being carried into the Town Hall.

Wilhelm was at the Kiel Regatta racing yachts when he heard the terrible news. He was entertaining a squadron of British battle cruisers and the town was full of fraternising German and British officers. When he heard that his closest friend Franz Ferdinand had been murdered, he was visibly shocked and distressed.

Nicky was on his annual Baltic summer cruise and 9-year-old Alexei had fallen while jumping from a ladder and twisted his ankle. He was screaming with pain and his mother was white with worry. They also had just heard that a madwoman had stabbed Rasputin and everyone on the boat, except Alix and Nicky, was hoping that he would die. With everything else going on around them, news of Franz Ferdinand's assassination barely registered with Nicky and his family.

George was preoccupied as well. He had been having bitter arguments over the fate of Protestants in six northern counties in Ireland, which had threatened to fight if they were separated from Britain. Guns had been smuggled into the north and George was obsessed with what might happen if his army had to fire on British citizens.

Although everyone was shocked at the news, no one expected the assassination to escalate to all-out war. Certainly initially, there was rage and sympathy for Austria but everyone expected it to blow over. Even if the murder could be traced back to Serbia, the 19-year-old assassin had admitted he had killed Franz Ferdinand because he was an enemy of the Southern Slavs.

The Austrian government, however, saw things differently. To them it was an opportunity not to be missed. Serbia had doubled in size after the Balkan wars and was constantly proclaiming itself leader of the Southern Slavs, which meant it was a threat to the Hapsburg Empire. Austria had asked Germany to help them crush Serbia on three separate occasions since 1913 and Wilhelm had refused every single time. With this new turn of events however, the Austrian army was quite enthusiastic for war, as were most of the German officers.

A week after the assassination, the Austrian ambassador came to Wilhelm with a confidential letter from Emperor Franz Joseph of Austria, requesting their support to launch a quick war to punish Serbia while Europe was on its summer holidays. Germany's only role was to make sure no other powers would feel tempted to get involved. It would be all over before anyone knew about it, they assured him.

Give Wilhelm his due: he hesitated. Even if it *was* for only a moment. Then he made a fateful decision. He told the ambassador that they could rely on German's full support if Austria acted fast.

His decision must have come from a deep sense that Germany was trapped and had nowhere else to go to avenge his friend's death. And like the army, he was obsessing about Russia as a future threat. He would have been well aware of the risk he was taking, even if the war was quick and localised. He knew that Russia was not ready for war and would think twice about it.

Convinced that the mere *threat* of war would be enough, Wilhelm set off the next day for his annual yachting trip along the Norwegian coast. The little boy with the damaged arm, who was put in a metal cage and stretched as a small child to strengthen his back, was taking his own personal revenge.

Two weeks went by with the three cousins totally unaware that Austria was desperately trying to find evidence to incriminate Serbia in the assassination. At midnight on 19th July, the matter was taken out of their hands. The Austrians had delivered their ultimatum and the ferocity of the demand stunned Europe. Austrian officers were to be allowed to enter Serbia to conduct their own investigation, all Serb nationalist societies were to be disbanded and all Serbian military officers, regarded as anti-Austrian, were to be dismissed. The Serbs had 48 hours to respond.

The specific demands made Russia sit up and take notice. With Russia and Serbia sharing borders, this new ultimatum meant that war against

Russia could be imminent. The Russian Foreign Minister, Sergie Sazonov, was even sure the Germans were the ones stirring the pot. They were the ones who were encouraging Austria because it was Germany who wanted to dominate the continent. Convinced that if Russia did not make a stand, she would be laughed at by other powers, he called a meeting of Russian Council Ministers to discuss possible action. After the last Japanese humiliation, another one would be too much to bear. With his ministers backing, Sazonov tried to head off the conflict.

There was nothing threatening in the wording of his letter. He politely asked the Austrians to extend the deadline and recommended the Serbs to accept as many Austrian demands as they could. As an afterthought, he suggested everything be adjudicated on neutral grounds in The Hague. Then he appealed to the German Foreign Office to mediate, sure in the knowledge that Germany was Austria's backup.

His reply from the German ambassador was not what he expected at all. The ambassador insisted that Germany knew nothing about the ultimatum and that this conflict was between Serbia and Austria and had nothing to do with Germany. The Austrians were simply teaching Serbia a lesson and if Russia wished to intervene, they should negotiate with Austria directly and not through Germany.

Nicky dreaded a conflict and he was sure that Wilhelm did as well. While the countdown ticked on, he tried to continue life as usual. He played tennis, canoed with his daughters and had tea with relatives. But inside, he was sick with worry.

When Wilhelm returned on 27th July, he was shaken to discover that Austria had ordered a partial mobilisation of its army before Serbia had even had time to reply to the ultimatum. Not just that, but his army chiefs were arguing over what they would do next. Most of them were convinced it was time to fight and if they did, Germany would have two aggressors simultaneously, France and Russia. Their plan was to knock out France early then wheel around and attack Russia, who was known to be slow to mobilise its huge army.

Wilhelm knew the plan would have devastating consequences. Firstly, regardless of whether France was even involved, it would be invaded. The same went for the neutral states of Luxembourg and Belgium, who were en route to France. Secondly, the plan meant Germany would have to mobilise before anyone else did and rush in to eliminate France. All Wilhelm could hope for was that Serbia backed down.

He didn't have to wait long. The Serb's reply to the ultimatum came the next day. It was breathtakingly humble and had acceded to everything the Austrians could reasonably have asked. Everyone, including Wilhelm, breathed a sigh of relief.

But not for long.

On a beautiful sunny August bank holiday weekend in England, the world began to fall apart. On August 1st, while the German ambassador, Friedrich Pourtales, was having lunch with the British ambassador George Buchanan in St Petersburg, explaining to him that the Germans assumed the Russians would not want to get involved, news from the Austrian government arrived. Austria had rejected the Serb reply to the ultimatum and they refused Sazonov's requests for mediation. War was on.

With Serbia agreeing to everything that Austria demanded, their answer could only mean that they meant to engage in a war all along. It also meant that Austria would expect the backing of Germany in their declaration of outright war on Serbia, which in turn would flow down to war on Russia who supported Serbia.

There was nothing that Nicky could do. He had to protect his country and the only way to do that was to order the partial mobilisation of Russian troops along his borders. The plan was to move Russian soldiers to the Austrian frontier while carefully keeping them away from the German borders so as not to give offence to the over-excitable Wilhelm.

George had been so preoccupied with the escalating civil war in Ireland due to the introduction of Home Rule two years before, he had not realised they were on the brink of war in Europe. As he was telling his wife that he'd have to cancel his annual trip to Goodwood Races and was regretting the loss of his weekend sailing at Cowes, Sir Edward Grey was telling Parliament that the minute the conflict spread beyond Austria and Serbia, it would become the greatest catastrophe that had ever befallen Europe. He did not need to tell Parliament that he now believed that Britain had an obligation to come to France's aid.

Initially sympathetic to making Serbia pay for its role in the assassination, Sir Edward Grey was now determined to prevent the war. He hoped, was actually convinced, that Berlin's intentions were honourable and they had no wish either to support a war. He endorsed the request for the matter to go to The Hague.

Once again, the Austrians rejected the offer. Then they bombed Belgrade.

George made one last attempt to close down the war. Dressed in a brown dressing gown over a nightshirt, he read a telegram from Berlin stating that despite Wilhelm's readiness to mediate, Russia had mobilised. He forwarded the German message on to Nicky and added: *'I cannot help thinking that some misunderstanding has produced this deadlock. I am most anxious not to miss any possibility of avoiding the terrible calamity, which at present threatens the whole world. I therefore make a personal appeal to you, my dear Nicky, to remove the misapprehension, which I feel must have occurred, and to leave still open grounds for negotiation and possible peace. If you think I can in any way contribute to that all-important purpose, I will do everything in my power to assist in reopening the interrupted conversations between the Powers concerned.'*

But Nicky was a hard man to get hold of in his isolated home outside St Petersburg. By the time the British ambassador had managed to deliver the message, war had already been declared on Russia and Wilhelm was no longer answering telegrams.

As war seemed unstoppable, Nicky and Wilhelm exchanged telegrams, each appealing to the other to stop the conflict. Nicky still hoped that if Germany pulled its support from Austria, war could be stopped. He also sent a letter to George asking for support from Britain if the Russians found themselves at war and assured George he was doing everything he could to avoid it. Wilhelm telegrammed Nicky back and assured him that Germany was doing its best to try to bring about an agreement.

What Wilhelm didn't know was that while he was reassuring his Russian cousin, his Foreign Office had advised the Austrians to go to war.

Most of the Wilhelm's army chiefs were keen to go to the next level and prepare for mobilisation but Wilhelm argued hotly against it. He'd received a message telling him that Britain would try to keep out of the conflict but that same afternoon, the foreign office received a telegram from Sir Edward Grey stating that if Germany and France became involved in the war, Britain would not be able to remain aloof.

It was far from being a threat but coming straight after news that the

Russians were mobilising, the foreign minister was convinced that the conflict was escalating too fast. He sent three desperate telegrams to Vienna asking the Austrian army to stop at Belgrade. Unbeknownst to him, the German Chief of Staff, Helmuth Moltke, had already telegrammed the Austrian Chief of Staff telling him to go to full mobilisation. By then it was too late for the German Chancellor, Bethmann-Hollweg, to change the course of history.

It was a horrible instance of the confusion in the German government. In a final effort to head off British involvement, Bethmann-Hollweg asked the British to remain neutral and if they did, the Germans would not invade Holland and while perhaps invading France, the Germans wouldn't take any British territories.

It was almost as if Germany had admitted that they were going to invade France.

Meanwhile, still under the illusion that he could mediate between Russia and Austria and that the Austrians would stop at Belgrade, Wilhelm sent another telegram to Nicky, begging him to remain a spectator.

Nicky cabled back asking for clarification but when he didn't receive an answer, he sent another one stating that he had allowed partial mobilisation to go ahead. He did, however, promise that Russian troops would not take the offensive as long as talks with Austria continued.

As you can imagine, when Wilhelm got the message, he took it badly. Very badly. He flew into a ferocious tantrum. In a panic, he assumed that Russia was ahead of him and *that* he would never stand for. What he should have realised, if he was thinking clearly, was that Russia, like the Austrians, took weeks to get their troops ready. Nicky's threat of mobilisation was just a warning that they *might* do something. Nicky's idea of mobilisation meant that they would march up and down their borders waving their guns in the air indefinitely. But when Germany said *'mobilisation'*, they actually meant *'war'*.

That evening, two days after the telegram had arrived, Wilhelm was shown the telegram of Grey's warning that if France became involved, Britain would as well. Once again, he exploded. Everyone was ganging up on him. Where was George's promise of neutrality? Where was Nicky's promise of being a spectator? For Wilhelm, Grey's warning and Russia's mobilisation brought back old anxieties.

But even then, Wilhelm hesitated. It was his chancellor who insisted that war should be declared even if Russia agreed to negotiate. And it was Wilhelm's war minister who pressed him to order their own ultimatum to Russia to halt her mobilisation within twelve hours ... or else.

The next day, Nicky sent one last telegram pleading with Wilhelm to negotiate. But it was too late.

Wilhelm actually *did* draft another telegram suggesting talks may take place if Russia halted its mobilisation. The problem was that it was not sent until late that evening. By then the German ambassador in Russia had already tearfully delivered the German declaration of war to the Russian ambassador Sazonov.

When Nicky heard the news, he turned pale and Alix began to weep, which set all the daughters crying as well. Later that night, when Wilhelm's delayed telegram had arrived, Nicky saw it as duplicity. No one was aware that in the future, this lack of understanding would explode on the battlefields of the First World War.

To his last breath, Wilhelm would always insist that Nicky had wanted war all along. But George, Nicky and Alix always believed that it was Wilhelm who was responsible for the war. And that was almost true. When it came down to it, he just couldn't stop it. Forces beyond his power had begun to dictate the direction his country was going. For 26 years, he had built a powerful army, conscious of its own strength. He had initiated a shipbuilding program and that had created bitter hostility with Britain where there had been none before. Virtually every decision he made was a result of vulnerability and a craving to look powerful and strong.

Each of the cousins had duties on 4th August 1914 when Britain declared war on Germany. George and Mary went for a short drive down the Mall to Trafalgar Square where huge crowds greeted them uproariously. To quieten the crowds, they had to show themselves three times on their balcony.

At the same time, Nicky appeared on the balcony of the Winter Palace and the vast crowd fell to their knees. The barricades had disappeared and the revolutionaries had melted away. The country had not been so vibrantly alive and united since Napoleon's invasion in 1812.

In Germany, the crowds cheered Wilhelm at the Brandenburg Gate. In a rush of enthusiasm, the Reichstag voted to give its power to the council of German princes, effectively allowing Wilhelm and the army free rein.

How Britain came to fight alongside Russia and against Germany is one of the great mysteries of the 20th century. Because of blood connections, they had been traditional allies, allies that shared many historical events, not to mention family ties, for over two hundred years. But in one month, between the assassination of Franz Joseph and the outbreak of World War 1, control had gradually slipped out of the fingers of Wilhelm, Nicky and George. What happened was the beginning of a terrible family tragedy that dragged the world into an abyss. Their friendships, and above all, their poisonous rivalries would play a key role in the realignment of Europe.

While London united and was filled to the bursting point with soldiers, the extended royal family of Europe was anything but united. In Russia, Alix was cut off from her sisters and her brother. George and Nicky's cousin, Ernest of Cumberland who had married Wilhelm's daughter Victoria, took the German side with his father-in-law. So did Charles Edward, the British cousin who had inherited the dukedom of Saxe-Coburg-Gotha after Affie's death, by taking a commission in the German army. The German-born Louis of Battenberg, but British citizen for many decades, was forced to resign his position as Admiral in the British navy due to xenophobia from the tabloid press, the clubs and the public. There had been accusations that he was sending secret signals to German ships and other allegations of allegiance to the Germans and he was being blamed for every ship sunk and every man drowned. No one had forgotten that his wife was the daughter of the Grand Duke of Hesse and Rhine, and no one had forgotten that his wife's sister had once caught the eye of her elder cousin Kaiser Wilhelm who had asked her to marry him. Both were Queen Victoria's granddaughters. It was Louis Battenberg, along with all of George's German relations, who lost his peerage and title, and it was Louis who was forced to change his name to the more English name of Mountbatten and retire to the Isle of Wight. It was also Louis whose eldest daughter Alice had married Prince Andrew of Greece and Denmark and who had five children, the youngest being a son by the name of Phillip who would meet, fall in love and marry George's eldest granddaughter, Elizabeth, in the future.

Of the 120 of Queen Victoria's descendants alive in 1914, 42 were living in enemy countries and 11 would fight against Britain including Alix's own brother. Four years later, more than 10 million people would die and Victoria's extended family would be ripped apart.

England had not forgotten the last cousin's war, the War of the Roses. They had not forgotten the cruel battles, the harvest of heads that followed and they had certainly not forgotten the sight of wounded and defeated soldiers returning from the battlefields. There was nothing noble about those battles. Nothing like the romantic ballads depicting quixotic knights. During the last cousin's war, heads were cleaved open by battle-axes and bellies were ripped open by swords. Men swinging great swords, war axes and pikes defended themselves against family members who only a decade before had been regarded as friends. It was a savage mess of brutish men killing each other for power. This time it would be more civilised. This time they would use guns and cannons and trench warfare as they scrambled in the mud over barbed wire towards enemy lines in an attempt to thrust a bayonet into the armpit or chest of the enemy. But the meadows would still be littered with corpses and the rivers would still run red as the snow fell softly on everything like frozen tears. Men would still hack and stab at each other. This time, instead of white and red roses, there would be blood-red poppies bobbing their heads knowingly.

Sometimes we learn. Sometimes we don't.

George and Mary surprised Britain by throwing themselves into the war effort. George renounced the theatre, closed Balmoral and turned the gardens at Frogmore into a potato field. He turned the lights off at Buckingham Palace, used paper napkins to save on washing, ate boiled fowl instead of lamb and took a pledge not to drink alcohol for the duration of the war. The gestures allowed him to hand back £100,000 to the Treasury.

But while he made a positive difference with some of his actions, his influence in other areas had tragic affects. His worst mistake was to support General Haig, his Chief of the General Staff, and General Robertson who were men committed to trench warfare. Their belief that conscripted soldiers could do little else than stand in a line and walk forward meant hundreds of thousands of men would climb over the top of their trenches and walk to their deaths in the Somme and at Passchendaele through 1916 and 1917. At Passchendaele alone, there were between 240,000 and 260,000 British casualties and barely a foot of territory was won to justify it. They lived in holes in the ground. They were cold, wet and hungry as bombs, artillery, gas and air missiles fell around them with nothing in front of them except barbed wire and machine guns. And they barely survived in a world of pain, mentally unprepared to face the gas attacks, the extensive trenches with their unsanitary conditions and diseases and the shrapnel that blew bodies, faces and limbs apart. The very nature of trench warfare (where soldiers could and did look over the edge of the trench) was conducive to massive, disfiguring facial injuries. The stress sent many mad. Literally. Haig's only excuse for failure was that he didn't have enough men.

Along with these brave soldiers, were the equally brave nurses who offered their unbelievable services. Some were very close to the front. They were cold. They were wet. They were exhausted. And they knew fear. They could hear the guns rumbling not very far away and sometimes they worked for days without sleep because the patient loads were staggering. Though they were trained nurses, the horrific wounds to which they tended were unlike anything they had ever experienced in their training. They worked with patients suffering from exposure to mustard gas, fire burns, shrapnel wounds and the mangled tearing of flesh associated with them. They were grateful that Haig did not have enough men. The ones he already had were suffering enough as it was.

The German invasion of Belgium produced monstrous tales of women raped, children's hands cut off, priests butchered and even a Canadian soldier crucified by German troops. Wilhelm, who had only wanted his British relatives to love him, was now hated more than he could ever have imagined. Propaganda posters showed him hunched over the dead, mutilated bodies of women and children or goose-stepping in front of burning libraries.

Wilhelm's war effort was less than dramatic. Within days of the war's beginning, he joined the army at military headquarters as his grandfather had before him, then promptly collapsed and took to his bed. He had spoken of leading his men into battle but barely a week into the war, he told the German General of Staff that the war was their responsibility, not his.

Once again, he became unpredictable. One moment, he was demanding that his soldiers should take no prisoners and then the next, he was plunged into a deep depression, knocking back sleeping pills to help him sleep. He pinned on medals and shook hands and found pointless projects to keep him occupied. The generals kept him close because they needed him to sign papers. But that was all. The Austrian foreign minister even called him *"a prisoner of his generals"*. Eventually, they talked him into submarine warfare against neutral shipping, which only served to bring America into the war. For a man who had been so sure of his own strength in battle, he was totally out of his depth.

Like Wilhelm and George, Nicky became a viewer. He was a pinner of medals as well and a visitor to munitions factories and hospitals, sometimes seeing 3,000 people a day. Like Wilhelm, he had fantasied over leading his army and like Wilhelm, he installed himself in the artificial office of Russian army headquarters, packed with aristocrats with whom he had once gotten drunk with in his youth and with whom he had run naked with in the snow before marrying Alix. There he thought he was in the thick of things. He took long walks, ate hearty lunches, and lingered over conversations while smoking cigars and organised boat races. While he charmed visitors, men were dying by the hundreds of thousands on the battlefields.

Within three months, the Russian war effort was a disaster. Vast sums of money were being poured into the army but war planning was a dismal failure. Before long, there was a supply crisis with no provision being made for winter uniforms, guns or boots. Ammunition began to run out by 1915 and soldiers were being told to limit themselves to ten bullets a day. Losses were huge and pointless. At one time, 1,800 new recruits arrived at the front without a single rifle to hand over to them. Instead, they were handed wooden replicas. They had to wait for casualties and deaths to receive a real gun. By then, 1,600 of the initial 1,800 were dead. Nicky's sister, a nurse on the Austrian front, said that Russian soldiers were sent to meet German machine guns with sticks in their hands. There were no medical supplies and generals came to her begging that she ask Nicky for reinforcements. Most of the soldiers shivered in the trenches without warm clothes or boots, clutching their wooden guns as the sub-zero winter months slowly approached.

As the losses mounted, morale collapsed and the nine million men who were called up in the first year of the war alone were asking themselves why they were there at all.

Like Wilhelm, Nicky could have filled a role as a civilian leader, caring for the wounded and refugees but like Wilhelm, he had no idea where to start. He was in thrall of the romance of the army but overwhelmed when it came to actually doing anything worthwhile.

By the end of the war, the three men were showing the effects of the war. For Wilhelm, it had been too much from the very start and by 1916, he was a broken man, swinging from violent and unpredictable rages to depressed and lethargic isolations. His attempt to show the world that he was a consistent leader had been destroyed. Two of his major generals had threatened to resign if he didn't rid Germany of its chancellor and as usual, Wilhelm threw a wobbler. The chancellor resigned anyway and his generals replaced him with someone *they* wanted, as well as taking away Wilhelm's title of 'Supreme Warlord' and giving it to Hindenburg. Resolutely, he clung onto his shaky dictatorship and they began to call him a 'Shadow Emperor.'

As millions of people died in the trenches, Wilhelm's depression worsened, not from remorse, but because of his declining popularity. Through the hot days of July 1916, he continued to pin medals on his troops and scrambled from front to front, egging his men onto greater atrocities.

As for George, he was looking ten years older than his age. His beard had gone completely white and his face was lined and haggard. But his dogged unsmiling face appeared every year on a gruelling visit to the Western Front where he visited ammo depots, railway depots and hospitals. The carnage absolutely overwhelmed him. Then in October 1915, he had an accident where the horse he was riding got frightened and reared up, falling on him. It was an accident he would never fully recover from and the pain would only make him grumpier.

Through the late months of 1916, everyone in Russia was trying to alert Nicky to the dangers around him and the malign influence of Rasputin. Of course, and as always, he and Alix refused to listen.

On 17th December, it was finally out of their hands. Rasputin was murdered. The assassins were Prince Felix Yusupov, a 29-year-old bisexual cross-dresser and Oxford graduate, who was the son of the richest woman in Russia, and one of Nicky's cousins who was a right-wing anti-Semitic monarchist. The plan was to save the monarchy by killing Rasputin, then put Alix into a mental institution.

One freezing night as snow drifted softy over the quiet city, they lured Rasputin to a party where they laced a cake with cyanide and poisoned his glass of Madeira. When that failed to kill him, they shot him in the back.

When he amazingly staggered up again, they panicked and fired an entire gun barrel into him, wrapped him in chains and then threw him into the Neva River.

Russia had become a seething hub of anger. It was the third year of war and everyone was thoroughly sick and tired of it. Millions had died on the battlefields and the civilian population of Russia and Germany were suffering terrible shortages. Neither food nor fuel was arriving and it brought industry to a standstill. In January, 150,000 people hunger-marched as temperatures plunged to minus thirty-five degrees. Some food prices had more than quadrupled and no one could afford the basic necessities anymore.

If things weren't bad enough, on 8th March an angry mob of women marched determinedly demanding food and crowds of people poured into the streets from their homes to support them. At army headquarters, Nicky had his mind on other things. His children had come down with measles and all he could do was think about them, especially his sickly son Alexei. It seemed easier to just overlook it all and say the riots were minor.

Hindsight is a wonderful thing and I'm sure if Nicky had the time over again, he would have paid attention to what his people were asking and not swept the matter under the carpet. The next day, soldiers shot dead 200 people across the capital and the crowds grew even angrier. Almost at the same time, the Petrograd garrison mutinied and several units shot their own commanding officers. The crowds were baying for his blood and his voluntary abdication looked to be the only solution to stabilise the situation. What the crowd wanted, he was told, was a soviet. A union.

Nicky looked vacant and went for his usual afternoon walk, returning for tea at the usual time. This time however, when he returned, he was a different man. He was unnervingly calm, as if he had come to a difficult decision, but was happy with the outcome. The next day he left for St Petersburg where he signed the document of abdication on the evening of 15th March on behalf of himself and his son Alexei, leaving his younger brother Grand Duke Peter, or Misha as he called him, as the heir. Several hours later, when Misha saw the angry crowds that had gathered, he stepped down as well. Throughout Russia, bells rang, people sang and flags waved as statues and insignias were torn down.

It was a rather ignominious end for a dynasty that had lasted 304 years but it was not going to be a revolution America-style where a highly literate and fairly well-to-do population was separating from the Mother Country. This was an impoverished country with enormous peasantry and a growing minority of poor industrial workers and most of Western Europe viewed them as an undeveloped and backward country run by a corrupt government.

In France and Britain, the abdication was greeted with relief. A democratic Russia was less likely to make a deal with Germany and even the United States, who had just entered the war, enthusiastically recognised the new government.

That same day, soldiers surrounded the imperial palace and Nicky and his family were put under house arrest. Even then Nicky still believed it was only temporary. The plan, he was told, was to get the family to the Finnish border and then the coast, only a few hours away, then send them off to England on a British steamer.

Nicky should have read the writing on the wall. If he had, he would have known that something wasn't quite right. When he arrived back home at Tsarskoe Selo, there were no soldiers standing to attention anymore. When he tried to go for a walk, six soldiers surrounded him and prodded him with their rifles while he stood quiet and expressionless. Later that night, three armoured cars of excited soldiers arrived to take Nicky and his family to St Peter and Paul Fortress after first exhuming and burning Rasputin's body.

Nicky spent his days cutting wood, gardening, reading and wandering the woods with stoic calmness and greeted his new life with a kind of relief. He'd never wanted to be tsar in the first place. This new life suited him much better where he could view his children splashing happily in the lake and watch silent films with his son Alexei. What he didn't know was that beyond Tsarskoe Selo, Russian soldiers were mutinying at an alarming rate. By 3rd July those same soldiers had taken to the streets of Petrograd where the provisional government struggled to stay in control and angry rumours abounded that the Romanovs were planning to escape the country and leave their people to their own dismal futures.

The rumours had some substance. In fact, only weeks before, Nicky's ministers had pleaded a second time for England to grant asylum to the tsar and his family. King George was his first cousin after all and they had once been very close.

It all came at a very inconvenient time for George who was being super sensitive to insinuations that his family might not be as entirely loyal to Britain as he intimated. He had a German sounding name and all of his ancestors, not to mention the long list of his family living in Europe, were German. When the second request for the Romanovs to be granted asylum arrived, George was deep in the process of changing his foreign sounding name from Saxe-Coburg-Gotha to the entirely made up name of Windsor. The new name sounded British and solid and was the name of a residence that had been given to his three-quarters-German grandmother, Queen Victoria, by her German husband Albert, the Prince of Coburg. Choosing the new surname of Windsor was George's attempt to show Britain that the worrying link between the European royalty and Britain was no longer tolerated. What he was actually doing was stepping away from the fact that his father was Kaiser Wilhelm's uncle, his mother was Nicky's aunt and that all three men, Wilhelm and Nicky and George, were all first cousins.

You can understand why George panicked when he received the request. He knew only too well that harbouring his Russian cousin in Britain was not going to make him popular with his people and he didn't want to do anything to alienate them at this stage, especially with the unstable Russians. The subject was a virtual hot potato that George did not want to handle despite the fact that he had always put family ahead of everything, much like his grandmother. George knew that if he allowed Nicky and his family to come to Britain, he might very well come under the same pressure that Nicky was under with revolutionaries. He had learnt the hard way that being a constitutional king was only a title and there was no way he was going to let his association with the Romanov autocrats knock him off balance. He had taken great pains to build his reputation while Nicky had done the exact opposite. The truth was George was very sensitive about the monarchy. He was very aware that his most important job as a royal was to survive. Isn't that exactly what his ancestors had done?

And that's what he did. The British ambassador was told to inform Russia that it was impossible for the Romanovs to come to Britain. The South of France was suggested as a better retreat. When Nicky heard the reply from George, there was no bitterness and no words of reproach.

A week after the request was rejected, H.G. Wells wrote to *The Times* stating that Britain should rid itself of *"the ancient trappings of throne and sceptre"* and described George's court as *"alien and uninspiring"*. George's reply was uncharacteristically witty. *"I may be uninspiring but I'll be damned if I'm an alien."*

As George was putting his signature on the document that would change his foreign sounding name forever, Nicky was being patient and polite to his captors while Wilhelm was having a nervous breakdown in Germany. His title of Supreme Warlord had been taken off him and Hindenburg had replaced him as the absolute leader. Wilhelm had become just as essential as a flimsy fig leaf.

George's refusal of sanctuary meant that Nicky and his family actually *did* have to leave and they were packed up and ready to move to Tobolsk in Siberia, appropriate when you think of the thousands of enemies who had been transferred to the barren wasteland by the Romanovs over the past century. By then, Nicky and his family were living in the governor's mansion, nowhere near as comfortable as their Imperial palace, but they had a household of maids and chefs at their disposal and there was room to exercise where everyone was respectful.

November 1917 was a confusing month for Nicky. The Bolshevik victory hardly registered with Nicky until Lenin began peace talks with Germany. As Nicky watched Germany snatch a million miles of Russian territory that contained virtually all of Russia's assets of coal and oil and half of her industry along with a third of her population, he must have been wondering why he had been forced to abdicate at all.

November also marked the month that his captivity became noticeably harsher. Luxuries disappeared and soldiers became unfriendly while windows were painted over so that the family could not look out. They were subjected to regular searches of their belongings, they were not permitted access to their luggage and attempts were made to forcibly remove Alix's and her daughter's gold bracelets from their wrists. They were required to ring a bell every time they wished to use the bathroom and Alix and the girls were even escorted there by guards who had graffitied drawings on the walls of them all having sex with Rasputin. Rations were mostly tea and black bread but by then, Alix could not have cared less. She was barely able to walk without help and she spent days in bed while the girls did whatever they could to keep going. Recently, it is believed that the guards sexually abused the women and the shrieks that were heard at night tend to confirm this. Anything more horrible cannot be imagined.

Five months later, everything changed again.

As the light faded on the evening of 29th April 1918, a train halted in the remote railway station of Lyubinskaya on the Trans-Siberian railway line. There was nothing outwardly remarkable about the first-class railway carriage except the presence of a heavily armed guard outside the door. Sitting quietly inside was Nicky and Alix, their four pale daughters dressed in white lace and their hair tied back with satin ribbons and a sickly Alexei dressed in a sailor suit, leaning on his father.

The engine started, and the train took a decisive direction. At that moment, all lingering hope inside Special Train Number 8 would have evaporated. The train was lumbering not towards a trial in Moscow or foreign exile, as they had been led to believe, but to the bleak Urals, specifically Ekaterinburg, the historic hub of Russia's old penal system. Unbeknownst to them, they were making their final journey. In just 78 days, 100 years ago, they would be facing a firing squad.

Stepping off the train in Ekaterinburg after a bone-rattling five-day journey, an exhausted Nicky, Alix and the children were received into the hands of local soviets, along with their doctor, maid, valet and footman. It would be a far cry from the sumptuous winter and summer palaces, banqueting halls and glorious gardens the Imperial Family had previously enjoyed. Ominously, it would be referred to by a Bolshevik euphemism, *dom osobogo znachenie* - The House of Special Purpose.

As their car drew up to their new home, they looked backwards over their shoulders to the outside world for the last time. It was Passion Week and the Easter bells of the Orthodox Church rang out merrily across the city. As the gates to his new prison slammed shut, Nicky was curtly told: *'Citizen Nicholas Romanov, you may enter.'* Hidden behind a high wooden fence, its windows blacked out, the Romanov's new home would be a gloomy prison consisting of five rooms.

Gradually, the family settled in to their new lodgings. The private house, though hardly a palace, was nonetheless regarded as one of the most modern in the city because it possessed a flushing toilet. The family were allowed to keep their bed linen bearing personalised monograms and the Imperial crest, as well as fine porcelain dinner plates bearing the name Nicholas II. Alix had also brought supplies of her favourite English eau de cologne by Brocard, as well as cold cream and lavender salts.

These were not the only potions on which Alix had become reliant. Plagued by migraines, heart palpitations, insomnia and sciatica, she was hopelessly addicted to a whole range of drugs. She had long ago admitted to being *'saturated'* with Veronal, a barbiturate. She also took morphine and cocaine for menstrual pain. It has been speculated that Nicky, too, was cushioned from reality by narcotics. It was said that his almost childlike indifference to losing the throne was the result of smoking a mixture of hashish and the psychoactive herb henbane administered to him by Rasputin to counter stress and insomnia.

Life in The House of Special Purpose was severely restrictive. They were not allowed visitors, they were to talk no language other than Russian (Alix liked to speak to her children in English) nor were they allowed to go outside the building except during a predetermined hour. Spirited and bored, the Romanov girls, aged between 17 and 22, ignored warnings not to peek out of an unsecured top-floor window until a sentry fired a warning shot at Anastasia's head. On that occasion, a laundry-woman witnessed Anastasia sticking her tongue out at the guard. Alix complied with this directive not to speak English but she refused point blank to obey an edict to ring a bell every time she went to use the bathroom.

Daily life became a matter of endurance. The young princesses' clothes were becoming increasingly threadbare. The white dresses and pretty hats that they used to wear every summer at their palace in the Crimea, a seaside paradise where the air was thick with the scent of roses and honeysuckle, had long since disappeared. Lively and vivacious, the girls still beguiled their guards with one saying they could not have looked prettier *'even if they had been covered in gold and diamonds'*.

The family had one consuming obsession: Alexei's fragile health. Since April, the 13-year-old had been suffering from a recurring haemorrhage in his knee, causing him agonising pain, so a splint was lackadaisically applied. Doctors had already cautioned Nicky that Alexei would not reach sixteen because of his debilitating illness, but the child half-heartedly rallied nonetheless. Of late, he seemed to be at death's door and the family was exhausted by a relentless round of all-night sessions at his bedside. Eventually, the splint was taken off his leg and he could be carried out to the garden. But he would never walk again.

By early July, the daily ritual of life at the House had taken on a numbing predictability. The family rose at eight in the morning and breakfasted on tea and black bread, as they had for many months. The days were filled with endless games of cards, patience and the French game bezique, which was a family favourite, while Alexei played with his model ship and tin soldiers. During their hour in the small garden, the girls and their father, the man who had ruled 8.5 million square miles of empire now master of a single room, would walk the 40 paces back and forth in the small, scrappy garden, eager to make the most of their exercise time. Nicky would watch his children play, his soft blue eyes full of tears while Alix took on the look of a broken woman. Each evening after a meagre supper, there were prayers and Bible readings, more games, diary writing, embroidery and sewing. Unbeknownst to their guards, the Romanov women spent long, furtive hours concealing gemstones and pearls into the linings of their dresses to fund the life in exile of which they dreamed.

Beyond the walls, civil war raged. The ranks of the White Army, which opposed the Bolsheviks, had been swelled by Czech deserters from the Austro-Hungarian army and were rapidly gaining ground on Ekaterinburg. Food in the city was rationed and typhus and cholera had taken a firm grip.

On the outside, the mood was growing increasingly ugly. Forty-five members of the local Orthodox diocese were murdered, their eyes gouged out, tongues and ears hacked off and their mangled bodies thrown in the river, but inside the House of Special Purpose an air of unreality reigned. The family had learnt to be stoical, but their awful fate loomed.

It was getting hotter and hotter, and the inhabitants of the building had now settled into a state of restless boredom. In America, the Washington Post published rumours that they had already been executed. In Britain, George was unaware that his decision to refuse his cousin asylum meant the Romanovs' fate hung in the balance.

At the House of Special Purpose, the guard book recorded the activities as it had for many days: *'Vse obychno'* - *'Everything is the same'* - but ominous preparations were under way. A nearby mineshaft was being examined and a doctor was procuring 400 lb of sulphuric acid.

Tuesday, July 16 began uneventfully for the Romanovs in their five rooms. Not so for their guards. Outside, they were assembling an armoury of guns in order to carry out their task and ordering 50 eggs from local nuns to *'help give them strength for the task ahead'*. At 3 pm, the family walked around the strip of unkempt garden for the last time and after evening prayers, they went to bed.

At 1.00 in the morning, their torture finally ended. Nicky, Alix, and all that remained of their household from doctor to cook, were woken and told to dress and gather their belongings before being led down to the basement. In his arms, Nicky carried his sleeping son while his youngest daughter, Anastasia, carried her sister's little Pekinese dog, Jemmy. Nicky was heard to say to his daughters reassuringly: *"Well, we're going to get out of this place"*.

As they gathered in the cellar of their mansion lit by a single naked bulb with the windows nailed shut, still wiping the sleep from their eyes, they could hear the boom of guns in the background. Outside, their assassins were downing shots of vodka. Alix, once again sick, asked for a chair and Nicky, noticing Alexei's pallor, asked for one as well so he could sit with his son on his lap. The confused group stood huddled together almost as if they were posing for a family portrait. It would have been an anxious several minutes as the puzzled family stared around in shock and confusion, questions forming in their minds. They didn't have to wait long for answers. The local secret police came into the room with an eleven-man squad, each armed with a rifle and read out a statement sentencing the family to death. Then it all became frightening clear what was happening. It was obvious there would be one gun for each of them.

Nicky was stunned. This couldn't be happening. It wasn't until the order came to shoot that Nicky reacted. He called out an incredulous *'What? WHAT?'* before he was shot point blank in the chest and as his body crumbled to the ground, the rest of the men started firing. An ashen-faced Alexei, too crippled to move and splattered with blood, survived the first volley of bullets, protected by both his father's body and jewels sewn into his underwear and cap as did his sisters, protected by 1.3 kilograms of diamonds sewn into the bodices of their dresses.

But it was only a temporary reprieve. When the gun smoke and plaster cleared, sobs and whimpers were heard as Alix and the children huddled together against a wall covering their heads in terror. It was then the guards realised they'd botched the slaughter.

None of the remaining Romanovs died a quick or painless death. One by one, the guards moved from person to person bayoneting them first then shooting them in head, disfiguring their faces to prevent identification. Their bodies were then taken fourteen miles away and burnt, dowsed in sulphuric acid and buried in two unmarked graves.

Inside a year, Russia had gone from monarchy, to democracy, to socialism to chaos.

The day that Nicky and his family were assassinated, George was watching the balloon-training wing of the RAF. He was to hear of his cousin's murder three days later when the Bolsheviks announced it.

Wilhelm's downfall would come three months later in October when he took his family from the Berlin army headquarters to Spa. To everyone in Berlin, it looked like Wilhelm was running away. Austria had stated their terms to him that week and it had already been decided that Wilhelm had to go. Up to that point, he had accepted the fact that he would most likely have to give up the imperial crown but he still hoped to retain the Prussian kingship. On 9th November that hope became a distant dream.

Wilhelm was having lunch, staring vacantly out of the window, when his chancellor walked silently into the room. As he anxiously bit his lips, Wilhelm knew without a doubt what the news would be: he would have to abdicate.

Wilhelm had never given up without a fight. He'd spent his whole life fighting with someone. Sometimes his grandmother. Sometimes his uncle. And always his mother. And he wasn't about to give up now. As obstinate as ever, Wilhelm refused to move. It was only when he heard that foreign troops were just a few miles away that he finally conceded. He and his family were driven quietly to the Dutch border and unceremoniously told to leave. By then, Wilhelm was completely crushed. He would spend the rest of his life in exile in Holland.

He was not the only one who had been forced to abdicate. Elsewhere in Europe, the kings of Greece, Bulgaria and Austria, had been deposed and the ruling dukes of Coburg and Hesse had been forced to abdicate as well. The Duke of Mecklenburg-Strelitz committed suicide by shooting himself.

When the crowds came to Buckingham Palace on Armistice Day, November 11th 1919, to mark the end of hostilities on the Western Front, their cheers were deafening. George was the only monarch still standing on his balcony. But it had come at a huge price. His family had suffered humiliation and death and his cousin Nicky, whom he had shared so many happy childhood memories with, now lay mutilated with the rest of his family. Although he disapproved of how Wilhelm had been treated, he did not intervene on his cousin's behalf. In the four-year war, George had lost all sympathy for his German cousin. When Wilhelm's son shot himself two years later and Wilhelm's wife died soon afterwards, there was no letter of sympathy sent from George. Throughout the war, eight and a half million soldiers had died, another 21 million were wounded and at least another million civilians had been wounded around the world, not to mention the death of Nicky and his family. *That* he put at Wilhelm's doorstep.

In the end, George was the only one who had managed to hang on to his throne. But by doing that, he had become serviceable, dutiful and utterly powerless. That was the price he had paid to survive. Never again would the peace of Europe hinge on the lottery of birth.

The worst was by no means over for George. A generation of young men were dead and there was still anger at low war pensions, a housing shortage and high inflation. The war was won but the empire was still unravelling. The Irish government were still fighting and would continue until 1922 for Irish independence and India was pushing for independence as well. Revolution was still imminent.

The war permanently changed George. It left him grey, haunted and baggy-eyed and he refused to give up the past, a fact that made him strangely popular. In a new world of dancing to jazz music, smart social women cutting their hair short, shorter dresses and smoking in public, he was the anchor of stability, reliability and old-fashioned values that Britain had always wanted and needed. But although he was being hailed as the one who had won them the war, he never lost his sense of fragility in his position as monarch during those dreadful post-war years and he threw himself into the project of establishing the British monarchy as the solid creation it is today.

But the war had also taken its toll on George's health. He was seriously injured in October 1915 when he was thrown from his horse during a troop review in France, breaking his pelvis, and his heavy smoking only exacerbated his recurring breathing problems, suffering from chronic pulmonary disease and pleurisy.

What worried George the most was his eldest son Edward, nicknamed

David by close friends and family. David had begun a love affair with a married Parisian courtesan Marguerite Albert who it turned out had kept a collection of his 'indiscreet' letters after he'd broken off the affair to begin one with an English married woman, Freda Dudley Ward, a textile heiress. Years later, tongues would wag during a spectacular murder trial after she shot and killed her husband in the Savoy.

David's womanising during the 1920s and 1930s constantly agitated George, not to mention the Prime Minister. Even David's private secretary for eight years commented, *"for some hereditary or physiological reason, his normal mental development stopped dead when he reached adolescence"*. George was disappointed by his elder son's affairs with married women and his failure to settle down while his younger brother, Albert (nicknamed Bertie), was married to Lady Elizabeth Bowes-Lyon, the daughter of the Scottish Earl of Strathmore and Kinghorne, and already had two daughters.

It wasn't as if he wasn't aware of his son's appeal to the nation. David had charisma and an informal style that made him a crowd pleaser wherever he went but it was exactly what George despised the most. His ominous words were *"After I am dead, the boy will ruin himself in 12 months"* followed closely by *"I pray to God that my eldest son will never marry and have children, and nothing will come between Bertie and Lilibet and the throne."*

While David's name was being connected to a long list of married women, George went on a crusade to stabilise the country. He made himself visible to his people, created charities and as each of his family came of age, they too were given projects. In an attempt to settle his son down, he gave David the lease of Fort Belvedere in Windsor Great Park (which eventually became the base for his relationships with more married women) then sent him to tour the Commonwealth. His second son Albert was sent to factories and shipyards. George put up a map at Buckingham Palace marking family visits and at the end of the year, he drew up a chart showing who had done the most work. In 1932, he left his comfort zone and made his first radio broadcast from a script written by Rudyard Kipling as his hands shook nervously in apprehension. To his surprise, it was a huge success.

But there were things he wouldn't do. He would never shake hands with the Soviets who were *"the murderers of his relatives"* and he would not meet his son's latest mistress, the chic, young, quick-witted and vivacious Wallis Simpson.

It took George quite some time to realise just how powerful a personality she was. At this stage, the fact that she was divorced mattered very little to him. He thought she was just another mistress in a long line of mistresses. By then the relationship between father and son had completely broken down, very reminiscent of previous Hanoverian monarchs. All through 1934, David flaunted his relationship with Wallis and by 1935, George was worn down and his health was seriously failing. Given all the political strains he'd endured, it was ironic that the thing that came close to breaking him was the failure of his eldest son to man up to what he should be doing.

Since before George's reign, smoking had become a hugely popular habit. Cigarette consumption had risen and doctors were beginning to see the connection between tobacco and lung disease. And like his father, George's heart was weak and he was a heavy smoker. To top it off, he'd never fully recovered from his illness of septicaemia seven years before. Still there was the feeling that he could hang on. That is, until the death of his eldest sister Victoria in December which sent him into the depths of depression and seemed to almost finish him off. On 15th January, a worn-out George complained of a cold and took himself to his bedroom at Sandringham House. Five days later, he was drifting in and out of consciousness and gradually growing weaker. The situation was obviously dire, so his eldest son and heir was called for.

To say his family were deeply concerned is understandable and the subtle words spoken by Queen Mary and David to his physician Lord Dawson, an admired and respected doctor of his generation, could have been misconstrued. They told Lord Dawson that they did not want George's life needlessly prolonged if his condition was fatal. There was nothing explicit but the way was left clear for Doctor Dawson *"to do the right thing"* and he clearly understood this. He even phoned his wife an hour before George died that night to tell her to get *The Times* to hold back its front page for a formal announcement.

Much like Doctor White in the library with a pearl handled pistol in his hand, it opened up the possibility of suspicious death and everything could, and would, eventually point to him.

This was still an era when treason was punishable by execution and the means, motive and opportunity were undeniably there. Let's not forget that euthanasia is still not accepted by the law to this day so what Doctor Dawson was planning was unquestionably murder and a very bold decision to make, considering the consequences. To say he was very sure of the subtle intent from George's family is an understatement. In fact, George's last conscious words to the doctor as he came to administer the lethal injection of morphine and cocaine were *"God damn you"* which would point to the fact that he was never consulted about the manner of his passing and that he had a suspicion how the treatment would end for him. In fact, it points towards the fact that he was still hanging on to life.

The set of circumstances is not difficult for us to understand. Doctor Dawson believed his patient was suffering and he'd been told to *"do the right thing"* if that was the situation. But murdering a monarch in this day and age was not something anyone would consider without the consent of that monarch's successor and that successor was David who hated his father. In actual fact, the feeling was mutual.

Being rather superstitious, I wonder what David was thinking days later when he saw the Imperial State Crown fall from the top of his father's coffin and land in the gutter as the funeral cortege turned into New Palace Yard. Would he have seen it as a bad omen? Was he aware of his father's words *"After I am dead, the boy will ruin himself in 12 months?"*

When Wilhelm heard of George's death, he took the opportunity to make contact once more to his estranged family and sent his grandson Fritzie, (who would in the future marry into the Guinness family and become a British citizen in 1947), to the funeral. Throughout his life, he continued to read English papers, drink English tea and dotted his conversations with *"ripping"* and *"damned good fellow"*. In 1938, he even wrote that God guided Neville Chamberlain. Twelve days later, when Hitler ordered Germany to march into Czechoslovakia, he wrote that he was horrified at events. In November that same year, he told visitors that it would all go wrong for Hitler but when war actually broke out the next year, as Germany ploughed across Europe again, Wilhelm must have thought that old scores were being settled at last. When Germany marched into Paris, he sent a telegram of congratulations to Hitler.

Fifty years before, George, Nicky and Wilhelm were born into a world of undeniable hereditary monarchy which should have guaranteed peace and harmony between the families. In the end, it had only lead to brutality. In fact, Nicky would be the last Tsar and Wilhelm would be the last Kaiser because of a war that would be called the most violent in the history of the world.

Up until then, all three cousins had wielded more power than perhaps any individual should have and all three had begun their rule ill-equipped and ill-prepared to deal with the modern world and democracy. The monarchy, as it was, was dying and the courts of Europe were turning against the halls of conservatism. They were being left behind in the great technical innovations and breakthroughs, scientific theories and the arts. Einstein, Stravinsky, Freud, Yeats and Picasso were taking over. As revolutions were taking place, the three cousins had tried desperately, and failed, to keep the world out and cling on to the past.

As the world took over, Wilhelm and Nicky had led their countries into a conflict that tore their countries apart and destroyed all illusion of family relationships. In England, their cousin George had been powerless to do anything but watch.

EDWARD VIII

Born 1894
Reign Jan 1936 – Dec 1936

On 21st January 1936, the people of Great Britain woke to the startling news that the man who had guided them through the 1st World War, their beloved king, George V, was dead. Businesses remained closed and shutters were drawn out of respect as the country went into mourning for their king. Against the odds, George had sealed their future through war, scandal and political upheaval and the public loved him for it. They were told that he'd lost his long-fought battle against lung disease and that he had died a painless death. His eldest son, David, would be their new king and would come to the throne as King Edward VIII. No one could possibly have known that George's prophecy of his eldest son not lasting a year could possibly come true.

At the time of David's birth at White Lodge, Richmond Park, he was the third in line of succession to the throne, behind his grandfather and father. He was baptised Edward Albert Christian George Andrew Patrick David in honour of his late uncle 'Eddy', his grandfather Albert, his great grandfather King Christian IX of Denmark, and four Patron Saints of England, Scotland and Wales. But his family and close friends always knew him by his last given name, David.

At an early age, David must have realised the full extent of his extraordinary legacy. At 15 years old, he had marched up the hill behind his father and beside his younger 14-year-old brother Albert, both boys dressed in their naval-cadet uniforms, showing dignity beyond their years, as they attended the funeral ceremony of their grandfather King Edward VII. As first in line to the throne after his father, he would have been very aware of the very public role he would have when his father died. Even his mother was confident her eldest son would assume the role with surety when his time came. His grandmother however, had her doubts. She had already warned her daughter-in-law that her eldest son had the potential to dominate his brothers and sisters.

As his grandmother predicted, David's dominance appeared early and had an effect on his younger brother Albert. Albert was a shy, nervous child, suffering from a debilitating stammer from the age of 8 and as such, was failing to blossom in his older brother's shadow. His only solace was that as the second son, he would never have to step out of the shadows. He could avoid the limelight that shone so brightly on his older brother. He could wait in a darkening room without having to face the daunting task of asking the palace staff to light the lamps.

At the age of 18, David was invested as Prince of Wales at a special ceremony at Caernarvon Castle marking him as the heir to the throne and at 20, when World War 1 broke out, David had reached minimum age for active service and was keen to participate. He joined the Grenadier Guards and showed a willingness to serve on the front lines although the Secretary of State for War, Lord Kitchener, refused to allow it, citing the immense harm that could occur if the enemy captured the heir to the British throne. Despite this, David witnessed trench warfare first-hand and attempted to visit the front line as often as he could. For this he was awarded the Military Cross in 1916, although he had never fired a single shot. Even then, no one had a bad word for him. He was popular among veterans, and undertook his first military flight in 1918, and later gained a pilot's licence.

As the Prince of Wales, his blond good looks, rank, easy charm and unmarried status gained him quite a bit of public attention and at the height of his popularity, he was the most photographed celebrity of his time. The pinup boy of his day and the ultimate bachelor. Everywhere he went rapturous crowds greeted him, keen to welcome the son of the British king. He visited poverty-stricken areas of the country and undertook 16 tours to various parts of the Empire between 1919 and 1935. He was a man who knew his place in the world and he was idolised by the working class as the champion of the underprivileged cause. He was Britain's shining star and as the heir to the throne, he represented a shining future for the British royal family, a symbol as strong as the towering walls of Windsor Castle. The people had high hopes for David. Unfortunately, like his grandfather, he was also every woman's romantic daydream and by the age of 26, his name was being linked with many prominent married women.

David's first public love affair was during World War 1 with a married Parisian 'escort', Marguerite Alibert who produced a cache of 'indiscreet' letters when the affair was concluded. He had begun a new affair with an English married woman, Freda Dudley Ward, a textile heiress and Marguerite Alibert was not the least bit happy about it. Years later, Marguerite would be acquitted in a spectacular murder trial after she shot her husband in the London Savoy. And didn't tongues wag.

David's womanising had both worried his father and disappointed him. David's younger brother Albert had already settled down with Lady Elizabeth Bowes-Lyon, daughter of the Scottish peer, Claude Bowes-Lyon 14th Earl of Strathmore and Kinghorne and together they had produced two beautiful girls. David looked far from doing the same. In an attempt to settle his son down, his father had given him the lease of Fort Belvedere in Windsor Great Park but from there, David had used it as a base to continue his relationships with married women, including Freda Dudley Ward and Lady Thelma Furness, the American wife of a British peer. It was Lady Furness who fatefully introduced David to her friend and fellow American, Wallis Simpson.

Wallis Simpson was not the woman David's father had dreamed of for his son. She was born in 1896 and her real name was actually Bessie Wallis Warfield. She was the daughter of a flour merchant, born in a hotel across the road from the Monterey Country Club in Pennsylvania. Her father passed away when she was four months old and she and her mother moved in with her rich uncle, Solomon Davies Warfield, and her grandmother. She was educated at the most expensive school in Maryland, which is where she started her life as a socialite after befriending the heiress of Kirk Silverware, Mary Kirk, the daughter of Senator T. Coleman du Pont and Renee du Pont.

Even at a young age, Wallis was memorable. She was married at 20 years old to a US Navy aviator, an alcoholic by the name of Earl Winfield Spencer Jr., and after many periods of separation, and an affair with a Count while visiting Beijing which left her pregnant, she'd had a botched abortion which left her infertile and was divorced by 1927. By the time her marriage to Spencer was dissolved, she was already involved with Ernest Aldrich Simpson, an Anglo-American shipping executive and former officer in the Coldstream Guards. Six months after Wallis's divorce, Ernest Simpson divorced his first wife to marry Wallis and the happy couple were saying their vows in July 1928 at a Registry Office in Chelsea London. They set up home in a furnished house in Mayfair with four servants and settled down to wedded bliss.

One year later in 1929, while visiting her sick mother in the United States, the Wall Street Crash happened and Wallis's family investments were wiped out. Back home in England however, the shipping business was booming and the Simpsons moved into a larger house in Mayfair with a larger staff of servants. It was around this time that Wallis's wandering eye had noticed David and through Lady Thelma Furness (David's current mistress), she wangled an introduction. Over the next three years, they met at several parties and David's own eyes had continually wandered in her direction on many occasions. By then, the Simpsons had been living beyond their means and Ernest's business was encountering serious financial difficulties. With creditors knocking on the door, they were forced to fire a succession of servants to make ends meet.

It wasn't love at first sight with David. You see he already had Thelma as his girlfriend. But something about Wallis intrigued him enough that while her friend was away in New York in January 1934, Wallis stepped into her place as David's mistress.

Bad news always travels fast and David's father soon heard the rumours. By then, George was feeling his age and his health was seriously failing. He smoked too much and his heart was weak but his temper was still something to behold. When confronted by his father about the affair, David denied everything, despite his staff seeing them in bed together and despite distancing himself from Thelma and his former lover Freda Dudley Ward in order to be in Wallis's company.

David was absolutely besotted with Wallis. He found her overbearing American manner and abrasive irreverence towards his position refreshingly appealing and he was so infatuated with her that he showered her with money, jewels and luxury holidays on the French Riviera. He'd been in love before but this was something entirely different for him. She treated him almost with indifference and he found it exciting and invigorating. She bossed him and treated him with distain when his other mistresses had fallen at his feet and he was absolutely intrigued with the new phenomenon. It became her lure and she reeled him in.

Perhaps he had some idea of what the reaction would be because as he continued his public duties, he was keeping Wallis out of the public eye. It was only at a party at Buckingham Palace when he introduced her to his mother that his father King George realised just how serious the affair had become.

His father was both alarmed and furious with his son and it was enough for him to bring in the Special Branch to spy on her. What George found infuriated him even further. Not only did Wallis have a shady marital history but it would seem she was also having an affair with a car-selling, moustachioed, lounge-lizard by the name of Guy Marcus Trundle at the same time as his son.

Of course, we all know the reputation of journalism when it comes to making up stories to sell papers. And this story had three vital ingredients: sex, snobbery and royalty. But as everyone knows, where there's smoke, there's fire, and Wallis was supplying plenty of kindling. While The Daily Mirror had a field day with photos of Trundle calling it the *"greatest royal sex scandal ever"*, Wallis was denying everything by stating it had apparently only been an *"outing"* between her and the car salesman. Photos showed her sitting in a car with a dapper man wearing a trilby jauntily cocked over one eye, his trouser creases sharp as a knife and his two-toned shoes shining almost as brightly as the smile spread across his face.

Trundle seems to have had no compunction against talking freely. Despite openly admitting to the affair, arrogantly boasting that *"every woman falls for me"*, no one seems to have seen Trundle and Wallis anywhere near a bed and she insisted there were perfectly innocent explanations as to why she might have spent the early hours of one morning in his house in Bruton Street. As for Trundle, he stated that he met Simpson *"quite openly at informal social gatherings as a personal friend but secret meetings were made by appointment where intimate relations took place."*

Special Branch delved even further and what they found shocked his father even more. Wallis had lived at two London addresses under the name of Mrs Earle Spencer (her first husband) and was *"regarded as a person very fond of the company of men"*. Her husband meanwhile was said to be *"bragging"* that he expected to get *"high honours"* for sharing his wife. He mentioned he *"expects at least to be created a Baron."* Apparently, he was even more talkative after a few drinks.

Still, David and Wallis weathered the storm while his father and his courtiers watched on in horror. As the investigation heated up and reports from the Special Branch flooded in, the affair began to interfere with David's official duties. One year later, the investigation came to an abrupt halt with his father's rather sudden death.

George's health had been seriously failing for years. He smoked too much, his heart was weak and he'd fallen from his horse seven years ago and broken his pelvis. His anger at his son and his depression over the death of his eldest sister Victoria seemed to finish him off. On 15th January, he took to his bedroom at Sandringham House complaining of a cold and there he remained, gradually growing weaker and drifting in and out of consciousness for five days.

Understandably, the family was deeply concerned and the carefully worded sentence spoken to his father's physician, Lord Dawson, was meant to assure the doctor that they did not want George's life needlessly prolonged if he was suffering unnecessarily. Despite no explicit command to end his life, that night Doctor Dawson injected George with a lethal injection of morphine and cocaine.

The set of circumstances is not difficult for us to understand. He believed his patient was suffering and he'd been told to *"do the right thing"* if that was the situation. But murdering a monarch in this day and age was not something anyone would consider doing without the consent of that monarch's successor. Obviously, he believed he had that consent when David whispered the words that he did not want told his father to suffer.

The suspicious part is that David hated his father and in actual fact, the feeling was mutual.

The next day, watching the proclamation of his accession to the throne from a partially hidden window of St James's Palace, was the still-married Wallis Simpson, sitting beside him with a smile on her face. Not only did David break strict protocol by including Wallis, but standing behind her was his cousin, Charles Edward, Duke of Saxe-Coburg and Gotha, a senior Nazi officer and Hitler's emissary.

World War 1 had caused a conflict of loyalties for Charles Edward. He was the son of Leopold, Queen Victoria's favourite son who had died from complications from a fall due to haemophilia and as such a member of the aristocracy impressively titled Duke of Albany, Earl of Clarence and Baron Arklow. He was raised and educated at Eton College as a Prince for the first 15 years of his life and made a Knight of the Garter by his uncle King Edward VII just prior to his 18th birthday. As a grandson of Queen Victoria, he was the first cousin of George V, Queen Maud of Norway, Grand Duke Ernst Ludwig of Hesse, Empress Alexandra of Russia, Queen Marie of Romania, Queen Victoria Eugenia of Spain, Queen Sophia of the Hellenes, Crown Princess Margaret of Sweden, Queen Wilhelmina of the Netherlands, and Kaiser Wilhelm II of Germany. At the age of 16, Charles had inherited the ducal throne of Saxe-Coburg and Gotha when his uncle Alfred died and he, his mother and sister had moved to Germany. From then on, his education was overseen by Wilhelm and even dubbed Wilhelm's 'seventh son'. When he came of age, he married Wilhelm's wife's niece Victoria and joined the German army.

Despite his strong British blood, during World War 1 he broke off relations with his family in the British and Belgian courts and supported his wife's German family. It was three years later in 1917 that his cousin George V would change the name of the British Royal House from Saxe-Coburg and Gotha to the more British one of Windsor in an anti-German gesture. That same year, the Privy Council were empowered to investigate *"persons who had borne arms against His Majesty or His Allies"* and of course, Charles Edward's name popped up. All he and his family entitlements to British peerage and titles, including Prince and Princesses of the United Kingdom, were removed and one year later again, on 11th November 1918, his abdication from Coburg was demanded. Effectively exiled from the

United Kingdom and fearful of the communist threat, he started looking for a new political home.

It wasn't until October 1922 that he met Adolf Hitler for the first time and joined the Bund Wiking, a paramilitary organisation. And you can believe that Hitler was very interested in Charles and his connection to the British royalty. Ten years later, Charles was an integral part of the Nazi Party as a member of the Brownshirts, calling on voters to support Hitler in the presidential election.

Even before George died, Charles had introduced himself as Hitler's emissary and stated he would open up all lines of connection between David and Hitler. The danger of David going behind his government's back was becoming very apparent.

On a cold winter's day in January, as George's coffin was taken from Westminster to be buried at Windsor, David walked slowly behind with his mind in turmoil. He was madly in love, he hated the stuffy tradition of the old court and more than anything else he wanted it changed. In the procession behind him walked his friend and cousin Charles Edward who outraged everyone by wearing his Nazi uniform. In such unsettled times, it was a blatantly obvious statement to make. As distressed as his mother and brother Albert were, David ignored everyone.

At this crucial moment, Hitler had a fair idea from Charles Edward that David was on his side and was busy moving his troops across the bridge into the Rhine belt, a zone controlled by France since the end of the First World War.

It is just another nail in David's coffin (sorry for the pun) when it comes to whether his father's death was mercy or murder. It would seem his father's death had come at a very opportune moment. By then, his family, Prime Minister Stanley Baldwin and the Government were nervously watching David and Charles' camaraderie and they were suspicious that David was sympathising with Germany. And then there was the Wallis problem to consider. It wasn't just Chancellor Neville Chamberlain who knew something had to be done, Stanley Baldwin knew as well.

Baldwin came from a very different generation. He had come into power during World War 1 and stayed in power while family members of David's generation had been killed on the battlefield. He'd entered politics at a relatively late age, already a wealthy man who had inherited the directorship of the Great Western Railway upon the death of his father in 1908, but because of his unending devotion to his country, his rise to the top was very rapid. So, on one hand you have a young king who wanted to make changes to the system but felt maddeningly stuck with elderly courtiers and on the other hand you have elderly ministers who wanted things to stay exactly the same. It was a situation full of disharmony and disagreement and it was a turning point for David. He was determined that as he was now the king, he could do what he wanted despite the consequences. A head on collision between David and the establishment was inevitable.

Albert knew full well what his elder brother was like. He'd grown up in David's shadow and was used to being intimidated by him. But this new David was someone else entirely. This David was going against everything his father and his father's father had advocated. The whole dynasty actually. And he was powerless to do anything but watch. More and more he was being called on to fulfil duties that David was abandoning rather than miss out on any time spent with Wallis.

As for Albert's wife Elizabeth, she detested everything about Wallis. She could not believe her brother-in-law had taken up with a harpy and her one desire was that she should disappear in a puff of smoke. They met at one memorable dinner during a Balmoral holiday when she and Albert had only just arrived. It was far too early to make snap judgements but that's exactly what Elizabeth did. Wallis came forward to greet them and upon seeing the smiling woman, Elizabeth instantly took a dislike to her. Sweeping past her in an undeniable snub, Elizabeth uttered the words, *"I've come to dine with the king."*

By October that year, they knew for certain what path David was going down. Wallis had filed for a divorce from her second husband on the grounds that he had committed adultery with her childhood friend Mary Kirk and the decree was granted. By December, she was free, her relationship with David was public knowledge and the press was hounding her. With reporters hot on her tail everywhere she went, she fled to France and for the next three months, she was under siege at the home of close friends in Cannes. Even David's Lord-in-Waiting, Lord Brownlow, followed her and had a press statement ready for her to sign renouncing her relationship with David.

It seemed nothing that Wallis could do would alter David's opinion about her. Throughout the dreadful press releases, the accusations of her scheming her way into his life and the horror of her past, cupid's arrow had hit David fair and square in his heart and he was determined to marry Wallis. She was exciting and radiated a sense of freedom so different from his own life and his stuffy English culture, he revelled in. She was the one he'd been waiting for all his life and no one who was going to stop him from having her. He couldn't live without her.

And then the bombshell arrived in the form of a demand to Stanley Baldwin that David be allowed a morganic marriage to Wallis Simpson. The frightful words silenced government ministers and stunned family members. No one had been sure how long the infatuation was going to last but most were holding their breath and praying that it would end soon, like all the other affairs David had had.

The law at the time stated that the monarch of the United Kingdom has the title of 'Supreme Governor of the Church of England' and until 2002, the Church of England did not permit the remarriage of divorced people who had living ex-spouses. For the British government, the wording couldn't have been more important. Wallis was a two-time divorcee and a woman of 'limitless ambition' who was pursuing the King because of his wealth and position. Not only that, she was politically, socially and morally unsuitable as a prospective consort. As a monarch with the title 'Supreme Governor of the Church of England', it meant that any proposed marriage between David and Wallis conflicted with the Church's teachings, something the government was very quick to point out.

To David, a morganic marriage seemed a simple answer to the complicated matter where the husband's titles and privileges are withheld from the wife and any children while he still remained king. And there were endless royals in Europe who had morganic marriages, he stated. Erik XIV of Sweden had married a servant in 1567. Ludwig Wilhelm, Duke of Bavaria had married an actress Henriette Mendel. Victor Emmanuel II of Italy married his principal mistress, a commoner, Rosa Guerrieri, and Archduke Franz Ferdinand of Austria whose subsequent assassination had triggered World War I, had married Sophie Chotek. And closer to home, what about Edward IV who had married the commoner Elizabeth Woodville? What about Edward III's son John of Gaunt who later married his mistress Katherine Swynford? That marriage had produced Henry VII. And what about James II who had eloped and married Anne Hyde? With all the information supplied, he confidently insisted he had the right to marry the woman of his choice. And then, at the end of his tirade, he spoke the words that he would remember for the rest of his life. If the government opposed him, he stated, he would step down from the throne.

It was an arrogant, even risky, thing to say and he'd said and done some silly things in the past in his confidence as king. But hindsight is a wonderful thing and once the words were out there was no taking them back. It made Baldwin and his ministers step back and take a serious look at the situation.

Baldwin and his ministers loathed David's infuriating casual style and his dislike of royal protocol. They could see no end to the arguments and disagreements in the future. And they loathed Wallis and everything she represented. It's been said that all the world loves a lover, but it seems Neville Chamberlain and Stanley Baldwin were not to be included in that number. So, when David offered them this ultimatum in order to marry an unsuitable woman of dubious character, they had the perfect excuse to push another button. It was a Godsend to them and she was the perfect excuse. David had played straight into Baldwin's hands.

David had done his homework, no doubt about it, but it just wasn't enough. When the reply came, David found that it wasn't the answer he wanted to hear. In an unanimous decision between the Prime Minister of Britain, Australia, Canada and South Africa, it was decided that if the king went ahead and married Wallis against Baldwin's advice, the Government would resign, causing a constitutional crisis. This seemed to indicate that if David were to decide to go ahead and marry Wallis, he had no option but to abdicate.

There is no doubt that David believed he had been hustled into this position by a scheming Baldwin. But that's not what Baldwin was thinking at all. Baldwin's position was that no matter what David wanted, he was the head of the Church of England and as such, he had responsibilities to his country by following the laws like everyone else. There was no way around it: remarriage of divorced people with living spouses was a no-go zone. In fact, the people would not tolerate it, he stated. Despite his references to morganatic marriages throughout history, no British monarch had even suggested marrying a divorced woman. The choice was clear: either the throne or Wallis Simpson. Make the choice. He could not have both.

There was no doubt in anyone's mind that Wallis was the brains behind the negotiations for David to both marry her and keep the throne and there was no doubt that she was urging him to appeal to the country. He was after all, their Prince Charming.

The ploy backfired spectacularly. Even when things were looking at their worst, everyone believed she was the one demanding certain conditions. The words *"adequate financial provision"* could only be hers, were the whispers, and because of these murmurs, there weren't too many people who didn't believe she was a selfish, calculating, ambitious and scheming woman who had ruined their beloved king and stolen his future.

For the first time in his life, David was unsure of what to do. He longed to talk to Wallis but she had escaped the press and England to stay with friends on the French Riviera. All he wanted to do was hear her voice. Palace lines were kept open in case she called and his days were spent in agitation as they spun out of control. He was becoming desperate and all he could think was what would Wallis do?

Then after weeks of vacillation, he made a decision. His ordered existence as the heir to the throne had disintegrated. The crisis had come to a head. He was going to marry the woman he loved and nothing was going to stop him from doing exactly that.

As David worried and fretted, disturbing rumours surfaced about Wallis and why she had left Britain. The latest one was that she was pro-Nazi and she was having an affair with Hitler's new ambassador to Britain, Joachim von Ribbentrop. As with the moustachioed car salesman, David ignored the rumours.

After only 325 days on the throne, on 10th December 1936, David stood forlornly in a room in his beloved Fort Belvedere not quite believing it had finally come down to this. He was the most eligible bachelor in history and his charms were intoxicating. As Prince of Wales he was idolised. His face had appeared in posters and newspapers and although he was shorter than his brothers, his confidence in his birth right shone brightly from his eyes. In January that year, he had inherited not just a throne but the devotion and loyalty of a nation who had watched him for 25 years during his extensive travels. The world had been at his feet and his downfall was so appallingly impulsive, it was as though his emotions had not yet caught up with the events as they unfolded.

In the presence of his three surviving brothers, Albert Duke of York, Henry Duke of Gloucester and George Duke of Kent, David signed the Instrument of Abdication and the law was finalised. The next day, David made a radio broadcast.

"*I have found it impossible to carry the heavy burden of responsibility, and to discharge my duties as King as I would wish to do, without the help and support of the woman I love.*"

Exhausted, David then left, bowing formally to his brother Albert, Duke of York who had become the new king.

Only Duke of Kent broke the formality of it, shouting out to his brother as he left: "*This is quite mad…It isn't possible! It isn't happening.*"

GEORGE VI

Born 1895
Reign 1936–1952

Early morning fog lay heavily over the Thames on Friday 11th December 1936. It wound sluggishly as dark clouds collected on the horizon, turning the river dishwater grey in the gathering gloom. The fog slowly lifted revealing Fort Belvedere in Windsor Great Park as a rambling turreted lodge. The fort had been built as a folly but still managed to maintain the air of a castle, in spite of David's lavish recent refurbishments. It was where David anchored himself, where he had felt most comfortable away from the formality of Buckingham Palace or Windsor Castle. Here, he could surround himself with his friends. For his younger brother, 40-year-old Albert, 10th December was the most distressing day of his life.

For days before, Albert had not been welcome at Fort Belvedere, even though he had tried repeatedly to talk to his brother. When he arrived, the press were already camped outside and a myriad of flashbulbs went off simultaneously to catch a glimpse of the distraught prince for a worldwide audience. Everyone knew that the British monarchy was being shaken to its very core. Once inside the gates, the uproar ceased as Albert was led through a hallway to where his brother waited for him. A few officials whispered quietly in respectful conversations but as Albert entered, they ceased talking. The unseen presence in the room was Wallis. Albert had no doubt that it was *she* who was the catalyst that was bringing the four brothers together that morning. *She* was the presence who had brought David to this point to sign away his birth right.

David had a reputation for being calm under the most stressful of circumstances. This proved correct as he showed no emotion whatsoever and remained remarkably composed. Neither of their brothers, Prince Henry Duke of Gloucester or Prince George Duke of Kent had arrived so the meeting would have to wait until all four brothers were present.

On a writing table, small elegant crystal glasses and a jug of water waited on a gleaming silver tray. Beside them sat copies of the Instrument of Abdication ready for David to sign. Each copy had to be signed and witnessed by each of his brothers as the kingdom and empire was transferred from one brother to the other, making Albert the next king as King George VI. All that was needed was David's signature to make it official.

Albert was in shock. Nothing had prepared him for this calamity. Although painfully aware of his own weakness, he fully understood his older brother's failings. The passion that burnt in Albert's chest had never burnt brightly in David's. There were too many rules and too many regulations for him. It had been less than a year since his father had died and Albert shared his mother's bewilderment that the monarchy was being plunged headlong into this crisis. His mother and father had brought all boys up to believe that the monarchy was *"something sacred"* and every monarch had the responsibility and obligation to put the country before anything else. But here was David, abdicating because his wish was to marry a divorced woman already in possession of *"two husbands living"*. The newspapers had exploded with the news and the scandal had been splashed over the headlines in every paper, both in Britain, in Europe and throughout the Commonwealth. Suddenly, the monarchy was tainted, perhaps destroyed. But in that room on that morning, there was no hint that David was bending under the strain.

David had approached the role of king like a spoilt child. He was lazy and unwilling to cooperate and Documents of State were regularly returned unread. He offended the Church by failing to attend services or take

Communion on the rare occasions that he did attend. More importantly, he had expressed his pro-German view when Adolf Hitler became Chancellor, then Head of State and finally Supreme Commander of the Armed Forces. Hitler had just reintroduced conscription in Germany and announced the German Air Force in direct contravention of the Treaty of Versailles signed after the First World War. David seemed unconcerned with the queasy facts and blind to Hitler's ambitions.

Albert still couldn't believe what was happening. In his eyes, his oldest brother had qualities that he would never have. Just one week before, David was the life and soul of a dinner party, while Albert was happy to stay quiet, dull and reserved. As always, David had dazzled everyone as he talked about labour problems in South Wales. Albert never imagined he would be able to match his legendary older brother, much less replace him. For most of his life, he had never lived up to anyone's expectations of being a royal.

Albert Frederick Arthur George was on born 14th December on the Sandringham Estate on the 34th anniversary of his great-grandfather, Albert's death. When his 76-year-old great-grandmother Queen Victoria was told of the birth, she was visibly distressed. She had mourned for her husband every day of the 34 years since his death and now she was expected to rejoice at the birth of another grandchild on that dreaded anniversary instead. She was mollified by the proposal to name the new baby Albert in his honour and quickly nicknamed him 'Bertie'. At the time, Albert was fourth in line to the throne behind his grandfather, father and elder brother David.

At the age of 2, he became His Royal Highness Prince Albert of York but it was pretty obvious Albert was nothing like his elder brother. Albert was soft hearted and often suffered from ill health, was easily frightened and prone to tears. He developed a stammer that lasted for years and was forced to write with his right hand although he was naturally left-handed. He suffered from chronic stomach problems, probably due to nerves, as well as knock-knees. To correct this, he had been forced to wear painful splints adding to his lack of self-esteem. When Queen Victoria died in 1901 and his grandfather became king, he moved up the line to third to the throne after his father and elder brother. No one ever dreamed it would be any other way.

When his grandfather Edward VII died in 1910, Albert was attending the Royal Naval College as a naval cadet and was about to come 61st out of 67 in the final examination. The death meant he was elevated to second in line to the throne after his elder brother David. At this stage, David his elder brother and heir was making a name for himself as the Prince Charming with an endless line of woman vying for his attention. Albert and his insecurities were far removed from the throne.

A year after his commission, he began his service in the First World War and was mentioned in despatches for his action as a turret officer during an indecisive engagement with the German navy in the Battle of Jutland in 1916. That was to be his last commission during the war due to a duodenal ulcer for which he had an operation in November 1917. Still he was desirous of serving while the war was still in progress. For the closing weeks of the war, he served in the Independent Air Force in France and in July 1919, he qualified as an RAF pilot and gained a promotion to squadron leader the following day.

Albert's father, George V was determined to make himself visible to his people after the war. He created charities and as his family came of age, they too were given projects. His father put up a map at Buckingham Palace marking family visits and at the end of the year, he drew up a chart showing who had done the most. David was already displaying a disturbing habit of courting married women and in an attempt to settle his son down, he gave David the lease of Fort Belvedere in Windsor Great Park (which David then used as a base for his relationships) and was then sent to tour the Commonwealth. Albert was sent to factories and shipyards.

Albert remembered well his first speech on the wireless on 31st October 1925. It was the closing of the British Empire Exhibition, a triumphant showcase for the empire. Thousands of people had filled Wembley stadium and ten million more were listening for his voice on the wireless. When the band finished, the crowds fell silent and the world waited for the 29-year-old Duke of York to speak.

His voice failed him. He opened his mouth but nothing had come out except a series of garbled sounds and half words. Spasms started in his mouth and jaw and his throat closed up. Albert, representing the Crown, was inarticulate and the humiliation was something he would never forget. He'd suffered from a stammer for so long that it seemed just a part of his personality. And his father yelling, *"Get it out, boy!"* had certainly not helped.

Six months later, Lionel Logue, an Australian speech therapist, had been engaged and eighty-two appointments had followed over the next fifteen months. The unorthodox method of practised breathing, tongue twisters and gargling had worked. But heavy duties lay ahead and Albert knew well there could be unpredictable setbacks under the stress. His stammer could humiliate him and he was in constant dread that he would lose his own mind due to the pressure. How could a man who could not even control his own speech possibly imagine he could be a king?

Disrupting Albert's thoughts, his 36-year-old brother Henry Duke of Gloucester was shown into the room. As an army man, Henry knew all about the time-honoured role of the monarch. He had never been close to David but he'd expected him to do his duty. His father had done his duty, as had his grandfather but his brother seemed hell-bent on breaking all the rules. But as he was shown in, he appeared composed as he prepared to do his unpleasant duty of witnessing his brother's signature.

The fourth and youngest brother, the glamorous 33-year-old Prince George Duke of Kent was still missing. Always attempting to lighten the mood, David remarked, *"George would be late".*

His lateness was characteristic. The Duke of Kent was unpredictable, volatile and flamboyant, and totally alien to his solemn, quiet brother Albert. Kent had no sense of duty, but he was film-star handsome and a playboy whose irresistible good looks had attracted a series of women. His closeness to his older brother was the fundamental guiding force in his life and how he would react to the news was anyone's guess. It was Albert's job now to keep his brothers in line and do all he could with or without their support to face the crisis.

To Albert, the storm his brother created was excruciating. He felt trapped. David was known the world over while Albert had managed to stay in the background so when David had stepped down, pictures were hastily found of Albert and the newspapers played the family card. Pictures of the awkward Duke, his wife Elizabeth and his pretty daughters, 10-year-old Elizabeth and 6-year-old Margaret were discovered and overnight the family became public property. Pictures surfaced of his wife on a blanket with her Welsh corgi, looking motherly, as she played in the garden with the dark-haired princesses in identical dresses. She looked plain, not elegant like Wallis, but to Albert she was utterly wonderful. Only the day before, crowds had gathered outside their Piccadilly home, hoping for a glimpse of their new king, and he had felt like he was on the edge of an abyss.

Albert had different standards from his brothers. Like his brothers, he'd had affairs before his marriage all that had stopped once he met Lady Elizabeth Bowes-Lyon. She was the 19-year-old daughter of a Scottish aristocrat with many admirers and all through the summer of 1920, he'd courted her shyly until he found the courage to propose. He'd had to propose three times before she finally accepted him. And since they'd married, he had remained loyal and faithful to her.

Albert had seen the danger in the approaching months as David paraded Wallis on his arm around London. He knew that behind the figure-hugging satins was a determined, strong woman with an incredible belief in herself. Life out of the limelight was not what she had in mind. She wanted to be royal and acknowledged in every bow and every curtsey. At the very least, she wanted her royal sisters-in-law to show her *some* sort of respect. She was the one who had captured David's heart and she wanted everything that he had promised her. And she was prepared to fight for it.

Now the dreaded event was becoming a reality and he was trapped, swept up in the confusion. There would be expectations he never expected to be able to fulfil and there would be demands. The events of just the past week had almost sent him over the edge. He'd maintained his dignity in public but by the time he reached his mother at Marlborough House, he was barely coping. Once again, words failed him as he tried to explain everything to her. Like a child he wept on his mother's shoulder despite being the future King of Great Britain, Emperor of India, Head of the Church of England and Commander in Chief of the Armed Forces. He was caught up in grief and even his mother could not console him.

One hour later, the doors burst open and George Duke of Kent was shown into the room. That morning, he was uncharacteristically subdued. He was the youngest and closest to his oldest brother but still, he'd been unable to reach David during his self-imposed isolation until two days before. He'd wanted to talk to David before he made an irrevocable decision but when he finally met with him, David was anguished, chain-smoking and stressed beyond reason. But he was definite. He was going to abdicate. There was nothing that would convince him to give up Wallis.

Albert watched as his youngest brother swaggered into the room. He knew Kent had hidden himself away with David for most of the weekend and he'd heard the whispers from various factions that the Prime Minister was considering altering the succession to bypass both Albert and his equally unsuitable third brother Henry so that Kent, with his regal bearing, self-assurance and charm, could inherit the throne. Would the abdicating king leave easier if his favourite brother were to sit on the throne? Was it possible that Kent had even suggested it? That morning as he walked into the room, Kent certainly looked and sounded confident. Could Albert even trust him?

With Kent's arrival, the formalities commenced and an air of unreality took over. The time had come for David to sign the pages that would change history. Albert watched as David moved slowly towards the writing table and the room fall silent as he picked up the pen. His brothers simultaneously held their breath, hardly daring to move, as the pen poised over the page. Then without any more delay, the pen scratched over the page and it was done. In that one moment, the world tilted and Albert and David swapped places in history.

Watching his brother sign the document was painful for Albert. It meant a change in his quiet life with his beloved family and it meant accepting a role he had never wanted. Even his wife Elizabeth saw it as a horror. She was terrified for him and had been ill in bed the previous week while she stressed and worried for him. He certainly did not feel confident in stepping into the shoes of the man widely believed to be the most popular person in the British Empire.

As soon as David put the pen down, he glanced at Albert as if trying to see inside his heart. To anyone watching the pair, David looked like a swimmer coming up for air while Albert stared in dread at his brother. Without another word spoken, the four brothers shook hands and parted.

As Albert rode back to Piccadilly, women were crying in the streets and he knew his own mother would be doing the same thing in Marlborough House. Only the day before, she had dressed in funeral black for photos as Albert's daughters, Elizabeth and Margaret, had watched solemnly from a top window.

For Albert, the degradation of the monarchy was uppermost in his mind. His head was full of the vicious gossip suggesting Wallis had been involved with Hitler's new ambassador to Britain, Joachim von Ribbentrop, and he could hardly believe it. Here was his brother, handsome, charming and charismatic, and there was Ribbentrop, a 43-year-old Nazi who was a former whiskey and champagne salesman with a receding hairline and expanding waistline. What on earth did she see in him? But if the gossip was to be believed, Wallis had been courted with gifts and flowers and Ribbentrop was sending her seventeen carnations a day representing the number of times they had slept together. But this awkward man had won the trust of Adolf Hitler and understood how much Hitler wanted rearmament. And whether the gossip was true or not, she had taken it upon herself to arrange a meeting between Ribbentrop and David at his former mistress's house. It fuelled the gossip that Wallis was acting for the Nazis and it made Baldwin puff his chest out with pride that he had stopped the conniving woman from becoming queen.

Two days after David had signed the papers, Albert, now reigning as George VI, announced that David would be styled as the 'Duke of Windsor' with the style of *Royal Highness*. Wallis, however, would not hold the same title. His decision to create David as a royal duke ensured that he could neither stand for election to the House of Commons nor speak on political subjects in the House of Lords. He wanted this to be the first act of his reign.

If Albert thought the royal family could rest easily and out of the limelight for a while as he settled into his role, he was sadly mistaken. Just twenty days into his reign, Albert woke up on New Year's Day to provocative headlines in The Daily Express ... "*Who is Mrs Allen?*" When he read further, he could hardly believe what he was reading. His youngest brother Kent had his name splashed across the tabloid alongside a woman of extraordinary beauty, the very much-married Mrs William Allen, the wife of a rich ex-MP.

Her flimsy lace dress hid nothing Albert noted as he gazed in horror at the photo placed in the centre of the front page. Mrs Allen was Paula Gellibrand and she was described as "*Britain's most painted woman*". Her exquisite beauty and Kent's "*warm*" relationship was noted, along with her "*two previous marriages*" and coming just weeks after David's abdication due to his association with Wallis, the implication was clear. Was Mrs Allen the new Wallis Simpson? The story went one step further with a string of other beauties the duke had courted including a jazz pianist Edythe Baker who had originally been involved with David. But according to the News Review, Edythe was even dearer in Kent's affections than Mrs Allen. And she was recently divorced.

Albert threw the paper on the table and rested his head in his hands. Kent's wife, Princess Marina, daughter of Prince Nicholas of Greece and related to the Danish and Russian royal family, had only just given birth to their second child, Alexandra, barely a week old. Their first child Edward was only fifteen months old. Marina had become a devoted mother and was no longer interested in the social whirl but it seemed his brother was still enthralled with the playboy life-style. Just when Albert was trying to promote the royal family as solid and reliable, Kent's many transgressions were there for the world to read, describing him as the archetypal royal bad boy. After Wallis Simpson, the gloves were off and the press was no longer holding their tongues when it came to royal indiscretions.

It was hard for Albert to know when Kent had changed from the sensitive boy he once was to the thrill-seeking celebrity he had become. Then he remembered their youngest brother John again and he realised it had been *his* death that had brought a change in Kent.

John had been the youngest of the five brothers and had suffered from epilepsy, seen in those days as a form of mental illness. It was also seen as a weakness and something to be ashamed of and as his condition had deteriorated, their father George V had insisted John be moved to a separate household on the Sandringham Estate away from the rest of the family.

The truth about John's life is difficult to separate from the rumours that were circulated and anything on the little boy has to be pieced together from tiny fragments because he was barely mentioned in history. Rumours say he was shut away when diagnosed with epilepsy at the age of 4. But is that actually the truth?

Epilepsy was stigmatised much more than it is today, seen as a sign of simple-mindedness. But for the young, endearing boy, related by blood to 20 reigning monarchs throughout Europe, being separated from his family at the age of 9 must have made him feel isolated and alone. At the time of his life when his condition was worsening, terrible events were unfolding in Europe in the summer of 1914 and Britain was experiencing the horror of a coming war. For the next four years and the rest of his life, his father's duties and his mother devotion to the war efforts would take them away from home and the family. He was also becoming more isolated from his siblings who were either away at boarding school or in the armed services. As he lost touch with his family, he began to slowly disappear from public view.

Kent had been very fond of his youngest brother but after John's sudden death at 13 years of age in 1919, Kent had changed almost overnight. He became unruly and bored with their father's choice for him in the Royal Navy so he had joined forces with his eldest brother at the heart of the high-society set. The two handsome brothers became inseparable, sharing the same pleasures and thrills, including an all-consuming interest in sex and married women.

As their father watched aghast, Kent acquired a long list of glamorous lovers, both men and women. His alleged affair with Noel Coward, as they walked the streets of London, only came to light after they were arrested for 'suspected prostitution'. Then there were claims of affairs with the future spy Anthony Blunt and their cousin Prince Louis Ferdinand of Prussia as well as a number of other young men, all blond and all foreign.

By the late 1920s, Kent had gone one step further with the beautiful heiress in Kenya Kiki Preston, *"the girl with the silver syringe"* and they had dabbled dangerously in drugs. Kiki was taking heroin, cocaine and morphine and when she was running low on supplies, she would despatch her private plane for more. As he became enthralled with the heiress, he became dependent on morphine and cocaine as well. Rumours even had it that in 1926 Kiki gave birth to an illegitimate son that she put up for adoption and that the child was Kent's child.

As the responsible older brother, David went to great lengths to keep the lovers apart, even finding a discreet retreat in 1929 for his brother under the watchful eyes of medical staff. Kent reappeared eventually, cured of his drug addiction, but little else. He set up house with his older brother in York House with happy spirits and once again, the handsome prince set about to fully enjoy life with the immensely rich. His charmed circle included Douglas Fairbanks Junior, Laurence Olivier and John Gielgud as well as the songwriter Cole Porter and the brilliant dancer Fred Astaire.

But the event that transformed Kent was the luncheon arranged by Lady Emerald Cunard. One guest was the striking Princess Marina of Greece. She made every woman in the room, including Wallis Simpson, look plain and

Kent, never one to do things half-heartedly, set out to shamelessly woo her. And of course, Marina could not resist him. He was tall, handsome and irresistible and their engagement was announced in August 1934. Three months later they were married with all the pageantry expected of a royal wedding and soon there was a baby on the way. And then a second one. Everyone believed the playboy had finally grown up.

But Kent had taken the abdication badly. The Kents had stayed away from the Christmas celebrations and Albert had assumed it was because the new baby was due at any time. But Kent had confided in his brother-in-law that he was feeling wretched about it all. When he'd asked Albert for permission to visit David in Austria, Albert could only refuse him. He'd looked jumpy and edgy and Albert was nervous of further press interest, unable to quite believe his brother would not let him down somehow. And by the looks of it, he'd been right.

To add to Albert's problems with his youngest brother, in the months leading up to the coronation on 12th May, more distressing news came in regarding David, causing deeper disagreements. And as usual, it all came down to money.

David had deceived him, without a doubt. Not lied but deceived. Before David left, he had demanded a promise that as well as his title of Duke of Windsor, he would be given an annual pension of £25,000. What he hadn't mentioned was that he had taken twenty years of wealth with him that he'd accumulated through the Duchy of Cornwall as Prince of Wales and the amount had been estimated at a staggering £1,000,000. A fact he had failed to mention to anyone when he gave up the throne. And then incredibly, after poring over the paperwork, officials had found that David had settled around £900,000 of that money on Wallis who was threatening to let the world know of Albert's filthy treatment of his brother.

Albert was well aware of how much Wallis hated him. Two days after David officially abdicated on 10th December, Albert had been the one to state that David would hold the title of Duke of Windsor but Wallis was not to be styled HRH. During one phone call on 14th December, she was overheard telling David in no uncertain terms that the title of 'Her Royal Highness' was essential. Being a duchess like countless others roaming Europe in obscurity was not an option.

An inspector from Scotland Yard, providing her with protection at the time, overheard her talking to David at midnight on 14-15 December. *"If they don't give you this thing, I will return to England and fight it out to the bitter end"*, she said. *"The coronation will be a flop compared to the story that I shall tell the British press. I will publish it in every paper in the world so that the whole world may know my story."* Apparently a diminishing status was not on Wallis's agenda.

Money would always be the main issue for Wallis and if David was under the illusion that she was soft-centred, then he was in for a rude shock. That David admired her strength and confidence was well known and if he was shocked by her tone, it was never recorded. What David did feel was regret that he had brought this all down on her. She was being hounded out of England by the press. She was receiving hate letters, and even death threats, and there seemed no end to the humiliation as the backlash turned against them. Even that one request to be called *'Her Royal Highness'* had been rejected. David telephoned Windsor daily, fuelled on by Wallis, expecting to speak to his brother regarding this one issue. But Albert could not, perhaps would not, give David what he wanted and in the end, officials had to stop the calls. David would never forgive his brother the insult. It was like a keg of dynamite waiting patiently for someone to light the fuse.

It wasn't just the denial of the title that caused conflict. The financial settlement angered David as well. The government declined to include David and Wallis on the Civil List, a list of individuals to whom money is paid by the government, and David's allowance was to be paid personally by Albert. But David had compromised his position with Albert by concealing the extent of his financial worth when they informally agreed on the amount of the allowance. Albert had already bought Sandringham House and Balmoral Castle from David, which were David's personal property inherited from their father George V as heir to the throne. Those estates had remained with David and had not automatically passed on to Albert on his accession so he knew David was not short of cash. It was always Wallis in the background wanting more. How could David not see the scheming and the greed in Wallis that everyone else could see?

As the coronation approached, Elizabeth hid her anxiety for her husband. On the Sunday before, prayers were said throughout the country and the archbishop had given them both his blessing but despite this, as the morning of the coronation dawned, Albert was visibly upset.

He'd rehearsed for weeks, both retracing the steps of his ancestors down the long aisle and more importantly, the coronation broadcast. But even still, there was no way of approaching the microphone with confidence. Millions were listening to see if there was any truth in the rumours that he suffered from epilepsy as his youngest brother John had but as he stepped up to the microphone, with his therapist close behind, there was a heart-stopping pause before he began hesitantly, *"It is with a very full heart that I speak to you tonight..."*.

David finally left Britain and as the cliffs of Dover faded into the distance on his way to France, he must have found a certain degree of peace. He was on his way to France to start a new chapter in his life with the woman of his dreams and although things were still on shaky ground, they were moving in the right direction.

His new residence for a while was the home of Baron Rothschild, where he had remained apart from Wallis until there was no risk of compromising the granting of the 'decree absolute' in her divorce proceedings two months before. But there was always the telephone and they sat for hours, day and night, redesigning their world.

They were reunited in France on 4th May 1937 and were scheduled to be married one month later on 3rd June. The wedding date would have been his father's 72nd birthday and his mother believed it had been scheduled as a deliberate affront. David knew well what his father felt about Wallis and by marrying the woman on his father's birthday only went to show his utter contempt for his father. He'd shown disrespect when his father was alive and he was still doing it after his death.

As the offence festered in everyone's hearts, it slowly turned to outright insult and Albert could only agree with his government that the royal family should not attend David's wedding. Not him. Not Henry. Not even David's favourite brother Kent, although Kent had already visited David in February and the two brothers had toured Austria under the watchful eye of a *Times* correspondent. With government standing firm on the issue, their cousin Louis Mountbatten withdrew his offer to act as best man and many members of the 'old court' found a polite reason to decline the invitation.

Wallis must have been more than a little angry. It was her marriage to the most talked about man in the world and his family was still shunning her. All of a sudden, she went from being a celebrity to a nonentity and she laid the blame at Albert's feet. Even the society pages were filled with news of Duke and Duchess of Kent with no mention of her at all. It was as if she had been forgotten while life went on happily without her.

To add salt to the wound, one week later on 12th May 1937, Albert, the son named after his great-grandfather Albert and the man who dreaded public speaking because of his stammer, became King George VI to restore confidence in the monarchy and emphasise continuity with his father. It was almost like a deliberate slap in David's face.

In the weeks following the accession, it was difficult for David and Wallis to hide their humiliation and fall from grace. Over 200 reporters flocked to France to witness the wedding but few friends had been brave enough to appear and not one family member attended. To top it off, they received a letter the day before stating that there would definitely be no 'HRH' for Wallis and her face showed the strain. The only thing she'd demanded was a royal title and the letter meant it was official: no title.

It was far from the wedding she had planned with laughter, important guests and sparkling atmosphere and her sense of loss was tangible. She'd gone from being a social butterfly with the prospect of being Queen of Great Britain to the most hated woman in the world with giddy speed. You could understand why she found it hard to smile that day. As for David, he could only feel seething anger towards his younger brother.

Apart from the absence of guests at the wedding, there was something else missing too. There seemed to be no visible signs of the powerful love that David had proclaimed he and Wallis shared just months before at his abdication speech. Wallis looked somehow hard wearing a baby-blue couturier dress and draped in huge sapphires, while David just looked sad and a little awkward as he stood with his arms crossed defensively across his chest.

By way of compensation, David planned a romantic honeymoon with every conceivable comfort. Complete with 266 pieces of luggage, they headed off to the peaceful Wasserleonburg Castle in the enchanting mountainside of the Austrian Tyrol, via Venice. Still Wallis could not let go. She spent hours every day in the office proudly reading through letters and telegrams and replying to each and every one with her new logo, 'WE' capped with a crown.

Some visitors filled the terrible void but soon they left and the castle was empty again and they were left alone. Boredom confronted them in every room and in the void, Wallis relived every trauma of the past weeks like a post mortem. Letters were sent to Kent almost begging him to visit but were rejected with polite excuses. His wife Princess Marina felt uncomfortable in acknowledging the new Duchess of Windsor.

Days stretched into weeks and the spectacular views and scenery became mundane for Wallis. She even took to writing tender letters to her ex-husband, confessing, *"I think of us so much, though I try not to."* What she needed was a distraction and it arrived in a gleaming Rolls Royce one beautiful sunny day as sunshine streamed into the castle. Charles Bedaux was a lively millionaire and he had arrived with a proposal for them.

Bedaux understood David's anger at his brother and his proposal was meant to put David back on the world stage with a tour beginning in thriving Nazi Germany. David would once again be in front of the press and he would look like the man who was championing the cause for the working man in Germany. Meetings would be arranged to talk to senior leaders of the Nazi party and David would be the voice of the common man. From there, they would tour America and gain more support. The world was their oyster and David was overjoyed at the proposal.

The offer covered everything for David and Wallis. The tour promised excitement and celebrity status and started in a health spa at Bad Reichenhall close to Hitler's Eagle's Nest retreat near Berchtesgaden. What they didn't know, but should have realised given his reputation, was that Bedaux was attempting to cash in on the show. On 1st July, the arrangements were made and the German Bedaux Company, which had once been seized by the Nazis, reopened for business.

If anything was going to make things worse at Buckingham Palace it was the danger of an expanding Third Reich. Every cinema was showing newsreels of Adolf Hitler bellowing to exuberant crowns who were almost hysterically besotted by their leader surrounded by ominous swastikas. The louder he roared the more they loved it and many would have thought they'd died and gone to Valhalla. Watching his impassioned and almost manic speeches on the newsreels, it was impossible to know what he had in mind.

While Albert watched the newsreels of Hitler nervously, Hitler and his foreign minister Joachim von Ribbentrop were welcoming David and Wallis on their tour of Germany.

With every chess piece on the move in Europe, the former king turning up in Berlin was an unexpected windfall for Hitler. He was well aware of David's pro-German views, not to mention his relatives. Let's not forget Charles Edward, Duke of Saxe-Coburg, a member of the Nazi party and the Brownshirts, who had mingled with the royal family as they mourned the death of George V. During the visit, Charles Edward had uncovered a lot of useful information for Hitler from David. David had expressed *"an urgent necessity"* for a German-British alliance and was quite prepared to take matters into his own hands. That view had not changed with David's abdication.

On 11th October 1937, at Buckingham Palace, Albert watched his brother and an exquisitely dressed Wallis on a newsreel as they emerged all smiles from a Berlin train station. A large crowd thronged to see the man who had thrown away the British throne for love and the woman herself, who seemed to possess magic and charm. There were bouquets for Wallis and Nazi salutes for David, while the 'workingmen' sang German and British national anthems. The newsreader informed the world that there would indeed be a dinner for the 'Royal Highnesses' entertained by General Goering who would then give the visitors a special tour of his large hunting estate north of Berlin. Then they would move on to Berghof, Adolf Hitler's mountainside retreat.

To the world, including Albert, Goering looked like a benign Santa Claus, which was the perfect foil for his position as commander in chief of the *Luftwaffe* intending to speed up rearmament. He had founded the Gestapo but was well and truly hidden behind a rosy, magnanimous manner. While Goering and David chatted, Wallis gazed around and took in the opulence of the estate from the gym in the basement, the flock of maids in peasant dresses and the lavish art treasures, which included a Rembrandt over the four-poster bed.

For two weeks, the papers showed the Windsors as they visited weapon factories already making U-boats and observed a few of the elite Academies for training young Aryans as future leaders. They met Joseph Goebbels but it must have been the highlight of the tour when they met with Hitler himself at his mountain hideaway in Berchtesgaden near the Austrian border. Pictures showed Wallis resplendent on David's arm as Hitler looked like he was almost rubbing his hands together in glee. There was an abundance of hand shaking and the Windsors offered Nazi salutes in return. Wallis was even mentioned as having had tea with Rudolf Hess while the Duke was concealed privately with Hitler.

The American tour could not have been any more different. Their arrival with Bedaux on 1st November got off to a bad start when the IRS handed an outstanding tax bill of $487,976 to Bedaux. Then the press began asking him embarrassing questions regarding his labour-management system. Was the Duke seriously interested in working conditions or was he just Bedaux's glorified salesman? To round off the visit, Bedaux was presented with a lawsuit of $250,000 from a former lover. In hot pursuit was a further bill from the IRS for a further $202,718. With hostility spiralling out of control, Bedaux handed control over to his manager and fled the country. In a state of shock, Bedaux collapsed in a hospital in Munich only to learn that he was required to hand back Bedaux Germany to the Nazis again. His American tour with the Windsors had proven to be the catalyst that had finally destroyed his golden goose and it had cost him dearly. It was certainly not the glorious finish to the tour that Wallis had imagined.

Albert may have been feeling unsure of himself, but he wasn't stupid. He was well aware that Kent was using his wife's relations in Europe as an excuse to visit the Windsors in Austria, despite Albert's instructions to do the opposite, and he hadn't stopped there. The Times had revealed that Kent was having meetings with his second cousins, relatives of the Hesse family, Prince Philipp of Hesse and his younger brother Prince Christoph.

On the surface, it all looked innocent. They were close to Kent's age and both were great-grandsons of Queen Victoria through her daughter Vicky and her marriage to the German Emperor Frederick III, which made Wilhelm their uncle. The threesome had become quite chummy, socialising at art galleries and racing events while Kent stayed with them at the magnificent Hesse estate in Germany.

What *was* disconcerting was that the two Hesse brothers were playing roles of their own in the Nazi party. Philipp had joined the Brownshirts and Christoph had joined the SS and it wasn't just Albert who was watching the brothers closely as they married into prestigious marriages. Hitler was watching them closely too.

Philipp had married Princess Mafalda, daughter of the King of Italy, so the close link to Benito Mussolini and the Fascist regime of Italy was especially timely for Hitler. Philipp's star began to shine brightly and he quickly found himself a part of Hitler's inner circle as an intermediary between the Italian and German leaders. As for Christoph, he had fallen in love with Princess Sophia of Greece and Denmark, a cousin of Kent's wife Princess Marina, and he was flourishing in Goering's intelligence division where his task was to bug the phones of the Windsors when they were in Austria. While they thrived in Hitler's inner circle, they still remained a part of the British royal family, which was why Albert was keeping a very watchful eye on Kent. In the back of his mind was Kent's unfailing support of David and the obvious opportunity for David to exploit him.

Any good politician tries to find allies. Not only allies but allies that will not turn against them. For Hitler, he saw the chance to make allies with members of the British royal family. After all, weren't they fundamentally of German descent? It wasn't as if he wanted to actually invade Britain. He had his sights set on more worthwhile achievements. His idea was to gain enough power to rebuild Germany after the Treaty of Versailles at the end of World War I and sympathetic allies sitting on the British throne could help him achieve that goal and insulate his plans. Unfortunately, humans being humans, he had personal hates that overshadowed any good intentions he may have had. Once he gained that power, he abused it. By attempting to violate the Versailles Treaty, he went too far.

The Treaty of Versailles was signed at the end of the First World War in 1919 and was supposed to ensure a lasting peace by punishing Germany and setting up a League of Nations to solve diplomatic problems. Instead it left a legacy of insurmountable difficulties that have often been blamed for starting the Second World War.

The terms of the Treaty left Germany having no choice but to accept total blame for the war and pay £6,600 million in compensation. The victorious powers had spent a colossal sum of money and they wanted that money to be paid back. There was ruined landscape and economy to rebuild and France and Britain in particular were facing huge bills while the German economic heartlands had virtually escaped. When viewing their own sagging economy, the decision was easy. Germany had to pay.

When Germany was presented with the peace terms by the victorious powers, they were presented with a stark choice: sign or be invaded. Germany's wartime weapons were to be scrapped and their army was to be cut to 100,000 men. Their navy would be cut to 36 ships and there would be no submarines. As well as that, any land captured by Germany was to be returned. The Saar, an important German coalfield, was to be given to France for 15 years after which members of a specially formed electorate would decide ownership and Poland was to become an independent country with a corridor of land cutting Germany in two. The treaty meant Germany would lose 13% of its land, 12% of its people, 48% of its iron resources, 15% of its agricultural production and 10% of its coal.

From the very start, the terms of the Treaty caused anger, even hate, in parts of German society. They had offered an armistice to their enemies but instead they received something very different. With no chance to negotiate terms, they had to accept the peace given or suffer the consequences. So they signed but they always felt they had been stabbed in the back. And Hitler fed on this hate and took it to a new level.

It can be argued that Hitler would never have taken power without the massive economic depression that struck the world in the late 20s/early 30s. Hitler argued that Germany's economic troubles were due to the Treaty of Versailles and he promised a way out. After 15 years, Germany was ripe for a charismatic leader to inspire them for rebellion at the unfairness of the Treaty of Versailles restraints. And Hitler was that man. After being a foot soldier in the first World War, he moved into politics with a message that people wanted to hear. I'll rebuild the country, he bellowed. And the people of Germany listened raptly.

Albert was right to watch Europe closely. In March 1938, a crisis erupted without warning. Phones in Downing Street began ringing furiously when a rumour emerged that German troops in Bavaria had suddenly moved to the southern border of Austria. By lunchtime, while the Prime Minister, Neville Chamberlain, and another leading minister, Winston Churchill, were meeting with Ribbentrop, a message arrived saying that the Germans had entered Austria. By that evening, the Austrian government had stepped down and German troops were marching further to Vienna. The police who were keeping order were wearing swastika armbands as the Nazi flag flew over the Chancery and on the wireless, Viennese waltzes were changed to Hitler's favourite Stormtroopers song. Hitler had moved with lightning speed to take a German-speaking country for his Reich and by midnight, Austria had become part of Germany.

Albert sat in stunned silence waiting for further news to reach him. He was dependent on the *Times* for the latest developments and the next morning, he read that Austria's leading cities were entirely under control of the Nazis who were surging in vast masses shouting Nazi slogans, including anti-Jewish ones. Hitler had even begun a triumphal tour.

It had all been too easy for Hitler. Europe had been ripe and he took full advantage of the situation. Six weeks later, Czechoslovakia became his next conquest, more particularly the Sudetenland. This wide strip of land that bordered German (and Austria) was home to 3,000,000 ethnic German-speaking people comprising almost a quarter of the population of Czechoslovakia. In the Treaty of Versailles, the Sudetenland had been taken from Germany and given to the new Czechoslovak state, against the wishes of much of the local population, based purely on a French intent to weaken Germany.

Czechoslovakia was well aware Hitler had his eyes on the Sudetenland. It was an important strategic part of Czechoslovakia as most of its border defences, banks and heavy industrial districts were situated there. It would be a major loss and one they felt sure Britain and France fully understood.

Before anyone knew it, while Hitler gathered his troops on the border, Czechoslovakia mobilised their army. By the weekend, the world was holding its breath and waiting. Telegrams flew backwards and forwards between European embassies and Halifax, the Secretary of State for Foreign Affairs, told the Germans that if they attacked Czechoslovakia, Britain would support France. It was déjà vu of World War 1.

It was while these words were still ringing in everyone's ears that Albert and Elizabeth sailed on the HMS *Enchantress* bound for France. It was a show of solidarity to the French and the crowds gathered warmly to greet them. It was as though the whole of France had forgotten past wars and differences and were suddenly in love with the British royals. Albert spoke of peace and co-operation and the common purpose of the French and British people and on camera, his handsome features and slim figure looked regal and stately. His speeches, still halting and sometimes poorly delivered, stood for integrity and together, he and Elizabeth embodied hope from the threats of the dark forces of the Nazis.

As the unease of the summer moved onto September, Europe was trembling on the verge of war. Hitler was still demanding the Sudetenland and

Czechoslovakia were still refusing to hand it over. France was promising to march against Germany if Czechoslovakia was violated and Britain had promised to support France. As the delicate balance of peace quivered, Neville Chamberlain asked to have a meeting with Hitler and at 69 years of age, he came face to face with the Fuhrer at Berchtesgaden.

It would seem that Britain had little faith in Chamberlain accomplishing much because while Chamberlain talked peace with Hitler, gas masks were being distributed in London. Even Albert was fitted with one. Trenches were excavated in London parks, basements were turned into shelters, anti-aircraft guns were positioned on Westminster Bridge and air-raid systems were tested, its ominous wail echoing through the cities. The talk was only of war and scenes of Flanders and the Somme, buried by time, resurfaced.

Albert's stress was plain to see. He watched newsreels as Hitler, bloated with success, descended into Italy to meet with Mussolini amid giant swastikas and flags billowing above military parades and he watched the Nuremberg Rally in September where the square at Nuremberg was filled to capacity eagerly waiting for Hitler to appear and speak to them. When Albert heard the Fuhrer's impassioned speech under the huge dome of lights telling the vast audience that he knew he could trust them and that they could trust him, Albert was seriously alarmed. Hitler bellowed, *"May Germany live and may her future, which lives in you, be praised!"* And as Albert watched, they roared back, *"We will follow our leader."*

But while Hitler had only stated that if Czechoslovakia would not hand over Sudetenland, Germany would take it by force, he now added another demand. The claims of ethnic Germans in Poland and Hungary also had to be satisfied. And the deadline was 28th September.

Albert's worst fears had materialised. All he could do was wait until his worst nightmare began.

It was Neville Chamberlain who devised a way out. Four hours before the deadline, he advised the British ambassador to Italy to send a message to the Foreign Minister in Italy to request an urgent meeting with Mussolini, urging him to enter negotiations to urge Hitler to delay the ultimatum. Mussolini agreed and telephoned his ambassador to Germany, telling him *"Go to the Fuhrer at once, and tell him that whatever happens, I will be at his side, but I request a twenty-four hour delay before hostilities begin. Mean-*

while, I will study what can be done to solve the problem." On hearing the message, Hitler agreed to delay the invasion date until 1st October.

When the House of Commons assembled, Chamberlain waved an invitation for him to meet with Mussolini in Munich the next day. At the meeting, he said, he would agree to hand over Sudetenland if Hitler promised to stop advancing through Europe. Not knowing where else to go, Albert agreed with his Prime Minister.

The meeting in Munich was attended by British, French and Italian prime ministers ready to give Hitler what he wanted in the hope that he would not demand any more. The Sudetenland would be handed over to the Reich *"for the sake of peace",* but in return Hitler was to give his word that Germany would not make any further demands of territories in Europe. The next day, Chamberlain went to Hitler and asked him to sign a peace treaty between United Kingdom and Germany and as his interpreter read it to him, Hitler happily agreed.

Two days later, Chamberlain stepped off his plane from Munich with the sheet of white paper in his hand to the roar of ovation from the British people. His car was engulfed and everyone was ecstatic as he rode through the streets of London on the way to Buckingham Palace. Peace had been won, British honour was upheld and Hitler had promised not to advance any further.

It was unfortunate for Czechoslovakia that they had not been permitted to attend the conference with Hitler and you can forgive them for the anger that followed the decision. On that day, and with no input of their own, Czechoslovakia lost 70% of its iron and steel, 70% of its electrical power and 3.5 million citizens to Germany. When they were told of the decision, Britain added that imminent war had been avoided but if Czechoslovakia did not accept the agreement, France and Britain would consider Czechoslovakia to be responsible for the war that followed.

In the face of so much opposition and knowing that they could not stop Nazi Germany alone, President Edvard Benes submitted and Germany took the Sudetenland unopposed. Three days later, Benes resigned, realising that the fall of Czechoslovakia was inevitable. At the same time that Benes stepped out of his office, 115,000 Czechs and 30,000 Germans fled to the remaining rump of Czechoslovakia.

It wasn't just Czechoslovakia who was upset by the results of the

Munich conference. The Soviets, headed by Joseph Stalin, had a mutual military assistance treaty with Czechoslovakia and they felt betrayed by France who also had the same treaty. He felt the Soviets had been used by Britain and France and had actively colluded with Hitler to hand over the European country to the Nazis. His concern was that Hitler would pull the same stunt with his country in the future. And the French Prime Minister could only agree with him. He believed that no matter what Hitler promised, *"...Today it is the turn of Czechoslovakia. Tomorrow it will be the turn of Poland and Romania. When Germany has obtained all the oil and wheat it needs, she will turn on the West."*

In Britain, as Chamberlain basked in his new hero status, Winston Churchill was vehemently denouncing the Munich Agreement as *"a total and unmitigated defeat...you will find that in a period of time which may be measured by years, but may be months, the whole of Czechoslovakia will be engulfed in the Nazi regime. We are in the presence of a disaster of the first magnitude ... we have sustained a defeat without a war ... this is only the beginning of the reckoning. This is only the first sip, the first foretaste, of a bitter cup ... England has been offered a choice between war and shame. She has chosen shame, and will get war."*

The strained peace lasted for only a few weeks. A little over a month later, Churchill's words came back to haunt them. A wave of anti-Semitic violence erupted in Germany as both paramilitary and citizens attacked Jews and smashed Jewish homes, hospitals and schools with sledgehammers while the German authorities looked on without intervening.

It was a night named *Kristallnacht or "Night of the Broken Glass."* 1,000 Synagogues were incinerated from Vienna to Berlin, 7,000 Jewish businesses were destroyed and 30,000 Jews were arrested and sent to concentration camps. Amazingly, only 91 Jews lost their lives. As it was happening, accounts from foreign journalists working in Germany sent shock waves around the world. *The Times* wrote, *"... a blackguardly assault on defenceless and innocent people, which disgraced that country..."*

In hindsight, it all seemed inevitable because only months before, the German authorities had announced that residence permits for foreigners were being cancelled. This included German-born Jews of foreign origin and hot on Germany's tail, Poland stated that it would not accept Jews of Polish origin after the end of October.

The Jews have been targets for Christians for centuries since Jesus Christ. Jews ran the gold trade, the diamond trade and money lending and had their hands deep in a lot of European finances. While the average citizen in Germany was suffering from the reparation after World War 1, Jewish enclaves on the whole were better off than the average citizen and as such, they became easy targets for thugs and bullies who didn't need much encouragement to smash and burn. And a politician like Hitler who menacingly said the Jews had all the money while Germany had none, the motto of *"let's get rid of the Jews and take their money"* became very popular.

On 28th October, on Hitler's orders, 12,000 Polish Jews were ordered to leave Germany on a single night with only one suitcase per person to carry their belongings. As the Jews were taken away, their remaining possessions were seized as loot by both the Nazi authorities and their neighbours. They were taken from their homes to railway stations and were put on trains to the Polish border where Polish border guards sent them back over the river to Germany. The stalemate continued for days in the pouring rain with the Jews marching backwards and forwards between borders without food or shelter. Most decided to stay put on the border, not welcome in either country.

While Albert and his government were supporting appeasement at any cost, the Windsors seemed oblivious to what was happening around them. They were living it up in a magnificent villa in one of the most prestigious parts of the French Riviera near Cannes and as the New Year dawned, they were spending lavishly, recreating a royal palace of their own. As for Kent, he was once again ushering in the New Year with one of his glamorous women friends while Albert was watching an older and thinner Prince Philipp of Hesse rise higher and higher in the Nazi ranks, even appearing in newsreels with Hitler as part of his inner circle. Still, as the royal family gathered at Sandringham, Albert was happy that there was no Christmas speech to deliver that year. The general feeling was one of relief that the worst was over.

Until 14th March when disturbing news from Europe began filtering in again.

Nervous questions were being asked concerning Germany and a renewal of interest they were showing in Czechoslovakia and almost as a premonition, the Czech government had resigned. The next day, the question was answered. German troops arrived in Prague and Czechoslovakia, as the country was being wiped off the map.

Everything that Hitler had promised and Chamberlain had worked tirelessly to achieve in Munich was overturned and the conciliation, uneasy and tense in the past, was finally shattered. Although keeping a calm exterior, Chamberlain was heartbroken as he remembered the piece of paper clutched in his hand, fluttering in the breeze, as he waved it so proudly after his return from Munich. With this new German advance, it was utterly worthless.

Along with the rest of the world, Mussolini watched the Germans advance. He was never a man to be outdone, especially not by Hitler, and he wanted Albania, a little country that was a foothold to the Balkans sharing borders with Greece and Yugoslavia. And he wanted it just as much as Hitler had wanted Austria and Czechoslovakia. Three weeks later, every Albanian port was under fire from Italy and within hours of the onslaught, they had all surrendered.

It was Yugoslavia's turn to feel threatened now with borders on both Italy and Austria, especially since Hitler and Mussolini had signed an alliance in which Germany and Italy would come to each other's aid if war were declared.

In public, Albert and Elizabeth hid their worries but in private, Albert was more stressed than ever. Plans had been made for a tour of Canada and despite what was happening in Europe, he decided to go ahead with it, leaving his brother Henry as his Senior Councillor of State in his absence and Kent as Governor General in Australia.

Albert was only four days into the trip when David suddenly visited a World War 1 battlefield, *"as a soldier of the last war"* on NBC America. He was making a plea for world peace and millions listened to the magic in his voice as he spoke of *"dangerous political passions"*.

Everyone in Britain knew it was a deliberate attempt to upstage Albert. After seeing newsreels of the Windsors smiling and laughing with Hitler, there were few people left in Britain who could say they felt any sympathy for the tarnished pair. In Britain there was no applause at the end of his speech and the BBC refused to even air his statement. Everyone saw it as his chance to grab the limelight from Albert who was being seen by more than 15 million people in Canada. What England wanted was a leader they could trust. Not one who shook hands and smiled into the eyes of their worst enemy. David had once been their golden-haired ruler but he had turned his coat and deserted them. In his duplicity, they saw him through different eyes and what they saw they loathed. At Buckingham Palace, even Kent saw through him and did not support him. By Albert's return in late June, it was obvious that Britain looked up to him as their figurehead, which was something he had never thought possible.

****

The wedding of Princess Irene of Greece and the Duke of Spoleto of Italy in Florence was the most glittering event planned for the summer season in Europe that year. The date was set for 2nd July and the extensive guest list included the royal houses of Queen Victoria's many descendants, great and small.

It was as if Florence had not heard of the prospect of war as a radiant sun dawned for the spectacular royal wedding. Flags were flying and crowds were cheering jubilantly standing ready to applaud each royal party as they arrived in their finery as if there was no sign of imminent danger. Mingling among the guests, keeping an eagle eye on events as they happened, was Philipp of Hesse hoping for a quiet word with his cousin Kent.

Over the two days, ambassadors missed the two cousins talking discreetly in quiet conversation. Perhaps because of the happy occasion of the wedding with no threat of imminent danger, Kent felt relaxed. It was in this peaceful idyllic setting that he revealed enough of the British position to his cousin to send him scurrying back home to Germany demanding an immediate appointment with Hitler. It wasn't until the end of August that Philipp of Hesse finally stood in the Fuhrer's inner sanctum and confided everything he had learned from Kent. A German attack on Poland would force Britain to declare war, he said, and that could lead Germany to ruin. The message was clear. If there was a move on Poland, the result would not be a local war. It would be the start of a second World War.

Given the nature of the secrets Kent had whispered to his cousin, it should have been seen as warnings *not* to proceed with an invasion of Poland. 'There would be consequences' was the inference and if Hitler had been listening, it would have stopped him in his tracks. But it wasn't Hesse that Hitler was listening to. It was Ribbentrop who was holding his full attention. Ribbentrop had managed a non-aggression pact with the Soviet Union making Hitler and Germany feel safe behind the Soviet Union's skirts because Britain would not possibly take on Germany with such a powerful country now on their side. In Hitler's excitement, Kent's warning was pushed aside and Hesse was dismissed.

Albert knew it was all too late for a remedy. World leaders were being swept helplessly along and persistent threats hung heavily in the air as heavy-weight dictators moved dangerously closer to war. He looked and felt weary and a resigned acceptance hung uncertainly in the House of Commons. Churchill, head in hands, knew that war was now inevitable. The irrevocable had happened and the world was trapped in a fatal, cataclysmic whirlpool of the unknown.

In the ominous quiet emanating from Europe, while Germany and the Soviet Union were busy making the pact, a fresh wave of volunteering began in Britain as people hurried to help with evacuation plans, first-aid units, defence and millions of other necessities. By 31st August, hundreds of machines had excavated earth to fill sandbags and the familiar outlines of London were transformed with sandbag walls as searchlights were secured in position. Traffic lights were screened with hoods and white lines were painted on footpaths for guidance during blackouts. Children with knapsacks on their backs and gas masks in their hand crammed into railway stations rehearsing evacuation plans that would certainly become a reality. Those with no shelters dug trenches and windows were boarded up, crisscrossed with sticky tape as protection when a blast happened. Even at Buckingham Palace staff organised the blackout of 700 windows.

As Britain prepared for the worst, Kent and Henry returned to Albert's side representing a united front while in France, David remained beside the sparkling Mediterranean Sea, listening to the sounds of soft waves lapping on the golden beach, unwilling to return home to England unless his demands were met regarding Wallis. Until that day, he stated, he would remain where he was.

One by one, David's small court said their good-byes before the sounds of war approached. He remained immovable even when a call came to him on the phone telling him that Albert was sending his private plane to bring him home. Once again, he repeated that there was only three things that would induce him to return: he was to be invited to stay at Windsor Castle and both the invitation and plane were to be sent personally by Albert. And of course, Wallis was to have the title she deserved.

If it had been hundreds of years in the past, Albert would have needed to watch out for himself. David was virtually standing with his sword at the ready, more than willing to avenge the honour of his wife, fuelled on by her indignation. But by then, Albert had become just as unrelenting.

On 1st September at five in the morning, the sleepy Polish port of Danzig woke up to the full force of the destructive force of Germany's Luftwaffe as armoured cars began streaming into Poland. At the same time, as heavy guns from a German warship pounded the Baltic coast, the Windsors were stretching and yawning on the Riviera, wondering how they were going to fill their day, while Londoners were blacking themselves out, trying to hide the glittering city and winding river, silver in the moonlight, as they awaited Hitler's next move.

For England, September 3rd is a date that keeps returning infamously over and over in history. Oliver Cromwell began his cold-blooded, brutal attack on Drogheda on September 3rd 1649. It was the anniversary of both the Battles of Dunbar and the Battle of Worcester, one year apart from each other, and it was on 3rd September that Elizabeth, Charles I's daughter, had first contracted the cold that had turned into pneumonia and killed her. It also seems somehow befitting that Cromwell's painful death from septicaemia should come in the middle of a howling storm on September 3rd as thunder roared and lightning flashed. It was also the date when Charles II woke in the pre-dawn hours and stood at his bedroom window watching London blazing below him as showers of hot ash filled the night skies. As he stared down in shock at the chaos the Great Fire of London had caused, a thought must have crossed his mind. The date was September 3rd again and all hell had broken loose once more.

This September 3rd, 1939, dawned glorious and church bells rang throughout the country. It was a Sunday and a vicious storm had raged the night before. That morning, at 11 am, the summer skies were the essence of tranquillity as an announcement from a BBC presenter spoke. *"You will now hear a statement by the Prime Minister."*

Chamberlain's voice began querulously, marking the gravity of the message. Hitler would not withdraw from Poland and Britain was at war with Germany, he stated. There was no pause and no hesitation in his voice and as he spoke, the penetrating whine of air-raid sirens cut through his voice, bringing with it the terrible reality. In the chaos, Albert and Elizabeth made their way down to the palace basement converted into an emergency shelter clutching their gas masks.

That night, it was Albert's turn to address the nation. His words were hesitant, his voice was flat but the message was clear. Germany had forced Britain into a conflict. His stirring words resonated around homes and offices and people fell silent, awed at the immensity of what their king was saying.

"FOR THE SAKE of all that we ourselves hold dear, and of the world's order and peace, it is unthinkable that we should refuse this challenge. It is to this high purpose that I now call my people at home and my peoples across the Seas, who will make our cause their own ... We can only do the right as we see the right, and reverently commit our case to God."

HIS WORDS WERE HEARD all around the world. The Pacific Dominions declared war on Germany at the same time as Australia, New Zealand, South Africa and Canada. A few days later France followed. The next day, Albert and his wife, tired and disorientated, retraced their steps to their shelter in the small hours of September 4th as the sirens wailed again, penetrating the darkness.

In Berlin, Hitler was astonished at the declarations of war coming from all over the world. Although Philipp of Hesse had been one of many who had tried to warn Hitler, it was Ribbentrop who had fuelled Hitler's fantasy that Britain would not fight. Goering too had urged for a negotiated settlement and as war declarations flooded in, he simmered with rage. He had been unable to counter Hitler's belief that he could invade Poland with impunity.

Ribbentrop had stepped on a political banana peel. In just one week, he had gone from being revered by Hitler for the German pact with Russia to being banished from Hitler's presence when Britain affirmed their support for Poland. Mussolini too had declared that Italians would not fight, something no one had expected.

In the end, it was Churchill who indirectly brought the Windsors back to Britain by asking Louis Mountbatten to intervene. But if the Windsors thought it would be to a riotous fanfare, they were terribly disappointed. A length of red carpet *was* hastily procured and a brass band *did* play a short version of the National Anthem as they arrived. But at the end of the carpet, there was no family waiting or welcoming warmth to greet them. Not even Kent, David's favourite brother, or his mother, waited to welcome them. And there was no chauffeured car to whisk them off to Fort Belvedere.

The two brothers, David and Albert, met on 14th September in Buckingham Palace and to everyone who observed, it was clear David had not lost his swaggering confidence. But childhood recollections, full of insecurity and vulnerability at David's dominance, slowly flooded Albert's memory. He had always been in his older brother's shadow and the feeling that he was never quite good enough had always been hovering just below the surface. In the back of his mind also would have been the fact that his brother had fostered relations with the enemy in Germany and when looking hard at his brother, he would not have seen any signs of remorse. On the contrary. The association had put him in the limelight and in the starring role where he felt entitled, comfortable and deserving.

It took only two weeks for David to realise he wasn't welcome in England anymore. At the end of that fortnight, he headed back to France just in time for news that the Soviet Red Army had invaded Poland with a 465,000 force. Poland was being crushed: the Nazis on one side and the Communists on the other.

As the Soviets were flexing their muscles, Hitler was beginning to show ominous signs of instability. On one hand, while he gloated over the success of the German Blitzkrieg in Poland, (a short powerful form of armoured warfare), he was talking of his desire for peace and how it was England who had first seized the opportunity to resume a fight with Germany. This jumble of sentiments was making people begin to wonder at the sanity of it all and whether Hitler was just a little disconnected from reality. When he suggested that British negotiators should come to Berlin to talk, people were looking at each other in amazement. It was at that moment when the Red Army marched further into Finland in November with 450,000 troops.

While Europe struggled through the chaos, Britain remained in a state of uneasy calm. Harvest time came, evacuees returned home and then the

Christmas speech was upon them again. Still the Blitzkrieg did not come. As Albert tried to bolster morale at home, his younger brother Henry lingered in France with troops waiting perpetually for the Germans to attack. Through the winter months, the roads remained glassy, clothes never dried and everyone seemed to have the flu while they braced themselves for their worst fears. It was an interminable wait for Henry, a man used to activity but now he was forced to endlessly peer through bare trees across a barren landscape during snow and ice storms for any movement on the horizon in the coldest winter for forty-five years.

Still London remained intact. The Thames froze over like a white icy sheet threading its way through London as people walked about seemingly carefree. But while mothers walked with babies in prams, people walked dogs and children skated on the ice, the Finns were fighting for their lives with indomitable spirit. They were dressing in white as camouflage and skiing into Russian camps, emerging from frozen landscapes with frightening speed to hurtle a new type of petrol bomb called a 'Molotov cocktail' as machine guns blazed fiercely. Dubbed the 'White Death' by the Soviets, the Soviets could freeze to death once injured and tens of thousands did exactly that. Still the British government did not take action. They simply waited their turn.

Waiting was not David's way of doing things. Still smarting from his cool reception in Britain and already feeling like he was being overlooked, he needed to keep himself in the thick of things. The neutral countries of Europe, in particular Belgium, were the perfect launchpad for him. He knew there was an Allied War Council due to discuss strategy and he couldn't resist attending.

As it turned out, Albert had been wise to advise his government not to give his brother any information concerning British policy. Not that it made any difference to David. He felt confident enough to grandstand the meeting of members of the Council and state that his timid brother would not proceed to war, even if provoked, and that the Allies would not occupy Belgium if the Germans invaded. And Ribbentrop, eager to be in Hitler's good books once again and delighted to have insight into the Allies strategy, passed the information on to Hitler. In actual fact, the truth was the exact opposite. If Germany attacked, Allied troops would defend Belgium at any cost.

As David bluffed his way through German politics, his brother Henry was throwing his weight into war preparations in France. He was inspecting storage facilities for ammunition and supplies in Rennes. He visited workshops for vehicle maintenance in Nantes and at Le Havre and he inspected the repairs of guns and tanks. Through the bitter chill of winter as the cruel winds howled, he tried his best to bolster morale, despite his own low spirits separated from his wife and family.

Spring brought bad news to the Allies. The Soviet Union had increased their endless number of troops and by mid-March, they invaded Finland. Britain's promise of help had come too late and the eight bombers promised were never going to be enough. The Russians were now in possession of critical industrial lands, immense saw mills and power stations while German propaganda offered up a continual flow of ominous threats of German merchant ships being adapted to carry troops. To Albert, no matter what he did, things went from bad to worse.

As men were dying agonisingly a thousand miles away over Easter and Albert worried himself sick, David was walking into Cartier in Paris with jewels clinking in his pockets ready to order a new creation for Wallis. He wanted something showy with diamonds, rubies, emeralds and sapphires. Wallis liked showy things, he said. A complicated flamingo brooch perhaps? One with tail feathers and retractable legs so that it would not dig into Wallis as she leant over? As David was pinning the trinket on Wallis, news came in that Germany had attacked the neutral countries of Norway and Denmark and troops had already arrived in Copenhagen.

It only took two hours for Denmark to surrender since they had little more than a police force and with that fresh success, the nagging worry was for Norway and Albert's uncle. Albert had last seen his 'Uncle Charles', King Haakon VII of Norway, on a cold wintery day in November 1938 at the funeral of his wife, Princess Maud, the youngest daughter of Edward VII and Alexandra of Denmark. Before the day was out, Albert learned that his 68-year-old Uncle Charles was fleeing from Oslo. What he didn't know was that Hitler had given strict instructions that the monarch should not escape. German warships had entered the fjord at Oslo and a team of Gestapo agents were under instruction to capture the Norwegian king.

If Hitler thought Norway would be as easy to conquer as Denmark, he had another thing coming. King Haakon took a different view from his brother, King Christian of Denmark. He would never surrender, and Norway would resist the Germans as long as possible, whatever the consequences.

The Luftwaffe went into overdrive, bombing villages where they thought the king was staying. Mercifully, he and his son escaped into the surrounding countryside in heavy snowfall, heading for the northern tip of Norway within the Arctic Circle where they hid in a log cabin deep in the forest. Still the bombs kept coming and still Britain waited.

While Norway struggled, the British MPs turned on Chamberlain. One by one, the members of the House fumed at him, venting their anger at his handling of the war and demanding his resignation. He had been buckling under the strain of being Prime Minister for years but giving up his post was something he refused to do. That is, until a bright sunny day on 8th May when he quietly walked out of the House of Commons, looking bowled over by the lack of support from his loyal allies. As the doors closed solidly behind him, he could hear the humiliating cheers and chants reverberating. The next day, he offered his resignation. In the shadows, Winston Churchill was waiting his turn.

Winston Churchill could trace his heritage back a long way. Not only was he born into a branch of the noble Spencer family, he could trace his ancestors back to the first Duke of Marlborough, John Churchill, who had married Queen Anne's notorious companion, Sarah Jennings.

Sarah had been Anne's long-time confidante during her numerous stillbirths and miscarriages when James II was plotting to retrieve his throne back from Anne's sister and husband, William and Mary of Orange. For their devotion and service to Anne, John and Sarah were given Blenheim Castle and the title of Duke and Duchess of Marlborough. It was also one of Sarah and John's daughters, Anne, who married Charles Spencer, 3rd Earl of Sunderland, and had a daughter they named Diana.

With a grandmother as influential as Sarah Churchill, her granddaughter Lady Diana was at the top of the list of eligible high society brides. She had beauty and breeding and it was no wonder that she had many suitors. So when the first round of negotiations for a bride for Prince Frederick, the son of King George II, fell through, Sarah Churchill pushed very hard for a proposed marriage between Frederick and Diana. Diana's early years had been spent in close contact with the children of George II, despite the initial aloof relationship between her grandmother and his family, so Sarah felt it was a given that the couple should marry since they already knew each other so well. With her granddaughter married to Frederick, she would reach the pinnacle of power when Diana finally became the Queen.

For someone like Sarah, whose humble beginnings were well known, it was a huge achievement and the idea almost consumed Sarah. As an added enticement, Diana's already massive dowry was raised to £100,000, which would undoubtedly help erase Frederick's huge gambling debts. The ceremony was arranged to take place in secret in the lodge of the Windsor Great Park and the date was set and agreed upon.

Robert Walpole was the Prime Minister at the time and he had an impressive spy system. When he heard of the upcoming nuptials, he strongly vetoed them. Not only had Diana's father been involved in the notorious South Sea Bubble fiasco, he had been implicated in what had become known as the Atterbury Plot of 1722 aimed at restoring the Stuarts to the throne. The Duke of Orleans, Regent of France, had made it known to Walpole's Secretary of State that the Jacobites had asked him to send 3,000 men in support of a coup d'état to take place in May of that year. Charles Spencer's papers had been seized and a letter of thanks addressed to him had come to light. Besides all of that, Walpole much preferred a European match anyway.

So instead of marrying Frederick, Lady Diana married the Duke of Bedford. A few years later, Lady Diana would die from tuberculosis and Wimbledon House, her inheritance according to her grandmother's will, passed instead to her brother John. In 1961, her brother's descendant, Edward John Spencer, 8th Earl of Spencer, styled Viscount Althorp, would become the father of a beautiful baby daughter whose name was chosen a week after her birth. The infant would be christened Diana after her ancestor, Lady Diana, Duchess of Bedford. Through another of Sarah's grandchildren, a boy by the name of Charles Churchill, a son would be born in a bedroom in Blenheim Place in 1874 and christened Winston Churchill.

From an early age, Winston Churchill was independent and rebellious by nature and generally had a poor academic record in school. The stocky boy with red hair who talked with a lisp and who had dentures specially designed to aid his speech grew into a young man who tried and failed three times in 1893 to pass the entrance exam in order to attend the Royal Military College in Sandhurst.

Forty-seven years later, in May 1940, Churchill was being summoned to the palace and as he drove through the streets, newspapers proclaimed: *"Brussels bombed", "Lille bombed"* and even *"Bombs in Kent".* Through the darkness in the middle of the night, the German tanks and infantry had crossed into the Lowlands and the front blazed with gunfire throughout Belgium, Netherlands and Luxembourg. German bombers had dived over airfields unleashing terror.

The attack had taken the Netherlands by surprise. Despite the Dutch neutrality, high above the sleeping towns the Luftwaffe soared, circling to bomb Dutch airfields while German planes dropped 5,000 paratroopers to glide silently down to the leading industrial port of Rotterdam. Their mission was to seize bridges and airfields and then move onto The Hague. Allied soldiers had been sent to Belgium in anticipation that Germany would attack France through Belgium.

When Churchill arrived at the palace gates, there was no crowd. He was swiftly taken to Albert who had received a call from the Netherlands during the night saying they were under attack Blitzkrieg fashion. He needed Churchill to step up and take over the role of new prime minister immediately and with a great deal of relief, Albert watched as Churchill immediately set about forming his War Cabinet as the battle intensified in the Netherlands and Belgium.

It turned out to be in the nick of time. Days later, three German divisions broke through at Sedan in France near the Belgian border, 150 miles north-east of Paris and the French, lulled by nine months of inactivity, were flung into a deadly fire of bombing. They had managed to do it just as the Luftwaffe exploded Rotterdam in a fireball.

Churchill took over at a time when Britain was at its most vulnerable. He'd only been in office five days when he received a call in the early hours of the morning from the French Premier in Paris. The words from the other end of the phone sent chills up and down his spine. *"We have been defeated. We are beaten. We have lost the battle."* As the news began to sink in, he heard that Amsterdam and Utrecht had suffered the same fate. At 11am, the Dutch had lain down their arms.

Henry Duke of Gloucester was driving through Belgium when he heard the news about the Netherlands, unaware of the catastrophe unfolding behind them in France. Suddenly Henry was in the thick of it all. With no warning at all, bombers were overhead and around them bombs began to fall. Buildings were exploding into flame as planes dived low to drop their bombs. Suddenly his car was on fire and somehow, he and his driver managed to escape. Dodging falling debris and unable to see anything but clouds of dust, they dashed for cover in a nearby alleyway as the ground began to vibrate. Before their eyes, the car was engulfed in flames.

Paris as well was in chaos. People were fleeing and the roads were jammed with cars brimming with household treasures and the people without cars, ran with infants in their arms, carrying anything they could, driven by fear of the enemy so close behind them.

While Albert and his prime minister struggled with the news of the German attacks, Henry was running for his life. Kent had also managed a transfer to the Royal Air Force hoping to be close at hand to raise morale in the troops. David was neither with British or French troops. He had decided that fashionable Biarritz in the south of France was well away from the noise of battle. There was a wonderful sandy beach with beautiful casinos, which was a much better setting for his bejewelled wife with her stunning flamingo brooch. It was obvious that David did not feel any threat from the Nazis.

At 65 years of age, an old man by military standards, Churchill was larger than life and a man on a mission. He had a lot to do and not much time left to put things right. With the memory of the French Premier's panicked voice still ringing in his ears, Churchill flew under gloomy skies to Paris. What he found stunned him. He was greeted with an air of hopelessness. The Germans were expected within days and the French were already burning their State archives. It was as though they had given up and were already defeated.

Albert was still waiting at the palace, desperate for news, when Henry walked confidently unannounced into the room. He had waited for the noise to cease before emerging from his hiding place and as soon as he could, he'd fled on foot, bleeding badly. He'd managed to get to the French port of Boulogne before making his way home.

Probably for the first time, Albert saw his brother in a new light. He was his usual unflappable self, full of bravado, and he was putting everything in a positive light to help Albert's frayed nerves. Though optimistic, his news from France was not good. German tanks had reached the French coast only 100 miles south of Dunkirk and at the gates of Boulogne. There was a chance to save the troops through Calais and Dunkirk but it was a race to reach the ports before the Germans. Calais was a mere 20 miles north of the Germans and Dunkirk the same distance again. The evacuation would mean the loss of guns, tanks and ammunition in France but the troops safety far outweighed this problem.

For Albert, it was hard to believe that a battle of life and death was playing out just across the English Channel and the enemy was in such close proximity. He was looking grey and tired and ageing quickly but he felt ready for the fight and was determined to persevere whatever the cost. His intention was to fight to the end and under no circumstance would Britain surrender.

From deep inside the white cliffs of Dover, Vice Admiral Ramsay was putting a plan into action at the same time as Albert was giving a stirring broadcast over the radio. Ramsay's job was to safeguard the Straits of Dover, and the ancient tunnels underneath Dover Castle were his headquarters. The warren consisted of white chalk passageways, cold and musty, with a few tables and chairs, no staff and barely any communication. Across the channel, he could hear guns raging and his main objective was to save as many men as he could against impossible odds. But apart from personal vessels of 'various sorts', there were just thirty passenger ferries, twelve naval drifters and six small coasters available. What Ramsay *did* have was a secret plan: Operation Dynamo. And on 26th May, he put it into action.

Ramsay wasn't about to wait another day. He had another forty small Dutch boats in addition to the passenger vessels he'd already commandeered and sea-transport officers were in the process of carrying out a survey across Britain's harbours to find more fishing boats, tugs and barges that could be used. From the depths of Dover Castle, his team worked through the night, determined to succeed.

In the dead of night, the first boats slipped into the darkness towards Calais to the sound of anti-aircraft fire. It was obvious that Calais was in enemy hands and there was every chance that the Germans would reach the beaches first. Even if the Allies got to the beaches, the Luftwaffe could use their firepower to annihilate them. The evacuation needed a miracle.

Resolutely, his aim was to rescue 45,000 men in just a few days before enemy fire could bring a halt to the rescue. Prayers were being said in Westminster Abbey and Churchill, seated in the choir, was full of pent up emotion.

Across northern France, the remains of British Expeditionary Force, nicknamed the BEF, were converging on Dunkirk and at last, the Windsors had heard about the defeat of Belgium. They decided to travel east to their home at Chateau de la Croe on the Riviera, not far from the Italian border. As they drove, they passed thousands of refugees with carts crammed with possessions heading the other way. People were terrified because Mussolini was on the move and he wanted his share of the alpine regions. Seemingly untroubled by the danger, the Windsors continued.

British soldiers had received their orders: they were to make their way to Dunkirk the best way they could and evacuate France. Amid the ominous rumble of bombing and the flash of gunfire, they came in their thousands via roads and paths despite hunger, thirst and exhaustion. Some walked briskly, others emerged as a disorderly rabble while others who were wounded, waited hopelessly by the roadsides for help. Mile after mile stretched ahead of them. Their eyes would have been fixed on the skies above them watching out for German dive-bombers on the horizon who would lunge and release bombs over the scattered soldiers.

Near Dunkirk, fires blazed as soldiers destroyed anything they thought the Germans could use. The acrid smell of burning fuel hung in the air as transport vehicles were disabled, guns were smashed and horses were shot. The harbour had already been bombed and strewn before their eyes were the wrecks of half-sunken ships. Dark shapes stood on the beaches in long queues stretching into the sea, waiting their turn to board vessels. Those closest to the vessels stood in water up to their necks. To the men pouring onto the beaches, it must have looked like hell instead of rescue.

From deep in the white cliffs of Dover, Operation Dynamo was struggling. There were not enough ships for the thousands of men waiting on the Dunkirk beaches. On one day alone, Monday 27th May, 7,669 men had arrived back safely but there were still thousands waiting. More boats were needed and as word circulated through the sleepy towns and inlets of the imminent catastrophe, everyone with any sort of craft wanted to be a part of the rescue.

Albert kept a record in his diary. On Wednesday 29th May, 30,000 men had been safely evacuated but there were still a quarter of a million remaining in France. On the same day, the Windsors reached their little oasis of La Croe, manned with a small army of staff to the grounds stretching lazily to a shimmering Mediterranean, far away from the horror unfolding on the beaches of Dunkirk. *"The sky is blue, the sea is smooth,"* Wallis wrote to her Aunt Bessie. *"Everyone is calm and the gardeners (all Italian) are planting flowers for the summer"*. Not so long ago, Wallis had shown fear at the hostility of the press when David had abdicated but in the face of an advancing German Blitzkrieg, she remained composed, seemingly unaware (or was it just uncaring) of the uncertainty of a quarter of a million English soldiers only a few hundred miles away.

As Albert despaired, ships began turning up at Dover ready to make the journey across the channel. Yachts, fishing boats, barges, motorboats, even dinghies arrived ready to do anything they could. Men too old to fight but who had no intention of missing this mission hauled anything that would float into the water. Finally, hundreds of craft crossed the channel under the waning moon homing in on the beach and the soldiers waiting. As Albert watched, it was like a white glow that ran from Britain across the channel to France.

On Thursday 30th, the total had risen to 80,000 men rescued off the beaches, more than Albert had ever imagined. By Friday, an extraordinary spirit had gripped the whole country. Volunteers were coming forward in their hundreds and a further flotilla of small craft had joined the great tide of vessels. By Friday 31st, more than 133,000 men of the BEF and 11,000 Frenchmen were saved and it was beginning to look like salvation.

Still the line continued in France converging on the beach drawn by a column of grey smoke rising above the town. They emerged with blistered feet and boots heavy with sand to an unbelievable sight. As far as the eye could see, the beach was covered with tens of thousands of men and in the watery queues, men stood exhausted and freezing with their eyes scanning the skies for the bombers. They did not know that as they queued, an air battle was under way. As many as 50 aircraft were making four or five trips a day in an effort to halt the German fighters from getting through but even as they tried, some Stukas were still diving among the men waiting desperately to get home.

By Saturday 1st June, 175,000 British and 34,000 Frenchmen had been rescued despite German bombers bearing down with deadly accuracy.

Thirty-one ships were sunk that day, many laden with troops who had waited in the cold water for almost 5 days.

By the following Wednesday, the final tally was 335,000 and the atmosphere was euphoric. It was nothing short of a miracle and Albert made an unexpected but jubilant visit to Aldershot Command who had been at the heart of the rescue mission. But despite the elation, the overall situation was still critical. The Germans were just 21 miles across the Channel, holding the coastline and poised to attack. In Norway, Albert's Uncle Charles and his cousin Olav finally left their homeland as the country surrendered after two months of fighting. As well as Norway, Poland, Finland, Denmark, the Netherlands, Luxembourg and Belgium being taken, France was still on the threshold.

Then, one week later, Mussolini declared war on Britain and France and Albert wrote in his diary *"May he rue the day when he gave the order."* Four days later, swastikas hung from the Arc de Triomphe.

Everyone knew what was coming. Albert never doubted that Britain was next and many wealthy families agreed with him. They hurried to send their children to safety in Canada and America but Albert and Elizabeth stood firm. Their daughters, Elizabeth and Margaret, would stay with them, united, and the four of them would stand firm by Churchill and his ministers, waiting for the onslaught. As well, both Henry in the army and Kent in the RAF were ready to do all they could. No one knew the precise whereabouts of David. It was as if he had disappeared.

Days later, a telegram arrived. David was safe in Madrid and despite a swift reply from Churchill, stating that he should come home as soon as possible, David was in no hurry to return home. He had just stepped through the polished doors of the baroque palace of the Ritz Hotel in Madrid, and that's where he and Wallis intended to stay.

Heady with the victories of the past week, Ribbentrop knew exactly where David and Wallis were staying and he had no hesitation in passing on the information to Hitler to help enhance his position. He was waiting at Hitler's side in the bright sunlight outside the French Armistice wagon, savouring the moment with Goering and Hess who could barely suppress their excitement as terms were read out to the French, their faces set like stone.

Hitler had chosen the exact site for the Armistice ceremony north of

Paris. Compiegne Forest was where Germany had suffered the humiliating defeat in 1918 but this time, the roles would be reversed. Germany would occupy a vast part of the north and west of France, including Paris and all Channel ports, and almost two million French men would become German prisoners of war.

As the unending line of armed Aryan youth marched down the Champs-Elysees against the backdrop of a giant swastika, Ribbentrop could barely contain himself. David's appearance in Spain was very convenient and he could see a path to even greater personal triumph through an intriguing telegram marked *"Strictly Confidential"* sent to Madrid. He knew Hitler wanted to settle the 'British question' and he felt in a unique position with his earlier acquaintance with David and Wallis. He also knew David's most ardent desire was to re-establish himself.

With Britain on the point of invasion, David was in no hurry to return home. He'd decided it was the perfect opportunity to make another stand with his brother in Buckingham Palace and he was again making a list of demands. For himself, he wanted a suitable appointment. For Wallis, she must be regarded as a member of the royal family and be given the same treatment by the palace as the Duchesses of Gloucester and Kent. And as ever, money loomed large in the demands. Any increase in taxation, because he was no longer living overseas, must be compensated with additional income from public funds. Oh, and Wallis was to be given her title.

Give Albert his due, he tried to force his brother to come back to England to safety but David continued to refuse unless *"I know the result"*. David's haggling had finally made Albert realise that there would never be a compromise. He called Churchill in to meet with him, knowing that Churchill and David had been friends not so long ago, and spoke frankly. *"I do not see what job he could have in this country."*

It was while David and Wallis arrived in a villa owned by a wealthy Portuguese banker that he was to receive a telegram he would never forget. Forgotten were the magnificent views across the Atlantic with the sound of waves crashing on the rocks below. David had no time to take in the beauty of his surroundings as he opened the message from his friend, Winston Churchill.

"Your Royal Highness has taken active military rank and refusal to obey direct orders of authority that would create a serious situation. ... I most strongly urge immediate compliance with the wishes of the Government."

David was stunned. It was tantamount to a threat of court martial. Since his abdication he had assumed Churchill had seen his point of view. The first telegram was followed by a second bombshell. There was no longer a demand for him to come home. Instead, he was offered a post as the Governor of the Bahamas.

David was in a state of shock. Everyone knew the Bahamas was one of the least significant spots anywhere in the empire. As he read and reread the telegrams, he knew that this was a personal banishment. His choices were to either return to Britain and have Wallis excluded from court or he could take the post in the Bahamas and maintain a degree of distance and dignity from his family in Britain. There didn't seem a choice.

As David's ill-judged statement aired in Madrid, London and Washington, Ribbentrop was watching closely. It was the perfect opportunity to bend David's grievances to his own advantage. It was perhaps a high-risk game to be playing at this stage but Britain's ex-king was the greatest trophy of all and an accomplishment that Hitler could not overlook. And on his side, he had a golden goose: Wallis Simpson.

After months of wondering what Hitler was going to do, it was then a handwritten note arrived from the Foreign Office marked *"PM to see"*. The note was of sufficient concern that it needed to be sent straight on to Albert. The letter given to him stated that the Germans had been negotiating with *"her"* since June 27th. They were proposing to form an Opposition Government under the Duke of Windsor and they were certain that he, Albert, would abdicate during an attack on London.

Albert had no doubt in his mind who *"her"* was. But David? Was it possible that David would betray his own brother and country to the enemy because of Wallis desire *"at any price to become Queen"*.

Ribbentrop wasn't the only one watching the Aryan youth march down the Champ-Elysees. All of Britain was watching closely as well. It was like the awakening of a giant and Britain began to show a sense of humour. One newspaper wrote, *"French sign peace treaty. We're in the finals! And it's to be played on the Home Ground."*

Despite the humour, Albert knew Britain was vulnerable. From his daily briefing papers, he knew that 90,000 rifles, 1,000 guns, 2,000 tractors and 400 anti-tank weapons had been left behind on the Continent and he estimated that there were no more than 200 heavy tanks available across the country. And they were desperately short of pilots since Fighter Command had lost sixty pilots during the Dunkirk campaign alone. Britain was down to 700 fighters although they were being made at the formidable rate of 470 a month, there were grave fears the Germans could win the battle simply by wiping out Britain's radar stations, airfields and aircraft factories.

As Albert worried, David and Wallis were enjoying life at the Ritz in Madrid although Wallis was heard to say that she was terribly concerned that their two homes in France, along with their lavish collections of fine art, silver and other treasures would not be safe from looters. As for Henry and Kent, they were trying their best to create morale-boosting resourcefulness. Miles of coastline were being transformed with coils of barbed wire, thousands of concrete pillboxes had been hurriedly built and placed randomly, like bollards, on roads and railway lines and a 'Dad's Army' of Local Defence Volunteers had also signed up, equipped with not much else except pitchforks, homemade Molotov cocktails and potatoes studded with razor blades to obstruct the enemy. Napoleon had called the English *'a nation of shopkeepers'* but Churchill proudly took an entirely different view.

After six weeks, Churchill rose to address the House. He had toiled over the speech, crafting emotional phrases, acutely aware of the crisis and its importance. At 3.49pm the House fell silent as he stood and delivered it.

"The whole fury and might of the enemy must very soon be turned on us," he warned. *"Upon this battle depends the survival of Christian civilisation. Upon it depends our own British life and the long continuity of our institutions and our empire ... Failure could draw the whole world into the abyss of a new Dark Age. Let us therefore brace ourselves in our duties, and so bear ourselves that if the British Empire and its Commonwealth last for a thousand years, men will still say, This was their finest hour."*

EVERYONE KNEW WHAT WAS COMING. It had been advertised in cinemas and it had toppled the capitals of Europe. Blitzkrieg was another word for obliteration and now it looked like it was finally Britain's turn.

Along with the summer heat of 1940 came the Luftwaffe, operating out of new airfields from Norway to France, darkening the skies over England. It was Goering's 'Attack of the Eagle' aimed at demolishing Britain's airfields and it would be every bit as bad as they'd imagined it would be. The Battle of Britain was about to begin.

Between 24th August and 7th September, 103 pilots died, 128 were seriously wounded and 466 Spitfires and Hurricanes were destroyed or out of action as RAF bases became littered with debris and pockmarked with craters. With exhausted pilots and damaged infrastructure, no one knew how many more days the RAF could sustain. And then suddenly, Goering changed tactics.

On 7th September 1940, a distant throbbing drowned out any other sound from the channel. Overhead, a formation stretching a distance of twenty miles was homing in on its new target. The deafening sound of hundreds of aircraft paralysed Londoners as the first bombs fell. Overcrowded slums were demolished, docks were ablaze and the East end transformed into fields of fire under the brilliant red sky. Over 400 bombers and 600 fighters pounded the docks in the East End of London for 56 out of the following 57 days and night, and everyday life became penetrated with wailing sirens and screaming people.

If Albert and Elizabeth were frightened, they did not show it. While the people were slowly coming to terms with the horror and emerging from the shelters, they walked around London every day spending countless hours in the affected areas talking to people, she in dove grey and lilac dresses, Albert defiant and undefeated amidst the devastation that had swept centuries of work away in seconds. Until one rainy night on 13th September when a zooming noise was heard from the sitting room of Buckingham Palace as Albert sat with his private secretary. They only had time to register what the noise was before a deafening sound erupted near Albert's study. The courtyard was transformed with bricks and broken glass, water was gushing through broken windows and the chapel was completely destroyed. The German bomber had emerged under cover of heavy cloud and had flown in plain view towards its target. In quick succession, six more bombs dropped over Buckingham Palace close to where Albert regularly spent most of his time.

While Albert blessed his lucky stars his family hadn't been injured, suspicions began forming in his mind. The attack on the palace had been uncanny in its accuracy. Was it possible someone had passed on the layout to the Nazi? Apart from his German cousins Philipp and Christophe of Hesse, Charles Albert Duke of Saxe-Coburg and a smattering of royal relations in Europe, only David knew his routine.

If David thought his younger brother would run from the palace, he was disappointed. Albert could be reduced to a nervous wreck at the thought of making a speech, but when it came to his family's safety, a lack of courage was not an issue. In the battered palace, against a background of repair work being carried out, Albert and Churchill discussed their suspicions. While they talked, David and Wallis appeared oblivious as they sailed blue seas empty of threatening vessels on their way to the Bahamas.

The welcome in the Bahamas was more than Wallis had dreamed of. Bands played, flower girls threw roses on the path before them, British flags waved in the breeze and the mood was jubilant. The governor had been sensitive to instructions *not* to call Wallis 'Your Royal Highness' so instead he arranged for a dais to be erected halfway between the floor and another level, decorated with a heavy red cloth. From her elevated position, she could take in the scene. Before her were thousands of brightly dressed men and women, cheering happily in the brilliant sunshine among vivid tropical flowers. There were welcoming speeches, a military band, beaches fringed with palms and an ocean of blue stretching as far as the eye could see. Wallis had her own personal throne and she was in heaven.

From being overjoyed at the joyous welcome, Wallis found herself in despair when they were shown around their new residence, Government House. They walked from room to room, taking in the heavy Victorian furniture, the irritating whirring of electric fans that did nothing to reduce the heat and her disappointment at the lack of elegance and neglect was obvious. Surely they needed a large sum of money from the local House of Assembly to renovate?

It wasn't just Wallis who was upset with the situation. David soon found a secret telegram that had been sent instructing local officials not to curtsey to his wife. The well-worn groove of anger flared in his heart once again.

While David and Wallis seethed in the Bahamas and Henry worked hard on morale, terrible news arrived at Buckingham Palace.

Kent's wife had delivered their third child in July to complete the family circle and the child was christened Peter amid a series of photographs taken on an idyllic summer day to mark the occasion. The photos were stunning. The new prince gazed up into his mother's eyes and the handsome duke leaned in protectively as their younger children played in the background in a garden full of roses. But with the end of the celebrations, Kent was on the road again with a gruelling schedule of wartime visits across southern England and the Isle of Wight, with trips to Iceland planned and approved for by the prime minister and Albert at the end of August.

Henry had unfortunately been absent at the christening due to work commitments in Egypt but he had recently returned and his family joined Albert and Elizabeth at Balmoral for dinner on 25th August. During the dinner, Albert was called urgently to the phone and when he returned, he was ashen-faced and unable to speak. Kent was dead.

Details were sketchy but Kent had left his home on 24th August and taken the night train to Scotland as planned. The next day he boarded a Sunderland flying boat and had taken off near Invergordon at around 1.10 pm. The flying boat had crashed overland and exploded into a giant fireball and all but one was dead. Flight Sergeant Andrew Jack had somehow survived the collision and after wandering around the area aimlessly in the fog, disoriented and burned, had been found and taken to the local hospital. Later, Kent's identity bracelet and watch were found, both inscribed with his name, so there was no room for doubt that Kent had been on the flight and perished.

The death sent shock waves through Britain but with so many British families suffering terrible losses in active duty, the royal family could not call attention to their own bereavement. A simple ceremony was arranged at St George's Chapel in Windsor where friends and family grieved in private but as days passed, unanswered questions began to pop up at a Court of Inquiry about the doomed flight. The first question was: why was the plane flying overland in the first place? The usual route to Iceland was to fly over the North Sea, hugging the Scottish coastline for eighty-five miles before turning north. For some reasons, the course was changed, taking the plane over land far too early. The plane's altitude was a mystery as well. It was hard to understand why an experienced pilot was flying at only 650 feet in a region known for its high hills and crags. Whey would Flight Lieutenant Frank Goyen, a pilot with more than a thousand flying hours to his credit in a Sunderland, risk flying so low near Eagle's Rock? At that point of the journey, it should have been over the sea and at an altitude of over 4,000 feet.

Then there were questions about the timing of the crash. The time was given as 1:10 pm but in fact, farmers nearby claimed that it occurred at 2.30 pm, almost an hour and a half later. Since Eagle's Rock was only twenty minutes flying time from the take off point at Invergordon, there was an hour unaccounted for. Had the plane flown inland for some other reason? Had they pickup up an extra passenger? Were they even going to Iceland at all?

The Court of Inquiry was held in secret and the findings have miraculously disappeared. However, a summary showed no fault with the aircraft and nothing wrong with the four engines or navigational equipment recovered at the crash site. Apparently, the pilot had changed flight-plan for unknown reasons and descended through cloud without first making sure he was even over water.

Flight Sergeant Jack was visited by two senior Royal Air Force officials while he was convalescing in hospital but no one knows what was said by either side. What we do know is that Jack refused to answer any questions about the flight for the rest of his life, only once alluding that he disagreed with the investigation's findings that the crash was the result of pilot error. Instead, he blamed it on the plane's captain, but without context.

But what did he mean? At the last minute, the flight crew had been joined by Wing Commander Thomas Mosley, who outranked the pilot. But then, so did Kent as an air commodore.

Of course, with no questions answered, rumours were rife that there was something more sinister hidden. At the time, Hitler was at the height of his powers. Europe was crushed and the Third Reich was laying waste to USSR, attacking the oil-rich region and threatening the Middle East. If ever there was a time for Britain to make peace, it was now. Speculation grew that Kent was not on an authorised RAF tour to Iceland at all but on a secret peace mission perhaps to Sweden. But if that was the case, where was the documentation?

Did Kent have a personal agenda to make plans after the war? Had the

Duke of Windsor enlisted the help of his youngest brother in peace negotiations with Hitler? Outrageous as the claim seemed, it was taken seriously considering the previous closeness of Kent with his oldest brother. Or was Kent on his way to Poland to seek peace since the British had encouraged talk between the Poles and the Czechs? There had been far-reaching rumours circulating about the possibility of a Polish monarchy being formed and it was thought Kent was the logical person to accept the Polish throne after the war. Was that where he was headed?

And then other stories began to surface as grist for the rumour mill. Kent and his German cousin, Philipp of Hesse, had had talks and it was well known that Philipp remained a close friend of Hitler during 1942 as his younger brother Christoph was rising to become head of Goering's signals intelligence agency. Were all three cousins involved in a plot to advance Nazi interests in Britain?

On the matter, Albert remained silent as he grieved. He could not bring his brother back from the dead and there would never be an answer to why he had changed course no matter how many inquiries they held. He had other problems to consider. He had the war in El Alamein where 2,300 British and empire forces had died along with 2,100 Germans and Italians. Over the course of 1943, the massive Allied North African offensive culminated in a victory on 13th May fought under hot African skies and Albert was jubilant.

Just how much Albert's style of monarchy meant to people became more evident during a trip he made to North Africa in June that year. He was tired and feverish on arrival but nonetheless elated. He dined with General Dwight Eisenhower, met Charles de Gaulle and rode in an open car along the North African coast to an ovation from more than 500 men on a beach in Algiers. He then moved on to Tripoli to knight the British General, Montgomery. From there he sailed by night across the Mediterranean to Malta, just sixty miles from Sicily where enemy aircraft were within reach.

Even at a distance from the deck of the *Aurora*, it was obvious the word had spread that Albert was close. The Maltese had made decorations from anything they could find. Flags, curtains and clothing hung from every window as people thronged from their bombed-out houses and cellars to cheer his arrival. The quayside was crammed to capacity. They had received persistent bombing to the point of annihilation but now their king had come to acknowledge their bravery. As the ship drew close, Albert stood on the bridge, a single figure, absolutely still in the dazzling sunlight, taking the salute and trying to swallow the lump in his throat as the crowd went wild. It was a moment he would never forget.

That July, the Allies launched their first offensive attack against Italy with the invasion of Sicily. Rome was bombed for the first time and eventually Mussolini was overthrown in a coup and arrested on the orders of the King of Italy. For a nation that had waited to step into the war, it was a surprising result and in London, everyone was dazed but jubilant.

But while England celebrated, news came in of a brutal murder of the wealthiest man in the Bahamas, the British baronet, Sir Harry Oakes, and once again David's name surfaced.

Sir Harry Oakes was an American-born Canadian gold mine owner, entrepreneur, investor and philanthropist who had made his fortune in Canada in the late 1930s and moved permanently to the Bahamas for tax purposes. He had a major role in expanding the airport, had built a golf course and a country club and developed new housing at a time when the economy had been struggling. He had even been seen with the American gangster boss, Meyer Lansky, and a property developer and legislator by the name of Harold Christie. There were whispers of negotiations for a casino among the men but for some reason Oakes had backed out of the discussions and was strongly opposing gambling in the Bahamas. David however could see nothing wrong with the project and had given his tick of approval to proceed with it.

Oakes was rich and influential so when his corpse was found bludgeoned to death, doused in petrol then set alight, the press went wild. Put that with his bloodied corpse covered in feathers from a pillow and only his pyjamas and mosquito net burnt, (his face and chest were simply scorched because the fire had failed to take) and you have dynamite.

Rather rashly, and for unknown reasons, David stepped in and tried to stop news of the murder leaking out only to become mired in the shocking headlines himself. He hired two detectives to investigate from Miami Homicide Bureau, despite British Security personnel stationed in New York who could easily have travelled to Nassau for an investigation, and met with them in private to discuss the case. With breathtaking efficiency, Oakes's son-in-law, playboy Count Alfred de Marigny, was arrested.

Count de Marigny, a notorious playboy, had eloped with and married Oakes daughter Nancy in New York without her parent's knowledge two days after her 18th birthday and bystanders had witnessed serious arguments between the pair. It seems de Marigny's lack of a meaningful career, his advanced age (he was 14 years older than Nancy) and the fact that he had been married twice before for remarkably short periods of time to wealthy women had rubbed Oakes up the wrong way. As such, there was no love lost between father and son-in-law.

Immediately after Oakes' funeral in Maine, de Marigny was committed to trial and a rope was even ordered for his hanging. His daughter Nancy had other ideas about the murder and she hired detectives and a lawyer of her own. A murder mystery of Agatha Christie proportions was about to unfold.

David's choice of detectives proved to be unfortunate. In a very detailed and thorough cross-examination at the trial, de Marigny's lawyer showed that David's detectives had not only fabricated the fingerprints at the crime scene but they forgot to mention that de Marigny hadn't visited his father-in-law for two years due to ill feeling and he was hosting his own dinner party at the exact time that the murder was being committed.

And that's when the brown stuff hit the fan.

During the trial, insinuations were presented that the gangster Lansky had sent his henchmen that night to 'rough up' and 'persuade' Oakes during a late-night meeting with Harold Christie, held aboard a powerboat, but things had gotten out of hand. Instead, Oakes had died. Add that to the fact that two medical examiners (ascertained by examination of blood work) stated Oakes had died elsewhere and his body moved to the bedroom after death and before the petrol dousing. You see blood simply does not flow uphill. During the trial, Harold Christie took the stand for extended periods but nothing could be proven and due to so much conflicting evidence, de Marigny was acquitted.

Significantly, David arranged to be away from the Bahamas while the murder trial was in progress so he was not available to be called as a witness. But people do talk. And they do speculate. A book written in 2005 by John Marquis, the editor of Nassau's leading daily newspaper for ten years, dismisses the Lansky theories and claims the murder was strictly a local affair. He believes David conspired to frame de Marigny by hiring two crooked Miami detectives to prevent inquiries by the FBI and Scotland Yard to investigate his own personal involvement in illegal money transfers to Mexico during wartime currency restrictions. Put that with the fact that plans for the casino went ahead and Harold Christie was later knighted for his contributions to the Bahamas and you have more than enough reason to suspect David's connection to the case. Suspiciously enough, the murder has never been solved because the case was simply dropped after de Marigny's acquittal.

David felt the slights, disgrace and humiliations deeply. While his brother had grown in stature, the papers regularly proclaimed the fact that David appeared visibly diminished and since his abdication, he had allowed himself to be led by the nose by Wallis. He had been cut off from his old life without knowing how to make his way back again and even long-standing friends were no longer keen to see him. Some would not even take his calls.

Churchill wanted to help the painful separation between the brothers and during a trip to Washington in 1943 he made time for David and spoke frankly. The king was *"unhappy over the family estrangement"* he said, and wanted to improve relations. But still David remained obstinate. His reply seems typical. *"I have taken more than my fair share of the cracks and insults at your hands."* Albert's first year or two was not easy, he acknowledged, but *"ever since I returned to England in 1939 to offer my services and you continued to persecute me and then frustrate my modest efforts to serve you and my country in war, I must admit that I have become very bitter indeed..."* It would seem that he had forgotten his little holiday with Hitler and could not see the olive branch when it was being waved in front of his face.

While David hoped to recover from what he saw as his humiliations, another great-grandson of Queen Victoria, Philipp of Hesse, suffered a swift downfall from which there appeared to be no return. His fate was linked with that of Mussolini since it was Philipp's father-in-law, King Victor Emanuel III of Italy, who had ordered the arrest of Mussolini. Hitler wasn't about to forget *that* little detail.

On the night that Philipp and Hitler had an amicable conversation over dinner, there was no warning of the horror ahead. On Philipp's way back to his hotel, two SS men emerged from the blackness and told him he was under arrest. He had only just left Hitler's company minutes before so he shook off their hands, sure there had been some mistake. All had gone so well. When he was told the arrest was on Hitler's orders, realisation suddenly hit home. He was 'interviewed' by the Gestapo in Berlin and stripped of his Nazi rank, his title as a Prince of Hesse and even his papers were removed.

Philipp of Hesse disappeared that night and it was prisoner 'Herr Wildhof' who was escorted by the criminal police to Flossenburg concentration camp in Bavaria where a small gallows was placed within sight of his cell window. Just to remind him.

Death in Flossenburg was meted out without dignity. Carts were piled high with the corpses of emaciated men and women, all skin and bone with sunken eyes, prominent cheekbones and the yellowing skin of starvation diets. As well as hearing the frequent hangings, Philipp could hear the soft crack of gunfire just a few yards away from his cell. Every day his door opened, he expected to be shoved towards the gallows. He protested frequently to Hitler and Himmler but no one was listening to him anymore.

He was unable to get word to his family but the guards were kind enough to inform him of the death of his brother Prince Christoph who had been serving in the *Luftwaffe*. Christoph had seen action in France, the Soviet Union, North Africa and Sicily but on 7th October 1943, he had taken a flight from Rome after being suddenly and unexpectedly recalled to Germany. The plane never arrived. There was no apparent reason why the twin-engine light aircraft crashed into the Apennines near Ravenna. Philipp knew well that sabotage was hard to rule out but the most shocking treatment was yet to come.

His wife, Princess Mafalda, a daughter of the King of Italy, had travelled to Bulgaria to attend the funeral of her brother-in-law King Boris III. While there, she was informed of Italy's surrender to the Allied Powers and that her husband was being held under arrest in Bavaria.

She obviously saw the writing on the wall because she fled to the Vatican in Rome for refuge. If she had not taken the phone call telling her of an important message waiting for her at the German embassy from her husband, she would have survived. But of course, she answered it and left at once for the German embassy. On her arrival, she was arrested for subversive activities and transported to Berlin for questioning and finally to Buchenwald concentration camp. It would be her death sentence. A year later, in August 1944, an ammunition factory inside Buchenwald was bombed by the Allies and some 400 hundred prisoners were killed. Mafalda had been one of the 'lucky' ones not to be killed but had been buried up to her neck in debris, suffering serious injuries to an arm. She bled profusely during an operation to amputate the arm but she never regained consciousness. Her naked body was then dumped in the crematorium.

In the Scottish Highlands, Princess Elizabeth's family struggles in Germany seemed far away. On her 18th birthday on 21st April 1944, it almost seemed possible for the 18-year-old to imagine a future. She was old enough to become a Councillor of State in her own right, one of five members of the royal family appointed to take on certain responsibilities for the monarch and she no longer needed her Uncle Henry to act as regent in the event of her father's death. She was rather hoping the Christmas break would bring something exciting.

She wasn't disappointed.

She joined her father in Buckingham Palace on 23rd December for the usual tradition of giving the servants their presents before heading back to Windsor. That year however they were joined by a handsome lieutenant from the Royal Navy by the name of Prince Philip.

She had already met Philip when she was 13 years old. He was closely connected to the royal family through his mother, Alice, (whose grandmother had been Victoria of Hesse who was in turn Queen Victoria's granddaughter) and his uncle, Lord Louis Mountbatten, (whose sister had been Alice and whose mother had been Princess Victoria of Hesse) – yes it is complicated - had gone out of his way to create opportunities for the young couple to see each other.

Albert saw the effect Philip had on his serious older daughter. She seemed delighted to see him again. As he watched his daughter blush, Albert's hope was that she would take her time before making any choice, at least until the war was over.

The New Year bought disappointment as any hope for an end to the war faded. Albert found himself immersed in fresh meetings with General Eisenhower and General Montgomery, as well as Admiral Sir Bertram Ramsay, the mastermind behind Dunkirk, and it was during these meetings that Operation Overlord was born. Their plan to launch an army across the Channel into Normandy in northern France, the very heart of enemy territory, seemed fraught with danger. It was the largest ambition of all time and it would involve 5,000 vessels in the sea and an army of 160,000 men to move into enemy territory. To land allied troops on five different beaches across a fifty-mile stretch of Normandy involved transportation plans, airforce plans, contingency plans and deception plans and the more Albert learned, the more he became alarmed. The odds could tip towards disaster in a wind change. Eisenhower however was sure it would not fail.

During the countdown to 6th June, called D-Day, Albert was pre-occupied with visiting his troops. Southern England was turned into an immense military camp and training became intense. He knew there would be high casualty rates on the beaches and he was warned that it could be as high as 20,000 deaths on the first day alone. Knowing he could be sending these young men to their death wasn't easy for him and although he focused on the practicalities of the mission, their self-sacrifice was clearly understood.

On the morning of Monday 5th June, the entire D-Day plan looked to be in jeopardy. A storm was blowing in from the Atlantic and strong westerly gales were whipping the English Channel into a frenzy of wind and rain. High seas would make it almost impossible for the landing craft to convey the troops from the ship to the relative safety of the beaches. Thick cloud would even jeopardise the bombing missions.

Finally, weather stations in the western and northern Atlantic sent news of a clearing in the weather, even though wind and rain was still battering windows in England. Eisenhower had a serious decision to make. Did he trust the prediction and proceed with the plan, hoping the Germans hadn't seen the forecast? Or did he wait until the rain had definitely passed? Finally, at dusk, he made his decision and gave the order to proceed. The operation thundered into life.

Aircraft roared out into the darkening night and paratroopers and glider-borne troops were the first to land in Nazi-occupied France, targeting bridges and enemy communications. Minesweepers would work their way towards Normandy in choppy seas in the small hours of the morning while aircraft hunted down U-boats. From Buckingham Palace, the noise of overhead aircraft was deafening.

While the Allies boomed into life, Rommel, Commander of the German defences, was away from his headquarters, believing the Allies wouldn't dare make any sort of a move on such an unstable day. That belief was just what Eisenhower was hoping for. By making that one decision not to send the German navy out that night, it left the way open for the Allies to slip in virtually unnoticed. In fact, if the Allies hadn't crossed that night, they would have needed to postpone for another two weeks and that would have taken them into the worst storm the channel had seen for over 40 years. It could have been the most appalling disaster in military history. As it was, it caught the Germans unprepared for the onslaught.

The first landing craft found themselves in the thick of the battle, tossed in heavy surf as men struggled to land amid mines, barbed wire and enemy fire. But they had one thing on their minds: destroy the German resupply system, which in turn would mean the Germans would be constantly short of rations, fuel and ammunition. They all knew it would have a huge effect on the German fighting capability.

The landing of so many thousands of troops on an enemy-occupied country, all in one day, after crossing a very large channel of water to get there, was unprecedented in history but once they were ashore, British victory became inevitable. They had overwhelming air power and they had massive artillery, which was able to smash through so many counterattacks. Albert, familiar with every detail of the plan, could only wait and pace the floor and wait for news about the most decisive battle of the war.

While Albert paced and fretted, David was fighting a private battle of his own. Increasingly, he was finding Wallis was not cut out for a life in the Bahamas. *"Some days,"* she confided to her aunt, *"I feel I can't resist slapping everyone in the face."* Two months later, she wrote, *"being shut up here is like being a prisoner of war only worse."* The final straw appeared as an article in the *American Mercury* in June 1944, which was scathingly unflattering to both of them. Spelled out in black and white, Wallis was scorned and their relationship trivialised.

The reporter, Helen Worden, wrote, *"In the ninth year of her reign over David, her face has taken on harsher lines....Her jaw, if anything, is squarer because of decisions which have been hers, not David's."* For the readers of the *Mercury*, Wallis was made to look shallow and nothing more than a *"clothes horse"*. Worden wrote that since moving to Nassau, Wallis had *"averaged a hundred dresses a year. Most of them cost about $250 a piece though some ran higher...She also has complete sets of rubies, emeralds, diamonds, topaz, onyx and turquoise, one for each day of the week."* When asked to travel lightly, Wallis *"turned on the man who dared to suggest this with supreme scorn in her voice. 'You are out of your mind,'* she stormed. *She insisted on at least thirty-*

one trunks for one weekend. Her lavish spending on herself is vastly in contrast to her thriftiness towards her staff."

David looked like a fool in front of the American public and Wallis was portrayed as cheap, vain and tawdry whose lack of love for her husband was finally exposed. According to one Englishman interviewed by Worden, *"the stoning of her house on Regent's Park at the time of the king's abdication would be as nothing to the reception she would get today."*

But David had a blind spot when it came to Wallis. Far from seeing any defect in his wife, all he could see was a conspiracy against her. He felt bruised as he turned to the FBI to investigate and files show that David discussed the article at great length with J. Edgar Hoover. To David's discredit, he appeared to suspect there might be a Jewish influence against his wife and told the FBI *"that he believed that Miss Helen Worden, author of the article, was Jewish."*

The difficulties with the press on top of everything else brought urgency to David's need for a new position away from the Bahamas. He knew ministers in London were preoccupied with the battle raging in Normandy but he wanted to resign his commission and seek a more prestigious role elsewhere. He was well aware that it was a critical time for Albert because he had seen pictures of his brother, apparently crowned in glory with the heroic troops in their moments of triumph, both on the beaches of Normandy in June and in Italy in July and August. Papers showed Albert stepping down from a plane to a fanfare of trumpets, giving salutes to British and American troops in the brilliant sunshine, touring Naples, inspecting cruisers and congratulating the army. And it smarted.

David desperately wanted a piece of the action. Why, he reasoned to his solicitor, was it not possible for an ex-king of England to have a role where he too could hold his head high? Even his younger brother Henry was Governor of Australia representing the king. Surely some sort of roving diplomatic post could be found for him in America? Was that too much to ask? A diplomatic post would have the added advantage of bestowing tax immunity, he added. As a private individual, he would be required to pay tax.

David was delighted to meet with Churchill in Washington in September. Churchill praised David's work in the Bahamas and acknowledged that of course he should feel free to resign. But when pressed to know what future role David might have, Churchill was difficult to pin down. The idea of a role in the British embassy in Washington was discreetly dropped and the Canadians had no diplomatic role available. Churchill suggested the idea of appointing him as Governor of Ceylon until another governor with superior credentials appeared. Another idea was Governor of Madras until someone delicately pointed out that several Indian princes had already been deemed unsuitable on account of their 'marriage arrangements'.

Equally troublesome was the question of where David should live. Paris, hardly touched by the bombing, was liberated on 25th August but British officials were unsure if post-war France would welcome the Windsors. David's greatest hope was still pinned on reunification with his family but he seemed totally unaware that by signing his abdication papers, as well as fraternising with the enemy, he had effectively committed himself to a life of permanent alienation.

Still he pushed on with the hope of coming back into British society. It was at this delicate time that he made another serious blunder when he should have been keeping his counsel. Yet again, he requested that Wallis be recognised as an HRH. Since the monarchy was no longer in jeopardy, he reasoned, surely *"family jealousy"* would not prevent him returning to his home country with some measure of courtesy extended to his wife? He had done everything in his power to heal the breach, he rationalised.

Buckingham Palace took a very different view to David. The answer came from Albert's private secretary, Lascelles. *"There is in the British cosmos, no official place for an ex-king"* and the Windsors' presence would be *"a constant agony to the present king."* As one of the richest men in the world, the duke could do almost anything, he concluded, *"but there is no room for two Kings of England."*

Churchill disagreed. *"Nothing that I am aware of can stop him returning to this country."*

On Christmas Day 1944, Albert made his way to the broadcasting room shortly before 3pm. His speech coach was waiting, full of apprehension, but when the moment came, Albert's voice filled the room, full of assurance. He talked proudly and gratefully of his fighting men and he spoke of the wounded, of prisoners of war and families torn apart by the calamities of war. *"The defeat of Germany and Japan is only the first half of our task,'* he said. *'the second is to create a world of free men untouched by tyranny."*

Central to Albert and Elizabeth's belief was that they were fighting a righteous war and that the Nazis were *"forces of Evil."* Soviet troops fighting their way across Poland could only agree. They had discovered Auschwitz.

Auschwitz was the largest of the concentration camps where the remaining citizens were little more than walking skeletons. They were surrounded by mountainous piles of naked dead bodies, awaiting what appeared to be ovens. There were no rosy plump-cheeked children, just terrified victims of horrific scientific experiments. Agonisingly tight skins and protruding bones marked them all. The overwhelming stench of illness and death hung over the camp and near the gas chambers and crematoria were 348,000 men's suits and 836,000 women's dresses neatly folded, along with piles of eye glasses, shoes, dentures and even seven tons of human hair.

The scale of the horror is hard to imagine and it continued to unfold before a stunned world when the American troops entered Buchenwald, Dachau and Mauthausen. Still there were more: Treblinka, Sobibor and Belzec and Bergen-Belsen were discovered as well as labour camps in cavernous underground chambers where prisoners never saw the light of day.

A story surfaced of a Polish nurse in Poland by the name of Irena Sendler who had declared war on Hitler. Nazis had begun walling off the Warsaw Ghetto where 380,000 Jews were imprisoned. 10 feet high walls were topped with barbed wire guarded by Nazis and Jews were fed only 180 calories a day. As a result, 5000 Jews died every month. Anyone caught trying to escape was shot on the spot and anyone caught trying to smuggle Jews to safety were executed. Irena decided to help. She gathered five of her co-workers and said *"Listen. We have to declare war on Hitler!"* First Irena gained permission to work in the Warsaw ghetto as a plumbing/sewer worker. Then once inside, she begged mothers to give up their children to give them a chance of survival and to grow up. Irena turned everyday objects into life-saving cradles to smuggle the children out. Small children were hidden in her toolbox. Larger children were hidden in burlap potato sacks in the back of her truck. She kept a dog in the back that she trained to bark when the Nazi soldiers let her in and out of the ghetto. The soldiers wanted nothing to do with the dog but the barking covered the children's noises. Irena saved 2,500 Jewish children and when the Nazis finally caught her, she was tortured. They broke her legs and arms and beat her mercilessly.

Albert was appalled by the brutality. He was told of camps where troops had found bodies littered about the camps and bodies already stacked in the ovens. Eisenhower wrote, *"the German people don't seem to know what they have allowed their leaders to do."*

From his concentration camp in Flossenburg, Albert's cousin, Philipp of Hesse, had watched the hangings from outside his window. Stripped of their identity, Jews and other prisoners were taken naked from the guard room to the place of execution. In April, Philipp was herded on to a transport van and taken south to Dachau concentration camp but with the advance of the Americans, he was ordered into a truck and driven around the Alps as the Nazis made frantic efforts to evade the enemy. He was told he would be killed before they were captured. It was then he heard the fate of his wife in Buchenwald. Finally, he was saved by the Americans.

Soviet soldiers were caught on newsreels shaking hands with the Americans on the River Elbe on 25th April and the electrifying finale of the war was captured. Three days later, Italian partisans shot Mussolini and his mistress and their battered bodies were hung upside down by his heels on meat hooks in a petrol station and beaten horrifically before a vengeful crowd.

In the depths of his safe underground bunker in the centre of Berlin, where the noise of the fast approaching Allies was dulled, Hitler was told of the vengeance wreaked on the body of his former ally. Himmler had already betrayed him and the German people had fallen short of what was required of them. The glorious Third Reich, which he had created and built so brilliantly, was crumbling all around him. The Soviets were yards away, revelling in laying Germany to waste and it would be his turn soon.

Beside Hitler in the bunker was his mistress Eva Braun, wearing the dress he loved so much, pledging to share his fate. The mood in the bunker was calm as they both took cyanide and just to be sure that he didn't survive, he shot himself. There was no remorse in his heart, no laments and no self-doubts for the 60 million sacrificed for his dreadful dreams. His secretary, Traudl Junge, later recalled Hitler's extraordinary dissociation from the calamity he had caused, making his exit from life with the ease of putting on a new jacket and leaving the room.

The world waited for the Nazi leaders to be hunted down. Joseph Goebbels and his wife poisoned their six young children then killed themselves in the bunker shortly after Hitler. Heinrich Himmler attempted to flee but was eventually detained by the British and committed suicide by biting into a cyanide capsule. On 6th May, Hermann Goering surrendered to the Americans and ten days later Robert Ley, a politician who headed the Labour Front, was arrested in his pyjamas. Somehow, in the chaos, Joachim von Ribbentrop, a key architect of this immense catastrophe, and Josef Mengele, the butcher of children at Auschwitz, slipped through the net of the foreign armies, on the run in the crumbling ruins of their country.

The war was ending and it was hard to know what peace would feel like after six years of conflict. But gradually the idea filtered through and plans were being made. Albert had the balcony repaired and tested and almost everyone was planning a victory party. Music and lights came on again and there was a last-minute rush for flags ready for the party. Through the celebrations, Albert looked worn out.

The announcement of the unconditional surrender came on 8th May and Big Ben struck the hour at 3pm as London fell quiet, ready for Winston Churchill's speech to the nation. Afterwards, bells rang out and tugs sounded their horns and as Churchill made his way back to Downing Street, an excited crowd engulfed his car bringing it to a standstill. Outside Buckingham Palace, the crowds chanted, *"We want the king...we want the king"* and as the balcony doors opened, a mighty roar greeted Albert and his family. The people gazing up at him were in their best and brightest clothes and even dogs had victory bows around their necks. People climbed lampposts to see them and the royal family emerged eight times on the balcony before the crowds would quieten. For the first time in many years, floodlights fell across the lawns in the gathering dusk, and the crowd quietened ready for Albert's speech.

To close family members, the strain and fatigue on Albert's face was evident as he began his delivery. Through heart-stopping pauses and audible gulps, his efforts to control his speech was visible in his face.

"THERE IS great comfort in the thought that the years together, that the years of darkness and danger in which the children of our country have grown up, are over, and please God, for ever... In the hour of danger we humbly committed our cause into the hand of God and He has been our strength and

shield. Let us thank Him for His mercies and in this hour of victory commit ourselves and our new task to guidance of that same strong hand".

THE CROWD ROARED THEMSELVES HOARSE. The Duke of Kent was dead, the Duke of Gloucester was on the other side of the world in Australia and the former king was destroyed in all but name, bitter about his apparent continuing exile. But Albert, their King George VI, appeared to have risen to new heights, redefining the monarchy. But it had come at a huge price.

The toll of the stress during the last six years of war and the heavy smoking had left Albert exhausted. He and Churchill had pushed themselves beyond their limits to deal with every emergency but the vitality had drained from Albert's face, leaving him looking tired and gaunt, and for a man of only 49 years old, he looked old beyond his years.

There was another deeply painful matter that rose that spring. In the closing weeks of the war, an American army in the Harz Mountains in Germany stumbled across a large hoard of German archives and took them to Marburg Castle in the state of Hesse. In the documents were damaging papers and telegrams relating to David's dealing with the Nazis. Two copies exist today: one sent to the vaults of the Foreign Office and the other to the US State Department.

Albert was privy to the documents although he already knew about David's behaviour in both Spain and Portugal after the fall of France through British Intelligence. But the papers revealed so much more. David's views, his sense of entitlement, his hunger for money and status were all laid out before Albert. What was surprising was the German records appeared to condemn him. The German Ambassador Stohrer wrote in 1940, *"The Duke was considering making a public statement disassociating himself from the present English policy and breaking with his brother".* Even more shocking was the idea of David waiting as the compliant *"king across the water"* ready *"for any personal sacrifice"* once bombing brought the British to the negotiating table. The Duke *"had agreed upon a code word"* with his Portuguese host, Santo Silva, *"on receipt of which he would immediately come back over".*

Sitting in his study in Buckingham Palace, Albert wondered what would have happened if he and his family had perished in the Battle of Britain. Would it have been possible that his brother would have been conveniently waiting in the wings as a pro-Nazi prospective monarch? It was hard for him to believe that the brother he had shadowed in his youth, who he'd grown up with and looked up to, could do such a thing.

But Albert's eyes were finally open. After his brother's appalling behaviour there was only one recourse. He sat with his mother on 23rd September and said, *"we must take the line that he cannot live here."*

The time came on 5th October when the brothers met with their mother. If David thought there would be a reconciliation, he was to be sadly mistaken. Unaware of the telegrams, tucked away in the Marburg file, David waited for his moment until after dinner to raise the issue. First he spoke of Wallis. Would his mother receive her?

The silence in the room lasted a little too long. It filled the room and allowed everyone to reflect on the importance of the answer. An immeasurable time lapsed before Queen Mary brought herself to answer. She replied that she could never do so as nothing has happened to alter the circumstances which had led to his abdication.

David knew the decision was final. He could see it in his mother's face and he could see it in Albert's face. His return to England to create a permanent home with Wallis was unwelcome.

Just how much Albert revealed about the telegrams is unknown. He did not raise his voice or lose his calm. It seems likely he did reveal them to make his brother understand why his damaging actions had hurt his family and I'm sure David realised it was not the time to bring up his old demands for Wallis. And if David was shocked that captured German documents were being held against him, just when there was a chance of returning to his old life, no one will ever know. The issues were discussed thoroughly and quietly and the frosty distance between them was palpable. They were brothers in name only.

That David allowed the matter to drop so readily would suggest he recognised the dangers of the incriminating file. And yet, it must have been hard to accept that the doors to palaces he had once taken for granted as a child were no longer open to him. He had once been offered a post in *"a third class British colony"* but it was now unclear whether he would be offered anything at all.

David waited for a post as Wallis busied herself with post-war renovations in Paris but nothing ever came. They were still waiting in the spring when they moved to their villa at La Croe in the South of France. From his window of the plane David would have been able to see the flags of the Allies flying where gigantic Nazi banners had once waved in the breeze.

In the aftermath of the war, David got off lightly. Ribbentrop was reunited with Hermann Goering, Dr Ley and other members of the Nazi leadership and flown across Germany to stand trial at Nuremberg. Three days after the indictment, Ley strangled himself in his prison cell using a noose made by tearing a towel into strips and fastened to the toilet pipe in his cell. Goering was found guilty of war crimes and sentenced to death by hanging but he committed suicide by taking cyanide the night before his punishment. Ribbentrop, the man who had once courted Wallis Simpson with seventeen carnations and presumably bed, was found guilty of war crimes against humanity and became the first Nazi leader to be led to the execution chamber in the Nuremberg jail. As Fate would have it, his hanging was bungled and some witnesses claim it took nearly twenty minutes for him to die. Rudolf Hess was given life imprisonment as Prisoner No. 7 mainly due to the state of his mental health. Appeals to have him released were turned down.

Despite two years in a Nazi concentration camp, Prince Philipp of Hesse faced a post-war world where he was to be known as No. 53 on the list of most wanted Nazis and moved from camp to camp giving evidence against others during the trials. During his incarceration, his family were given four hours to leave their imposing castle at Schloss Friedrichshof, the seat of family pride and security. Looting had already begun on a small scale but eventually the family's famed jewellery collection vanished. Philipp suffered stiff penalties and fines that stripped him of more than 30% of his assets and his legal costs, on top of the penalties, left him almost penniless.

Charles Edward, Duke of Saxe-Coburg, was not forgotten. He had first befriended then influenced David and had continued to represent the Nazi party throughout the war. And let's not forget his sons who fought on the German side. The Americans imprisoned him and his atonement payment left him impoverished as most of his property was confiscated.

But throughout the trials, there was one great-grandson of Queen Victoria who managed to escape punishment or being stripped of his wealth. In a wonderfully British desire to protect and safeguard the monarchy and to avoid embarrassment, there was sustained effort to suppress David's misdemeanours evident in the Marburg file. Yes, David got off lightly.

Albert's fading health was all too evident as his eldest daughter Elizabeth walked down the aisle of Westminster Abbey to marry Prince Philip on 20th November 1947. All eyes were on the silk clad figure whose dress had taken 3,000 clothes coupons and bore 10,000 pearls. It was the largest gathering of royalty, over 2,000 guests, since the time of Queen Victoria and from across Europe they came, many of them direct descendants of the formidable queen.

Absent from the guest list were David and Wallis, spurned just as Philip's German relations were spurned. To make up for the slight, David took Wallis on a long holiday to America to avoid the humiliation but you can believe they were watching the newsreels and would have realised that his Mountbatten cousins had eclipsed him.

It was painfully obvious that Albert was suffering. He had severe pain in his feet and debilitating cramps in both legs. Many months lapsed in which Albert found he could help his circulation by banging his leg against the desk during prolonged periods of sitting. But by October 1948, he could not ignore the problem any more.

The medical experts were brutal. Albert was suffering from such severe obstruction in blood vessels to his feet and legs that he was in danger of developing gangrene. The likely cause of the inflammation and clotting at such a relatively young age of 53 was tobacco. They believed amputation was almost inevitable. Six months later, surgeons performed an operation to relieve the conditions in his legs by severing a nerve in the lower spine that controlled blood flow.

From Europe, David and Wallis watched Albert's declining health closely. Letters from their close friend, Kenneth de Courcy, alerted Wallis that *"those around him will gain greater and greater power."* De Courcy noted Louis Mountbatten's unstoppable rise in popularity and to counter it, he advised the Windsors to buy an estate in England.

But returning to England without an HRH for Wallis was an insurmountable block for David and despite the fact that his brother was ill, David again requested an HRH for Wallis one last time.

It was winter before the brothers met. David did not appear to notice signs of his brother's deteriorating health although it was obvious he was ill.

Albert was a shell of a man, gaunt without vitality, with cheekbones chiselled out of a hollow face. Instead of seeing a brother who was obviously suffering, David saw a brother who was surrounded by everything that was once his: the palace, the court and the titles. Not only had he lost everything to his brother, but Albert had chosen not to share it, not even an HRH. And that's when David vented his feelings.

For most of his life, Albert had been slow to anger but this latest request, on top of all the other rejected requests at inappropriate times, tipped him over the edge. Maybe he'd just had enough or maybe it was the state of his health. He sent a letter back to David, with capitals and italics highlighting his feelings. David had shaped his own life, Albert wrote. He had failed to acknowledge the *"ghastly VOID"* his selfish exit had caused, a decision that was *"your own."* Wallis had been bestowed the highest rank in the English peerage but if she were to receive an HRH now, *"there is no reason why she should not have become Queen in 1937."* There would NEVER be an HRH for Wallis.

While David battled with his brother, a handsome man was fast becoming a constant companion of Wallis. A 35-year-old playboy by the name of Jimmy Donahue, heir of the Woolworth fortune, had appeared on the scene and the pair went everywhere together, utterly absorbed in each other. Wallis bloomed like a movie star in the attention and as David watched, he visibly diminished. Pictures of her slim figure shown off to the best effect in stunning dresses were flaunted as she appeared on the arm of the millionaire playboy in glamorous Manhattan nightclubs.

The greatest romance of all time was now in question. Wallis was infatuated with a younger, taller, richer man but David could still not bring himself to pull out of the embarrassing threesome. He'd given up so much for her, had always been besotted with her, that the need for her outweighed her disgraceful treatment of him. The way he willingly, and quite honestly embarrassingly, followed her and Donahue around, meant he had accepted the relationship on any terms. Journalists who had politely averted their eyes at David's antics in the 1920s now adopted a no-holds-barred approach to him. He was trashed and ridiculed by crude comments in the papers and rumours circulated that Wallis intended to leave him, like a moth drawn to the Woolworth flame. As her collection of furs and jewels grew ever more resplendent, so did her undisguised devotion to Jimmy. She no longer took the trouble to hide it and David seemed obliged to tag along behind until the small hours of the morning to the point of exhaustion. It became pretty obvious that David had given up his throne and inheritance for a woman whose passion was for wealth and money, something he had been warned about twelve years before.

David's unrest did not go unnoticed. He could not sleep or concentrate and while he wrote his memoirs, Wallis travelled to New York with Jimmy. An editor of *Life* magazine, Charles Murphy, wrote that he feared the ex-king might commit suicide because he was tied to this woman he could not live without and in so doing, he had condemned himself to trail forlornly around after her.

While David was becoming a sad figure to the world, in Buckingham Palace Albert was failing to regain his vigour. Onlookers saw a frail man struggling to hide the signs of his serious illness. Still there was no rest for him. Fears that a war in Korea in 1950 between the communist North supported by Chinese troops, and the South, supported by US, British and Commonwealth troops would spark a Third World War consumed him.

He had developed a debilitating cough and a soaring temperature and it was hoped that the summer break at Balmoral would help. Still the cough persisted despite the crystal air of the Highland moors. Reluctantly he returned to London in September 1951 for a series of tests.

The news was not good. His bronchial tubes were blocked and he required an urgent operation to remove his left lung. It was a dangerous operation for a man already suffering ill health. There was the danger of a fatal blood clot happening and by removing the blockage, nerves to the larynx might also need to be severed, making him unable to speak.

Only his wife knew the truth. The blockage was in fact a cancerous tumour.

Amazingly, the operation was a success. Although tired and frail, he felt strong enough at the end of January to wave goodbye to Princess Elizabeth and Prince Philip, who were setting off on a tour of Australia and New Zealand by way of Kenya, taking them away for five months. He then went up to Sandringham in Norfolk and went out hare-shooting in a cheerful frame of mind with a group of friends on a bright, cold day on February 5th. After planning the next day's sport, Albert enjoyed dinner with his wife and youngest daughter Margaret before retiring to bed at about 10.30 that night.

He never woke. Early the next morning he was found dead in bed of a coronary thrombosis. He was 56 years old and had been King for fifteen years since December 1936, in which time, the shy, stammering and unprepared man had earned the greatest respect the nation could give him.

Elizabeth and Philip had only just returned to their Kenyan home, Sagana Lodge when Philip broke the news to Elizabeth of her father's death and her immediate accession to the throne. When asked to choose a reign name, she said Elizabeth, *"of course."*

Across the country, cars stopped in the streets and people were openly weeping. Flags were adjusted to half mast, the BBC took its programmes off air and cinemas, restaurants and theatres closed their doors. Dark shapes hunched against the perishing cold and rain, gathered outside Buckingham Palace to mourn.

On February 11th, Albert's coffin was moved from the church at Sandringham to Westminster Hall in London to lie in state while more than 300,000 people filed past. Foreign royalties and heads of state gathered in London for the funeral.

David arrived at Southampton on the 13th aboard the Queen Mary, without Wallis, who had not been invited, but still he brought his grievances. The palace had been in no particular hurry to inform him of his brother's passing and he had to hear of it from journalists demanding a statement at the Waldorf Towers in New York, where he was seeing the winter through.

In London David had arrived and opted to stay with his mother, the 85-year-old Queen Mary at Marlborough House. *"Mama is as hard as nails but failing,"* he noted and reported to Wallis and his reception by the family had been *"entirely correct and dignified."* There was a nasty shock, however, when he was told that the allowance of £10,000 a year, which he had been receiving from the palace, had been a personal favour from Albert and would now cease. Wallis wrote to him on the 15th, *"I hope you have not taken the expensive trip to lose the £10,000 and to be insulted."* She had also heard that he would not be permitted to walk in uniform behind the coffin in the funeral procession.

The 15th, a Friday, dawned cloudy and misty. At 9.30 the mile-long cortege began its slow journey from Westminster Hall as Big Ben tolled 56 times – once for each year of Albert's life – and artillery salutes of 56 guns were fired in Hyde Park and at the Tower of London. The route along the Mall passed by Marlborough House, where Queen Mary watched from a window, and continued past St James's Palace to Piccadilly, Hyde Park Corner, Marble Arch, Edgeware Road and by Sussex Gardens to Paddington Station. Detachments from the services lined the route and headed the cortege. In the procession walked four field-marshals (Alanbrooke, Ironside, Montgomery and Slim), four admirals of the fleet and four marshals of the Royal Air Force. An escort of the Household Cavalry, pipers and the band of the Scots Guards preceded the Earl Marshal along with some of the Albert's personal servants, walking immediately in front of the gun-carriage bearing the coffin on which rested the imperial crown, orb and sceptre.

In a carriage behind the coffin came the new Queen Elizabeth, the Queen Mother, Princess Margaret, all shrouded in black and followed on foot by the closest male members of the family – Philip, Henry and David. Behind them came heads of state, foreign royalties, diplomats and other dignitaries, with more cavalry and detachments from the police and the fire services bringing up the rear.

In the 1950s, an ageing Churchill could not stop the inevitable publication of David's Marburg file. Plans were made to publish the paper in 1957 under the unexciting title of *Documents on German Foreign Policy, Volume X, Series D* and according to Albert's wishes and foresight, David was warned and given a chance to see the documents beforehand and prepare his response.

For the first time, David saw with clarity the course he had chosen in 1940 when it looked like England would be defeated. Even to an unprejudiced eye, his behaviour was treacherous with the amount of correspondence between Ribbentrop and his Nazi agents implying his involvement. It was all there in black and white. Later when he was outraged at the lack of a prestigious job and the continued withholding of an HRH for Wallis, David had blamed Albert who said nothing about the file. David had seen Albert as the key perpetrator of an unreasonable prejudice against him and he had complained bitterly that it was Albert's attitude that lay behind the insults and humiliations heaped on him. Far from being his enemy, Albert had done his best to protect him. David was not a man prone to flashes of insight, given his abdication over his marriage to Wallis, but if he did feel any regret or remorse, there was nothing he could do now with his brother's coffin laying in the Royal vault at Windsor.

Of course, David released statements denying the claims and in a breezy rebuttal printed in *The Times*, he declared they were *"in part complete fabrications"* and *"gross distortions of the truth..."*. While these denials were grudgingly accepted at the time, British intelligence have since demonstrated the collaboration between the Windsors and the Nazis over their possessions in the summer of 1940. It is hard to put any other interpretation on the Windsors erratic course through Europe during the worst of the war in 1940 other than they were looking for the best deal and most historians stop short of using the word 'traitor' to describe the Duke of Windsor.

Stepping up to the mark now was a young woman who would soon prove to the world just how intelligent she really was. Her romantic love match had enchanted the world when she made the most important decision of her life, against the wishes of her mother, who would have preferred a titled English aristocrat for a son-in-law.

But from the moment the 13-year-old first met the strikingly handsome 18-year-old Prince Philip, she never looked at anyone else.

ELIZABETH II

Born 1926
Reign 1952–2023

As Elizabeth walked down the aisle of Westminster Abbey on 2nd June 1953 in a dress embroidered with the English Tudor rose, Scots thistle, Welsh leek, Irish shamrock, Australian wattle, Canadian maple leaf, New Zealand silver fern, South African protea, lotus flowers for India and Ceylon and Pakistan's wheat, cotton and jute, I wonder if she remembered the words spoken by her younger sister Margaret in December 1936 when Elizabeth was 10 years old. Their grandfather George V had died eleven months before and her uncle, Edward VIII, had just abdicated in a rather spectacular way.

The whole family had been thrown into chaos and the disruption meant her father, worried and unnerved, was the new king, reigning as King George VI. It also meant that she was the first in line to the throne.

"Does that mean that you will have to be the next queen?" her sister Margaret had asked when their father became king.

"Yes, someday," Elizabeth replied.

"Poor you," said Margaret.

As the daughter of the second son of George V, she was never destined to touch the sceptre at all but there she was, walking down the aisle. Her life was about to change forever.

When first seeing Elizabeth, people were often surprised at her small stature. She was only five feet four but like her great-great-grandmother Queen Victoria, she had a bearing that made her size inconsequential. She walked with an intentionally measured step emphasising her authority yet paradoxically it was because of her inner modesty. In her youth, her laughter filled the palace, she never wore a hard hat when riding horseback and she never used a seat belt in her cars as she drove on the private roads *"like a bat out of hell"*. And to her credit, she aged gracefully without the help of a surgeon, showing consistency and confidence.

To uphold her position for such a long time, Elizabeth II must have been an extraordinary person. She reigned, rather than ruled, with a commitment to serve until her death. But it came at a huge price. There was never a moment in her life when she was not the Queen, putting her in a rather solitary position. Because of this, she remained scrupulously neutral in everything – not just about politics but innocuous matters such as songs, television shows and books. Because of this, she managed to float above politics and controversy.

For the past 123 of the past 174 years, two formidable women, Queen Victoria and Queen Elizabeth II, have dominated the British monarchy. Between them, they have symbolised Britain far longer than the four men who occupied the throne between them.

I wonder if Elizabeth sometimes considered the 'what ifs' in her life. What if her uncle Edward VIII hadn't married the barren Wallis Simpson? What if he'd married someone else and had children? If indeed, there had been children, what would her role have been?

* * *

A PLUMP ELIZABETH ALEXANDRA MARY of York arrived by Caesarean section into the world at 2.40am on the morning of 21st April 1926. Crowds were cheering outside the house and her parents were overjoyed, especially her mother who had especially wanted a daughter. She was a wonderful blessing into a happy marriage, officially third in line to the throne but never expected to worry about that possibility. First in line to the throne, one in front of her father, the prime spot went to her Uncle David who was expected to marry and provide the Crown with future heirs. It meant that she could have a relatively normal life and be brought up to be a good aristocratic wife in the future with an education very much like her mother, Elizabeth Bowes-Lyon.

But if some were cheering the new arrival, there were others who hated the monarchy because of their obvious privilege. Britain was in a time of worker unrest and the monarchy was seen as tottering at the top of an unfair system. Mine owners had informed their employees that their wages would be lowered and their hours would be increased. The unions were threatening industrial action and Prime Minister Stanley Baldwin's government had authorised a royal commission into the matter. A general strike was on the horizon, calling out all workers, including railway men, printers, dockers and miners, and it was a matter they were determined to win.

It was during this post World War I turmoil that Elizabeth Bowes-Lyon, the 25-year-old wife of Albert, Duke of York, delivered their first child after three years of marriage. They were eager for her first name to be Elizabeth, but not for what we would see as the obvious reason. The name was chosen because of her mother's name, not Queen Elizabeth I. Her initials were even the same as her mother: E.A.M. She was named after consorts and wives, not a past ruling queen because her only destiny at that time was to make a good marriage (possibly to a foreign royal family) and to become a supportive wife and mother like her mother, the Duchess of York, her grandmother Queen Mary and her great-grand-mother, Queen Alexandra. After her grandfather, and then after the death of her uncle David, the title of King or Queen of England would go to her Uncle David's children.

King George V and Queen Mary visited their first granddaughter, (their daughter, the Royal Princess Mary, had already delivered two sons to her husband Viscount Lascelles) and the baby was announced a *"little darling with a lovely complexion and pretty hair"* by her grandmother.

In the true Hanoverian tradition, George V and his eldest son David, fought incessantly. In the words of the Royal Librarian to Sir Harold Nicolson, George V's biographer, *"The House of Hanover, like ducks, produce bad parents and ... trample on their young."* They weren't the first of their dynasty to be at loggerheads with each other.

Her Uncle David disliked everything the Royal family stood for. He hated the pageantry and he hated the traditions and it turned him into a rebellious, unhappy young man. At his father's death, he was already in love with a twice-divorced woman by the name of Wallis Simpson and he took the throne with the full intention of marrying her and making her his queen. And Wallis couldn't have been happier. Until Parliament stepped in.

Elizabeth was only 10 years old when her father became an accidental king just four days before his 41st birthday. His elder brother, ruling as King Edward VIII, had abdicated in order to marry Wallis a mere ten months after having accepted the throne following his father's death. Suddenly, Uncle David never visited them anymore and her father was always tired and strained, locking himself away in his study, much like his own father used to do. Her mother had been unwell with a bad bout of influenza and her grandmother, Queen Mary, looked cross all the time.

The abdication crisis threw the family into turmoil, not just because of the terrible scandal but because it upset the rules of succession to the throne. Like Queen Victoria and Prince Albert, Elizabeth's father was consumed with sending a message of stability and continuity to his people. But he had never been groomed for the role. He was in tears when he talked to his mother about the new responsibilities that would be his and he had told his cousin Louis Mountbatten that he had never wanted this to happen. All he knew was how to be a Naval officer. He was too shy, too reserved and he was plagued by anxiety. He had a severe stammer and sometimes couldn't get the words out. How was he supposed to talk to the millions of his people without falling apart?

Yet, for all his insecurities, her father was dutiful and with his wife's strong support, he set about performing his tasks and helping Lilibet – Elizabeth's name within the family – to be ready to succeed him when her time came if he did not have a son before he died. She learned timeless lessons of perseverance, courage and duty from her father, realising at an early age that living in Buckingham Palace was like living in a glass house where everyone has full view of you.

Elizabeth was only 13 when Britain declared war on Germany on September 3rd, 1939 (doesn't that date keep coming up in history?) and 14 years old when German troops surged into Holland, Belgium and France. Prime Minister Neville Chamberlain resigned that same year leaving the way open for Winston Churchill to succeed him and it was the year that she and her sister Margaret were sent to the medieval fortress of Windsor Castle to wait out the war in safety, away from the whistle and screaming of falling bombs. Her parents had already resolved to continue working in London, despite exposing themselves to considerable danger, endearing them to the British populace. It was a wise decision because Buckingham Palace was hit nine times in the summer of 1940 with one bomb falling on the Palace chapel, almost killing her parents.

But Elizabeth didn't shirk her duty. At 18, she received a three-week stint of training at the Mechanical Transport Training Centre, acquiring pivotal skills in driving a three-ton truck in heavy London traffic, changing wheels and spark plugs, understanding ignition systems and bleeding brakes, her face grimy from grease as she saluted senior officers.

When the war came to an end, Elizabeth was barely 19 years old. She had watched her parents braving bombed areas and she in turn had taken on new responsibilities as the heiress presumptive. She had entered the war a little girl and had exited a mature young woman prepared to do her utmost for her country.

Elizabeth and Philip first met at a family occasion when she was just 8 years old at the wedding of Princess Marina of Greece (Philip's cousin) and Prince George, Duke of Kent (Elizabeth's uncle). Five years later, in July 1939, the 13-year-old princess accompanied her parents to the Royal Naval College at Dartmouth, where 18-year-old Philip was a cadet, and she later told her cousin Margaret Rhodes that he seemed like *"a Viking god"*. As for Philip, he told his naval commander that he might marry the future queen. It was the first emergence of Philip's uncle, Louis Mountbatten.

Mountbatten and his wife Edwina had the most extravagant life imaginable with the jazz age full of cocktails and dancing. He was the great grandson of Queen Victoria while Edwina was the heir to a fabulously wealthy financier. They loved the nightclubs and dances and loved living it up with the top royals of their generation. He was a charmer but he also had ambition that had roots in childhood trauma.

At the beginning of World War I, Louis' father, Louis Battenberg, as well as many family members of German origin, had been forced by King

George V to change their names and surrender their German titles. Louis Battenberg was forced to stand down as Sea Lord of the Admiralty and change his name to Mountbatten.

Philip's uncle never quite got over the humiliation. He was terribly hurt and he wanted to raise himself up to at least the same rank as his father to vindicate him. The abdication crisis in 1936 presented him with an opportunity.

Mountbatten had been friends with David, then King Edward VIII, but when David abdicated in favour of his younger brother Albert, Mountbatten took notice. There was a new king, George VI, and he had a daughter, Elizabeth, now first in line to the throne. It opened up intriguing possibilities for him. There was a limited pool of potential husbands for Elizabeth. A few senior aristocrats and a few international princes but Mountbatten had the perfect candidate: his nephew, Prince Philip of Greece, the son of his sister Alice.

Mountbatten saw his nephew as the obvious consort for Elizabeth, believing his good looks and his ancestry more than qualified him for the role. And it was at Dartmouth Naval College on July 22nd 1939 that he succeeded in engineering the historic meeting between his nephew and Elizabeth by shoving Philip to the forefront at eye level to the extremely susceptible young princess. His intention was to strike the spark that day and it worked magnificently.

There was no question the 13-year-old would fall in love with the 18-year-old Adonis. But many were far less keen on seeing the romance flourish.

Prince Philip was born on the Greek island of Corfu in 1921. Although his uncle was King of Greece, Philip didn't have a drop of Greek blood in his veins, being a descendant from both German and Danish royalty. In his favour though, he was directly related to Queen Victoria through her daughter Alice.

In 1942, a revolution broke out in Athens and the King, Philip's grandfather, was overthrown while Philip's father, Prince Andrew, was arrested. His father was a scapegoat, a soldier accused of poor leadership and of disobeying an order and his trial ended with him being sentenced to death. It was only the intervention of George V that saved his life. It would mean being perpetually exiled and it would mean Philip and his family would have to flee Corfu aboard a British battleship to save their lives. But the alternative was not worth thinking about.

This was only 5 years after the Russian revolution where Tsar Nicholas and his family had been murdered and a lot of European royals were on the run as well. Although still upset with the death of his favourite cousin, Tsar Nicholas, George was not eager to have exiled royalties roaming around London spreading the idea that royalty could be overthrown. So, Phillip's family moved in with relatives in Paris and as the feeling of insecurity deepened, his parent's relationship deteriorated.

It was at this time that his mother began to show signs of mental illness. It was 1930 when Philip went out one day and on coming home, found his mother had been taken to a mental asylum and his father had moved in with his mistress. His father had decided that the best place for him was Monte Carlo in the South of France where he could sip champagne and watch the waves lap the beach. The move left 9-year-old Philip effectively an orphan, sent to boarding school under the care of his uncle Louis Mountbatten.

But his destiny lay in the balance. As 3rd in line to the Greek throne, he was torn between his English relatives and his birthright, although Mountbatten was very determined to keep his young nephew under his wing in England. He firmly steered him towards Dartmouth Naval College where his fate was to meet his 3rd cousin Elizabeth, the future Queen of England.

A few weeks later, World War II broke out and the handsome young prince was sent to war as a midshipman. Even then he knew his uncle had the idea that he could marry the 13-year-old and they wrote to each other every week. While Philip was earning distinctions in the war, Elizabeth was growing up.

She spent the war years at Windsor Castle and Philip was a regular visitor. Initially, the family was horrified at Philip's interest in Elizabeth but they knew the appeal of an exotic prince to a teenage girl leant more weight than a father's opinion of his suitability. Her family thought he was rough, ill-educated, bad mannered and probably not inclined to be faithful. And then there was his family.

Like the royal family, Philip's ancestry had a lot of German blood. But a second more serious problem was Philip's four elder sisters. All of them had married Germans and three of them had become Nazis. Two of them had even married into the aristocratic von Hesse family and moved to a new house outside of Frankfurt.

Elizabeth's mother had lost a brother in World War I and she was particularly hostile to Philip's German connections. She much preferred someone from the British aristocracy like her own. She could trace her own ancestry back to Edward Seymour, the elder brother of Jane Seymour who had provided Henry VIII with his only legitimate son and heir, Edward V.

But Philip still had one champion on his side, his Uncle Louis Mountbatten. But while Mountbatten was the Commander of the Allied Forces in the Far East, he still had an infinite capacity to incite suspicion in those around him. There were suspicions of his being a dangerous radical and suspicions of his cunning. As well as suspicions his ambitions. In the midst of the war, he had still found time to press his nephew's case with Elizabeth.

In 1944, Mountbatten approached Elizabeth's father, George VI, to open doors for the possible marriage and he was met with incredible resistance. One year later, with the end of the war, things became more serious between the two. He became a regular to the palace and everyone began to take notice of the intelligent, incredibly handsome 24-year-old with a wonderful career in the navy ahead of him, breezing confidently into the palace like a breath of fresh air.

It was the summer of 1946 when Philip was invited to Balmoral by his prospective royal in-laws and everyone could see that Elizabeth was clearly in love. And who could blame her? By then, even her father was won over by Philip's charm regardless of one gaff when Philip dropped into a deep curtsy to the king while wearing the traditional kilt.

But nothing mattered to Elizabeth. She was infatuated and besotted with him. That year he proposed to her before going to her father first and she accepted his proposal despite the fact that her father had doubts about 'Prince Philip of Greece'. He had a somewhat raffish reputation, his father had been forcibly rejected by his county leaving his family penniless exiles and then there was the role his ambitious uncle Mountbatten hoped to play. Not just that, there was his slightly awkward surname. His father Prince Andrew descended from the line of Schleswig-Holstein-Sonderburg-Gluchsburg (not an easy name to roll off the tongue) and one that had a strong Germanic sound to it.

It was Mountbatten who had a suggestion. Why not change Philip's name to Mountbatten? It was Phillip's mother's name after all. And Philip agreed.

Elizabeth's father had a few suggestions of his own to make. Before announcing her betrothal, he wanted her to go away on a long South Africa tour first. Not just that, he wanted the thoroughly British 'Lieutenant Philip Mountbatten RN' to renounce his nationality, his name and his Greek Orthodox religion. Once all that was done, the marriage could go ahead.

It was a lot to ask and you can believe there were some complaints.

The suggestions were precisely and oddly equivalent to those that had greeted Prince Albert on his engagement to Queen Victoria. Albert too had a favourite uncle, and there were concerns over *his* German heritage, *his* title and *his* lack of funds, much the same as Philip. And then there was the cost of the wedding, echoing those of Victoria and Albert. All relating directly to the end of the Second World War and the sad state of the treasury.

In post war Britain, George VI would have been concerned over how Phillip would be accepted into the royal household. He was, after all, born in Greece with German relatives despite considering himself Danish.

They needn't have feared. He did everything that George had requested. Upon engagement, he dropped his Greek and Danish royal titles, became a naturalised British subject and took the surname Mountbatten from his maternal grandparents. He transformed himself into Prince Philip Mountbatten of Greece and Denmark and the world loved him.

At the end of yet another horrific war, this happiness was what the world needed. Crowds around the world rushed to the cinemas to feel a part of what the commentator described as a "fairy tale". And as Elizabeth and Philip made their way down the aisle of Westminster Abbey before the British public, it was seen for the first time on newsreel cameras. Perhaps the only fly in the ointment were the tensions that meant Philip's three surviving sisters, all married to German princes, were not invited to the wedding.

Despite all the intensive planning, the event did not go off without incident. Elizabeth's tiara snapped on the morning of the wedding and Phillip was stopped for speeding through central London on the day of the rehearsal dinner the day before. *"I'm sorry officer,"* he said to the policeman as an excuse. *"But I've an appointment with the Archbishop of Canterbury".*

It was a magical story but behind the images of smiles and laughter, tension was brewing. Mountbatten and Philip knew there would be battles ahead over the role Philip would play as the husband to the future Queen. Battles that could drive a wedge between the young couple. There had been no Prince Consorts since the days of Queen Victoria and her husband Prince Albert, and many believed that Mountbatten would encourage his nephew to want more once his wife was on the throne. Many believed that Philip had hit the dynastic jackpot.

These fears came to the fore in 1946 when King George fell seriously ill. The issue surfaced that there was the possibility that a regency may be required until the king recovered. Princess Elizabeth was the obvious candidate but it was also assumed that she would be under the control of her husband and his uncle, Louis Mountbatten. Traditionalists within the Royal Court were terrified of the consequences.

That fear hatched an extraordinary plot (recently uncovered by historian Christopher Wilson) by a minor aristocrat and scoundrel by the name of Kenneth de Courcy and the exiled Duke of Windsor and Wallis Simpson. The plot that emerged would have the Duke return to Britain, buy an estate, and settle down to wait for others (i.e. Kenneth de Courcy and his supporters) to suggest that he should be the one to ascend the throne once again.

The first written evidence of the treacherous scheme comes in a typed letter from the Duke of Windsor to de Courcy, dated March 19th 1946 and signed 'Edward', which makes a thinly veiled reference to what had effectively been a treasonable private conversation. Referring to *"the subject we discussed in Paris"*, the Duke added: *"It certainly is a situation of great delicacy but, at the same time, one in which it would seem I hold fifty per cent of the bargaining power in order that the Duchess and I can plan for the future in the most constructive and convenient way. For obvious reasons, I prefer to say no more in this letter but look forward to another talk with you when there is an opportunity which I hope may be soon ......"*

Barely a decade before, the Duke of Windsor had sat atop the most powerful empire in the world and had remained deeply ambitious for a return to public life, and to the adulation he felt was still his by right. The news of her brother-in-law's failing health would not have troubled Wallis Simpson greatly. Humiliated by George VI's aloofness during the war, she and David were now riding out the early years of peacetime in limbo, waiting in vain to be invited home to Britain by the British Royal family.

There is no doubt that Wallis was also in on the plot. In a hand-written note to de Courcy, in July that year, she said, *"We are always busy turning things around and around in our heads – there's no doubt that something must be done – perhaps a good thunderstorm would clear the atmosphere. Anyways I can't sit by and see the Duke of Windsor wasted."*

By Spring 1949, George VI, the reluctant king who had cried on his mother's shoulder when he learned the job was his, lay in bed in Buckingham Palace following an operation to cut a nerve at the base of his spine. It was designed to counteract the arteriosclerosis the king now suffered as a result of too much stress and too many cigarettes.

Just weeks after the major operation, the plot thickened. In a letter dated May 13, 1949, de Courcy wrote to the Duchess of Windsor saying: *"The King is gravely ill and out of circulation and he will not be in circulation again…the King faces the fearful tragedy of losing first one leg then the other… The king will be able to do extremely little and moreover that those around him will gain greater and greater power. I may tell you most confidentially that a Regency has already been discussed and it seems likely enough that presently a Regent will be appointed."*

The situation mirrored the position of King George III during his years of serious madness – still a king in name but unable to reign. It was his highly unpopular, greedy son who became regent for many years while he waited for the throne to be his.

De Courcy continued: *"The Duke could, in these difficult circumstances be a decisive influence for good – making it absolutely impossible for the Mountbattens to become the decisive political and social influence upon the Regency and the future Monarch,"* he argued sweetly.

The ball was in the Windsor's court. In the thirteen years since his abdication, the Duke had never ceased to complain about his lot, often stating his country still needed him. The war had muddied the water, but now at last the moment to strike back had arrived. His actions in buying an agricultural property near London would appear innocent enough and if a constitutional crisis erupted within the Palace, well, he was right there ready to help if needed.

It was his one big change to re-assert his place and it failed. Within weeks, his younger brother was on the road to temporary recovery. By the time his brother died, the Duke of Windsor and Wallis Simpson had embarked on fruitless journeys which was to occupy the rest of their lives, wafting from Paris to New York to Palm Beach in the company of rich, bored, vacuous people.

The death of King George in 1952 came as a shock to the world. His death came as Elizabeth and Philip were touring Kenya and the couple rushed back for the funeral. As Elizabeth grieved, Philip had his own anxieties. It effectively meant the end of his naval career.

Philip wasn't the only one who knew there were changes coming. Days later Mountbatten gave a dinner party at his residence and made it obvious to the world of his belief. He said: *"The House of Mountbatten now reigns!"*

It was a terribly indiscreet thing to say so soon after the death of a king and it was almost treacherous, in a way. The next morning, Ernst August of Hanover, a guest who had been present at the party, surreptitiously went to see Queen Mary, Elizabeth's grandmother.

She was appalled at the suggestion that the House of Windsor, the house her husband had initiated to save the Royal monarchy's reputation, would change from Windsor to Mountbatten. After a sleepless night, she contacted the Prime Minister Winston Churchill (not Philip's greatest fan by the way) who immediately brought pressure on the young queen. She was a very young monarch and he was a very old politician and he wasn't about to lose this important battle.

It wasn't just her grandmother Queen Mary and Winston Churchill who opposed the change. Her mother did as well. Within days, it was publicly announced that the House of Windsor would remain the House of Windsor.

And of course, tension grew even more between the young couple. He'd never expected to be king but he'd also never expected to be so sidelined. He was furious. *"I am the only man in the country not allowed to give his name to his children. I am nothing but a bloody amoeba."*

It tore at the young queen's heart strings until 1960, at the birth of Prince Andrew when an announcement was made. In the future, the children's names would be Mountbatten-Windsor.

Philip spent most of his life walking two steps behind Elizabeth and it's possibly not how he imagined his life to be. It's not surprising his temper flared at times and his frustration has shown. But the marriage survived.

As a couple, Queen Elizabeth and Prince Philip moved gracefully through events like a royal Ginger Rogers and Fred Astaire, expertly turning and smiling and making it look so absolutely effortless. He was the strawberry in her champagne with his often irreverent and sometimes hilarious comments and he was the only man in the world who treated her simply as another human being.

THE CIRCLE OF BLOOD

I wonder if Elizabeth realised how utterly correct she was when the 13-year-old spoke to her cousin Margaret Rhodes about her visit to the Royal Naval College at Dartmouth and her meeting with an 18-year-old cadet by the name of Philip. She told her cousin that he seemed like *"a Viking God"*.

Settle back and get comfortable because I'm going to tell you a long story that shows how the histories of both Queen Elizabeth and Prince Philip are entwined.

We all know that for Queen Elizabeth to be where she was, there had to be a long line of kings and queens in her ancestry. But do you know that she's not the only one with a strong link back to the Vikings?

Drumroll please.

Although my story begins in January 1448 when Prince Phillip's ancestor, King Christian I of Norway, Denmark and Sweden pulled out the major prize from a lucky dip. There are 400 years of Viking kings (and one queen) before him threading their way back through history that I will explain more fully later on. But for now, let's go straight to King Christopher III of Denmark, Sweden and Norway who died suddenly at 32 years of age without heirs, resulting in the break-up of the three kingdoms which all went their separate ways. Even in the confusion, everyone knew that *someone* had to accept the vacant throne. It was first offered to Duke Adolphus of Schleswig being the most prominent lord of Danish dominions, but being relatively old and childless, the duke declined and recommended his nephew, Count Christian of Oldenburg.

The Council of the Realm considered the suggestion at great length and came up with a few stipulations. The first: Christian had to promise that in the future, the same person could not be both ruler of the Duchy of Schleswig and Denmark simultaneously. And secondly: he had to marry the widow of his predecessor Christopher III, dowager queen Dorothea of Brandenburg.

Now it's not as grim as it sounds. Forget the word 'dowager' because Dorothea was only 15 years old when she married 30-year-old Christopher III and according to a Swedish historian by the name of Ericus Olai, the marriage was in fact not sexually active, hence no children. Three years later, Christopher died suddenly and 18-year-old Dorothea became regent until a successor could be found. King Casimir IV of Poland and Albert VI Archduke of Austria had both proposed to the 18-year-old but she declined the offers in order to marry the dashing Christian. Together the couple had five children, the first two boys dying as infants, leaving two boys and a girl.

I know you're asking where this is going, but bear with me. This is the beginning of the interesting part of the story. As we know, in Medieval times, the sole purpose of life for a king's daughter was to cement alliances by making good marriages and producing children, and this is where their 4-year-old daughter Margaret steps in to the picture. For years, there had been talk of betrothing her to King James III of Scotland as a means to stop a feud regarding the debt Scotland owed Denmark over the annual taxation of the Hebrides and Isle of Man. So, in July 1469, at the age of 13, Margaret was married to James III at Holyrood Abbey in Scotland and all of the Scottish debt was cancelled.

Unlike her parent's marriage, the relationship between Margaret and James III was not a happy one. She was a popular queen by all accounts, described as beautiful, gentle and sensible, and later historians regarded her as far better qualified to rule than her spouse. She was just not very fond of James. It would be four years later that the first of three sons was born and named James. Seeing a definite bonus in keeping the English on their good side, a marriage alliance was agreed upon between Edward IV of England

and James III by which his son James, the future James IV of Scotland, would marry Edward's daughter, Princess Cecily of York. At the time, James was 1 year old and Cecily was 4.

Five years later, while James and Cecily were busy growing up and the War of the Roses was raging furiously as English kings battled and butchered each other, the alliance collapsed. Not about to let the insult be forgotten, Edward IV found the time to launch a full-scale invasion on Scotland led by his brother Richard of Gloucester. Fortunately for Scotland, Richard was unable to take Edinburgh Castle and the English army returned unsuccessfully to England due to the lack of money, leaving the Stuarts in relative, but wary, peace. Instead, James IV of Scotland married Margaret Tudor, Henry VII's eldest daughter and the Stuart line continued through their son James V to Mary Queen of Scots.

It was *her* son, James VI of Scotland who became James I of England and who would marry Anne of Denmark, the daughter of the current King of Denmark, King Frederick II, the ancestor of Prince Philip. It would be the second link between Elizabeth and Philip after the marriage of Margaret of Denmark to James III of Scotland. James I of England and Anne of Denmark would in turn have a son who would become Charles I and a daughter Elizabeth who would marry Frederick V, Elector of Palatine.

As a king who firmly believed in his Diving Right to rule, Charles had many issues that finally led to his execution but Elizabeth's marriage to Frederick was an enormously popular match. The wedding ceremony lived up to everyone's expectations and was an occasion for an outpouring of public affection for the young couple on the streets of London. Elizabeth was dressed in cloth of silver lined with taffeta, with a crown *"of immense value"* on her head. Sixteen noble bridesmaids, dressed in white satin carried her train. Her hair hung in plaits down to her waist, and between every plait was a roll of gold spangles, pearls, rich stones and diamonds, many of inestimable value. The sleeves were embroidered with more diamonds that dazzled and amazed the eyes of all beholders. When she departed five days later, Elizabeth was presented with a collection of gems and pearls, together with tapestries, damask table linen, tableware and household furnishing to the value of £10,000 (well over £1m in today's money).

Six years later, in late 1619, Frederick and Elizabeth were crowned King and Queen of Bohemia (today part of the Czech Republic) only to be driven from their court in Prague and deprived of everything the following year by the Hapsburg Emperor, Ferdinand. They have been called "The Winter King and Queen" because their reign lasted just one single winter.

Half a century after her death, when it became clear the last of the Stuart dynasty, Queen Anne, would die without heirs, Elizabeth's youngest daughter Sophia (who had married the Elector of Hanover) was designated heir-presumptive to the British throne, once again to put paid to a Catholic claimant. It would be Sophia's son, George, who subsequently became King of Great Britain and Ireland in 1714 as King George I, making all British monarchs ever since descended from Elizabeth Stuart, daughter of James I.

Years down the track, Frederick VII of Denmark would die childless, just as Christopher III had, and King Christian IX was offered the prize of the Danish throne because his wife Louise who, although being the direct descendant, was not eligible to reign because she was a woman.

Now we come to that amazing part I promised you. It was King Edward VII, Queen Victoria's son, who would join the two countries together for a third time by marrying Christian IX's daughter, Alexandra, who could trace her family's lineage back through the centuries to 1013 AD.

As we know from my story about Edward VII, Alexandra's ancestor was King Sweyn II of Denmark, son of Sweyn Forkbeard, King of Denmark, and nephew of King Canute the Great, the first Viking King of England who stole the throne of England in a series of bloody battles with King Edmund I, King Ethelred II the Unready and Edmund's son King Edwig. Through Sweyn Forkbeard's daughter Estrid, the Viking line has continued through centuries in the Danish line - Alexandra's family - until the present day. When Elizabeth married Phillip, and delivered their first son Prince Charles, Charles became a firm link going back in time to the first Vikings who ransacked England in 1016 AD.

While that is amazing in itself, it is also noteworthy that Prince William's children, Prince George, Princess Charlotte and Prince Louis, are the 14th great-grandchildren of Marie Stuart, Queen of Scots. While the English throne eluded the Stuarts of Scotland after 1701 with the death of childless Queen Anne, the bloodline extends back through Marie Stuart's paternal grandmother Mary Tudor to Owen Tudor's bloodline, and through her Stuart ancestors as far back as Robert The Bruce of Scotland.

Another thread in the cobweb is Princess Diana Spencer, the mother of

Prince William and Prince Harry, who was a descendent of King Charles II. Charles left no legitimate children but we know of a dozen by his ten mistresses. The present Dukes of Buccleuch, Richmond, Grafton and St Albans descend from Charles II in a direct male line and Diana descended from two of Charles's illegitimate sons: the Duke of Grafton and the Duke of Richmond. Prince William, now first in line to the current throne, is likely to be the first monarch who is descended from Charles II. When he becomes king in the future, strong Stuart blood will once more course through the veins of future kings and queens of England. I can't help but think that Charles would be proud.

Rather insightfully, 101 years ago George V decided to relax the policy on prospective spouses marrying into the royal family. Previously, Britain's kings, to keep the bloodline pure and impeccably noble, had tended to marry their royal German cousins but with the gene pool becoming not only soupier but politically awkward after World War I, George initiated a sharp rebound. He changed the name to the more British one of Windsor and made it easier for heirs to marry away from the broader aristocracy.

So when I ask, 'Why are we so enthralled with British monarchy?', let's wind the clock back to 1952 at the coronation of Elizabeth II. Despite the post war severity, there was pomp and ceremony, jewels, anthems and trumpets. No expense was spared. So my question is, how could a population that was subjected to food rationing and economic hardship react so amazingly when the hereditary monarch seemed to be wealthy beyond belief? Didn't they feel like they were having their noses rubbed in to how much wealth the monarchy enjoyed?

The answer is no. They loved it. Britain - battered, bruised and almost broken - appeared to be determined to embrace its new monarch and hang the cost. They were happy to accept the cost because in their hearts, they loved tradition. And they loved the monarchy. And Elizabeth did not disappoint.

For those who followed Queen Elizabeth II, it is fascinating to speculate on the degree to which the Queen's 'stiff upper lip' was natural. I think most will argue that one of her strengths and reasons for her enormous success was her ability to detach and her sense of duty. But at what emotional cost was this to her and to those she loved?

It is not often realised that Queen Elizabeth II actually came to the throne as a Mountbatten, not a Windsor. After marrying Philip in November 1957, she became Elizabeth Mountbatten, having consulted all precedents including the Act of 1917 that had changed the royal family's name from Saxe-Coburg-Gotha to Windsor. So, when Phillip's uncle, Louis Mountbatten, stood up at a dinner party in 1952 and said, *"The House of Mountbatten now reigns"*, he was quite correct. This event and comment is based on an historical account by Ernst August of Hanover who was present at the dinner party and took the news to Queen Mary (the widow of King George V, the Queen's grandmother and one of the surviving co-founders of the House of Windsor), she was having none of it. The House of Windsor was restored on the 7th April 1952, two months into Elizabeth's reign.

At the heart of our present are the stories of our past. It's a story of all people, in all places, at all times and because we know of that history, we can decide what may happen in the future. It shows us models of good and responsible behaviour as well as teaching us how to learn from the mistakes of others. The more we know about the past the better prepared we are for the future because by remembering the past, we realise that we are responsible for building a legacy for the generations that follows us.

These stories are of ruthless kings, favoured queens, warriors, generals, battles and wars. But standing tall above them all are the strong, stable ones who have persevered. The quiet ones. The resilient ones. The irrepressible ones. And at the top of that list stood one woman.

Queen Elizabeth II.

www.ingramcontent.com/pod-product-compliance
Lightning Source LLC
Chambersburg PA
CBHW052220090526
44585CB00015BA/1039